SRA
Reading Mastery

Signature Edition

Language Arts
Presentation Book B
Grade 2

Siegfried Engelmann
Karen Lou Seitz Davis
Jerry Silbert

D1376891

Columbus, OH

SRAonline.com

 SRA

Send all inquiries to this address:
SRA/McGraw-Hill
4400 Easton Commons
Columbus, OH 43219

ISBN: 978-0-07-612565-4
MHID: 0-07-612565-3

1 2 3 4 5 6 7 8 9 10 BCM 13 12 11 10 09 08 07

The *McGraw-Hill* Companies

Table of Contents

Scope and Sequence *following final lesson*

> **Materials:** Starting on lesson 68, students will also need a textbook and lined paper.

Objectives

- **Discriminate between sentences that report on a picture versus sentences that convey an inference.** (Exercise 1)
- **Identify the part of a sentence that names.** (Exercise 2)
- **Follow conventions for using lined paper (numbers with periods before the margin, sentences with capitals and periods after the margin).** (Exercise 3)
- **Write appropriate subjects in sentences.** (Exercise 4)
- **Complete a simple deduction.** (Exercise 5)
- **Listen to a familiar story and answer comprehension questions.** (Exercise 6)

WORKBOOK

EXERCISE 1 Reporting

1. Everybody, open your workbook to lesson 66. ✔
   Look at the picture in part A.
   Remember, if the sentence tells you about something you can touch in the picture, the sentence reports.

2. Listen: One man was standing in the boat. That sentence reports. Touch the part of the picture that shows: One man was standing in the boat. ✔
   - Listen: One woman was standing in the boat. Everybody, does that sentence report? (Signal.) *No.*
     Right, nothing in the picture shows a woman standing in the boat.

3. Listen: Three dogs were swimming next to the boat. Everybody, does that sentence report? (Signal.) *No.*
   - Listen: Two men were sitting in the boat. Everybody, does that sentence report? (Signal.) *Yes.*
     Touch the part of the picture that shows two men sitting in the boat. ✔
   - Listen: All the men wore hats. Everybody, does that sentence report? (Signal.) *Yes.*
   - Listen: Two of the men were hungry. Everybody, does that sentence report? (Signal.) *No.*

- Listen: The men were going to have fish for dinner. This is tricky. Everybody, does that sentence report? (Signal.) *No.*
- It doesn't report because the picture doesn't **show** what they will have for dinner or even if they'll catch any fish. Maybe that man standing up in the boat is catching a turtle or an old tire.

4. Everybody, touch sentence 1 below the picture. Sentence 1. ✔
   I'll read sentence 1: The three men were brothers. Everybody, does that sentence report? (Signal.) *No.*
   - The sentence does not report, so circle the words **does not report.** Find the words **does not report** on the same line as sentence 1. Then make a circle around those words. ✔

5. Everybody, touch sentence 2. ✔
   I'll read sentence 2: Three men fished from a boat. Everybody, does that sentence report? (Signal.) *Yes.*
   - The sentence reports, so circle the word **reports** on the same line as sentence 2. Find the word **reports** and circle it. ✔

6. Touch sentence 3. ✔
   I'll read sentence 3: The men were going to have fish for dinner. Everybody, does that sentence report? (Signal.) *No.*
   - That sentence does not report. So what words are you going to circle for sentence 3? (Signal.) *Does not report.*
   - Do it. Circle **does not report.** ✔

7. I'll read the rest of the sentences. Touch each sentence as I read it. Don't circle anything. Just touch the sentences.
Sentence 4: A big dog stood in the boat.
Sentence 5: All the men wore hats.
Sentence 6: One man held a net.
Sentence 7: One fishing pole bent down toward the water.
Sentence 8: A large fish was on the end of the line.

8. Your turn: Circle the right words for the sentences. Read each sentence to yourself. If the sentence reports, circle **reports.** If the sentence **does not report,** circle **does not report.** Raise your hand when you're finished.
(Observe students and give feedback.)

9. Let's check your work. Make an **X** next to any item you missed.
I'll read each sentence. You tell me whether you circled **reports** or **does not report.**
- Sentence 4: A big dog stood in the boat. What did you circle? (Signal.) *Does not report.*
- Sentence 5: All the men wore hats. What did you circle? (Signal.) *Reports.*
- Sentence 6: One man held a net. What did you circle? (Signal.) *Reports.*
- Sentence 7: One fishing pole bent down toward the water. What did you circle? (Signal.) *Reports.*
- Sentence 8: A large fish was on the end of the line. What did you circle? (Signal.) *Does not report.*

10. Raise your hand if you got no items wrong. Great job.
- Raise your hand if you got only 1 item wrong. Good work.
- Listen: Fix up any mistakes you made in part A. Do it now. Circle the right words for any items you missed.
(Observe students and give feedback.)

EXERCISE 2   Subject

The Part That Names

1. Everybody, pencils down.
You're going to learn about sentences.
Every sentence has a part that names.
2. Here's a sentence: **The woman** (pause) went to the store. Say that sentence. (Signal.) *The woman went to the store.*
- (Repeat step 2 until firm.)

3. Listen: **The woman** (pause) went to the store.
Here's the part of the sentence that names: **the woman.**
Listen: The woman went to the store. Everybody, what part names? (Signal.) *The woman.*

4. New sentence: **The old man** (pause) went to the store. What part names? (Signal.) *The old man.*
- New sentence: The man and the boy (pause) went to the store. What part names? (Signal.) *The man and the boy.*
- New sentence: A man (pause) ran in the park. What part names? (Signal.) *A man.*
- New sentence: Two girls (pause) ran in the park. What part names? (Signal.) *Two girls.*
- (Repeat step 4 until firm.)

5. New sentence: A big dog is running in the park. What part names? (Signal.) *A big dog.*
- New sentence: The rabbit and the squirrel are running in the park. What part names? (Signal.) *The rabbit and the squirrel.*
- New sentence: Four yellow birds flew to a tree. What part names? (Signal.) *Four yellow birds.*
- New sentence: A bird and an elephant ate dinner. What part names? (Signal.) *A bird and an elephant.*
- New sentence: A gray elephant went swimming in the lake. What part names? (Signal.) *A gray elephant.*
- (Repeat step 5 until firm.)

6. Everybody, find part B. ✔
Touch each sentence as I read it.
Sentence 1: The old man went to the store.
Sentence 2: The man and the boy went to the store.
Sentence 3: The horse jumped over the fence.
- Make a circle around the part of each sentence that names. Circle the part that names. Raise your hand when you're finished.
(Observe students and give feedback.)

7. Let's check your work. Make an **X** next to any item you missed.
- Sentence 1: The old man went to the store. Everybody, say the part you circled. (Signal.) *The old man.*
- Sentence 2: The man and the boy went to the store. Say the part you circled. (Signal.) *The man and the boy.*

- Sentence 3: The horse jumped over the fence. Say the part you circled. (Signal.) *The horse.*
8. Raise your hand if you got no items wrong. Super job.
- Everyone else, fix up any mistakes you made in part B.
(Observe students and give feedback.)

EXERCISE 3   Paper Set-Up

1. Everybody, pencils down. Turn your workbook page and find part C. ✔
- The lined paper at the top is filled out correctly. Below it is lined paper that you're going to fill out.
2. Look at the sheet that is filled out correctly. Touch the ball on the paper. ✔
- That ball is on a line that goes up and down. That up-and-down line is the margin. What is the up-and-down line? (Signal.) *The margin.*
- Run your finger up and down the margin. ✔
3. Here's the rule about the margin: You start writing words just after the margin. The only things that go before the margin are numbers. Everybody, what's the only thing that you write before the margin? (Signal.) *Numbers.*
- Where do you start writing words? (Signal.) *After the margin.*
4. Touch the lined paper you're going to fill out. ✔
- Write your name on the top line.
(Observe students and give feedback.)
5. Everybody, touch the margin on the sheet you're filling out. Run your finger up and down the margin. Remember, the up-and-down line is the margin. ✔
- Listen: Write the number **1** and a period on the line below your name. Remember, the number and period go just in front of the margin.
(Observe students and give feedback.)
- Now copy sentence 1 just as it's written above. Remember, start the sentence just after the margin. Begin the sentence with a capital **H.** Don't write capital letters anywhere except at the beginning of the sentence. Put a period at the end of the sentence. Raise your hand when you're finished with sentence 1.
(Observe students and give feedback.)

6. Now copy sentence 2 and sentence 3. Remember, first write the number and the period in front of the margin. Then write the sentence. Start with a capital letter and end with a period. Be sure to spell all the words correctly. You have a minute and a half.
(Observe students and give feedback. Praise students with specific comments such as:) Good starting with a capital; good starting just before the margin; good spelling; good putting a period at the end of the sentence.
7. (After one and a half minutes, say:) Everybody, stop writing. Raise your hand if you finished copying all the sentences.
- Good for you. If you didn't finish, you can copy the rest of the sentences when we finish the lesson.
8. Here's the rule about things you'll write in the rest of this program. You'll have a chance to fix up any mistakes you made before you hand the paper in. You may have some mistakes, but if you fix them up before you hand in the paper, you'll get a **super** grade for the paper. If I find mistakes on your paper, you'll get less than a **super** paper. So here's your chance to check all the things you should have written.
9. Here's the first check: Did you write the numbers 1, 2 and 3 before the margin and is there a period after each number? Check your paper. If you made a mistake, use your pencil and fix up the mistake. Make sure you have the numbers 1, 2 and 3 before the margin and you have a period after each number. Raise your hand when you're finished with check 1.
(Observe students and give feedback.)
10. Here's the next check: Does each sentence start with a capital letter and end with a period?
- Sentence 1 should start with a capital **H** and have a period at the end.
- Sentence 2 should start with a capital **A** and have a period at the end.
- Sentence 3 should start with a capital **D** and have a period at the end.
Check your sentences and make sure they all start with a capital and end with a period. Then look at your sentences and make sure those are the only capital letters

you wrote. Fix up any mistakes. Raise your hand when you're sure that all your sentences are right.
(Observe students and give feedback.)

11. Now comes the hardest check. Listen: Check your sentences to make sure you copied **all the words** and spelled them **correctly.** Touch each word you wrote. Then look at the paper at the top of your page and see if you copied the word and spelled it correctly. Check your work carefully and fix up any mistakes you find. Raise your hand when you're finished.
(Observe students and give feedback.)

12. If you did all the checks, you'll get a super paper. Next time, we'll find out how many super papers we get.

EXERCISE 4   Sentence Completion

The Part That Names

1. Everybody, pencils down. Find part D. ✔
You're going to use the picture to complete sentences.

2. Touch sentence 1.
It says: Blank stood next to the mother deer. Everybody, look at the picture and touch the animal that stood next to the mother deer. ✔
• Everybody, read the name of the animal that stood next to the mother deer. (Signal.) *The baby deer.*
• I'll say the whole sentence about the baby deer: The baby deer stood next to the mother deer. Your turn: Say the whole sentence. (Signal.) *The baby deer stood next to the mother deer.*

3. Touch sentence 2.
It says: Blank hopped over a log. Look at the picture.
• Everybody, read the name of the animal that hopped over a log. (Signal.) *A rabbit.*
• Now say the whole sentence about **a rabbit.** (Signal.) *A rabbit hopped over a log.*

4. Touch sentence 3.
It says: Blank sat on a log. Look at the picture.
• Everybody, read the name of the animal that sat on a log. (Signal.) *A frog.*
• Now say the whole sentence about **a frog.** (Signal.) *A frog sat on a log.*

5. Complete all the sentences in part D. Write the correct words in the blanks. Remember to start each sentence with a capital. Be sure to spell the words correctly. Raise your hand when you're finished.
(Observe students and give feedback.)

6. Let's check your work. Make an **X** next to any sentence you missed.
• Everybody, touch sentence 1.
Capital **T,** The baby deer stood next to the mother deer.
• Touch sentence 2.
Capital **A,** A rabbit hopped over a log.
• Touch sentence 3.
Capital **A,** A frog sat on a log.

7. Raise your hand if you got no items wrong. Great job.
• Everyone else, fix up any mistakes you made in part D.
(Observe students and give feedback.)

EXERCISE 5   Deductions

1. Everybody, pencils down. Find part E. ✔
You can draw a conclusion from these two sentences. I'll read the sentences: All **vehicles** can move. A **car** is a vehicle. Here's the conclusion: So a **car** can move.
• Listen again: All **vehicles** can move. A **car** is a vehicle. So a **car** can move.

2. Your turn to read both sentences and say the conclusion.
• First sentence. (Signal.) *All vehicles can move.*
• Next sentence. (Signal.) *A car is a vehicle.*
• Conclusion. (Signal.) *So a car can move.*

3. Let's do that one more time.
• First sentence. (Signal.) *All vehicles can move.*
• Next sentence. (Signal.) *A car is a vehicle.*
• Conclusion. (Signal.) *So a car can move.*
• (Repeat step 3 until firm.)

4. (Call on several students:) See if you can say the whole thing—two sentences and the conclusion. *All vehicles can move. A car is a vehicle. So a car can move.*

5. Your turn: Write the conclusion. The word **so** is already written with a capital. You don't have to start the next word with a capital. Remember to end the conclusion with a period. Raise your hand when you're finished.
(Observe students and give feedback.)

6. Check your work. I'll read the conclusion you should have on the last line: Capital **S,** So a car can move, period. Fix up any mistakes you made in part E.
(Observe students and give feedback.)

EXERCISE 6   The Bragging Rats Race

Storytelling

- I'll read a story that I read to you before. The story I'll read is titled **The Bragging Rats.** Let's see how well you can remember things that happened.

A bunch of rats lived near a pond that was on a farm. The rats got along well, except for two of them. The other rats called these two the bragging rats because they were always bragging, quarreling and arguing about something.

One day they'd argue about who could eat the most. Another day they'd squabble and quarrel over who was the best looking. Neither one of them was very good looking. One was a big gray rat with the longest tail you've ever seen on a rat. The other one wasn't big, but he had the biggest, yellowest teeth you ever saw.

- The other rats didn't pay much attention to the bragging rats until they started to argue about something for days. What was that? (Call on a student. Idea: *Who was the fastest.*)

The other rats in the bunch didn't pay much attention to the bragging and quarreling until the two rats started bragging about who was the fastest rat in the whole bunch. This quarrel went on for days, and the other rats got pretty sick of listening to the rats shout and yell and brag about how fast they were.

On the third day of their quarrel, the two rats almost got into a fight. The rat with the yellow teeth was saying, "I'm so fast that I could run circles around you while you ran as fast as you could."

The big gray rat said, "Oh, yeah? Well I could run circles around your circles. That's how fast I am."

- Who remembers who told the rats how to settle their argument? (Call on a student. *The wise old rat.*)
- What did the wise old rat tell them to do? (Call on a student. Idea: *Have a race.*)

The two rats continued yelling at each other until a wise old rat said, "Stop! We are tired of listening to all this shouting and yelling and bragging. There is a way to find out who is the fastest rat on this farm."

The wise old rat continued, "We will have a race for any rat that wants to race. Everybody will line up, run down the path to the pond, then run back to the starting line. The first rat to get back is the winner. And then we'll have no more arguing about which rat is the fastest."

The rats agreed, and early the next morning they were lined up, ready for the big race. Six rats entered the race. The bragging rats were lined up right next to each other, making mean faces and mumbling about how fast they were going to run.

- Who remembers which rat won this race? (Call on a student. *A little black rat.*)

The rats put their noses close to the ground, ready to take off like a flash.

"Everybody, steady," the wise old rat said, "Everybody, ready. Go!"

The rats took off toward the pond. The big gray rat got ahead of the others, with the yellow-toothed rat right behind him. But just before they got to the pond, the yellow-toothed rat stepped on the long tail of the gray rat, and both rats tumbled over and over in a cloud of dust.

They tumbled down the dusty path and right into the pond.

The other rats finished the race. The winner was a little black rat. It was hard for her to finish the race because she was laughing so hard over the bragging rats who were still splashing and sputtering around in the pond.

After the race, all the other rats went back to the pond. The bragging rats were still splashing and sputtering. The wise old rat said to them, "So now we know who the fastest runner on this farm is. It's neither one of you, so we will have no more arguments from either of you about who can run the fastest!"

- Did this race stop the bragging rats from arguing? (Call on a student. *No*.)
- What did they argue about next? (Call on a student. Idea: *Who was the fastest swimmer*.)

The bragging rats looked at each other. Then the rat with yellow teeth suddenly smiled and said, "I may not be the fastest **runner** in this bunch, but there is no rat in the world that can **swim** as fast as I can."

"Oh, yeah?" said the gray rat. "I can swim so fast that I could go all the way across this pond without even getting my fur wet."

The wise old rat and the other rats just walked away from the pond, slowly shaking their heads.

Note:
- Collect the students' workbooks.
- Check the students' workbooks before the next language period. Mark any mistakes.
- Write **super** on lessons that have all mistakes corrected. Write **good** or **pretty good** on lessons that have only 1 or 2 mistakes.

Objectives

- Discriminate between sentences that report on a picture versus sentences that convey inference. (Exercise 2)
- Identify the part of a sentence that names. (Exercise 3)
- Follow conventions for using lined paper. (Exercise 4)
- Write appropriate subjects in sentences. (Exercise 5)
- Complete a simple deduction. (Exercise 6)
- Listen to a familiar story and answer comprehension questions. (Exercise 7)

WORKBOOK

EXERCISE 1   Feedback On Lesson 66

1. (Hand back student workbooks.)
2. Open your workbook to lesson 66. ✔
   Raise your hand if I wrote **super** on that page.
   - The **super** means that you checked over your work and fixed it up so it was perfect. If you didn't get a **super,** look at the mistakes you made and be more careful next time. (Pause.)
3. Now turn to lesson 67 in your workbook. ✔

EXERCISE 2   Reporting

1. Look at the picture in part A. Remember, if a sentence tells about something that you can touch in the picture, the sentence **reports** on the picture. If the sentence does not tell about something you can touch, the sentence **does not report.**
2. Listen: A boy sat at a picnic table. That sentence reports. Touch the part of the picture that shows: A boy sat at a picnic table. ✔
   - Listen: The boy wanted to go home. Everybody, does that sentence report? (Signal.) *No.*
     Right, nothing in the picture shows: The boy wanted to go home.
3. Listen: Two dogs sat on the ground. Everybody, does that sentence report? (Signal.) *No.*
   - Listen: Cups and plates were on the table. Everybody, does that sentence report? (Signal.) *Yes.*

Touch the part of the picture that shows: Cups and plates were on the table. ✔

- Listen: A girl gave something to a dog. Everybody, does that sentence report? (Signal.) *Yes.*
- Listen: A boy ate with his sisters. Everybody, does that sentence report? (Signal.) *No.*
  It doesn't report because the picture doesn't show the girls are the boy's sisters. Maybe they are friends or cousins.

4. Everybody, touch sentence 1 below the picture. Sentence 1.
   I'll read sentence 1: The children had been camping for three days. Everybody, does that sentence report? (Signal.) *No.*
   - The sentence does not report, so circle the words **does not report.** Find the words **does not report** on the same line as sentence 1. ✔
5. Everybody, touch sentence 2.
   I'll read sentence 2: A girl gave something to a dog.
   Everybody, does that sentence report? (Signal.) *Yes.*
   - The sentence reports, so circle the word **reports** on the same line as sentence 2.
6. I'll read the rest of the sentences. Touch each sentence as I read it. Don't circle anything. Just touch the sentences.
   Sentence 3: The girls liked chicken.
   Sentence 4: Two girls and a boy sat at a picnic table.
   Sentence 5: Cups and plates were on the table.
   Sentence 6: The boy petted the dog.
   Sentence 7: The boy wanted to go home.

7. Your turn: Circle the right words for the sentences. Read each sentence to yourself. If the sentence reports, circle **reports.** If the sentence does not report, circle **does not report.** Raise your hand when you're finished.
(Observe students and give feedback.)

8. Let's check your work. Make an **X** next to any item you missed.
I'll read each sentence. You tell me whether you circled **reports** or **does not report.**

- Sentence 3: The girls liked chicken. What did you circle? (Signal.) *Does not report.*

- Sentence 4: Two girls and a boy sat at a picnic table. What did you circle? (Signal.) *Reports.*

- Sentence 5: Cups and plates were on the table. What did you circle? (Signal.) *Reports.*

- Sentence 6: The boy petted the dog. What did you circle? (Signal.) *Does not report.*

- Sentence 7: The boy wanted to go home. What did you circle? (Signal.) *Does not report.*

9. Raise your hand if you got no items wrong. Great job.

- Raise your hand if you got only 1 item wrong. Good work.

- Listen: Fix up any mistakes you made in part A.
Do it now. Circle the right words for any items you missed.
(Observe students and give feedback.)

EXERCISE 3 Subject

The Part That Names

1. Everybody, pencils down.
I'll say some sentences. Then you'll tell me about the part that names.

2. Here's a sentence: A man (pause) ran down the street. Say that sentence. (Signal.) *A man ran down the street.*

- (Repeat step 2 until firm.)

3. Here's the part of the sentence that names: **a man.** Listen: A man ran down the street. Everybody, what part names? (Signal.) *A man.*

4. New sentence: A little dog (pause) is running down the street. What part names? (Signal.) *A little dog.*

- New sentence: A boy and a girl (pause) are running down the street. What part names? (Signal.) *A boy and a girl.*

- New sentence: Two girls (pause) are eating ice cream. What part names? (Signal.) *Two girls.*

- New sentence: The man and the boy (pause) ate ice cream. What part names? (Signal.) *The man and the boy.*

- (Repeat step 4 until firm.)

5. New sentence: A little rabbit ran under the fence. What part names? (Signal.) *A little rabbit.*

- New sentence: A dog and a cat ran under the fence. What part names? (Signal.) *A dog and a cat.*

- New sentence: My brother went to the store. What part names? (Signal.) *My brother.*

- (Repeat step 5 until firm.)

6. Everybody, find part B in your workbook. ✔
Touch each sentence as I read it.
Sentence 1: Two girls are eating ice cream.
Sentence 2: A black cat ran under the fence.
Sentence 3: A man and a woman sat on the porch.
Make a circle around each part of each sentence that names. Circle the part that names. Raise your hand when you're finished.
(Observe students and give feedback.)

7. Let's check your work. Make an **X** next to any item you missed.

- Sentence 1: Two girls are eating ice cream. Everybody, say the part you circled. (Signal.) *Two girls.*

- Sentence 2: A black cat ran under the fence. Say the part that names. (Signal.) *A black cat.*

- Sentence 3: A man and a woman sat on the porch. Say the part that names. (Signal.) *A man and a woman.*

8. Raise your hand if you got no items wrong. ✔
Super job.

- Everyone else, fix up any mistakes you made in part B.
(Observe students and give feedback.)

EXERCISE 4   Paper Set-Up

1. Everybody, pencils down. Find part C. ✔
The lined paper at the top is filled out
correctly. Below it is lined paper that you're
going to fill out.

2. Look at the sheet that is filled out correctly.
Touch the ball on the paper. ✔
   - That ball is on a line that goes up and
down. What is the up-and-down line
called? (Signal.) *The margin.*
   - Run your finger up and down the margin. ✔

3. Remember the rule about the margin: You
start writing words just after the margin.
The only things that go before the margin
are numbers. Everybody, what are the only
things that you write before the margin?
(Signal.) *Numbers.*
   - Where do you start writing words? (Signal.)
After the margin.

4. Touch the lined paper you're going to fill
out. ✔
   - Write your name on the top line.
(Observe students and give feedback.)

5. Everybody, touch the margin on the sheet
you're filling out. ✔
   - Listen: Write the number 1 and a period
on the line below your name. Remember,
the number and period go just in front of
the margin. Then copy sentence 1 just as
it's written above. Remember, start the
sentence just after the margin. Begin the
sentence with a capital **A.**
Don't write capital letters anywhere except
at the beginning of the sentence. Put a
period at the end of the sentence. Raise
your hand when you're finished with
sentence 1.
(Observe students and give feedback.)

6. Now copy sentence 2 and sentence 3.
Remember, first write the number and the
period in front of the margin. Then write the
sentence.
Start with a capital letter and end with
a period. Be sure to spell all the words
correctly.
You have a minute and a half. Raise your
hand when you're finished.
(Observe students and give feedback.
Praise students with specific comments
such as:) Good starting with a capital;
good starting just after the margin; good
spelling; good putting a period at the end
of the sentence.

7. (After one and a half minutes, say:)
Everybody, stop writing. Raise your hand if
you finished copying the sentences.
   - Good for you. If you didn't finish, you can
copy the rest of the sentences when we
finish the lesson.

8. Remember the rule about things you'll write
in this program. You'll have a chance to fix
up any mistakes you made before you hand
the paper in. If you fix them up before you
hand in the paper, you'll get a **super** paper.
So here's your chance to check all the
things you should have written.

9. Here's the first check: Did you write the
numbers 1, 2 and 3 before the margin, and
is there a period after each number? Check
your paper. If you made a mistake, use
your pencil and fix up the mistake. Make
sure you have the numbers 1, 2 and 3
before the margin and you have a period
after each number. Raise your hand when
you're finished with check 1.
(Observe students and give feedback.)

10. Here's the next check: Does each sentence
start with a capital letter and end with a
period?
Sentence 1 should start with a capital **A**
and have a period at the end.
Sentence 2 should start with a capital **M**
and have a period at the end.
Sentence 3 should start with a capital **S**
and have a period at the end.
Check your sentences and make sure
they all start with a capital and end with a
period. Then look at your sentences and
make sure those are the only capital letters
you wrote. Fix up any mistakes. Raise
your hand when you're sure that all your
sentences are right.
(Observe students and give feedback.)

11. Now comes the hardest check. Listen:
Check your sentences to make sure you
copied **all the words** and spelled them
correctly. Touch each word you wrote.
Then look at the paper at the top of your
page and see if you copied the word
and spelled it correctly. Check your work
carefully and fix up any mistakes you find.
Raise your hand when you're finished.
(Observe students and give feedback.)

12. If you did all the checks, you'll get a super paper. Next time, we'll find out how many super papers we get.

EXERCISE 5   Sentence Completion

The Part That Names

1. Everybody, pencils down. Find part D. ✔ You're going to use the picture to complete sentences.
2. Touch sentence 1.
   It says: Blank held the kite string. Everybody, look at the picture and touch the person who held the kite string. ✔
   • Everybody, read the name of the person who held the kite string. (Signal.) *Tim.*
   I'll say the whole sentence about Tim: Tim held the kite string. Your turn: Say the whole sentence. (Signal.) *Tim held the kite string.*
3. Touch sentence 2.
   It says: Blank climbed the tree.
   Look at the picture.
   • Everybody, read the name of the person who climbed the tree. (Signal.) *Susan.*
   • Now say the whole sentence about Susan. (Signal.) *Susan climbed the tree.*
4. Complete all the sentences in part D. Write the correct words in the blanks. Remember to start each sentence with a capital. Be sure to spell the words correctly. Raise your hand when you're finished.
   (Observe students and give feedback.)
5. Let's check your work. Make an **X** next to any sentence you missed.
   • Everybody, touch sentence 1.
   Capital **T,** Tim held the kite string.
   • Touch sentence 2.
   Capital **S,** Susan climbed the tree.
   • Touch sentence 3.
   Capital **A,** A kite was stuck in a tree.
6. Raise your hand if you got no items wrong. Great job.
   • Everyone else, fix up any mistakes you made in part D.
   (Observe students and give feedback.)

EXERCISE 6   Deductions

1. Everybody, pencils down. Find part E. ✔ You can draw a conclusion from these two sentences. I'll read the sentences: All **fish** have fins. A **bass** is a fish. Here's the conclusion: So a **bass** has fins.

• Listen again: All **fish** have fins. A **bass** is a fish. So a **bass** has fins.
2. Your turn to read both sentences and say the conclusion.
   • First sentence. (Signal.) *All fish have fins.*
   • Next sentence. (Signal.) *A bass is a fish.*
   • Conclusion. (Signal.) *So a bass has fins.*
3. Let's do that one more time.
   • First sentence. (Signal.) *All fish have fins.*
   • Next sentence. (Signal.) *A bass is a fish.*
   • Conclusion. (Signal.) *So a bass has fins.*
   • (Repeat step 3 until firm.)
4. (Call on several students:) See if you can say the whole thing—two sentences and the conclusion.
   All fish have fins. A bass is a fish. So a bass has fins.
5. Your turn: Write the conclusion. The word **so** is already written with a capital. You don't have to start the next word with a capital. Remember to end the conclusion with a period. Raise your hand when you're finished.
   (Observe students and give feedback.)
6. Check your work. I'll read the conclusion you should have on the last line: Capital **S,** So a bass has fins, period.
7. Fix up any mistakes you made in part E. (Observe students and give feedback.)

EXERCISE 7   Sweetie and the Birdbath

Storytelling

• I'll read a story. The story I'll read today is titled, "Sweetie and the Birdbath." Let's see how well you can remember things that happened.

   A woman named Bonnie loved birds. One day she noticed some birds cleaning themselves by splashing in a puddle on the sidewalk.

• Who remembers what idea Bonnie got as she observed these birds? (Call on a student. Idea: *Getting a bird bath.*)

   She said, "Those birds shouldn't have to splash in a puddle to get clean. They need a birdbath." That was a good idea.

The more Bonnie thought about getting a birdbath, the more she liked the idea. "I will get a birdbath big enough for all the birds that want to take a bath."

So Bonnie went to the pet store and looked at birdbaths. She picked out the biggest birdbath they had.

The next day, a truck delivered the birdbath. Bonnie set it up in her backyard, and soon some birds saw it. They called to their friends and, the first thing you know, all kinds of birds were splashing in the bird bath—red birds, yellow birds, spotted birds and little brown birds.

- Who remembers what happened when all those birds got in the birdbath? (Call on a student. Idea: *Sweetie saw the bird.*)
- What plan did Sweetie have? (Call on a student. Ideas: *Sneak over to the birdbath; jump up and grab some birds.*)

A big yellow cat lived in the house next to Bonnie's house. That cat's name was Sweetie, but that cat was anything but sweet. Sweetie loved to chase birds. When Sweetie saw all the birds in Bonnie's birdbath. Sweetie said to himself, "Yum, yum, look at all those little birds. I'm going to sneak over to that birdbath, jump up before they know I'm around and grab a couple of birds. Yum, yum."

So Sweetie crouched down and went through a hole in the fence. Then Sweetie snuck through some bushes that were near the birdbath—closer, closer and closer until he was almost underneath the birdbath.

Sweetie heard some chirping and fluttering, so he crouched down and waited—very still, without moving anything but the tip of his tail, which moved back and forth.

Well, Sweetie couldn't see what was happening in the birdbath because Sweetie was in the bushes.

- What happened while Sweetie was sneaking through the bushes? (Call on a student. Idea: *A huge eagle flew into the birdbath.*)

But all that fluttering and chirping came about because a huge eagle decided to take a bath in the birdbath. So the eagle swooped down. And as soon as the other birds saw this huge eagle, with its great beak and its huge claws, they took off—fluttering and chirping.

Sweetie didn't know it, but there wasn't a group of little birds in that birdbath any more. There was one huge bird—about three times as big as Sweetie.

Things were quiet now, so Sweetie got ready to leap up to the edge of the birdbath and grab a couple of tiny birds. Sweetie crouched down and, with a great leap, shot out of the bushes and landed on the edge of the birdbath.

- What happened next? (Call on a student. Ideas: *Sweetie jumped; The eagle grabbed Sweetie.*)

He landed with his claws out, grabbing at the first thing he saw. He grabbed the eagle, and, before Sweetie knew what was happening, that eagle grabbed **him.** The eagle picked Sweetie up and slammed him down into the middle of the birdbath. Splash!

Sweetie hated water, and he was all wet. He put his ears back and shot out of that birdbath so fast he looked like a wet yellow blur. He darted across the yard and through the hole in the fence. Then he just sat there with his mouth open and his eyes very wide.

"What happened?" Sweetie said to himself. One second he was grabbing at something and the next second he was getting slammed into the birdbath.

While Sweetie was trying to figure out what happened, he wasn't looking at the birdbath. He didn't see the eagle. That eagle finished bathing and took off.

- What happened just after the eagle finished taking a bath? (Call on a student. Idea: *The little birds returned to the birdbath*.)

As soon as the eagle left, all the little birds returned to the birdbath.

So when Sweetie finally peeked through the hole in the fence, he didn't see the eagle. He saw a bunch of little birds, twittering and splashing around in the water.

Sweetie looked and looked at those birds for a long time.

- Had Sweetie seen the eagle in the birdbath? (Call on a student. *No*.)
- Who did he think slammed him around? (Call on a student. *The little birds*.)

Then he said to himself, "From here those birds look pretty small and helpless. But when you get close to them, they are really big and strong. I don't think I'll go near that birdbath again."

So now Bonnie is happy because her birdbath always has a lot of birds in it. The birds are happy because they can meet all their friends and have a nice bath whenever they want. Sweetie is the only one who is not all that happy. He looks at the birds in Bonnie's yard a lot, but he never goes over there, and he spends a lot of time trying to figure out how those birds could look so small but be so big and strong.

Note:
- Collect the students' workbooks.
- Check the students' workbooks before the next language period. Mark any mistakes.
- Write **super** on lessons that have all mistakes corrected. Write **good** or **pretty good** on lessons that have only 1 or 2 mistakes.

Note: **Beginning on lesson 68, students will work in textbooks as well as workbooks. Each student will need a piece of lined paper with a margin.**

Note: Students will begin working in their textbook on this lesson. They will need lined paper with a margin.

Objectives

- Identify the part of a sentence that names. (Exercise 2)
- Write appropriate subjects in sentences. (Exercise 3)
- Complete a simple deduction. (Exercise 4)
- **Copy item numbers and sentences onto lined paper.** (Exercise 5)
- Write whether sentences report on a picture or do not report. (Exercise 6)
- Listen to a familiar story and answer comprehension questions. (Exercise 7)

WORKBOOK

EXERCISE 1   Feedback On Lesson 67

1. (Pass out textbooks and hand back student workbooks.)
2. Starting today, you'll do work in your workbook and your textbook. We'll always do the workbook activities first. Then we'll do the textbook activities. We start with the workbook.
3. Look at lesson 67 in your workbook. Raise your hand if I wrote **super** on that page. The **super** means that you checked over your work and fixed it up so it was perfect. If you didn't get a **super,** look at the mistakes you made and be more careful next time. (Pause.)
4. Now turn to lesson 68 in your workbook. ✔

EXERCISE 2   Subject

The Part That Names

1. Here's a sentence: **The horse** (pause) jumped over the fence. What part names? (Signal.) *The horse.*
- New sentence: **A little girl** (pause) ate two apples What part names? (Signal.) *A little girl.*
- New sentence: A cow and a horse ate grass. What part names? (Signal.) *A cow and a horse.*
- New sentence: A red bird flew over the house. What part names? (Signal.) *A red bird.*
- New sentence: The airplane had four engines. What part names? (Signal.) *The airplane.*
- (Repeat step 1 until firm.)

2. New sentence: My brother was washing the dishes. What part names? (Signal.) *My brother.*
- New sentence: That big bear licked the dishes. What part names? (Signal.) *That big bear.*
- New sentence: A kite went high in the sky. What part names? (Signal.) *A kite.*
- New sentence: An old man threw a stick to his dog. What part names? (Signal.) *An old man.*
- (Repeat step 2 until firm.)
3. Everybody, find part A in your workbook. ✔ Touch each sentence as I read it.
   Sentence 1: A little girl ate two apples.
   Sentence 2: A cow and a horse ate grass.
   Sentence 3: A kite went high in the sky.
   Sentence 4: My brother washed the dishes.
   Your turn: Circle the part of each sentence that names. Raise your hand when you're finished.
   (Observe students and give feedback.)
4. Let's check your work. Make an **X** next to any item you missed.
- Sentence 1: A little girl ate two apples. Everybody, say the part that names. (Signal.) *A little girl.*
- Sentence 2: A cow and a horse ate grass. Say the part that names. (Signal.) *A cow and a horse.*
- Sentence 3: A kite went high in the sky. Say the part that names. (Signal.) *A kite.*
- Sentence 4: My brother washed the dishes. Say the part that names. (Signal.) *My brother.*

5. Raise your hand if you got no items wrong. Great job.
- Everybody else, fix up any mistakes you made in part A.
(Observe students and give feedback.)

EXERCISE 3   Sentence Completion

The Part That Names

1. Everybody, find part B. ✔
Look at the picture. Then complete all the sentences in part B. Remember to start each sentence with a capital. Be sure to spell the words correctly. And start writing just after the margin. Raise your hand when you're finished.
(Observe students and give feedback.)
2. Let's check your work. Make an **X** next to any item you missed.
- Everybody, touch sentence 1.
Capital **A,** A sad clown rode a bicycle.
- Touch sentence 2.
Capital **A,** A bear juggled three balls.
- Touch sentence 3.
Capital **A,** A monkey walked on the rope.
- Touch sentence 4.
Capital **K,** Kathy laughed at the clown.
3. Raise your hand if you got no items wrong. Great job.
- Everybody else, fix up any mistakes you made in part B.
(Observe students and give feedback.)

EXERCISE 4   Deductions

1. Everybody, pencils down. Find part C. ✔
You can draw a conclusion from these two sentences. I'll read the sentences: Every **worker** uses tools. A **plumber** is a worker. Here's the conclusion: So a **plumber** uses tools.
- Listen again: Every **worker** uses tools. A **plumber** is a worker. So a **plumber** uses tools.
2. Your turn to read both sentences and say the conclusion.
- First sentence. (Signal.) *Every worker uses tools.*
- Next sentence. (Signal.) *A plumber is a worker.*
- Conclusion. (Signal.) *So a plumber uses tools.*

3. Let's do that one more time.
- First sentence. (Signal.) *Every worker uses tools.*
- Next sentence. (Signal.) *A plumber is a worker.*
- Conclusion. (Signal.) *So a plumber uses tools.*
- (Repeat step 3 until firm.)
4. (Call on several students:) See if you can say the whole thing—two sentences and the conclusion. *Every worker uses tools. A plumber is a worker. So a plumber uses tools.*
5. Your turn: Write the conclusion. Raise your hand when you're finished.
(Observe students and give feedback.)
6. Check your work. I'll read the conclusion you should have on the last line: Capital **S,** So a plumber uses tools, period.
- Fix up any mistakes you made in part C.
(Observe students and give feedback.)

EXERCISE 5   Copying Sentences

1. Open your textbook to lesson 68. ✔
- You're going to copy the sentences in part D onto a sheet of lined paper. Take out a sheet of lined paper. Write your name on the top line of the paper. Raise your hand when you're finished.
(Observe students and give feedback.)
2. Now run your finger up and down the margin of your paper. ✔
- Remember, write the numbers and the periods before the margin. Write the sentences just after the margin. Copy the sentences. Do it carefully. You have 3 minutes.
(Observe students and give feedback.)
3. (After 3 minutes, say:) Everybody, stop writing. Raise your hand if you finished copying the sentences.
(Praise students who raise their hands.)
4. Here's your chance to fix up any mistakes.
- Here's check 1: Did you write the numbers 1 and 2 before the margin, and is there a period after each number? Check your numbers and fix up any mistakes. Raise your hand when you're finished with check 1.
(Observe students and give feedback.)

- Here's check 2: Does each sentence start with a capital and end with a period? Look at each sentence and make sure it starts with a capital and ends with a period. Fix up any mistakes. Raise your hand when you're finished with check 2.
(Observe students and give feedback.)
- Here's the hard check: Did you copy **all the words** and spell them **correctly?** Remember how to check your paper for the words and the spelling. Do it carefully and fix up any mistakes. Raise your hand when you're finished.
(Observe students and give feedback.)
- Who thinks they'll get a **super** paper? We'll see next time.

EXERCISE 6 Reporting

1. Everybody, skip a line after your last sentence and write the number 1. Remember where it goes—just before the margin. ✔
- Now number the next line 2 and the line after that 3. Go all the way to 6. Number your paper to 6.
(Observe students and give feedback.)
2. Everybody, pencils down. Find part E in your textbook. ✔
- You're going to figure out if sentences report on what the picture shows. The rule about sentences that report is in the box. Touch that rule.
- I'll read it: Sentences that report tell what the picture shows. Remember, if a sentence does not tell what the picture shows, it does not report.
- I'll read the instructions for part E: Write **reports** if a sentence reports on what the picture shows. Write **no** if the sentence does not report.
3. What are you going to write if a sentence reports? (Signal.) *Reports.*
- What are you going to write if a sentence doesn't report? (Signal.) *No.*
- (Repeat step 3 until firm.)
4. Touch sentence 1.
Tom sat in a wheelchair. Everybody, does that sentence report on what the picture shows? (Signal.) *Yes.*
- So what do you write after number **1** on your paper? (Signal.) *Reports.*
Write **reports** after number **1.** ✔

5. Touch sentence 2.
Tom's sister walked next to him. Everybody, does that sentence report on what the picture shows? (Signal.) *No.*
- So what do you write after number **2** on your paper? (Signal.) *No.*
Write **no** after number **2.** ✔
6. Do the rest of the items in part E. Read each sentence carefully. Look at the picture. Write **reports** if the sentence reports. Write **no** if it doesn't report. Raise your hand when you're finished.
(Observe students and give feedback.)
7. Let's check your work. Make an **X** next to any item you missed.
- Sentence 3: A nurse pushed a wheelchair. What did you write? (Signal.) *Reports.*
- Sentence 4: The nurse felt very warm. What did you write? (Signal.) *No.*
- Sentence 5: Tom was hungry. What did you write? (Signal.) *No.*
- Sentence 6: Tom wore slippers and a hat. What did you write? (Signal.) *No.*
8. Raise your hand if you got no items wrong. Great job.
- Raise your hand if you got 1 item wrong. Good work.
- Fix up any mistakes you made in part E.
(Observe students and give feedback.)

EXERCISE 7 Clarabelle and the Bluebirds

Storytelling

- The story I'll read today is titled, "Clarabelle and the Bluebirds." Let's see how well you can remember things that happened.

> This is a story about a cow named Clarabelle. Clarabelle looked like the other brown-and-white cows on the farm. But Clarabelle was really different.

- Who remembers how she was different? (Call on a student. Idea: *She was always trying to do things that other animals did*.)

She was always trying to do things that other animals did. In fact, she felt sad about not being a bird or a frog or a student.

One day, Clarabelle was looking at the bluebirds that were sitting on a wire that went from the barn to a large pole.

- What did Clarabelle do next? (Call on a student. Idea: *She said that she wanted to sit on the wire with the bluebirds.*)

Clarabelle said, "I would love to sit on that wire with those bluebirds."

Some of the other cows heard Clarabelle talking to herself and they said, "Don't do it, Clarabelle. Remember what happened when you tried to swim like a duck in the duck pond?"

"Yeah," another cow said, "when you jumped **in** the pond, all the water jumped **out** of the pond."

Another cow said to Clarabelle, "And what about the time you tried to crow like the roosters? That was a real laugh. They were all saying 'cock-a-doodle-doo.' And you were saying, 'cock-a-doodle-moo.'"

"Ho, ho, ho." All the cows laughed until they had tears in their eyes.

"That's not very funny," Clarabelle said. "And if I want to sit on the wire with those bluebirds, you can't stop me."

So Clarabelle went into the barn and up to the window by the wire. While she was getting ready, all the farm animals gathered around. One goat said, "We're in for another great show by Clarabelle."

And so they were.

- Who remembers what the wire did when Clarabelle walked on it? (Call on a student. Idea: *The wire went down almost to the ground.*)

Clarabelle tiptoed out onto the wire, but Clarabelle was heavier than one

thousand bluebirds, so the wire went down, lower and lower, until it was almost touching the ground.

Well, the bluebirds were really angry. One of them said, "What are you doing, you big, fat cow? You've bent our wire almost to the ground."

"Yeah," another bluebird said. "This wire is for bluebirds, not brown-and-white cows."

Meanwhile, the farm animals were laughing and howling and rolling around on the ground. "Look at that," they said and rolled and laughed some more.

Clarabelle was not happy. She said, "This wire is not as much fun as I thought it would be." Clarabelle looked back up at the barn and said, "Wow, it's going to be hard to walk all the way back up there."

- How did Clarabelle finally get off the wire? (Call on a student. Idea: *She jumped off.*)
- What happened to the birds when she did that? (Call on a student. Idea: *The wire shot up so fast it sent the birds up into the clouds.*)

Then Clarabelle looked down and said, "I'm close to the ground, so maybe it would be easier for me to jump off and land in that haystack."

While she was trying to figure out what to do, all the bluebirds were yelling at her and saying things like, "Well, do something. Get off our wire so we can sit in peace!"

"All right, all right," Clarabelle said. "I'm leaving. Right now."

And with that, she jumped off the wire. Well, when she jumped off, the wire sprang way up into the air. It shot up so fast that it sent the bluebirds way up into the clouds, leaving blue tail feathers fluttering this way and that way.

And the farm animals almost died from laughter. "Did you see that?" a horse said as he rolled around on the ground. "Did you see those birds go flying up to the clouds?"

- Most of the animals thought it was very funny. Some animals did not think that. Which animals are those? (Call on a student. *The bluebirds.*)

Everybody laughed except for a bunch of bluebirds and one brown-and-white cow. That cow pouted and kept saying, "It's not **funny.** It's not funny."

But let me tell you: It was too—**very** funny.

Note:

- Collect the students' workbooks.
- Check the students' workbooks before the next language period. Mark any mistakes.
- Write **super** on lessons that have all mistakes corrected. Write **good** or **pretty good** on lessons that have only 1 or 2 mistakes.

Objectives

- **Change regular present-time verbs to past-time verbs by adding the suffix –ed.** (Exercise 2)
- **Draw conclusions based on different concrete examples.** (Exercise 3)
- **Identify the part of a sentence that names (subject) and the part that tells more (predicate).** (Exercise 4)
- Write whether sentences report on a picture or do not report. (Exercise 5)
- **Construct sentences by combining given parts that name and parts that tell more.** (Exercise 6)
- Listen to a familiar story and answer comprehension questions. (Exercise 7)

EXERCISE 1   Feedback On Lesson 68

- (Hand back the students' work from lesson 68.)
- Look at what I wrote on your lined paper. Raise your hand if I wrote **super.**
- If you didn't get a **super,** look at the mistakes you made and be more careful next time.

WORKBOOK

EXERCISE 2   Suffixes –ed

1. Everybody, pencils down. Open your workbook to lesson 69 and find part A. ✔
2. The words in part A tell what people do. You can make the words tell what people **did** by adding the letters **e-d** to the end of each word. What letters do you add to make the words tell what people did? (Signal.) *E-d.*
3. Touch word 1. ✔
   What word? (Signal.) *Burn.*
   If you add the letters **e-d** to **burn,** the word says **burned.**
4. Touch word 2.
   What word? (Signal.) *Fill.*
- What letters do you add to make the word tell what people did? (Signal.) *E-d.*
- When you add **e-d,** you get a word that tells what people did. That word is **filled.**
   Spell **filled.** (Signal.) *F-i-l-l-e-d.*
5. Touch word 3.
   What word? (Signal.) *Push.*
- **Push** tells what people **do.** Say the word that tells what they **did.** (Signal.) *Pushed.*
- Spell **pushed.** (Signal.) *P-u-s-h-e-d.*

6. Go back to word 1.
   The word that tells what people do is **burn.**
   What's the word that tells what they did? (Signal.) *Burned.*
- Write the word **burned** in the blank after **burn.**
   (Observe students and give feedback.)
7. Touch word 2.
   The word that tells what people do is **fill.**
   What's the word that tells what they did? (Signal.) *Filled.*
- Write the word **filled** in the blank after **fill.**
   (Observe students and give feedback.)
8. Write the rest of the words that tell what people did. Raise your hand when you're finished.
   (Observe students and give feedback.)
9. Let's check your work. Make an **X** next to any item you missed.
- Everybody, touch item 1.
   Say the word that tells what people did. (Signal.) *Burned.*
   Spell **burned.** (Signal.) *B-u-r-n-e-d.*
- Touch item 2.
   Say the word that tells what people did. (Signal.) *Filled.*
   Spell **filled.** (Signal.) *F-i-l-l-e-d.*
- Touch item 3.
   Say the word that tells what people did. (Signal.) *Pushed.*
   Spell **pushed.** (Signal.) *P-u-s-h-e-d.*
- Touch item 4.
   Say the word that tells what people did. (Signal.) *Licked.*
   Spell **licked.** (Signal.) *L-i-c-k-e-d.*
- Touch item 5.
   Say the word that tells what people did. (Signal.) *Started.*
   Spell **started.** (Signal.) *S-t-a-r-t-e-d.*

- Touch item 6.
  Say the word that tells what people did.
  (Signal.) *Scratched.*
  Spell **scratched.** (Signal.) *S-c-r-a-t-c-h-e-d.*
10. Raise your hand if you got no items wrong.
   Great job.
   - Raise your hand if you got 1 item wrong.
     Good work.
   - Fix up any mistakes you made in part A.
     (Observe students and give feedback.)

EXERCISE 3   Deductions

1. Everybody, pencils down. Find part B. I'll
   read the deduction. Listen: All **vehicles**
   can move. A **blank** is a vehicle. So a **blank**
   can move.
   - To draw a conclusion we must put the
     name of a vehicle in the blanks. I'll name
     a vehicle: a truck. I'll say **truck** for each
     blank. Listen: All **vehicles** can move. A
     truck is a vehicle. So a **truck** can move.
2. Your turn to say all three sentences.
   - Everybody, say the first sentence.
     (Signal.) *All vehicles can move.*
   - Next sentence. (Signal.) *A truck is a vehicle.*
   - Conclusion. (Signal.) *So a truck can move.*
   - (Repeat step 2 until firm.)
3. That conclusion is true. We'll get other
   true conclusions if we put the name of any
   vehicle in the blanks. Here's a different
   vehicle: **a train.**
4. Say the whole thing with **train** in each
   blank.
   - First sentence. (Signal.) *All vehicles can
     move.*
   - Next sentence. (Signal.) *A train is a vehicle.*
   - Conclusion. (Signal.) *So a train can move.*
   - (Repeat step 4 until firm.)
5. The names of some vehicles are written
   below the deduction: **truck, boat, train,
   car, plane, bike.** Your turn to complete the
   deduction. Put the name of any vehicle you
   want in the blanks.
   (Observe students and give feedback.)
6. (Call on several students to read all three
   sentences.)

EXERCISE 4   Predicate

The Part That Tells More

1. Everybody, pencils down. Find part C.
   Sentences that report have two parts.

One part names; the other part tells more.
Remember, one part names; the other part
tells more.
2. Touch sentence 1. ✔
   The little cats were in bed. Everybody, what
   part names? (Signal.) *The little cats.*
   - The rest of the sentence tells more. Listen
     to that part: were in bed.
3. The little cats were in bed. Say that
   sentence. (Signal.) *The little cats were in
   bed.*
   Everybody, what part names? (Signal.) *The
   little cats.*
   What part tells more? (Signal.) *Were in bed.*
   - Touch sentence 2.
     They were in bed. Say that sentence.
     (Signal.) *They were in bed.*
     Everybody, what part names? (Signal.)
     They.
     What part tells more? (Signal.) *Were in bed.*
   - Touch sentence 3.
     Five birds sat in the tree. Say that sentence.
     (Signal.) *Five birds sat in a tree.* What part
     names? (Signal.) *Five birds.*
     What part tells more? (Signal.) *Sat in the tree.*
   - Touch sentence 4.
     A dog chased a cat. Say that sentence.
     (Signal.) *A dog chased a cat.* What part
     names? (Signal.) *A dog.*
     What part tells more? (Signal.) *Chased a
     cat.*
   - (Repeat step 3 until firm.)

LINED PAPER • TEXTBOOK

EXERCISE 5   Reporting

1. Everybody, take out a sheet of lined paper
   and write your name on the top line. Raise
   your hand when you're finished.
   (Observe students and give feedback.)
2. Now number your lined paper from 1
   through 7. Write 1 on the line under your
   name. Remember where the 1 goes. Then
   number lines 2, 3, 4, 5, 6 and 7. Raise your
   hand when you're finished.
   (Observe students and give feedback.)
   - Everybody, open your textbook to lesson
     69 and find part D. ✔
3. I'll read the instructions: Write **reports** if
   a sentence reports on what the picture
   shows.
   Write **no** if the sentence does not report.

- Read each sentence carefully and look at the picture. Write **reports** or **no** for each sentence in part D. Raise your hand when you're finished.
(Observe students and give feedback.)
4. Check your work. Make an **X** next to any item you missed.
- Sentence 1: The woman rode a horse. What did you write? (Signal.) *Reports.*
- Sentence 2: The horse was named Rusty. What did you write? (Signal.) *No.*
- Sentence 3: The woman wore a hat and sunglasses. What did you write? (Signal.) *No.*
- Sentence 4: The woman lived on a farm. What did you write? (Signal.) *No.*
- Sentence 5: A man sat on the fence. What did you write? (Signal.) *Reports.*
- Sentence 6: The man held a rope. What did you write? (Signal.) *Reports.*
- Sentence 7: The man wanted to ride the horse. What did you write? (Signal.) *No.*
5. Raise your hand if you made no mistakes. Great job.
- Raise your hand if you made 1 mistake. Good work.
- Fix up any mistakes you made in part D. (Observe students and give feedback.)

EXERCISE 6 **Sentence Completion**

The Part That Tells More

1. Everybody, skip a line after the last word and write the number 1. Number the next line 2 and the line after that 3. ✔
- Everybody, pencils down. Find part E in your textbook. ✔
2. You're going to write sentences that report on the picture. Your sentences will name and then tell more. The parts that tell more are written in the box under the picture. Touch that box. ✔
- I'll read the parts: **held an umbrella, chased a cat, fell on the sidewalk.** Get ready to complete each sentence by saying the part that names.

3. Touch sentence 1. ✔
- It says: **Blank** held an umbrella. Everybody, what name goes in the blank? (Signal.) *A tall woman.*
- Say the whole sentence. (Signal.) *A tall woman held an umbrella.*
- Touch sentence 2. ✔
It says: **Blank** chased a cat.
What name goes in the blank? (Signal.) *The dog.*
- Say the whole sentence. (Signal.) *The dog chased a cat.*
- (Repeat step 3 until firm.)
4. You're going to write sentence 1. Everybody, who held an umbrella? (Signal.) *A tall woman.*
- Say the whole sentence. (Signal.) *A tall woman held an umbrella.*
- Write sentence 1 on your lined paper. Remember to start with a capital and put a period at the end of the sentence. Raise your hand when you're finished. (Observe students and give feedback.)
- Everybody, read sentence 1. (Signal.) *A tall woman held an umbrella.*
5. Now write sentence 2. Copy the part that names from the picture and write the rest of sentence 2. Remember to start with a capital and put a period at the end of the sentence. Raise your hand when you're finished. (Observe students and give feedback.)
- Everybody, read sentence 2. (Signal.) *The dog chased a cat.*
6. Now write sentence 3. Copy the part that names from the picture and write the rest of sentence 3. Remember to start with a capital and put a period at the end of the sentence. Raise your hand when you're finished. (Observe students and give feedback.)
- Everybody, read sentence 3. (Signal.) *Bill fell on the sidewalk.*
7. Here's your chance to fix up any mistakes.
- Check 1: Did you write the numbers 1, 2 and 3 before the margin, and is there a period after each number? Check your numbers and fix up any mistakes. Raise your hand when you're finished. (Observe students and give feedback.)

- Here's check 2: Does each sentence begin with a capital and end with a period? Look at each sentence and make sure it starts with a capital and ends with a period. Fix up any mistakes. Raise your hand when you're finished.
  (Observe students and give feedback.)
- Here's the hard check: Did you copy **all the words** and spell them **correctly?** Remember how to check your paper for the words and the spelling. Do it carefully and fix up any mistakes. Raise your hand when you're finished.
  (Observe students and give feedback.)
- Who thinks they'll get a **super** paper? We'll see next time.

EXERCISE 7 Bleep Says Some Strange Things

Storytelling

- The story I'll read today is titled, "Bleep Says Some Strange Things." Let's see how well you can remember things that happened.

> Bleep was a robot that could do lots of smart things. He could answer questions. He could follow directions. You could tell him to get the ladder out of the garage and he'd get the ladder.

- Who remembers the name of the person who invented Bleep? (Call on a student. *Molly.*)

> The person who invented Bleep was named Molly. People called her Molly Mix-up because, although she invented lots of things, everything she invented had problems. She invented Bleep. And Bleep had a lot of problems.

- Who can name some of the problems he had? (Call on a student. Ideas: *He wouldn't always tell the truth. He said, "Bleep" every time he talked*.)

> At first, Bleep would not always tell the truth. You couldn't tell when he was lying and when he was saying things that were true.

He also said "bleep" every time he talked. If you asked him what color the grass was, he wouldn't say "green." He'd say, "Bleep. Green."

If you asked him what color the sky was, he wouldn't say "blue." He'd say, "Bleep. Blue."

Molly made adjustments so Bleep wouldn't say "bleep" all the time and other adjustments so he would tell the truth. She fixed him so he'd say "I don't know" if he didn't know the answer to something. That was a lot better than having Bleep make up some wild story when he didn't know the answer.

Each time Molly adjusted Bleep, she'd take off the top of his head and turn the screws that controlled the way he talked and thought. There were many screws. Each screw was a different color. For some adjustments, Molly would turn the blue screw. For other adjustments, she'd turn the yellow screw or the pink screw or sometimes more than one screw. Well, after many adjustments, Bleep seemed to work very well, except for a couple of small problems.

- What were those problems?(Call on a student. Idea: *He said, "Okay, baby."*)

> One problem Bleep had was that he would sometimes say "okay, baby." If you told him to get the ladder out of the garage, he would get the ladder all right, but, before he did, he might say "okay, baby." If you told him to sit down, he'd sit down all right, but, before he did, he might say something.
>
> Molly tried three or four times to fix Bleep so he wouldn't say "okay, baby," but she was not able to do it. Bleep kept right on saying "okay, baby."

One day, a school teacher came over to Molly's house. Bleep answered the door. Molly was in the garage working on a new invention. The school teacher said, "Is Molly Henderson at home?"

Bleep said, "Yes."

The school teacher said, "Would you ask her to come to the door?" Bleep said, "Okay, baby." The school teacher jumped. She said, "Oh . . . oh, what kind of talk is that?"

Bleep said, "Bleep-talk."

The teacher said, "Well, I don't think I like Bleep-talk very much at all."

Bleep said, "Okay, baby."

The school teacher jumped again. "Oh . . . oh," she said. "I'm leaving." And she did just that.

After the teacher left, Bleep started thinking about what she had said. She had said, "Well, I don't think I like Bleep-talk very much at all."

- How did Bleep think he could change his Bleep talk? (Call on a student. Idea: *Tinkering with the screws on his head*.)

Bleep said to himself, "Maybe I should change the way Bleep talks."

He had seen Molly do it many times. He knew that she took off the top of his head and tinkered around with the screws. He figured that he could take off the top of his head, tinker with the screws and change the way he talked.

- Who remembers what he did? (Call on a student. Idea: *He turned a red screw and a brown screw*.)

That's just what he did.

But he didn't know which screws to adjust. In fact, he wasn't even very sure about how he wanted to change the way he talked. So he just turned a red screw

a little bit and a brown screw a little bit. Then he put the top of his head back on.

Pretty soon, Molly came in from the garage. She said, "Did I hear somebody at the door a while ago?"

Bleep didn't say "yes."

- Who remembers what he said? (Call on a student. *Yus*.)

He said, "Yus."

Molly said, "Did you say 'yus'?"

Bleep said, **"Yus."**

Molly looked at Bleep and said, "Did you take the top of your head off and play with the screws?"

"Yus."

"Well, why did you do that?"

Bleep said, "I want to talk butter."

Molly said, "Well, you don't talk **better**. You sound awful. But I don't have time to fix you now." She handed him a letter and said, "Mail this letter right away."

"Okay, baby."

- What did Bleep say for the word *letter*? (Call on a student. *Lutter*.)

Then Bleep looked at the letter and said, "But there is no stamp on this **lutter.**"

"Well, put a stamp on it and then mail it."

- How would Bleep say the word *get*? (Call on a student. *Gut*.)

Bleep said, "Okay, baby. I'll **gut** a stamp."

Molly shook her head and said, "When you mail the letter, please don't talk to anybody. You sound awful."

Bleep put a stamp on the letter and took it to the mailbox. But just as he was mailing the letter, a neighbor walked by—an old man named Ben.

Ben said, "Hello, Bleep."

- What did Bleep say to Ben? (Call on a student. *Hello, Bun.*)

Bleep looked at Ben and said, **"Hullo, Bun."**

Ben blinked and stared at Bleep. Then he shook his head and walked away, saying, "What kind of talk is that?"

Bleep said, "Bleep-talk."

Then Bleep said to himself, **"Wull,** Molly will take the top of my **hud** off again and fix it so I talk **butter."**

And that's just what she did.

Note:
- Collect the students' workbooks and papers.
- Check the students' work before the next language period. Mark any mistakes.
- Write **super** on lessons that have all mistakes corrected. Write **good** or **pretty good** on work that has only 1 or 2 mistakes.

Objectives

- Change regular present-time verbs to past-time verbs by adding the suffix –ed. (Exercise 2)
- **Write past-time verbs for irregular present-time verbs.** (Exercise 3)
- Draw conclusions based on different concrete examples. (Exercise 4)
- Identify the part of a sentence that names (subject) and the part that tells more (predicate). (Exercise 5)
- Construct sentences by combining given parts that name and parts that tell more. (Exercise 6)
- Listen to a familiar story and answer comprehension questions. (Exercise 7)

EXERCISE 1   Feedback On Lesson 69

- (Hand back the students' work from lesson 69.)
- Look at what I wrote on your lined paper. Raise your hand if I wrote **super.**
- If you didn't get a **super,** look at the mistakes you made and be more careful next time.

WORKBOOK

EXERCISE 2   Suffixes –ed

1. Everybody, pencils down. Open your workbook to lesson 70 and find part A. ✔
2. The words in part A tell what people do. You can make the words tell what people **did** by adding the letters **e-d** to the end of each word. What letters do you add to make the words tell what people did? (Signal.) *E-d.*
3. Touch word 1. ✔
   What word? (Signal.) *Jump.*
   If you add the letters **e-d** to **jump,** the word says **jumped.**
4. Touch word 2.
   What word? (Signal.) *Pull.*
- What letters do you add to make the word tell what people did? (Signal.) *E-d.*
- When you add **e-d,** you get a word that tells what people did. Say the word that tells what they did. (Signal.) *Pulled.*
   Spell **pulled.** (Signal.) *P-u-l-l-e-d.*
5. Touch word 3.
   What word? (Signal.) *Play.*
- **Play** tells what people **do.** Say the word that tells what they **did.** (Signal.) *Played.*
   Spell **played.** (Signal.) *P-l-a-y-e-d.*

6. Go back to word 1.
   The word that tells what people do is **jump.** What's the word that tells what they did? (Signal.) *Jumped.*
- Write the word **jumped** in the blank after **jump.**
   (Observe students and give feedback.)
7. Touch word 2.
   The word that tells what people do is **pull.** What's the word that tells what they did? (Signal.) *Pulled.*
- Write the word **pulled** in the blank after **pull.**
   (Observe students and give feedback.)
8. Write the rest of the words that tell what people did. Raise your hand when you're finished.
   (Observe students and give feedback.)
9. Let's check your work. Make an **X** next to any item you missed.
- Everybody, touch item 1.
   Say the word that tells what people did. (Signal.) *Jumped.*
   Spell **jumped.** (Signal.) *J-u-m-p-e-d.*
- Touch item 2.
   Say the word that tells what people did. (Signal.) *Pulled.*
   Spell **pulled.** (Signal.) *P-u-l-l-e-d.*
- Touch item 3.
   Say the word that tells what people did. (Signal.) *Played.*
   Spell **played.** (Signal.) *P-l-a-y-e-d.*
- Touch item 4.
   Say the word that tells what people did. (Signal.) *Pushed.*
   Spell **pushed.** (Signal.) *P-u-s-h-e-d.*
- Touch item 5.
   Say the word that tells what people did. (Signal.) *Spilled.*
   Spell **spilled.** (Signal.) *S-p-i-l-l-e-d.*

- Touch item 6.
Say the word that tells what people did. (Signal.) *Tricked.*
Spell **tricked.** (Signal.) *T-r-i-c-k-e-d.*

10. Raise your hand if you got no items wrong. Great job.
- Raise your hand if you got 1 item wrong. Good work.
- Fix up any mistakes you made in part A. (Observe students and give feedback.)

EXERCISE 3   Past Time

Irregular Verbs

1. Everybody, pencils down. Find part B. ✔
Next to each number in the first column is a pair of words. The first word tells what people **do.** The second word tells what people **did.**
- Touch number 1.
The words are **find** and **found.** The word that tells what people do is **find.** The word that tells what they did is **found.**

2. Touch number 2.
The word that tells what people do is **give.** Everybody, what word tells what they did? (Signal.) *Gave.*
- Touch number 3.
Buy tells what people do. What word tells what they did? (Signal.) *Bought.*
- Touch number 4.
Dig tells what people do. What word tells what they did? (Signal.) *Dug.*
- Touch number 5.
Have tells what people do. What word tells what they did? (Signal.) *Had.*

3. For words 6 through 10, I'll say the word that tells what people **do.** You'll say the word that tells what they **did.**

4. Touch 6.
Buy. Everybody, tell me what they did. (Signal.) *Bought.*
- Touch 7.
Find. Tell me what they did. (Signal.) *Found.*
- Touch 8.
Dig. Tell me what they did. (Signal.) *Dug.*
- Touch 9.
Have. Tell me what they did. (Signal.) *Had.*
- Touch 10.
Give. Tell me what they did. (Signal.) *Gave.*
- (Repeat step 4 until firm.)

5. Do words 6 through 15. Next to each word, write the word that tells what people did. Remember to spell each word correctly. Raise your hand when you're finished. (Observe students and give feedback.)

6. Check your work. Make an **X** if you don't have the right word or if you didn't spell it correctly. Say the words that tell what people did.
- Touch 6.
What did you write for **buy?** (Signal.) *Bought.*
Spell **bought.** (Signal.) *B-o-u-g-h-t.*
- Touch 7.
What did you write for **find?** (Signal.) *Found.*
Spell **found.** (Signal.) *F-o-u-n-d.*
- Touch 8.
What did you write for **dig?** (Signal.) *Dug.*
Spell **dug.** (Signal.) *D-u-g.*
- Touch 9.
What did you write for **have?** (Signal.) *Had.*
Spell **had.** (Signal.) *H-a-d.*
- Touch 10.
What did you write for **give?** (Signal.) *Gave.*
Spell **gave.** (Signal.) *G-a-v-e.*

7. Touch **dig** in the next column. ✔
What did you write for **dig?** (Signal.) *Dug.*
- What did you write for **buy?** (Signal.) *Bought.*
- What did you write for **have?** (Signal.) *Had.*
- What did you write for **give?** (Signal.) *Gave.*
- What did you write for **find?** (Signal.) *Found.*

8. Raise your hand if you got no items wrong. Great job.
- Raise your hand if you got 1 item wrong. Good work.
- Fix up any mistakes you made in part B. (Observe students and give feedback.)

EXERCISE 4   Deductions

1. Everybody, pencils down. Find part C. ✔
You're going to draw a conclusion. The first sentence is: Every building has a roof.
- To draw a conclusion we must put the name of building in the blanks. I'll name a building: a house.
- Listen to the deduction: Every **building** has a roof. A **house** is a building. So a **house** has a roof.

2. Your turn to say all three sentences.
   - First sentence. (Signal.) *Every building has a roof.*
   - Next sentence. (Signal.) *A house is a building.*
   - Conclusion. (Signal.) *So a house has a roof.*
   - (Repeat step 2 until firm.)
3. That conclusion is true. We'll get other true conclusions if we put the name of any building in the blanks. Here's a different building: a store.
4. Say the whole thing with **a store.**
   - First sentence. (Signal.) *Every building has a roof.*
   - Next sentence. (Signal.) *A store is a building.*
   - Conclusion. (Signal.) *So a store has a roof.*
   - (Repeat step 4 until firm.)
5. Your turn to complete the deduction. The names of some buildings are written below the deduction. Put the name of any building you want in the blank. Then complete the last sentence. Raise your hand when you're finished.
   (Observe students and give feedback.)
6. (Call on individual students to read all three sentences. Praise students who have appropriate deductions.)

TEXTBOOK

EXERCISE 5   Predicate

The Part That Tells More

1. Everybody, pencils down. Open your textbook to Lesson 70. Find part D. ✔
   - Sentences that report have two parts. One part names; the other part tells more. Remember, one part names; the other part tells more.

2. Everybody, touch sentence 1. ✔
   Tom and his dog ran next to the lake. Say that sentence. (Signal.) *Tom and his dog ran next to the lake.* Everybody, what part names? (Signal.) *Tom and his dog.* What part tells more? (Signal.) *Ran next to the lake.*
   - Touch sentence 2.
     They jumped in the water. Say that sentence. (Signal.) *They jumped in the water.* Everybody, what part names? (Signal.) *They.*
     What part tells more? (Signal.) *Jumped in the water.*
   - Touch sentence 3.
     A little girl had a toy boat. Say that sentence. (Signal.) *A little girl had a toy boat.* Everybody, what part names? (Signal.) *A little girl.* What part tells more? (Signal.) *Had a toy boat.*
   - Touch sentence 4.
     Sally and Ginger were under a tree. Say that sentence. (Signal.) *Sally and Ginger were under a tree.* What part names? (Signal.) *Sally and Ginger.* What part tells more? (Signal.) *Were under a tree.*
   - Touch sentence 5.
     They were happy. Say that sentence. (Signal.) *They were happy.* What part names? (Signal.) *They.*
     What part tells more? (Signal.) *Were happy.*
   - (Repeat step 2 until firm.)

LINED PAPER

EXERCISE 6   Sentence Completion

The Part That Tells More

1. Everybody, take out a sheet of lined paper and write your name on the top line. ✔
2. Now number your lined paper 1 through 3. Raise your hand when you're finished.
3. Pencils down. Find part E in your textbook. ✔
   - I'll read the instructions: Write sentences that report on the picture. Each sentence should name and then tell more. The parts that name are in the picture. The parts that tell more are written in the box under the picture. Everybody, touch that box. ✔
   - I'll read the parts: **sat in a wheelchair; pushed the wheelchair; stood next to the man.** Get ready to complete each sentence by saying the part that names.

4. Touch sentence 1.
   It says: **Blank** sat in a wheelchair.
   Everybody, what name goes in the blank?
   (Signal.) *A sick man.*
   - Say the whole sentence. (Signal.) *A sick man sat in a wheelchair.*
   - Touch sentence 2.
   It says: **Blank** pushed the wheelchair. What name goes in the blank? (Signal.) *A nurse.*
   - Say the whole sentence. (Signal.) *A nurse pushed the wheelchair.*
   - (Repeat step 4 until firm.)
5. You're going to write sentence 1.
   Everybody, who sat in a wheelchair?
   (Signal.) *A sick man.*
   - Say the whole sentence. (Signal.) *A sick man sat in a wheelchair.*
   - Write sentence 1 on your lined paper. Remember to start with a capital and put a period at the end of the sentence. Raise your hand when you're finished.
   (Observe students and give feedback.)
   - Everybody, read sentence 1. (Signal.) *A sick man sat in a wheelchair.*
6. Now write sentence 2. Copy the part that names from the picture and write the rest of sentence 2. Remember to start with a capital and put a period at the end of the sentence. Raise your hand when you're finished.
   (Observe students and give feedback.)
   - Everybody, read sentence 2. (Signal.) *A nurse pushed the wheelchair.*
7. Now write sentence 3. Copy the part that names from the picture and write the rest of sentence 3. Remember to start with a capital and put a period at the end of the sentence. Raise your hand when you're finished.
   (Observe students and give feedback.)
   - Everybody, read sentence 3. (Signal.) *His sister stood next to the man.*
8. Here's your chance to fix up any mistakes.
   - Check 1: Did you write the numbers 1, 2 and 3 before the margin, and is there a period after each number? Check your numbers and fix up any mistakes. Raise your hand when you're finished.
   (Observe students and give feedback.)

- Here's check 2: Does each sentence start with a capital and end with a period? Look at each sentence and make sure it starts with a capital and ends with a period. Fix up any mistakes. Raise your hand when you're finished.
   (Observe students and give feedback.)
- Here's the hard check: Did you copy all the words and spell them correctly? Remember how to check your paper for the words and the spelling. Do it carefully and fix up any mistakes. Raise your hand when you're finished.
   (Observe students and give feedback.)
- Who thinks they'll get a **super** paper? We'll see next time.

EXERCISE 7 Paul Paints Pansies
Storytelling

- The story I'll read today is titled, "Paul Paints Pansies." Let's see how well you can remember things that happened.
- This story is about Paul. Who remembers the kinds of words Paul liked to say? (Call on a student. Praise reasonable responses.)
- What was his favorite letter? (Call on a student. *P.*)

One day Paul was in the country painting a picture of pink and purple pansies. He had a small can of pink paint and a very large can of purple paint.

He liked that big can of purple paint because he never knew when he'd have to use purple paint to fix up something that got paint on it.

Well, Paul was in the middle of a large pasture painting perfect little pansies. He said to himself, "Painting in a pasture is perfect."

A lot of brown-and-white cows were in that pasture, and one of them was very, very curious about what Paul was doing.

That cow, of course, was Clarabelle. She walked over to where Paul was painting and she looked at his picture and thought that painting pictures was a lot of fun.

But it was a warm day and the flies kept buzzing around Clarabelle.

- Who remembers how these flies helped Clarabelle paint something? (Call on a student. Idea: *She swished her tail at them*.)
- What did she paint? (Call on a student. Idea: *Purple bushes on Paul's paintings*.)

When the flies got on her back or on her side, she'd swish them away with her tail. She stood there for a long time, watching and swishing and watching and swishing.

Suddenly, Paul looked at his watch and said, "Oh, pooh." Paul had forgotten that he had promised his mother that he would pick up pickles for her. So he just left his paint and painting in the middle of the pasture and ran over to his bike.

He hopped on and he peddled away down the pebble path. He knew it wouldn't take him long to pick up the pickles.

As soon as he had left, Clarabelle looked at the painting and said to herself, "I don't have a paint brush to paint with, but . . . "

She looked at her tail. On the end of it was a large patch of hair. That would make a perfect paintbrush.

She dipped the end of her tail into the big can of purple paint. Then she turned around and swung her tail towards Paul's painting. The end of her tail hit the painting with a great plop. Her tail made a great splat that looked like a huge purple bush.

"Not bad," Clarabelle said to herself.

So she did it again, and again— dipped her tail into the can, swung that tail at the picture and plop. She made six purple bushes in the picture.

Then the flies started to get really bad. Biting flies were buzzing around her back and her side. Without thinking, Clarabelle swished her tail and splat. She made a purple bush on her side. Then splat, she made a purple bush on her back. Then splat, another purple bush on her other side.

She was getting ready to paint another bush in Paul's picture when Paul came peddling up the pebbled path on his bike. He got off and ran over to his painting. Then he stopped. He stood there and stared.

- What did Paul think when he saw the painting? (Call on a student. Idea: *His painting looked better*.)

Then he said, "Purple plants with my pansies. They're perfect."

He looked around to see who could have made those perfect purple plants. He saw Clarabelle with purple bushes on her back and her sides. He said to her, "You improved my painting, but you did a poor job of painting yourself.

- What did Paul think Clarabelle needed? (Call on a student. Idea: *Pink and purple pansies*.)

You have purple bushes on you, but you don't have any pink and purple pansies."

Clarabelle turned her head and looked at the purple plants. Then she turned back and looked at Paul. He was smiling.

He said, "Those purple plants don't look good without some pink and purple pansies."

Clarabelle agreed, so she nodded her head up and down.

Paul said, "Don't worry, brown-and-white cow. I can fix it up." And he did.

Now there is a large herd of brown-and-white cows in the pasture. Most of them look like ordinary brown-and-white cows. But one of them has a very pretty picture on her sides and back.

Note:
- Collect the students' workbooks and papers.
- Check the students' work before the next language period. Mark any mistakes.
- Write **super** on lessons that have all mistakes corrected. Write **good** or **pretty good** on work that has only 1 or 2 mistakes.

Objectives

• Write past-time verbs for irregular present-time verbs. (Exercise 2)
• **Change 2-word verbs in sentences to 1-word verbs.** (Exercise 3)
  Note: Most of what students write early in the program uses simple past-time verbs, not progressive verbs (for example, **was walking**). Later in the program, progressive verbs are introduced.
• Identify the part of a sentence that names (subject) and the part that tells more (predicate). (Exercise 4)
• Draw conclusions based on different concrete examples. (Exercise 5)
• **Select sentences that state the main thing that illustrated characters did.** (Exercise 6)
• Write whether a sentence reports on a picture or does not report. (Exercise 7)
• Listen to a familiar story and answer comprehension questions. (Exercise 8)

EXERCISE 1 Feedback On Lesson 70

• (Hand back the students' work from lesson 70.)
• Look at what I wrote on your lined paper. Raise your hand if I wrote **super.**
• If you didn't get a **super,** look at the mistakes you made and be more careful next time.

WORKBOOK

EXERCISE 2 Past Time

Irregular Verbs

1. Everybody, pencils down. Open your workbook to lesson 71 and find part A. ✔
• Next to each number in the first column is a pair of words. The first word tells what people **do.** The second word tells what people **did.**
• Touch number 1.
  The words are **give** and **gave.** The word that tells what people do is **give.** The word that tells what they did is **gave.**
2. Touch number 2.
  The word that tells what people do is **dig.** Everybody, what word tells what they did? (Signal.) *Dug.*
• Touch number 3.
  Find tells what people do. What word tells what they did? (Signal.) *Found.*
• Touch number 4.

Have tells what people do. What word tells what they did? (Signal.) *Had.*
• Touch number 5.
  Buy tells what people do. What word tells what they did? (Signal.) *Bought.*
3. For words 6 through 10, I'll say the word that tells what people **do.** You'll say the word that tells what they **did.**
4. Touch 6.
  Dig. Everybody, tell me what they did. (Signal.) *Dug.*
• Touch 7.
  Find. Tell me what they did. (Signal.) *Found.*
• Touch 8.
  Buy. Tell me what they did. (Signal.) *Bought.*
• Touch 9.
  Give. Tell me what they did. (Signal.) *Gave.*
• Touch 10.
  Have. Tell me what they did. (Signal.) *Had.*
• (Repeat step 4 until firm.)
5. Do words 6 through 10. Next to each word, write the word that tells what people did. Remember to spell each word correctly. Raise your hand when you're finished. (Observe students and give feedback.)
6. Let's check your work. Make an **X** if you don't have the right word or if you didn't spell it correctly. Say the words that tell what people did.
• Touch 6.
  What did you write for **dig?** (Signal.) *Dug.* Spell **dug.** (Signal.) *D-u-g.*

- Touch 7.
  What did you write for **find?** (Signal.) *Found.*
  Spell **found.** (Signal.) *F-o-u-n-d.*
- Touch 8.
  What did you write for **buy?** (Signal.) *Bought.*
  Spell **bought.** (Signal.) *B-o-u-g-h-t.*
- Touch 9.
  What did you write for **give?** (Signal.) *Gave.*
  Spell **gave.** (Signal.) *G-a-v-e.*
- Touch 10.
  What did you write for **have?** (Signal.) *Had.*
  Spell **had.** (Signal.) *H-a-d.*
7. Raise your hand if you got no items wrong. Great job.
- Raise your hand if you got 1 item wrong. Good work.
- Fix up any mistakes you made in part A. (Observe students and give feedback.)

EXERCISE 3   Editing Sentences

Changing the Verb

1. Everybody, pencils down. Find part B. ✔
   For things you'll write in this program, you'll tell what people **did,** not what they **were doing** or **are doing.** The words that are underlined in each sentence tell what people were doing or are doing. You're going to fix up those parts to tell what people did.
2. Sentence 1: Alicia was fixing her bike. What words are underlined? (Signal.) *Was fixing.*
- That tells what she was doing. Here's the word that tells what she did: **fixed.** What word tells what she **did?** (Signal.) *Fixed.*
- Sentence 2: The girl was talking loudly. What words are underlined? (Signal.) *Was talking.*
- That tells what she was doing. Everybody, what word tells what she **did?** (Signal.) *Talked.*
- Sentence 3: Miss Cook is finding her keys. What words are underlined? (Signal.) *Is finding.*
- That tells what she is doing. What word tells what she **did?** (Signal.) *Found.*
- Sentence 4: Her grandmother is smiling at the baby. What words are underlined? (Signal.) *Is smiling.*

- That tells what she is doing. What word tells what she **did?** (Signal.) *Smiled.*
- Sentence 5: Mr. Howard was buying a picture. What words are underlined? (Signal.) *Was buying.*
- That tells what he was doing. What word tells what he **did?** (Signal.) *Bought.*
- (Repeat step 2 until firm.)
3. Your turn: Cross out the underlined words in each sentence. Above those words, write the word that tells what people did. Raise your hand when you're finished. (Observe students and give feedback.)
4. Let's check your work. Make an **X** next to any item you missed.
- Sentence 1: Alicia was fixing her bike. Say the sentence so it tells what Alicia did. (Signal.) *Alicia fixed her bike.*
- Sentence 2: The girl was talking loudly. Say the sentence so it tells what the girl did. (Signal.) *The girl talked loudly.*
- Sentence 3: Miss Cook is finding her keys. Say the sentence so it tells what Miss Cook did. (Signal.) *Miss Cook found her keys.*
- Sentence 4: Her grandmother is smiling at the baby. Say the sentence so it tells what her grandmother did. (Signal.) *Her grandmother smiled at the baby.*
- Sentence 5: Mr. Howard was buying a picture. Say the sentence so it tells what Mr. Howard did. (Signal.) *Mr. Howard bought a picture.*
5. Raise your hand if you got no items wrong. Great job.
- Raise your hand if you got 1 item wrong. Good work.
- Fix up any mistakes you made in part B. (Observe students and give feedback.)

EXERCISE 4   Subject/Predicate

1. Everybody, pencils down. Find part C. ✔
   For each sentence in part C, you're going to **circle** the part that names and **underline** the part that tells more.
2. Everybody, touch sentence 1.
   Three tall girls sat on a horse. Say the part of the sentence that names. (Signal.) *Three tall girls.*
- Say the part of the sentence that tells more. (Signal.) *Sat on a horse.*
- (Repeat step 2 until firm.)

3. You're going to circle the part that names. Listen to the sentence again: Three tall girls sat on a horse. Circle the part that names. ✔
- Everybody, read the words you circled. (Signal.) *Three tall girls.*
- Now underline the part of sentence 1 that tells more.
(Observe students and give feedback.)
- Everybody, read the words you underlined. (Signal.) *Sat on a horse.*
4. Touch sentence 2.
They rode the horse across the field. Say the part of the sentence that names. (Signal.) *They.*
- Say the part of the sentence that tells more. (Signal.) *Rode the horse across the field.*
- (Repeat step 4 until firm.)
5. Circle the part of the sentence that names and underline the part that tells more. (Observe students and give feedback.)
- Everybody, read the part of sentence 2 that names. (Signal.) *They.*
- Read the part that tells more. (Signal.) *Rode the horse across the field.*
6. I'll read the rest of the sentences in part C. Touch each sentence as I read it.
Sentence 3: Their horse jumped over a fence.
Sentence 4: A girl and her horse went across a stream.
Sentence 5: She rested under a tree.
- For each sentence, circle the part of the sentence that names. Underline the part that tells more. Do it now. Raise your hand when you're finished.
(Observe students and give feedback.)
7. Let's check your work. Make an **X** next to any item you missed.
- Sentence 3: Their horse jumped over a fence. Say that sentence. (Signal.) *Their horse jumped over a fence.* What part names? (Signal.) *Their horse.*
What part tells more? (Signal.) *Jumped over a fence.*
- Sentence 4. A girl and her horse went across a stream. Say that sentence. (Signal.) *A girl and her horse went across a stream.* What part names? (Signal.) *A girl and her horse.*
What part tells more? (Signal.) *Went across a stream.*

- Sentence 5. She rested under a tree. Say that sentence. (Signal.) *She rested under a tree.* What part names? (Signal.) *She.* What part tells more? (Signal.) *Rested under a tree.*
8. Raise your hand if you got no items wrong. Great job.
- Raise your hand if you got 1 item wrong. Good work.
- Fix up any mistakes you made in part C. (Observe students and give feedback.)

EXERCISE 5 Deductions
1. Everybody, pencils down. Find part D. ✔ You're going to draw a conclusion. The first sentence is: Every bird has wings.
- To draw a conclusion we must put the name of a bird in the blanks. I'll name a bird: a robin.
- Listen to the deduction: Every **bird** has wings. A **robin** is a bird. So a **robin** has wings.
2. Your turn to say all three sentences.
- First sentence. (Signal.) *Every bird has wings.*
- Next sentence. (Signal.) *A robin is a bird.*
- Conclusion. (Signal.) *So a robin has wings.*
- (Repeat step 2 until firm.)
3. That conclusion is true. We'll get other true conclusions if we put the name of any bird in the blanks. Here's a different bird: a seagull.
4. Say the whole thing with **a seagull.**
- First sentence. (Signal.) *Every bird has wings.*
- Next sentence. (Signal.) *A seagull is a bird.*
- Conclusion. (Signal.) *So a seagull has wings.*
- (Repeat step 4 until firm.)
5. Your turn to complete the deduction. The names of some birds are written below the deduction. Put the name of any bird you want in the blank. Then complete the last sentence. Raise your hand when you're finished.
(Observe students and give feedback.)
6. (Call on individual students to read all three sentences. Praise students who have appropriate deductions.)

EXERCISE 6   Main Idea

1. Everybody, take out a sheet of lined paper and write your name on the top line. Then number your lined paper 1 and 2. Raise your hand when you're finished. ✔
   - Everybody, pencils down. Open your textbook to lesson 71 and find part E. ✔
2. Touch picture 1.
   One of the sentences next to the picture tells the main thing the person did. The other sentences tell about a detail.
   - First sentence: Mary held a glass. Say that sentence. (Signal.) *Mary held a glass.*
   - My turn: That's not the **main thing** Mary did. That's a **detail.**
   - Next sentence: Mary drank a glass of water. Say that sentence. (Signal.) *Mary drank a glass of water.*
   - That's the **main thing** Mary did.
   - Next sentence: Mary wore a belt. Say that sentence. (Signal.) *Mary wore a belt.*
   - Everybody, is that the **main thing** Mary did or **a detail?** (Signal.) *A detail.*
3. Touch picture 2.
   One of these sentences tells the **main thing** the person did. The other sentences tell about **a detail.**
4. First sentence: Jill bent her leg. Say that sentence. (Signal.) *Jill bent her leg.*
   - Everybody, is that the **main thing** Jill did or **a detail?** (Signal.) *A detail.*
   - Next sentence: Jill held the board with one hand. Say that sentence. (Signal.) *Jill held the board with one hand.*
   - Everybody, is that the main thing Jill did or a detail? (Signal.) *A detail.*
   - Next sentence: Jill sawed a board. Say that sentence. (Signal.) *Jill sawed a board.*
   - Everybody, is that the main thing Jill did or a detail? (Signal.) *The main thing.*
   - (Repeat step 4 until firm.)
5. I'll read the instructions for part E: For each picture, copy the sentence that tells the main thing the person did. Don't copy any of the other sentences. You have two minutes. Raise your hand when you're finished.
   (Observe students and give feedback.)

6. (At the end of two minutes, say:) Stop writing. Let's check your work. Make an **X** next to any sentence you missed.
   - Everybody, read the sentence that tells the main thing Mary did. (Signal.) *Mary drank a glass of water.*
   - Now read the sentence that tells the main thing Jill did. (Signal.) *Jill sawed a board.*
7. Raise your hand if you wrote the correct sentence for each picture. Good job.
8. Check your sentences. Remember, first check the numbers and the periods after them. Then check to make sure each sentence starts with a capital and ends with a period. Then check the spelling of the words. Raise your hand when you're sure that your sentences are right.
   (Observe students and give feedback.)

EXERCISE 7   Reporting

1. Skip a line on your paper. Then number the lines from 1 through 8. Raise your hand when you're finished. ✔
   - Find part F in your textbook. ✔
2. I'll read the instructions: Write **reports** if the sentence reports on what the picture shows. Write **no** if the sentence does not report. Remember, write **reports** or **no** for each sentence. Do it now. Raise your hand when you're finished.
   (Observe students and give feedback.)
3. Let's check your work. Make an **X** next to any item you missed.
   - Sentence 1: Mr. Jones stood in front of his desk. What did you write? (Signal.) *No.*
   - Sentence 2: Mr. Jones wore a shirt and tie. What did you write? (Signal.) *No.*
   - Sentence 3: Ned wrote on the chalkboard. What did you write? (Signal.) *Reports.*
   - Sentence 4: Ned was a very good speller. What did you write? (Signal.) *No.*
   - Sentence 5: One girl raised her hand. What did you write? (Signal.) *Reports.*
   - Sentence 6: Hilary held a piece of paper. What did you write? (Signal.) *Reports.*
   - Sentence 7: The room had desks in it. What did you write? (Signal.) *Reports.*
   - Sentence 8: Hilary raised her hand. What did you write? (Signal.) *No.*
4. Raise your hand if you got no items wrong. Great job.

- Raise your hand if you got 1 item wrong. Good work.
- Fix up any mistakes you made in part F. (Observe students and give feedback.)
5. Who thinks they'll get a **super** paper? We'll see next time.

EXERCISE 8   Bleep Says Some Strange Things

Storytelling

- I'll read another story about Bleep. Let's see how well you can remember things that happened.

> Bleep adjusted some screws in his head so that he would talk better. He turned the **red** screw and the **brown** screw. When he was done, he couldn't say the **e** sound in words like **egg** and **let.**

- What did he say instead of *egg* and *let?* (Call on a student. Idea: *Ugg and lut.*)

> After Bleep mailed the letter, he went back home and Molly took the top of his head off. Then she adjusted the screw for the **e** sound.

- Who remembers which screw Molly turned to fix the E sound? (Call on a student. Idea: *The red screw.*)

> That was the red screw. Molly didn't know that Bleep had also turned the brown screw. So she didn't adjust that screw.
>
> After she adjusted the red screw, she said, "Say the word **get.**"
>
> Bleep said, "Get."
>
> She said, "Say the word **yes.**"
>
> Bleep said, "Yes."
>
> She said, "Say the word **better.**"
>
> Bleep said, "Better."
>
> Then Molly said, "Well, I think you're all fixed up now."
>
> Bleep said, "Okay, baby."

> Molly didn't know it and Bleep didn't know it, but Bleep still had a problem because he had fiddled with the brown screw.

- Who remembers what sound got messed up when Bleep turned the brown screw? (Call on a student. Idea: *The L sound.*)

> Molly went into the garage to work on her new invention, and Bleep went into the kitchen to wash the dishes.
>
> Pretty soon, Molly heard a loud crashing sound from the kitchen. She went in there to see what had happened. And she saw a **big** mess. On the floor was a broken plate. She said, "Bleep, what happened?"

- If Bleep tried to say the word *slipped,* what would he say? (Call on a student. Idea: *Sipped.*)

> Bleep said, "The plate was wet. When I took it out of the water, it **sipped** out of my hand."
>
> Molly said, "It did what?"
>
> "It **sipped** out of my hand."
>
> "That's what I thought you said." Then Molly said, "Tell me, Bleep, was that plate **slippery?**
>
> "Yes," Bleep said. "Very sippery."
>
> "Oh, no," she said.

- How would Bleep say *slick?* (Call on a student. Idea: *Sick.*)

> "Oh, yes. That plate was very **sick.**" Molly wanted to make sure that she understood Bleep's problem. So she said to Bleep, "What's your name?"
>
> Bleep looked at her and said, "Bleep."
>
> Molly said, "Did you drop a pate or a plate?"
>
> Bleep said, "A plate."

Molly said, "Watch me and tell me what I do." She blinked. Then she asked, "What did I do?"

Bleep said, "Blinked."

Then Molly said, "What do I do during the night when I go to bed?"

Bleep looked at Molly and said, **"Seep."**

So Molly knew that Bleep could say some words with an **L** sound. He could say **plate, Bleep** and **blinked.** But he couldn't say **sleep**.

Molly said, "When you took the top of your head off, did you happen to fiddle around with more than one screw?"

Bleep said, "Yes."

Molly said, "Do you happen to remember the color of the other screw you messed with?"

"No," Bleep said.

"This is going to be a lot of fun," Molly said. She wasn't very happy because she wasn't sure which screw to adjust, and there were lots and lots of screws inside Bleep's head.

Molly said, "Well, clean up this mess and then come into the garage. I'll see if I can find the right screw."

Bleep said, "Okay, baby."

Molly started to leave the kitchen, but the floor was wet. Just as she started to walk, she slipped and almost fell on the wet floor. She banged her hand against the counter and hurt her wrist.

Bleep didn't see what happened, but he heard Molly slipping and banging into the counter. He turned around and said, "Did you **sip** on the floor?"

She said, "Yes, Bleep. I slipped."

"Did you hurt your wrist?"

"Yes, Bleep."

"Do you want to put your arm in a **sing?**"

"No, Bleep. I don't think I need to put my arm in a sling."

"Okay, baby." So after Bleep cleaned up the mess in the kitchen, he went into the garage, and Molly spent a lot of time fixing up his problem. At last, she found the right screw and adjusted it.

Then she tested Bleep to make sure he didn't have a problem. She said, "Say **slop.**"

Bleep said, "Slop."

Molly Said, "Say **slide.**"

Bleep said, "Slide."

Molly said, "I think you're fixed up now."

And you know what Bleep said.

- Everybody, what did he say? (Signal.) *Okay, baby.*

Objectives

- Identify the part of a sentence that names (subject) and the part that tells more (predicate). (Exercise 2)
- Change 2-word verbs in sentences to 1-word verbs. (Exercise 3)
- **Replace the subject of a sentence with a pronoun (he or she).** (Exercise 4)
- Select sentences that state the main thing that illustrated characters did. (Exercise 5)
- Write whether a sentence reports on a picture or does not report. (Exercise 6)
- Listen to a familiar story and answer comprehension questions. (Exercise 7)

EXERCISE 1   Feedback On Lesson 71

- (Hand back the students' work from lesson 71.)
- Look at what I wrote on your lined paper. Raise your hand if I wrote **super.**
- If you didn't get a **super,** look at the mistakes you made and be more careful next time.

WORKBOOK

EXERCISE 2   Subject/Predicate

1. Everybody, pencils down. Open your workbook to lesson 72 and find part A. ✔
- For each sentence in part A, you're going to **circle** the part that names and **underline** the part that tells more.
2. Everybody, touch sentence 1. ✔
   That sad clown rode on a bicycle. Everybody, say the part of the sentence that names. (Signal.) *That sad clown.*
- Say the part of the sentence that tells more. (Signal.) *Rode on a bicycle.*
- (Repeat step 2 until firm.)
3. Circle the part that names and underline the part that tells more.
   (Observe students and give feedback.)
- Everybody, read the part of sentence 1 that names. (Signal.) *That sad clown.*
- Read the part that tells more. (Signal.) *Rode on a bicycle.*
4. Touch sentence 2. ✔
   He had a monkey on his head. Everybody, say the part of the sentence that names. (Signal.) *He.*
- Say the part of the sentence that tells more. (Signal.) *Had a monkey on his head.*
- (Repeat step 4 until firm.)

5. Circle the part that names and underline the part that tells more.
   (Observe students and give feedback.)
- Everybody, read the part of sentence 2 that names. (Signal.) *He.*
- Read the part that tells more. (Signal.) *Had a monkey on his head.*
6. I'll read the rest of the sentences in part A. Touch each sentence as I read it.
   Sentence 3: The monkey went over to Sam.
   Sentence 4: Clowns and monkeys fell down.
   Sentence 5: They made people laugh.
- Circle the part of each sentence that names. Underline the part that tells more. Do it now. Raise your hand when you're finished.
   (Observe students and give feedback.)
7. Let's check your work. Make an **X** next to any item you missed.
- Sentence 3. The monkey went over to Sam. Say that sentence. (Signal.) *The monkey went over to Sam.*
   What part names? (Signal.) *The monkey.*
   What part tells more? (Signal.) *Went over to Sam.*
- Sentence 4. Clowns and monkeys fell down. Say that sentence. (Signal.) *Clowns and monkeys fell down.*
   What part names? (Signal.) *Clowns and monkeys.*
   What part tells more? (Signal.) *Fell down.*
- Sentence 5. They made people laugh. Say that sentence. (Signal.) *They made people laugh.*
   What part names? (Signal.) *They.*
   What part tells more? (Signal.) *Made people laugh.*
8. Raise your hand if you got no items wrong. Great job.

- Raise your hand if you got 1 item wrong. Good work.
- Fix up any mistakes you made in part A. (Observe students and give feedback.)

EXERCISE 3   Editing Sentences

Changing the Verb

1. Everybody, pencils down. Find part B. ✔ The words that are underlined in each sentence tell what the people were doing or are doing. You're going to fix up those parts to tell what the people did.
2. Sentence 1: He is giving her a kiss. What words are underlined? (Signal.) *Is giving.*
- That tells what he is doing. What word tells what he did? (Signal.) *Gave.*
- Sentence 2: We were having fun. What words are underlined? (Signal.) *Were having.*
- That tells what we were doing. Everybody, what word tells what we did? (Signal.) *Had.*
- Sentence 3: Boys and girls were buying lunch. What words are underlined? (Signal.) *Were buying.*
- That tells what they were doing. What word tells what they did? (Signal.) *Bought.*
- Sentence 4: The man is painting the house. What words are underlined? (Signal.) *Is painting.*
- That tells what he is doing. What word tells what he did? (Signal.) *Painted.*
- Sentence 5: Josh was finding his socks. What words are underlined? (Signal.) *Was finding.*
- That tells what he was doing. What word tells what he did? (Signal.) *Found.*
- Sentence 6: Miss Clark is digging in the garden. What words are underlined? (Signal.) *Is digging.*
- That tells what she is doing. What word tells what she did? (Signal.) *Dug.*
- (Repeat step 2 until firm.)
3. Your turn: Cross out the underlined words in each sentence. Above those words, write the word that tells what people did. Raise your hand when you're finished. (Observe students and give feedback.)
4. Let's check your work. Make an **X** next to any item you missed.
- Sentence 1: He is giving her a kiss. Say the sentence so it tells what he did. (Signal.) *He gave her a kiss.*

- Sentence 2: We were having fun. Say the sentence so it tells what we did. (Signal.) *We had fun.*
- Sentence 3: Boys and girls were buying lunch. Say the sentence so it tells what boys and girls did. (Signal.) *Boys and girls bought lunch.*
- Sentence 4: The man is painting the house. Say the sentence so it tells what the man did. (Signal.) *The man painted the house.*
- Sentence 5: Josh was finding his socks. Say the sentence so it tells what Josh did. (Signal.) *Josh found his socks.*
- Sentence 6: Miss Clark is digging in the garden. Say the sentence so it tells what Miss Clark did. (Signal.) *Miss Clark dug in the garden.*
5. Raise your hand if you got no items wrong. Great job.
- Raise your hand if you got 1 item wrong. Good work.
- Fix up any mistakes you made in part B. (Observe students and give feedback.)

EXERCISE 4   Pronouns

He and She

1. Everybody, pencils down. Find part C. ✔
- The person named in each sentence is underlined. You're going to change the underlined part to **he** or **she**.
2. Touch sentence 1.
The girl was running. Say the part of the sentence that names. (Signal.) *The girl.*
- Are you going to change **the girl** to **he** or **she**? (Signal.) *She.*
- Say the sentence with **she**. (Signal.) *She was running.*
3. Touch sentence 2.
My grandfather read a book. Say the part of the sentence that names. (Signal.) *My grandfather.*
- Are you going to change **my grandfather** to **he** or **she**? (Signal.) *He.*
- Say the sentence with **he**. (Signal.) *He read a book.*
4. Touch sentence 1 again.
Sentence 1 says: The girl was running. We change **the girl** to **she**. Write **she** in the blank. Start with capital **S**. (Observe students and give feedback.)

5. Start the rest of the sentences in part C with **he** or **she.** Remember to start each sentence with a capital. Raise your hand when you're finished.
(Observe students and give feedback.)

6. Let's check your work. Make an **X** next to any item you missed. I'll say the sentences that are written. You say them with the word you wrote.
- Sentence 1: The girl was running. Say your sentence. (Signal.) *She was running.*
Make sure you have capital **S.**
- Sentence 2: My grandfather read a book. Say your sentence. (Signal.) *He read a book.*
Make sure you have capital **H.**
- Sentence 3: Mary painted the wall. Say your sentence. (Signal.) *She painted the wall.*
- Sentence 4: Bill walked home. Say your sentence. (Signal.) *He walked home.*
- Sentence 5: My brother woke up. Say your sentence. (Signal.) *He woke up.*
- Sentence 6: His mother washed her hands. Say your sentence. (Signal.) *She washed her hands.*

7. Raise your hand if you got no items wrong. Great job.
- Raise your hand if you got 1 item wrong. Good work.
- Fix up any mistakes you made in part C. Make sure each sentence starts with a capital.
(Observe students and give feedback.)

LINED PAPER • TEXTBOOK

EXERCISE 5 Main Idea

1. Everybody, take out a sheet of lined paper and write your name on the top line. Number your lined paper 1 and 2. Raise your hand when you're finished.
- Everybody, pencils down. Open your textbook to lesson 72 and find part D. ✔

2. Touch picture 1.
One of the sentences next to the picture tells the main thing the person did. The other sentences tell about a detail.

3. I'll read the first sentence: Steve stood next to the tub. Everybody, is that the main thing Steve did or a detail? (Signal.) *A detail.*
- Next sentence: Steve gave the dog a bath. Everybody, is that the main thing Steve did or a detail? (Signal.) *The main thing.*
- Next sentence: Steve held a brush in one hand. Everybody, is that the main thing Steve did or a detail? (Signal.) *A detail.*
- (Repeat step 3 until firm.)

4. For each picture, copy just the sentence that tells the main thing the person did. You have two minutes. Raise your hand when you're finished.
(Observe students and give feedback.)

5. (At the end of two minutes, say:) Stop writing. Let's check your work. Make an **X** next to any sentence you missed.
- Everybody, read the sentence that tells the main thing Steve did. (Signal.) *Steve gave the dog a bath.*
- Now read the sentence that tells the main thing Martha did. (Signal.) *Martha painted part of the house.*

6. Raise your hand if you wrote the correct sentence for each picture. Good job.

7. Check your sentences. Remember, first check the numbers and the periods after them. Then check to make sure each sentence starts with a capital and ends with a period. Then check the spelling of the words. Raise your hand when you're sure that your sentences are right.
(Observe students and give feedback.)

EXERCISE 6 Reporting

1. Skip a line on your paper. Then number the lines 1 through 7. Raise your hand when you're finished.
- Everybody, find part E in your textbook. ✔

2. I'll read the instructions: Write **reports** if the sentence reports on what the picture shows. Write **no** if the sentence does not report. Remember, write **no** or **reports** for each sentence. Do it now. Raise your hand when you're finished.
(Observe students and give feedback.)

3. Let's check your work. Make an **X** next to any item you missed.
- Sentence 1: Bill and Carlos sat in chairs. What did you write? (Signal.) *Reports.*

- Sentence 2: Nancy read a book about horses. What did you write? (Signal.) *No.*
- Sentence 3: The dogs dreamed about a bone. What did you write? (Signal.) *No.*
- Sentence 4: Boots were on the floor. What did you write? (Signal.) *Reports.*
- Sentence 5: All the firefighters played cards. What did you write? (Signal.) *No.*
- Sentence 6: Everybody wanted to go home. What did you write? (Signal.) *No.*
- Sentence 7: Two dogs were lying on the floor. What did you write? (Signal.) *Reports.*

4. Raise your hand if you got no items wrong. Great job.
- Raise your hand if you got 1 item wrong. Good work.
- Fix up any mistakes you made in part E. (Observe students and give feedback.)

5. Who thinks they'll get a **super** paper? We'll see next time.

EXERCISE 7 Goober

Storytelling

- The story I'll read is titled, "Goober." Let's see how well you can remember things that happened.

Once there was a crusty old man named Gustaf Gutenberger.

- What did people call Gustaf Gutenberger? (Call on a student. *Goober.*)

But nobody called him Gustaf Gutenberger. Instead, they used the nickname, Goober. Goober lived by himself on a small farm.

- His farm was between two towns. What were their names? (Call on a student. *West Town and East Town.*)

That farm was right between two small towns. The town to the west of Goober's farm was called West Town. The town to the east of Goober's farm was called East Town.

The people in West Town and East Town had mixed feelings about Goober.

- Why did people have mixed feelings about Goober? (Call on a student. Ideas: *Goober's farm had a very bad smell; Goober played the violin very sweetly.*)

The reason they had mixed feelings was that Goober's farm had a very bad smell. He had dirty pigs that **never** took a bath. They didn't just smell sort of strong or kind of bad. They smelled **awful.** People would sometimes hold their nose when they walked near his farm. And when the wind blew **from** the east, the people in one of the towns would say, "Phew, what is that **awful** smell?"

And when the wind blew **from** the west, the people in one of the towns would say, "Phew. I wish the wind would change **soon.**"

It would be easy for people to hate Goober because of his smelly farm. But things were not that simple because of the violin. You see, although Goober's farm smelled so bad, Goober could play the violin so sweetly that people would just stop what they were doing and listen to the beautiful sounds that drifted on the breeze. Birds would stop singing because they were ashamed of their songs when they heard Goober's beautiful violin music.

Some people who lived in West Town and East Town **loved** Goober. The reason they loved him was that they couldn't **smell** his farm. The breeze **wouldn't** carry the **smell** for more than a mile. But the breeze **would** carry Goober's **music** for more than a mile. So the people who lived more than a mile from Goober's place could hear the music, but couldn't smell his pigs.

"Such wonderful music," they would say as they sat out on their porches in the evening, listening to the music.

Some people who lived in West Town and East Town were **confused** about Goober. They hated him and they loved him. They hated him because they lived less than a mile from Goober's farm.

- If the wind blew to the east, which town would not like Goober? (Call on a student. *East Town.*)
- If the wind blew to the west, which town would not like Goober? (Call on a student. *West Town.*)

So when the wind blew from Goober's farm, most of them wouldn't sit out on their porch in the evening listening to the music. They would go inside and close all the windows and the doors. They wouldn't be able to hear the music, but they felt that was better than having to breathe in all that terrible smell. Oh, there were some real music lovers who would put clothespins on their noses and sit outside to enjoy the music, but they would get sore noses because they had to make sure that their clothespins were very tight or some of the smell would come through.

So on a summer evening, Goober would get out his violin, sit on an old stump near his barn and start playing. If there was no wind, all the people in West Town and East Town would be on their porches listening to his wonderful music.

But, if the wind blew **to** the west, there would be a **lot** of people in East Town with **their** houses shut up tight.

Then one day, something very strange happened.

- Somebody came to Goober's farm. Who was that? (Call on a student. *A little girl from West Town.*)
- Why did she talk funny? (Call on a student. Idea: *She held her nose.*)
- Why was she holding her nose? (Call on a student. Praise reasonable responses.)

A little girl from West Town went over to visit Goober. That was very strange because **nobody** ever visited Goober. She took a big package with her and walked up to his barn where he was milking a cow. She held her nose and said, "Mr. Goober, you make nice music." But it didn't sound quite that way because she was holding her nose.

- What did she actually say? (Call on a student. *Bister Goober, you bake dice busik.*)

What she actually said sounded like this: "Bister Goober, you bake dice busic."

Goober looked up and said, "I do what?"

She said, "Bake dice busic."

He shook his head and said, "Well, I can't do anything about that."

She said, "Dough. You dote uderstad."

He said, "You know, if you'd stop holding your nose, maybe I could understand what you're trying to tell me."

So the little girl took a very deep breath, let go of her nose and said, very fast, "We love your music, but you need to clean up your pigs. They **stink.**"

Goober's eyes got wide and he stared at the girl for a long time. She was holding her nose again. At last he said, "Do my pigs really stink?"

She said, "Yes."

He said, "Golly. I didn't know that."

- What did the girl give Goober? (Call on a student. *Bars of pig soap.*)

Then she handed Goober her package and said, "Here are sub thigs for you." Then she said, "Good-bye," and ran away, holding her nose.

After she left, Goober opened the package. Inside were some bars of pig soap.

Goober smelled the soap and said, "What a great smell."

Then Goober shrugged, took the package with him down to his pond and called his pigs. They came running. Then he jumped into the pond with the pigs and scrubbed them until they were pink. He rubbed and scrubbed and he washed and he rinsed. When he was done, his pigs were as clean and sweet smelling as anybody in East Town or West Town. Goober sniffed the air and said, "Those pigs smell great." Goober took some of that great-smelling soap back to his house. "I can use this soap on me," he said.

Well, that's the story. If you ever go to West Town or East Town, you'll hear the sweetest violin music you've ever heard in your life. And you'll hear people saying wonderful things about Goober. And they also say some nice things about a little girl who visits Goober every week. She always takes a package with her, and the people in West Town and East Town are **very** grateful.

Note:
- Collect the students' workbooks and papers.
- Check the students' work before the next language period. Mark any mistakes.
- Write **super** on work that has all mistakes corrected. Write **good** or **pretty good** on work that has only 1 or 2 mistakes.

Objectives

- Identify the part of a sentence that names (subject) and the part that tells more (predicate). (Exercise 2)
- **Replace the subject of a sentence with a pronoun (he or she). (Exercise 3)**
- Change 2-word verbs in sentences to 1-word verbs. (Exercise 4)
- Draw a conclusion based on different concrete examples. (Exercise 5)
- Write past-time verbs for irregular present-time verbs. (Exercise 6)
- Select sentences that state the main thing that illustrated characters did. (Exercise 7)
- Listen to a familiar story and answer comprehension questions. (Exercise 8)

EXERCISE 1 Feedback On Lesson 72

- (Hand back the students' work from lesson 72.)
- Look at what I wrote on your lined paper. Raise your hand if I wrote **super.**
- If you didn't get a **super,** look at the mistakes you made and be more careful next time.

WORKBOOK

EXERCISE 2 Subject/Predicate

1. Everybody, open your workbook to lesson 73 and find part A. ✔
- For each sentence in part A, you're going to circle the part that names and underline the part that tells more.
2. Touch sentence 1.
   A boy and his dad went to a baseball game. Everybody, say the part of the sentence that names. (Signal.) *A boy and his dad.*
- Say the part of the sentence that tells more. (Signal.) *Went to a baseball game.*
- (Repeat step 2 until firm.)
3. Circle the part that names and underline the part that tells more.
   (Observe students and give feedback.)
4. I'll read the rest of the sentences in part A. Touch each sentence as I read it.
   Sentence 2: They ate lots of popcorn.
   Sentence 3: The boy caught a baseball.
   Sentence 4: One baseball player wrote his name on the ball.
   Sentence 5: Yesterday was a wonderful day.

- Circle the part of each sentence that names. Underline the part that tells more. Do it now. Raise your hand when you're finished.
   (Observe students and give feedback.)
5. Let's check your work. Make an **X** next to any item you missed.
- Sentence 1. A boy and his dad went to a baseball game. Say that sentence. (Signal.) *A boy and his dad went to a baseball game.* What part names? (Signal.) *A boy and his dad.*
   What part tells more? (Signal.) *Went to a baseball game.*
- Sentence 2. They ate lots of popcorn. Say that sentence. (Signal.) *They ate lots of popcorn.*
   What part names? (Signal.) *They.*
   What part tells more? (Signal.) *Ate lots of popcorn.*
- Sentence 3. The boy caught a baseball. Say that sentence. (Signal.) *The boy caught a baseball.*
   What part names? (Signal.) *The boy.*
   What part tells more? (Signal.) *Caught a baseball.*
- Sentence 4. One baseball player wrote his name on the ball. Say that sentence. (Signal.) *One baseball player wrote his name on the ball.*
   What part names? (Signal.) *One baseball player.*
   What part tells more? (Signal.) *Wrote his name on the ball.*

- Sentence 5. Yesterday was a wonderful day. Say that sentence. (Signal.) *Yesterday was a wonderful day.*
  What part names? (Signal.) *Yesterday.*
  What part tells more? (Signal.) *Was a wonderful day.*
6. Raise your hand if you got no items wrong. Great job.
- Raise your hand if you got 1 item wrong. Good work.
- Fix up any mistakes you made in part A. (Observe students and give feedback.)

EXERCISE 3   Pronouns

He and She

1. Everybody, pencils down. Find part B. ✔ The person named in each sentence is underlined. You're going to change the underlined part to **he** or **she**.
2. Touch sentence 1.
   His sister won the race. Say the part of the sentence that names. (Signal.) *His sister.*
- Are you going to change **his sister** to **he** or **she**? (Signal.) *She.*
- Say the sentence with **she**. (Signal.) *She won the race.*
3. Your turn: Fill in the blanks in part B with **he** or **she**. Remember to start each sentence with a capital. Raise your hand when you're finished.
   (Observe students and give feedback.)
4. Let's check your work. I'll say the sentences that are written. You say them with the word you wrote. Make an **X** next to any item you missed.
- Sentence 1: His sister won the race. Say your sentence. (Signal.) *She won the race.*
- Sentence 2: Her father went to the park. Say your sentence. (Signal.) *He went to the park.*
- Sentence 3: A tall boy washed the car. Say your sentence. (Signal.) *He washed the car.*
- Sentence 4: The young woman fixed the bike. Say your sentence. (Signal.) *She fixed the bike.*
5. Raise your hand if you got no items wrong. Great job.
- Raise your hand if you got 1 item wrong. Good work.
- Fix up any mistakes you made in part B. (Observe students and give feedback.)

EXERCISE 4   Editing Sentences

Changing the Verb

1. Everybody, pencils down. Find part C. ✔ The words that are underlined in each sentence tell what people were doing or are doing. You're going to fix up those parts to tell what people did.
2. Sentence 1: Two children are washing the car. What words are underlined? (Signal.) *Are washing.*
- What word tells what they did? (Signal.) *Washed.*
- Sentence 2: He is spelling a hard word. What words are underlined? (Signal.) *Is spelling.*
- What word tells what he did? (Signal.) *Spelled.*
- (Repeat step 2 until firm.)
3. Your turn: Cross out the underlined words in each sentence. Above those words, write the word that tells what people did. Raise your hand when you're finished. (Observe students and give feedback.)
4. Let's check your work. Make an **X** next to any item you missed.
- Sentence 1: Two children are washing the car. Say the sentence so it tells what they did. (Signal.) *Two children washed the car.*
- Sentence 2: He is spelling a hard word. Say the sentence so it tells what he did. (Signal.) *He spelled a hard word.*
- Sentence 3: Wendy is having a party. Say the sentence so it tells what Wendy did. (Signal.) *Wendy had a party.*
- Sentence 4: Nick is buying his sister a present. Say the sentence so it tells what Nick did. (Signal.) *Nick bought his sister a present.*
- Sentence 5: He is finding a pencil. Say the sentence so it tells what he did. (Signal.) *He found a pencil.*
- Sentence 6: She was filling the glass with water. Say the sentence so it tells what she did. (Signal.) *She filled the glass with water.*
5. Raise your hand if you got no items wrong. Great job.
- Raise your hand if you got 1 item wrong. Good work.
- Fix up any mistakes you made in part C. (Observe students and give feedback.)

EXERCISE 5 Deductions

1. Everybody, pencils down. Find part D. ✔
   You're going to draw a conclusion. The first sentence is: All trees have leaves.
   - To draw a conclusion we must put the name of a tree in the blanks. I'll name a tree: a spruce. Listen to the deduction: All **trees** have leaves. A **spruce** is a tree. So a **spruce** has leaves.
2. Your turn to say all three sentences.
   - First sentence. (Signal.) *All trees have leaves.*
   - Next sentence. (Signal.) *A spruce is a tree.*
   - Conclusion. (Signal.) *So a spruce has leaves.*
   - (Repeat step 2 until firm.)
3. Here's a different tree: a pine.
4. Say the whole thing with **a pine.**
   - First sentence. (Signal.) *All trees have leaves.*
   - Next sentence. (Signal.) *A pine is a tree.*
   - Conclusion. (Signal.) *So a pine has leaves.*
   - (Repeat step 4 until firm.)
5. Your turn to complete the deduction. The names of some trees are written below the deduction. Put the name of any tree you want in the blank. Then complete the last sentence. Raise your hand when you're finished.
   (Observe students and give feedback.)
6. (Call on individual students to read all three sentences. Praise students who have appropriate deductions.)

LINED PAPER • TEXTBOOK

EXERCISE 6 Past Time

Irregular Verbs

1. Everybody, take out a sheet of lined paper and write your name on the top line. Number your lined paper 1 through 5. Raise your hand when you're finished.
   - Everybody, pencils down. Open your textbook to lesson 73 and find part E. ✔
2. The words in part E tell what people do. You're going to write the words that tell what they did.
   - Word 1 is **give.** What word tells what they did? (Signal.) *Gave.*
     Write **gave** for number **1.** ✔

3. Write the rest of the words for part E. Read each word that tells what people do and write the word that tells what they did. Raise your hand when you're finished.
   (Observe students and give feedback.)
4. Let's check your work. Make an **X** if you wrote the wrong word or did not spell the word correctly. I'll say the word that tells what people do. You'll say the word that tells what they did.
   - Word 1: Give. Say the word that tells what people did. (Signal.) *Gave.*
     Spell **gave.** (Signal.) *G-a-v-e.*
   - Word 2: Dig. Say the word that tells what people did. (Signal.) *Dug.*
     Spell **dug.** (Signal.) *D-u-g.*
   - Word 3: Find. Say the word that tells what people did. (Signal.) *Found.*
     Spell **found.** (Signal.) *F-o-u-n-d.*
   - Word 4: Have. Say the word that tells what people did. (Signal.) *Had.*
     Spell **had.** (Signal.) *H-a-d.*
   - Word 5: Buy. Say the word that tells what people did. (Signal.) *Bought.*
     Spell **bought.** (Signal.) *B-o-u-g-h-t.*
5. Raise your hand if you got no items wrong. Great job.
   - Everybody else, fix up any mistakes you made in part E.
     (Observe students and give feedback.)

EXERCISE 7 Main Idea

1. Skip a line and number your paper 1 through 3. ✔
   - Everybody, pencils down. Find part F in your textbook. ✔
2. One of the sentences next to each picture tells the main thing a person did. The other sentences tell about a detail.
3. I'll read the sentences.
   Picture 1: Angela sat in a boat. Angela loved the water. Angela rowed a boat.
   Picture 2: A boy held a broom. A boy swept the floor. A boy wore long pants.
   Picture 3: Pam shoveled snow. Pam stood in the snow. Pam had a shovel.
4. For each picture, copy just the sentence that tells the main thing the person did. You have three minutes. Raise your hand when you're finished.
   (Observe students and give feedback.)

5. (At the end of 3 minutes, say:) Stop writing. Let's check your work. Make an **X** next to any sentence you missed.

• Everybody, read the sentence that tells the main thing Angela did. (Signal.) *Angela rowed a boat.*

• Now read the sentence that tells the main thing a boy did. (Signal.) *A boy swept the floor.*

• Now read the sentence that tells the main thing Pam did. (Signal.) *Pam shoveled snow.*

6. Raise your hand if you wrote the correct sentence for each picture. Good job.

• If you didn't write the correct sentence, cross out the sentence you wrote and write the sentence that tells the main thing the person did.

7. Check your sentences. Remember, first check the numbers and the periods after them. Then check to make sure each sentence starts with a capital and ends with a period. Then check the spelling of the words. Raise your hand when you're sure that your sentences are right. (Observe students and give feedback.)

• Who thinks they'll get a **super** paper? We'll see next time.

EXERCISE 8   The Bragging Rat Wants to be a Detective

Storytelling

• The story I'll read is titled, "The Bragging Rat Wants to be a Detective." Let's see how well you can remember things that happened.

• One of the bragging rats wanted to be a detective. Which rat was that? (Call on a student. *The gray bragging rat.*)

One day the gray bragging rat decided that he wanted to be a detective. He told the rat with the yellow teeth about his plan.

The rat with the yellow teeth said, "You can't be a detective. You don't know how to figure things out."

"I do, too," the gray rat said. "I can figure out anything. In fact, I'm so good at figuring things out that I could beat anybody in the world in a figuring-out contest."

"Oh, yeah," the rat with the yellow teeth said. "If you're so smart, where is Betty the frog?"

"I don't know."

"Ha, ha," the rat with the yellow teeth said. "You don't know, and you don't even know how to figure it out."

"I do, too. I just don't feel like doing it right now."

The yellow-toothed rat said, "You don't know how to figure it out."

And that rat was right. The gray rat didn't have any idea how to figure out where Betty the frog was.

Finally, the gray rat said to the yellow-toothed rat, "Okay, if you're so smart, where is Betty the frog?"

"That's easy," the yellow-toothed rat said. "She's taking a snooze on a lily pad."

"You must have seen her there," the gray rat said.

• Who remembers how he figured it out? (Call on a student. *He made a deduction.*)

"I did **not** see her. I figured it out."

"How could you do that?"

"That's easy," the yellow-toothed rat said. "I know that, in the afternoon, all the frogs are on lily pads. Betty is a frog. So . . . what do you know about Betty?"

The gray rat said, "So, Betty is a frog."

"No, no," said the yellow-toothed rat. "You don't even know how deductions work. Listen again: In the afternoon, all the frogs are on lily pads. Betty is a frog. So . . . "

The gray rat was getting mad. He said, "So Betty is a frog."

"No, no," the yellow-toothed rat said. "Listen: In the afternoon, all the frogs are on lily pads. Betty is a frog.

- So what do you know about Betty? (Call on a student. *Betty is on a lily pad.*)

So in the afternoon, Betty is on a lily pad."

"You're just making that up," the gray rat said.

"I'll bet we find her on a lily pad," the yellow-toothed rat said.

"I'll bet," the gray rat said.

- Where did they find Betty? (Call on a student. *On a lily pad.*)

So the two rats went down to the pond and looked at the frogs sitting on lily pads. And there was Betty, sitting on a lily pad.

The yellow-toothed rat stuck out his chest and smiled. His big yellow teeth were sticking way out. "I was right," he said proudly, "because I know about deductions, and you don't."

- How did the gray rat find out how deductions work? (Call on a student. Idea: *He asked the wise old rat for help.*)

The gray rat was very sad. He walked around for a while. Then he decided to go to the wise old rat to learn about deductions.

He found the wise old rat resting on top of an old stump with four other old rats. It took the gray rat a while to find him, because he looked in five different places before he went to the stump.

The gray rat explained his problem to the wise old rat.

Then the wise old rat said, "How did you find me?"

The gray rat said, "I looked and looked until I found you."

The wise old rat said, "Didn't you know that, in the afternoon, all old rats sit on this stump?"

- Who can start with **every afternoon all old rats sit on this stump** and say the whole deduction? (Call on a student. *Every afternoon all old rats sit on this stump. The wise old rat is an old rat. Therefore, the wise old rat sits on this stump every afternoon.*)

"Sure, I knew that," the gray rat said. "Everybody knows that."

"Well," the wise old rat said, "you could have figured out where I was. Listen: In the afternoon, all the old rats sit on this stump. I'm an old rat. **So . . .** "

The gray rat said, "So you're an old rat."

"No, no," the wise old rat said, as all the other old rats tried not to laugh. "Listen to me: In the afternoon, all the old rats sit on this stump. I'm an old rat. So, in the afternoon, I sit on this stump."

The gray rat was very confused. The wise old rat said, "Try this one: Where is Henrietta the bluebird right now?"

"I don't know. Do you want me to go look for her?"

All the old rats started to chuckle.

The wise old rat said, "Don't you know where all the bluebirds are in the afternoon?"

"Sure," the gray rat said. "In the afternoon, all the bluebirds are in the oak tree."

"Well, then," the wise old rat said, "where is Henrietta the bluebird?"

"I don't know. Do you want me to go look for her?"

"No," the wise old rat said. "I want you to figure it out. Start with what you know about all the bluebirds in the afternoon and what you know about Henrietta."

The gray rat said, "In the afternoon, all the bluebirds are in the oak tree. Henrietta is a bluebird. So . . . "

• Everybody, say the whole deduction. (Signal.) *In the afternoon, all the bluebirds are in the oak tree. Henrietta is a blue bird. So, in the afternoon, Henrietta is in the oak tree.*

"So, what?" the wise old rat said.

"So Henrietta is a bluebird," the gray rat said.

All the old rats started laughing so hard that two of them rolled right off the old stump.

The wise old rat tried not to laugh. He said, "We'll work on that. You'll learn how to do it."

But the gray rat felt **very** sad. He no longer liked the idea of being a detective.

Note:

• Collect the students' workbooks and papers.

• Check the students' work before the next language period. Mark any mistakes.

• Write **super** on work that has all mistakes corrected. Write **good** or **pretty good** on work that has only 1 or 2 mistakes.

Objectives

- **Replace the subject of a sentence with a pronoun (he, she or it).** (Exercise 2)
- Change 2-word verbs in sentences to 1-word verbs. (Exercise 3)
- Identify the part of a sentence that names (subject) and the part that tells more (predicate). (Exercise 4)
- **Construct sentences that state the main thing that illustrated characters did.** (Exercise 5)
- Listen to a familiar story and answer comprehension questions. (Exercise 6)

EXERCISE 1 Feedback On Lesson 73

- (Hand back the students' work from lesson 73.)
- Look at what I wrote on your lined paper. Raise your hand if I wrote **super.**
- If you didn't get a **super,** look at the mistakes you made and be more careful next time.

WORKBOOK

EXERCISE 2 Pronouns

It

1. Everybody, open your workbook to lesson 74 and find part A. ✔
- Some of these sentences name a person. Other sentences name something that is not a person. Here's the word we use to refer to something that is not a person: **it.** Everybody, what word? (Signal.) *It.*
2. Everybody, touch sentence 1. That coat was covered with dirt. Say the part of the sentence that names. (Signal.) *That coat.*
- **That coat** is not **he** or **she. That coat** is **it.** Say the sentence with **it.** (Signal.) *It was covered with dirt.*
- (Repeat step 2 until firm.)
3. Touch sentence 2.
 The rubber ball fell off the table. Say the part of the sentence that names. (Signal.) *The rubber ball.*
- Are you going to change **the rubber ball** to **he, she** or **it?** (Signal.) *It.*
- Say the sentence with **it.** (Signal.) *It fell off the table.*

- Touch sentence 3.
 My mother sat in a chair. Everybody, say the part that names. (Signal.) *My mother.*
- Say the sentence with the word that refers to **my mother.** (Signal.) *She sat in a chair.*
4. Your turn: Fill in the blanks with **he, she** or **it.** Remember, start each sentence with a capital. Raise your hand when you're finished.
 (Observe students and give feedback.)
5. Let's check your work. Make an **X** next to any item you missed. I'll say the sentences that are written. You say them with the word you wrote.
- Sentence 1: That coat was covered with dirt. Say your sentence. (Signal.) *It was covered with dirt.*
- Sentence 2: The rubber ball fell off the table. Say your sentence. (Signal.) *It fell off the table.*
- Sentence 3: My mother sat in a chair. Say your sentence. (Signal.) *She sat in a chair.*
- Sentence 4: This book was very funny. Say your sentence. (Signal.) *It was very funny.*
- Sentence 5: The young woman rode a bike. Say your sentence. (Signal.) *She rode a bike.*
- Sentence 6: Susan's game ended early. Say your sentence. (Signal.) *It ended early.*
6. Raise your hand if you got no items wrong. Great job.
- Raise your hand if you got 1 item wrong. Good work.
- Fix up any mistakes you made in part A. (Observe students and give feedback.)

EXERCISE 3 Editing Sentences

Changing the Verb

1. Everybody, find part B. ✔
   I'll read the instructions: Fix up the sentences so they tell what people did. Nothing is underlined in the sentences. But all the sentences tell what somebody **is doing** or **was doing.** Find the words in each sentence that tell what somebody is doing or was doing. Cross out those words and write the word that tells what the person did. Do it now. Raise your hand when you're finished.
   (Observe students and give feedback.)

2. Let's check your work. Make an **X** next to any item you missed.
   • Everybody, touch sentence 1.
     He was having fun. Say the sentence that tells what he did. (Signal.) *He had fun.*
   • What did you cross out? (Signal.) *Was having.*
   • Sentence 2: She is looking at the sky. Say the sentence that tells what she did. (Signal.) *She looked at the sky.*
   • What did you cross out? (Signal.) *Is looking.*
   • Sentence 3: Alice was picking apples. Say the sentence that tells what Alice did. (Signal.) *Alice picked apples.*
   • What did you cross out? (Signal.) *Was picking.*
   • Sentence 4: She is buying a dress. Say the sentence that tells what she did. (Signal.) *She bought a dress.*
   • What did you cross out? (Signal.) *Is buying.*
   • Sentence 5: Ann is digging in the sand. Say the sentence that tells what Ann did. (Signal.) *Ann dug in the sand.*
   • What did you cross out? (Signal.) *Is digging.*
   • Sentence 6: She was folding the paper. Say the sentence that tells what she did. (Signal.) *She folded the paper.*
   • What did you cross out? (Signal.) *Was folding.*

3. Raise your hand if you got no items wrong. Great job.
   • Raise your hand if you got 1 item wrong. Good work.
   • Fix up any mistakes you made in part B.
   (Observe students and give feedback.)

EXERCISE 4 Subject/Predicate

1. Everybody, pencils down. Find part C. ✔
   For each sentence in part C, you're going to circle the part that names and underline the part that tells more.

2. Everybody, touch sentence 1.
   Carla and Tom rode their bikes to the park.
   Say the part of the sentence that names. (Signal.) *Carla and Tom.*
   Say the part of the sentence that tells more. (Signal.) *Rode their bikes to the park.*
   • (Repeat step 2 until firm.)

3. I'll read the rest of the sentences in part C. Touch each sentence as I read it.
   Sentence 2: They had a picnic with Mary and Beth.
   Sentence 3: A big dog took Tom's sandwich.
   Sentence 4: Rain started to fall.
   Sentence 5: The children went home quickly.
   • Circle the part of each sentence that names. Underline the part that tells more. Do it now. Raise your hand when you're finished.
   (Observe students and give feedback.)

4. Let's check your work. Make an **X** next to any item you missed.
   • Sentence 1. Carla and Tom rode their bikes to the park. Say that sentence. (Signal.) *Carla and Tom rode their bikes to the park.*
     What part names? (Signal.) *Carla and Tom.*
     What part tells more? (Signal.) *Rode their bikes to the park.*
   • Sentence 2. They had a picnic with Mary and Beth. Say that sentence. (Signal.) *They had a picnic with Mary and Beth.*
     What part names? (Signal.) *They.*
     What part tells more? (Signal.) *Had a picnic with Mary and Beth.*
   • Sentence 3. A big dog took Tom's sandwich. Say that sentence. (Signal.) *A big dog took Tom's sandwich.*
     What part names? (Signal.) *A big dog.*
     What part tells more? (Signal.) *Took Tom's sandwich.*
   • Sentence 4. Rain started to fall. Say that sentence. (Signal.) *Rain started to fall.*
     What part names? (Signal.) *Rain.*
     What part tells more? (Signal.) *Started to fall.*

- Sentence 5. The children went home quickly. Say that sentence. (Signal.) *The children went home quickly.*
  What part names? (Signal.) *The children.*
  What part tells more? (Signal.) *Went home quickly.*
5. Raise your hand if you got no items wrong. Great job.
- Raise your hand if you got 1 item wrong. Good work.
- Fix up any mistakes you made in part C. (Observe students and give feedback.)

LINED PAPER • TEXTBOOK

EXERCISE 5 Main Idea

1. Everybody, take out a sheet of lined paper. Write your name on the top line. Number the paper 1 through 2. Raise your hand when you're finished.
- Everybody, pencils down. Open your textbook to lesson 74 and find part D. ✔
2. The rule in the box for part D tells about sentences that report on the main thing a person did. Touch that rule. ✔
- I'll read: Sentences that report on the main thing a person did have two parts. The first part of the sentence **names the person.** The second part **tells the main thing the person did.** Remember, the first part names; the second part tells more.
3. You're going to say sentences that report on the main thing each person did. Remember, when you report, you can only tell what the picture shows.
- Everybody, touch picture 1. Name the person in that picture. (Signal.) *Beth.*
- Get ready to say a sentence that reports on the main thing Beth **did.** Don't say what Beth **is doing** or **was doing.** Start by naming Beth. Then tell the main thing Beth **did.** (Call on a student. Praise sentences such as: *Beth painted the ceiling.* For each good sentence: Everybody, say that sentence.)

4. Everybody, touch picture 2. Name that person. (Signal.) *Rosa.*
- Get ready to say a sentence that reports on the main thing Rosa did. Don't say what Rosa **is doing** or **was doing.** Make up a sentence that tells the main thing Rosa **did.** (Call on a student. Praise sentences such as: *Rosa read a book.* For each good sentence: Everybody, say that sentence.)
5. Touch the words in the vocabulary box as I read them: **painted, book, ceiling, read.** Be sure to spell those words correctly if you use them.
6. I'll read the instructions for part D. Write a sentence that reports on the main thing each person did.
- Next to number 1 on your paper, write a sentence that reports on what the person in picture 1 did. Do the same thing for picture 2. Be sure each sentence starts with a capital and ends with a period. You have 3 minutes. Raise your hand when you're finished.
  (Observe students and give feedback.)
7. (After 3 minutes, say:) Stop writing. If you didn't finish, you can write the rest of the sentences at the end of the lesson.
8. I'll call on students to read their sentences. Listen to each sentence and see if it **names** the right person and tells **the main thing** that person **did.** (Call on individual students to read the sentences they wrote for pictures 1 and 2. After each good sentence, tell the group:) Everybody, say that sentence.
9. (Write on the board:)

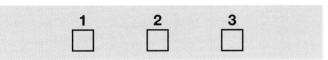

- Let's check your work. These are check boxes. Make boxes like these below your last sentence.
  (Observe students and give feedback.)
10. Everybody, touch the box for check 1.
- Here's check 1: Does each sentence begin with a capital and end with a period?
- Read your sentences. If they begin with a capital and end with a period, put a check mark like this in box 1 on your paper.
  (Make a check mark in box 1.)

- If you forgot any capitals or periods, fix up your sentences now and then make the check mark. Don't make a check mark until you've checked your sentences and fixed up any mistakes. Raise your hand when you're finished.
  (Observe students and give feedback.)
11. Now touch the box for check 2 on your paper.
    - Here's check 2: Does each sentence tell the main thing the person did?
    - Read over your sentences carefully. Each sentence should start out by naming the person. Then it should tell the main thing the person did. When all your sentences name and tell the main thing the person did, put a check mark in box 2. Raise your hand when you're finished.
      (Observe students and give feedback.)
12. Now touch the box for check 3.
    - Here's that check: Did you spell words from the vocabulary box correctly?
    - Look at each sentence. Make sure vocabulary words are spelled correctly. Fix up any mistakes and make a check mark in box 3. Raise your hand when you're finished.
      (Observe students and give feedback.)
13. Raise your hand if you think you'll get a **super** paper.
    - I'll read your sentences later and hand them back at the beginning of the next lesson. I'll mark any mistakes I find.
    - Also on the next lesson, you'll have a test. Here's the rule about the test: If you don't make any more than 2 mistakes on the test, you'll get a **super** on your test.

EXERCISE 6   Dot And Dud

Storytelling

- The story I'll read is titled, **Dot and Dud.** Let's see how well you can remember things that happened.

Once there were two St. Bernard dogs called Dot and Dud. Dot was Dud's sister. St. Bernards are great big work dogs. And Dot and Dud had a very important job. They lived in the mountains at the rescue station. During the winter, the mountains were deep with snow and very dangerous. Skiers and mountain climbers would sometimes get lost. That's when Dot and Dud were supposed to do their job. They were supposed to go into the mountains with the other St. Bernards and find the stranded skier or mountain climber. That's what they were **supposed** to do, but there was one problem.

- What was the problem? (Call on a student. Idea: *He wasn't a good rescue dog.*)

That problem was Dud. He was called "Dud" because that's what he was—a great big dud at doing his job. When he went out to find a mountain climber, everybody else would have to go out and find Dud. He'd get lost. Some other St. Bernard would find the mountain climber.

- Who was that? (Call on a student. *Dot.*)

That dog was usually Dot. She was the best rescue dog in all the mountains. But, after she found the stranded skier or mountain climber, she and the other St. Bernards would have to go on another rescue mission.

Dud was a dud because he didn't like to work. He didn't like to use his nose. Although his nose was nowhere near as good as a hunting dog's nose, it probably was as good at smelling things as the other St. Bernards' noses. But sniffing things and trying to figure out which way a trail led was a lot of hard work. You had to find the trail of the person who was stranded. Then you had to stick your nose in the snow, take a great sniff and make sure that you were still on the trail of the person you were trying to rescue. All that sniffing and figuring out gave Dud a headache. So he **pretended** to sniff and track, but his mind was not on his work. He was usually thinking of eating a great ham bone or sprawling out in front of a fireplace.

One time, the St. Bernards got **really** mad at Dud.

- Name some of the things they were mad about. (Call on a student. Idea: *They spent too much time rescuing Dud.*)

They were back at the rescue station in their kennel. The oldest St. Bernard said to Dud, "Do you realize we spend more time rescuing you than we do rescuing stranded mountain climbers?"

"Yeah," another St. Bernard said. "You don't even stay with the rest of us when we go out on a rescue. You're always going off and fooling around in the snow."

"Yeah," another St. Bernard said. "Last time, I saw you go behind some rocks and run around chasing your tail while we were trying to do our job."

"Yeah," another St. Bernard said, "and then you got so dizzy from chasing your tail that you got completely lost, and we had to spend two hours trying to find you."

"Yeah," another St. Bernard said, "and when we found you, you were less than half a mile from the rescue station, and you didn't even know how to get back home."

"Yeah," all the St. Bernards said—all of them except one. That one was Dot.

- Who stuck up for Dud? (Call on a student. *Dot.*)
- What did she say?(Call on a student. Idea: *Dud was her brother.*)

Dot said, "Stop picking on my brother. He may not be the best tracker, but he can learn, and he'll work harder from now on. Won't you, Dud?"

"I will," Dud said. "I'll work harder."

"Yeah," one of the St. Bernards said. "We've heard that before. 'I'll work harder.' The last time you said that, we caught you rolling snowballs down the mountain with your nose."

"Yeah," the other St. Bernards agreed.

But this time, Dud was serious. "I'll try harder," he said.

But you know what the other St. Bernards said.

Just then, the rescue alarm sounded. The ranger who was in charge of the St. Bernards came running out to the kennels where the dogs were. A mountain climber was stranded in the snow.

Now all the dogs knew that **mountain climbers** climbed mountains that were to the **north** of the rescue station.

- What was south of the ranger station? (Call on a student. *A ski lodge.*)

To the **south** of the rescue station was the ski lodge. So if a mountain climber was stranded, the dogs knew which way to go.

And if a **skier** got stranded, the dogs knew which way to go. That's the same direction as the ski lodge.

The ranger let the St. Bernards out of the kennel, and they all headed in the right direction, including Dud.

When they started up the mountain, they searched for the trail of the stranded mountain climber. All the dogs were sticking their nose in the snow and trying to find the scent of that mountain climber.

- Who remembers what Dud did? (Call on a student. *He played with his shadow.*)

Even Dud put his nose in the snow—a couple of times. But that snow was mighty cold, and it really took a lot of effort to sniff and snort and try to smell something. So, after a while, Dud walked slower and slower. He got farther and farther behind the other dogs.

Then Dud came to a large flat part on the side of the mountain. And he saw something that was far more interesting than the snow. It was his shadow. He jumped up, and the shadow moved. Dud pounced on the shadow. He rolled over on the shadow. He ran around in circles—faster, faster, faster. Wow, was this fun or what?

For about ten minutes, Dud and his shadow tore around in the snow, making circles and zigzags, making leaps and even somersaults. But then, his shadow disappeared.

Dud couldn't see the other St. Bernards. Dud knew they were going up the mountain to the north, but, after all that running around in circles, he didn't know where **north** was.

He looked around to see where the mountain was, but there were mountains all around him, and they all looked the same. And it was snowing harder now. Soon the snow was coming down so hard that Dud couldn't see any mountains. He couldn't see anything at all—just snow, snow, snow.

At last, he walked around in a large circle trying to find out which way was north. He couldn't tell, so he made a guess. And his guess was wrong, wrong, wrong. Instead of starting to go north, he went south. That silly dog was heading right back toward the rescue station, not to the mountain-climbing mountain.

- In which direction did Dud end up going? (Call on a student. *South.*)
- What was to the south? (Call on a student. *The rescue station and the ski lodge.*)

Note:

- Collect the students' workbooks and papers.
- Check the students' work before the next language period. Mark any mistakes.
- Write **super** on work that has all mistakes corrected. Write **good** or **pretty good** on work that has only 1 or 2 mistakes.

Objectives

- Construct sentences that state the main thing that illustrated characters did. (Exercise 2)
- Listen to a familiar story and answer comprehension questions. (Exercise 3)
- **Perform on a mastery test of skills presented in lessons 1–9.** (Exercise 4)
  Exercises 5–7 give instructions for marking the test, giving student feedback and providing remedies.

EXERCISE 1   Feedback On Lesson 74

- (Hand back the students' work from lesson 74.)
- Look at what I wrote on your lined paper. Raise your hand if I wrote **super.**
- If you didn't get a **super,** look at the mistakes you made and be more careful next time.

LINED PAPER • TEXTBOOK

EXERCISE 2   Main Idea

1. Everybody, take out a sheet of lined paper and write your name on the top line. Number your lined paper 1 through 3. Raise your hand when you're finished.
- Everybody, pencils down. Open your textbook to lesson 75 and find part A. ✔
2. You're going to say sentences that report on the main thing each person did. Remember, when you report, you can only tell what the picture shows.
- Everybody, touch picture 1. Name the person in that picture. (Signal.) *A zookeeper.*
- Get ready to say a sentence that reports on the main thing a zookeeper **did.** Don't say what a zookeeper **is doing** or **was doing.** Start by naming **a zookeeper.** Then tell the main thing a zookeeper **did.** (Call on a student. Praise sentences such as: *A zookeeper gave a banana to a monkey.*

For each good sentence:) Everybody, say that sentence.
3. Everybody, touch picture 2. Name that person. (Signal.) *Bob.*
- Get ready to say a sentence that reports on the main thing Bob **did.** Remember, don't say what Bob **is doing** or **was doing.** (Call on a student. Praise sentences such as: *Bob put cheese on a pizza.* For each good sentence:) Everybody, say that sentence.
4. Everybody, touch picture 3. Name that person. (Signal.) *A girl.*
- Get ready to say a sentence that reports on the main thing a girl did. (Call on several students. Praise sentences such as: *A girl put a log on a campfire.* For each good sentence:) Everybody, say that sentence.
5. Touch the words in the vocabulary box as I read them: **banana, pizza, cheese, campfire, log, built, gave, put, made.** Be sure to spell those words correctly if you use them.
6. I'll read the instructions for part A: Write a sentence that reports on the main thing each person did. Be sure each sentence starts with a capital and ends with a period.
- Next to number 1 on your paper, write a sentence that reports on what the person in picture 1 did. Do the same thing for pictures 2 and 3. Be sure each sentence starts with a capital and ends with a period. You have 5 minutes. Raise your hand when you're finished.
(Observe students and give feedback.)
7. (After 5 minutes, say:) Stop writing. If you didn't finish, you can write the rest of the sentences at the end of the lesson.
8. I'll call on students to read their sentences. Listen to each sentence and see if it **names** the right person and tells **the main thing** that person **did.**

- (Call on individual students to read the sentences they wrote for pictures 1, 2 and 3. After each good sentence say) Everybody, say that sentence.

9. (Write on the board:)

1	2	3
□	□	□

- Let's check your work. These are check boxes. Make boxes like these below your last sentence.
  (Observe students and give feedback.)

10. Everybody, touch the box for check 1.
- Here's check 1: Does each sentence begin with a capital and end with a period?
- Read your sentences. If they begin with a capital and end with a period, put a check mark like this in box 1 on your paper. (Make a check mark in box 1.)
- If you forgot any capitals or periods, fix up your sentences now and then make the check mark. Don't make a check mark until you've checked your sentences and fixed up any mistakes. Raise your hand when you're finished.
  (Observe students and give feedback.)

11. Now touch the box for check 2 on your paper.
- Here's check 2: Does each sentence tell the main thing the person did?
- Read over your sentences carefully. Each sentence should start out by naming the person. Then it should tell the main thing the person did. When all your sentences name and tell the main thing the person did, put a check mark in box 2. Raise your hand when you're finished.
  (Observe students and give feedback.)

12. Now touch the box for check 3.
- Here's the check: Did you spell words from the vocabulary box correctly?
- Look at each sentence. Make sure vocabulary words are spelled correctly. Fix up any mistakes and make a check mark in box 3. Raise your hand when you're finished.
  (Observe students and give feedback.)

13. Raise your hand if you think you'll get a **super** paper.

- I'll read your sentences later and hand them back at the beginning of the next lesson. I'll mark any mistakes I find.

EXERCISE 3 Dot And Dud *Part 2*

Storytelling

- I'll read another part of the Dot and Dud story. Let's see how well you can remember things that happened.
- In which direction was Dud going at the end of the last story? (Call on a student. *South.*)
- In which direction was he supposed to be going? (Call on a student. *North.*)
- What did he do to get himself turned around the wrong way? (Call on a student. Idea: *It was snowing hard.*)

Dud headed south through the snowstorm, and he went right past the rescue station. He came so close to the kennel that, if he'd taken a few steps to the **east,** he would have run right into the kennel. But it was snowing, and it was snowing hard. So Dud didn't see the rescue station. He didn't see anything but snow, and he was too lazy to use his nose. So he went right past the rescue station and kept heading south. After he'd trudged through that deep snow for three hours, he was starting to get very tired and very hungry. He kept dreaming of gnawing on a large ham bone. That silly dog thought that he was going in the right direction because he was going up, up, up a pretty steep mountain. He kept looking for the other dogs, but, of course, he didn't see them.

At last, he came down the other side of the mountain, and he saw something through the falling snow. It was a large building—the ski lodge.

"Uh-oh," he said to himself. "I must have gone in the wrong direction."

But at least he was at a place that had warm fireplaces and maybe even a great ham bone.

- What part of the lodge did Dud go to? (Call on a student. Praise reasonable responses.)

> Dud went up to the kitchen of the lodge. His nose worked pretty well when it came to finding kitchens. He stood outside the kitchen and let out a few deep barks, "Ruff, ruff."
>
> Pretty soon, the door opened and a woman peeked out. "What are you doing out here?" she said.
>
> Dud wagged his tail and licked his chops.
>
> "You must be hungry and tired," she said.
>
> He wagged his tail harder and gave his chops a great big lick.
>
> "Come in here," she said. "You poor dog."

- What did Dud do after she let him inside? (Call on a student. Praise reasonable responses.)

> She gave Dud a large bowl of leftover soup and a great pile of meat scraps. This was like a dream come true. Dud ate until he was full. Then he curled up in front of a warm, warm stove and fell asleep. He was one happy dog.
>
> But, in the meantime, things were not going that well for the other St. Bernards.

- What was Dot doing? (Call on a student. Praise reasonable responses.)
- What were the other dogs doing? (Call on a student. Praise reasonable responses.)

> Dot had found the trail of the stranded mountain climber, but, in the snowstorm, she got separated from the other rescue dogs.
>
> She followed the trail up slopes that were so steep that she'd sometimes slip and fall down a long way. But she'd

> get up and try again and again until she made it up the slope. Finally she came to a rocky place where the mountain climber was stranded. He was injured and couldn't walk.
>
> Dot barked to let the other dogs know that she'd found the mountain climber, but the other dogs couldn't hear her. They were over a mile away, and the sound of her barks was lost in the thick, falling snow.

- What did Dot do to keep the mountain climber from freezing? (Call on a student. Praise reasonable responses.)

> She didn't know what to do, so she curled up next to the mountain climber to keep him warm. And she waited. And she waited. And she waited. By evening, the snow stopped falling, and she still waited. But she was all alone with that mountain climber, and she couldn't move him without help.

Note:

- Collect **only** the students' papers.
- Check the students' work before the next language period. Mark any mistakes.
- Write **super** on work that has no mistakes. Write **good** on work that has only 1 mistake.

WORKBOOK

EXERCISE 4   Test

Reporting

1. The rest of the lesson is a test. You'll do the whole test and then I'll mark it. Open your workbook to lesson 75 and find part A. ✔
2. I'll read the instructions: Circle **reports** if a sentence reports on what the picture shows. Circle **does not report** if the sentence does not report on what the picture shows. Do it. Read each sentence. Then circle **reports** or **does not report.** Raise your hand when you're finished.

Irregular Verbs

1. Everybody, find part B. ✔
2. I'll read the instructions: Next to each word, write the word that tells what people did. Raise your hand when you're finished.

Subject/Predicate

1. Everybody, find part C. ✔
2. I'll read the instructions: Circle the part that names. Underline the part that tells more. Do it now. Circle the part of each sentence that names. Then underline the part that tells more. Raise your hand when you're finished.

Editing Sentences

1. Everybody, find part D. ✔
2. I'll read the instructions: Fix up the sentences so they tell what people did.
- Fix up the sentences. Remember to cross out the words that tell what somebody is doing or was doing. Then write the word that tells what the person did. Raise your hand when you're finished.
3. (When students finish the test, collect their workbooks.)

EXERCISE 5   Marking The Test

1. (Mark the test before the next scheduled language lesson. Use the *Language Arts Workbook Answer Key* to determine acceptable responses.)
2. (Write the number of errors each student made in the test scorebox at the beginning of the test.)
3. (Enter the number of errors each student made on the Summary for Test 7. Reproducible Summary Sheets are at the back of the *Language Arts Teacher's Guide*.)

EXERCISE 6   Feedback On Test 7

1. (Return the students' workbooks.)
- Everybody, open your workbook to lesson 75. Look at how I marked your test page.
2. I wrote a number at the top of your test. That number tells how many items you got wrong on the whole test. Raise your hand if I wrote **0, 1,** or **2** at the top of your test. **Those are super stars.**

- Raise your hand if I wrote **3** or **4.** Those are pretty good workers.
- If I wrote a number that's more than 4, you're going to have to work harder.

EXERCISE 7   Test Remedies

- (Before beginning lesson 76, provide any necessary remedies. After students complete the exercises specified for a remedy, check their work and give feedback.)

Test Part A   Reporting

If more than $\frac{1}{4}$ of the students made 2 or more errors in test part A, present the following exercises:
- Lesson 68, Exercise 6, Student Textbook page 1, Part E
- Lesson 69, Exercise 5, Student Textbook page 2, Part D

Test Part B   Irregular Past-Time Verbs

If more than $\frac{1}{4}$ of the students made 2 or more errors in test part B, present the following exercise:

- Lesson 73, Exercise 6, Student Textbook page 9, Part E

Test Part C   Subject/Predicate

If more than $\frac{1}{4}$ of the students made 2 or more errors in test part A, present the following exercises:

- (Direct students to part A on page 263 of the workbook.)
  Circle the part that names in each sentence.
  Underline the part that tells more.
- (Direct students to part B on page 263 of the workbook.)
  Circle the part that names in each sentence.
  Underline the part that tells more.

Test Part D Editing Sentences

> If more than $\frac{1}{4}$ of the students made 2 or more errors in test part D, present the following exercise:

- (Direct students to part C on page 264 of the workbook.)
  Fix up the sentences so they tell what the people did.
  Cross out the words that tell what somebody is doing or was doing.
- (Direct students to part D on page 264 of the workbook.)
  Fix up the sentences so they tell what the people did.
  Cross out the words that tell what somebody is doing or was doing.

Objectives

- Write past-time verbs for irregular present-time verbs. (Exercise 2)
- **Indicate the subject of sentences in a paragraph.** (Exercise 3)
- Replace the subject of a sentence with a pronoun (**he, she** or **it**). (Exercise 4)
- Change 2-word verbs in sentences to 1-word verbs. (Exercise 5)
- **Identify the set of pictures a sentence describes.** (Exercise 6)
- Construct sentences that state the main thing that illustrated characters did. (Exercise 7)
- Listen to a familiar story and answer comprehension questions. (Exercise 8)

EXERCISE 1   Feedback On Lesson 75

- (Hand back the students' sentence-writing assignment from lesson 75.)
- Look at what I wrote on your lined paper. Raise your hand if I wrote **super.**
- If you didn't get a **super,** look at the mistakes you made and be more careful next time.

WORKBOOK

EXERCISE 2   Past Time

Irregular Verbs

1. Everybody, open your workbook to lesson 76 and find part A. ✔
- Next to each number in the first column is a pair of words. The first word tells what people **do.** The second word tells what they **did.**
2. Everybody, touch number 1.
    The words are **wear** and **wore.** The word that tells what people do is **wear.** Everybody, what word tells what they did? (Signal.) *Wore.*
- Touch 2.
    The word that tells what people do is **see.** Everybody, what word tells what they did? (Signal.) *Saw.*
- Touch 3.
    Run tells what people do. What word tells what they did? (Signal.) *Ran.*
- Touch 4.
    Go tells what people do. What word tells what they did? (Signal.) *Went.*

- Touch 5.
    Sit tells what people do. What word tells what they did? (Signal.) *Sat.*
3. For words 6 through 10, I'll say the word that tells what people **do.** You'll say the word that tells what they **did.**
4. Touch 6.
    See. What word tells what they did? (Signal.) *Saw.*
- Touch 7.
    Sit. What word tells what they did? (Signal.) *Sat.*
- Touch 8.
    Go. What word tells what they did? (Signal.) *Went.*
- Touch 9.
    Wear. What word tells what they did? (Signal.) *Wore.*
- Touch 10.
    Run. What word tells what they did? (Signal.) *Ran.*
- (Repeat step 4 until firm.)
5. Do words 6 through 10. Next to each word, write the word that tells what people did. Remember to spell each word correctly. Raise your hand when you're finished. (Observe students and give feedback.)
6. Let's check your work. Make an **X** if you don't have the right word or if you didn't spell it correctly.
- Touch 6.
    What did you write for see? (Signal.) *Saw.* Spell **saw.** (Signal.) *S-a-w.*
- What did you write for **sit?** (Signal.) *Sat.* Spell **sat.** (Signal.) *S-a-t.*
- What did you write for **go**? (Signal.) *Went.* Spell **went.** (Signal.) *W-e-n-t.*

- What did you write for **wear?** (Signal.) *Wore.*
  Spell **wore.** (Signal.) *W-o-r-e.*
- What did you write for **run?** (Signal.) *Ran.*
  Spell **ran.** (Signal.) *R-a-n.*
7. Raise your hand if you got no items wrong. Great job.
- Everybody else, fix up any mistakes you made in part A.
  (Observe students and give feedback.)

EXERCISE 3   Subject/Predicate

1. Everybody, find part B. ✔
   You're going to circle the part of each sentence that names.
2. Touch the beginning of the first sentence. I'll read the sentence: Tina and Ginger wanted to play in the water. Everybody, what part names? (Signal.) *Tina and Ginger.*
- Circle **Tina and Ginger.** ✔
- Next sentence: The girls were wearing jeans. What part names? (Signal.) *The girls.*
- Circle **the girls.** ✔
- Next sentence: They went to the little pool. What part names? (Signal.) *They.*
- Circle **they.** ✔
- Next sentence: The two girls went into the shallow water. What part names? (Signal.) *The two girls.*
- Circle **the two girls.** ✔
3. Read the last two sentences. Circle the part of each sentence that names. Raise your hand when you're finished.
   (Observe students and give feedback.)
4. Let's check your work. Make an **X** next to any item you missed.
- Sentence 1. Tina and Ginger wanted to play in the water. Say that sentence. (Signal.) *Tina and Ginger wanted to play in the water.*
  What part names? (Signal.) *Tina and Ginger.*
  What part tells more? (Signal.) *Wanted to play in the water.*
  Put an **X** if you did not circle these words: **Tina and Ginger.**
- Next sentence: The girls were wearing jeans. Say that sentence. (Signal.) *The girls were wearing jeans.*
  What part names? (Signal.) *The girls.*
  What part tells more? (Signal.) *Were wearing jeans.*

- Next sentence: They went to the little pool. Say that sentence. (Signal.) *They went to the little pool.*
  What part names? (Signal.) *They.*
  What part tells more? (Signal.) *Went to the little pool.*
- Next sentence: The two girls went into the shallow water. Say that sentence. (Signal.) *The two girls went into the shallow water.*
  What part names? (Signal.) *The two girls.*
  What part tells more? (Signal.) *Went into the shallow water.*
- Next sentence: They started to splash each other. Say that sentence. (Signal.) *They started to splash each other.*
  What part names? (Signal.) *They.*
  What part tells more? (Signal.) *Started to splash each other.*
- Next sentence: Tina and Ginger were all wet when they left the pool. Say that sentence. (Signal.) *Tina and Ginger were all wet when they left the pool.*
  What part names? (Signal.) *Tina and Ginger.*
  What part tells more? (Signal.) *Were all wet when they left the pool.*
5. Raise your hand if you made no mistakes. Great job.
- Everybody else, fix up any mistakes you made in part B.
  (Observe students and give feedback.)

EXERCISE 4   Pronouns

He, She, It

1. Everybody, find part C. ✔
   The instructions say to fill in the blanks with **he, she** or **it.** What word can we use to refer to something that is not a person? (Signal.) *It.*
2. Fill in the blanks. Remember to start each sentence with a capital. Raise your hand when you're finished.
   (Observe students and give feedback.)
3. Let's check your work. Make an **X** next to anything you missed.
- Sentence 1: His big sister parked the car. Say your sentence. (Signal.) *She parked the car.*
- Sentence 2: Ted's car slid down the hill. Say your sentence. (Signal.) *It slid down the hill.*

- Sentence 3: That movie was interesting. Say your sentence. (Signal.) *It was interesting.*
- Sentence 4: Amanda's brother won the race. Say your sentence. (Signal.) *He won the race.*
- Sentence 5: The party was fun. Say your sentence. (Signal.) *It was fun.*
4. Raise your hand if you got no items wrong. Great job.
- Everybody else, fix up any mistakes you made in part C.
  (Observe students and give feedback.)

EXERCISE 5   Editing Sentences

Changing the Verb

1. Everybody, pencils down. Find part D. ✔
- I'll read the instructions: Fix up the sentences so they tell what people did.
2. Nothing is underlined in the sentences. All the sentences tell what somebody is doing or was doing. Find the words in each sentence that tell what somebody is doing or was doing. Cross out those words and write the word that tells what the people **did.** Raise your hand when you're finished. (Observe students and give feedback.)
3. Let's check your work. Make an **X** next to any item you missed.
- Everybody, touch sentence 1.
  Vanessa is giving the cup to him. Say the sentence that tells what Vanessa **did.** (Signal.) *Vanessa gave the cup to him.*
- What did you cross out? (Signal.) *Is giving.*
- Sentence 2: Carlos was jumping over a fence. Say the sentence that tells what Carlos did. (Signal.) *Carlos jumped over a fence.*
- What did you cross out? (Signal.) *Was jumping.*
- Sentence 3: Four children were buying apples. Say the sentence that tells what they did. (Signal.) *Four children bought apples.*
- What did you cross out? (Signal.) *Were buying.*
- Sentence 4: Mr. Lopez was painting a chair. Say the sentence that tells what Mr. Lopez did. (Signal.) *Mr. Lopez painted a chair.*
- What did you cross out? (Signal.) *Was painting.*

4. Raise your hand if you got no items wrong. Great job.
- Everybody else, fix up any mistakes you made in part D.
  (Observe students and give feedback.)

LINED PAPER • TEXTBOOK

EXERCISE 6   Clarity

Pictures for Sentences

1. Everybody, take out a sheet of lined paper and write your name on the top line. Number your paper 1 through 4. Raise your hand when you're finished.
- Everybody, pencils down. Open your textbook to lesson 76 and find part E. ✔
2. Look at the four pictures in part E. In each picture, a person held a tool.
- Touch picture A.
  Everybody, what tool did Jane hold in that picture? (Signal.) *A hammer.*
- Touch picture B.
  What tool did Seth hold in that picture? (Signal.) *A hammer.*
- Touch picture C.
  What tool did Seth hold in that picture? (Signal.) *A saw.*
- Touch picture D.
  What tool did Jane hold in that picture? (Signal.) *A saw.*
- The four sentences below the pictures tell about the pictures.
3. I'll read sentence 1: A person held a hammer. That sentence tells about **two** pictures. Find the two pictures. ✔
- Everybody, say the letters for the pictures that show: A person held a hammer. (Signal.) *A and B.*
- Sentence 2: Seth held a tool. That sentence tells about two pictures. Find the two pictures. ✔
- Everybody, which pictures show: Seth held a tool? (Signal.) *B and C.*
- Sentence 3: Seth held a hammer. Look at the pictures. Find the pictures that show: Seth held a hammer. ✔
- Everybody, how many pictures show: Seth held a hammer? (Signal.) *One.*
- Yes, only one. Which picture shows: Seth held a hammer? (Signal.) *B.*

- Sentence 4: A person held a tool. This is hard. Look at the pictures carefully. Find the pictures that show: A person held a tool. ✔
- Everybody, how many pictures show: A person held a tool? (Signal.) *Four.*
- Yes, all four. Every picture shows that a person held a tool—picture A, picture B, picture C and picture D.
- (Repeat step 3 until firm.)

4. I'll read the instructions: Read each sentence. Write the letter of each picture that shows what the sentence says.

5. Everybody, touch sentence 1.
   It says: A person held a hammer. Look at each picture. If a picture shows what that sentence says, write the letter of the picture. If a picture doesn't show what the sentence says, don't write the letter of that picture. Raise your hand when you've finished sentence 1.
- Everybody, which letters did you write for sentence 1? (Signal.) *A and B.*

6. Work the rest of the items in part E. Read each sentence. Then write the letter of each picture that shows what the sentence says. Raise your hand when you're finished. (Observe students and give feedback.)

7. Let's check your work. Make an **X** next to any item you missed. I'll read the answers.
- Sentence 1: A person held a hammer. The pictures are A and B.
- Sentence 2: Seth held a tool. The pictures are B and C.
- Sentence 3: Seth held a hammer. The picture is B.
- Sentence 4: A person held a tool. The pictures are A, B, C and D.

8. Raise your hand if you made no mistakes. Great job.
- Everybody else, fix up any mistakes you made in part E.
   (Observe students and give feedback.)

EXERCISE 7 Main Idea

1. Skip a line on your lined paper. Then number your paper 1 and 2. Raise your hand when you're finished.
- Everybody, pencils down. Find part F in your textbook. ✔
- You're going to write sentences that report on the main thing each person did. Remember, when you report, you can only tell what the picture shows.

2. Everybody, touch picture 1.
   Name that person. (Signal.) *Vic.*
- Get ready to say a sentence that reports on the main thing Vic did.
   Remember, don't say what Vic is doing or was doing. (Call on several students. Praise sentences such as: *Vic watered the plant.* For each good sentence:) Everybody, say that sentence.

3. Everybody, touch picture 2.
   Name that person. (Signal.) *A woman.*
- Get ready to say a sentence that reports onthe main thing a woman did. Remember, don't say what a woman is doing or was doing. (Call on several students. Praise sentences such as: *A woman chopped down a tree.* For each good sentence:) Everybody, say that sentence.

4. Touch the words in the vocabulary box as I read them: **watering can, watered, ax, plant, tree, hanging, chopped.** Be sure to spell those words correctly if you use them.

5. I'll read the instructions for part F: Write a sentence that reports on the main thing each person did. Write your sentences. You have 3 minutes. Raise your hand when you're finished.
   (Observe students and give feedback.)

6. (After 3 minutes, say:) Stop writing. If you didn't finish, you can write the rest of the sentences at the end of the lesson.
- I'll call on students to read their sentences. Listen to each sentence and see if it names the right person and tells the main thing that person did. (Call on individual students to read the sentences they wrote for pictures 1 and 2. After each good sentence, tell the group:) Everybody, say that sentence.

7. Let's check your work. Make 3 check boxes below your last sentence. ✔

8. Everybody, touch the box for check 1.

Here's check 1: Does each sentence begin with a capital and end with a period? Read your sentences. If they begin with a capital and end with a period, make a check in box 1 on your paper. If you forgot any capitals or periods, fix up your sentences now and then make the check. Don't make a check until you've checked your sentences and fixed up any mistakes. Raise your hand when you're finished. (Observe students and give feedback.)

9. Now touch the box for check 2. Here's check 2: Does each sentence tell the main thing the person did? Read over your sentences carefully. Each sentence should start out by naming the person. Then it should tell the main thing the person did. When all your sentences name and tell the main thing the person did, make a check in box 2. Raise your hand when you're finished.
(Observe students and give feedback.)

10. Now touch the box for check 3. Here's the check: Did you spell words from the vocabulary box correctly? Look at each sentence. Make sure vocabulary words are spelled correctly. Fix up any mistakes and make a check in box 3. Raise your hand when you're finished.
(Observe students and give feedback.)

11. Raise your hand it you think you'll get a **super** paper.

- I'll read your sentences later and hand them back at the beginning of the next lesson. I'll mark any mistakes I find.

EXERCISE 8 Dot And Dud *Part 3*

Storytelling

- I'll read another part of the Dot and Dud story. Let's see how well you can remember things that happened.
- Where was Dud at the end of the last part? (Call on a student. Idea: *In the kitchen of the ski lodge.*)

That evening, while Dud was snoozing next to the stove in the kitchen, full of food and dreaming about summertime, a truck pulled up to the ski lodge, and the ranger came inside to pick up Dud.

The cook had called the rescue station and left a message that one of their St. Bernards was at the ski lodge.

The ranger was not happy.

- Who else was in the truck? (Call on a student. *The other St. Bernards.*)
- Was Dot with the other dogs? (Call on a student. *No.*)
- Had they found the mountain climber? (Call on a student. *No.*)

He led Dud to the truck and put him in the back with all the other St. Bernards. They were coming back from their search. They hadn't found the stranded mountain climber, and they hadn't found Dot. The ranger decided that it was best to go home before it got dark in the mountains. They would go out again early in the morning.

Of course, Dud didn't know that Dot was stranded on the mountain. He got in the back of the truck with the other dogs. They didn't even look at him. They didn't start griping about how he didn't keep up with the others and got lost. They didn't remind him that he didn't even know north from south or that his nose was about as useful as another paw. They just sat there, weary from plowing through the snow all day and worried about Dot.

As the truck went down the road back to the rescue station, Dud tried to strike up a conversation with the other dogs. "How did things go today?" he asked.

Two of the dogs looked at him but didn't answer. The other dogs didn't even look at him.

"Did you find the mountain climber?"

No dogs looked at him.

"You look pretty tired. Have you had anything to eat?"

No answer.

"I had some great soup at the ski lodge. And a big plateful of meat scraps. And, after I ate that, I took . . . "

"Will you shut up?" the oldest dog said.

- Dud was about to discover something. What was that? (Call on a student. *Dot was not in the truck.*)

So Dud was quiet for a while. Then he looked around and noticed that Dot wasn't in the truck. "Hey," he said, "where's Dot?"

"Lost," one of the St. Bernards said.

"What do you mean? Where is she?"

The oldest St. Bernard said, "Somewhere on the mountain. We couldn't find her."

"Do you mean that she's out there all alone?"

Some of the dogs nodded yes.

This was no game. Dud loved Dot. He didn't always show it, but he loved her. As he sat in the back of that truck, he remembered her from way, way back when the two of them were little puppies. She always stuck up for him when the other puppies in the litter would pick on Dud. Dud remembered a lot of other things as that truck moved slowly down the snowy road. He remembered how sad he had been when Dot and Dud had to leave their mother and their other brothers and sisters. The only good thing about going to the rescue station was that Dot was there. She had always been there. But now . . . she was gone.

"No," Dud said out loud. "She **can't** be lost."

All the other dogs looked down. "Why didn't you find her? You can't leave her out there."

"She'll be all right—if we find her tomorrow."

Dud said, "But what if she found the mountain climber? Won't he freeze during the night?"

All the other dogs looked down.

Dud didn't say anything more.

- What did Dud plan to do? (Call on a student. Idea: *Find Dot.*)

But he did a lot of thinking. And the biggest thought he had was this: "If they can't find her, **I'll** find her." This wasn't one of those promises he made when he was only half serious and half embarrassed for being foolish. This wasn't one of those promises like "I'll try" or "I'll do better next time." This was a **real** promise: **"I'll** find her."

At last, the truck stopped in front of the rescue station.

- What did Dud do next? (Call on a student. Idea: *He ran north.*)

The ranger opened the back door, and out bounded Dud, just as fast as he could bound. He ran north. The ranger was shouting, "Dud, come back here! Where do you think you're going in the dark?"

The other dogs were yelling at him, too. "Yeah! Where do you think you're going in the dark?"

But Dud knew exactly where he was going—north.

- What did the other dogs do? (Call on a student. Idea: *They followed Dud.*)

Pretty soon, some of the other dogs started to follow Dud. Then the rest of the dogs started to follow. Then the ranger started to follow. And away everybody went, plowing through the deep snow and heading up that mountain.

Dud was all business. He said to himself, "I know Dot's smell better than any other dog in the world, and I'll find that smell. I **will.**"

He put his nose in the snow and he snorted and sniffed. He didn't care that the snow was cold. He didn't even **notice** that it was cold. Again and again—snort, sniff, snort, sniff. Then he did it the fast way—he just put his head deep into the snow and kept it there—like a snowplow—snorting and sniffing as he went up that mountain as fast as he could run. Then, suddenly he recognized a faint smell in the snow—very faint. But he knew that smell. It was Dot.

"Come on, you guys," he yelled to the other dogs. "Follow me."

And up the mountain Dud went once more, with his head in the snow like a snowplow. He followed that trail up, up, up the mountain. When he came to steep parts and slid down, he just tried again until he made it. Her smell was getting stronger in the snow. She was closer, and closer, and . . . suddenly, Dud came to the rocky part where Dot was lying with the mountain climber.

He called back down to the other dogs, "Up here, you guys. I found her."

- Did the cold bother Dot? (Call on a student. *No*.)
- What about the mountain climber? (Call on a student. Idea: *The climber was seriously injured*.)

While he waited for the others, he sat down next to Dot. "Are you okay?" he asked.

"Yes, but I'm sure glad you got here. This climber is seriously injured. I don't think he could make it through the night."

Then she looked at Dud and said, "What are **you** doing here?"

"Looking for you," Dud said.

She couldn't believe it. "And you found me without getting lost?"

"Well . . . " he said. "I got a little lost once."

Dot said, "Well, I'm sure glad to see you." She wagged her tail. He wagged his tail.

- How did they get the injured mountain climber down the mountain? (Call on a student. Idea: *They used a sled*.)

Soon, the ranger and the other St. Bernards made it up the steep slope. The ranger had a little sled. He put the injured climber on the sled. Then he and the dogs lowered the sled down the very steep part. Then the dogs pulled the sled back to the rescue station.

After the ranger took care of the injured climber, and all the dogs were back in the kennel, the oldest St. Bernard looked at Dud and said, "See? That shows what you can do when you put your mind to it. When you try hard, you're a pretty good rescue dog."

The other dogs said, "Yeah, pretty good."

Then the oldest dog said, "We're all glad that you found Dot. And here's our way of thanking you."

- How did they thank Dud? (Call on a student. Idea: *Gave him a ham bone.*)

The oldest dog picked up a great big ham bone, brought it over to Dud and dropped it in front of him.

Dud started to say, "Oh, I really can't accept that ham bone. I really shouldn't eat this great big . . . " But then he looked at that ham bone, and it **looked** so good and **smelled** so good that he stopped talking and started doing something else.

> **Note:**
> - Collect the students' workbooks and papers.
> - Check the students' work before the next language period. Mark any mistakes.
> - Write **super** on work that has all mistakes corrected. Write **good** or **pretty good** on work that has only 1 or 2 mistakes.

Objectives

- Indicate the subject of sentences in a paragraph. (Exercise 2)
- Write past-time verbs for irregular present-time verbs. (Exercise 3)
- Replace the subject of a sentence with a pronoun (**he, she,** or **it**). (Exercise 4)
- Draw a conclusion based on different concrete examples. (Exercise 5)
- Identify the set of pictures a sentence describes. (Exercise 6)
- Construct sentences that state the main thing that illustrated characters did. (Exercise 7)
- Listen to a familiar story and answer comprehension questions. (Exercise 8)

EXERCISE 1 Feedback On Lesson 76

- (Hand back the students' work from lesson 76.)
- Look at what I wrote on your lined paper. Raise your hand if I wrote **super.**
- If you didn't get a **super,** look at the mistakes you made and be more careful next time.

WORKBOOK

EXERCISE 2 Subject/Predicate

1. Everybody, open your workbook to lesson 77 and find part A. ✔
- You're going to circle the part of each sentence that names.
2. I'll read the first sentence: Carla was in the park. What part names? (Signal.) *Carla.* Circle **Carla.**
3. I'll read the rest of the paragraph: She played on the swings. She went down a slide. That tired girl rested on a bench. Carla walked home with friends.
- Your turn: Read the sentences. Circle the part of each sentence that names. Raise your hand when you're finished.
(Observe students and give feedback.)
4. Let's check your work. Make an **X** next to any item you missed.
- First sentence: Carla was in the park. Say that sentence. (Signal.) *Carla was in the park.* What part names? (Signal.) *Carla.* What part tells more? (Signal.) *Was in the park.*
- Next sentence: She played on the swings. Say that sentence. (Signal.) *She played on the swings.* What part names? (Signal.) *She.*

What part tells more? (Signal.) *Played on the swings.*
- Next sentence: She went down a slide. Say that sentence. (Signal.) *She went down a slide.* What part names? (Signal.) *She.* What part tells more? (Signal.) *Went down a slide.*
- Next sentence: That tired girl rested on a bench. Say that sentence. (Signal.) *That tired girl rested on a bench.* What part names? (Signal.) *That tired girl.* What part tells more? (Signal.) *Rested on a bench.*
- Next sentence: Carla walked home with her friends. Say that sentence. (Signal.) *Carla walked home with her friends.* What part names? (Signal.) *Carla.* What part tells more? (Signal.) *Walked home with her friends.*
5. Raise your hand if you made no mistakes. Great job.
- Everybody else, fix up any mistakes you made in part A.
(Observe students and give feedback.)

EXERCISE 3 Past Time

Irregular Verbs

1. Everybody, pencils down. Find part B. ✔ Next to each number is a pair of words. The first word tells what people **do.** The second word tells what they **did.**
- Everybody, touch number 1.
The word that tells what people do is **see.** Everybody, what word tells what they did? (Signal.) *Saw.*

2. Touch 2.
The word that tells what people do is **wear.**
Everybody, what word tells what they did?
(Signal.) *Wore.*

- Touch 3.
Sit tells what people do. What word tells
what they did? (Signal.) *Sat.*

- Touch 4.
Run tells what people do. What word tells
what they did? (Signal.) *Ran.*

- Touch 5.
Go tells what people do. What word tells
what they did? (Signal.) *Went.*

3. Do words 6 through 10. Next to each word,
write the word that tells what people did.
Remember to spell each word correctly.
Raise your hand when you're finished.
(Observe students and give feedback.)

4. Let's check your work. Make an **X** if you
don't have the right word or if you didn't
spell it correctly.

- Touch 6.
What did you write for **wear?** (Signal.)
Wore.
Spell **wore.** (Signal.) *W-o-r-e.*

- What did you write for **run?** (Signal.) *Ran.*
Spell **ran.** (Signal.) *R-a-n.*

- What did you write for **see?** (Signal.) *Saw.*
Spell **saw.** (Signal.) *S-a-w.*

- What did you write for **go?** (Signal.) *Went.*
Spell **went.** (Signal.) *W-e-n-t.*

- What did you write for **sit?** (Signal.) *Sat.*
Spell **sat.** (Signal.) *S-a-t.*

5. Raise your hand if you got no items wrong.
Great job.

- Everybody else, fix up any mistakes you
made in part B.
(Observe students and give feedback.)

EXERCISE 4 Pronouns

He, She, It

1. Everybody, find part C. ✔
The instructions say to fill in the blanks
with **he, she** or **it.** What word can we use
to refer to something that is not a person?
(Signal.) *It.*

2. Fill in the blanks. Remember to start each
sentence with a capital. Raise your hand
when you're finished.
(Observe students and give feedback.)

3. Let's check your work. Make an **X** next to
anything you missed.

- Sentence 1: His shirt was covered with dirt.
Say your sentence. (Signal.) *It was covered
with dirt.*

- Sentence 2: My new pencil fell off the table.
Say your sentence. (Signal.) *It fell off the
table.*

- Sentence 3: A boy sat in a chair. Say your
sentence. (Signal.) *He sat in a chair.*

- Sentence 4: Tamika's book was very funny.
Say your sentence. (Signal.) *It was very
funny.*

- Sentence 5: A young woman rode a bike.
Say your sentence. (Signal.) *She rode a
bike.*

4. Raise your hand if you got no items wrong.
Great job.

- Everybody else, fix up any mistakes you
made in part C.
(Observe students and give feedback.)

EXERCISE 5 DEDUCTIONS

1. Everybody, pencils down. Find part D. ✔
You're going to draw a conclusion. The first
sentence is: Every bird has wings.

- To draw a conclusion, we must put the
name of a bird in the blanks. I'll name a
bird: a robin.

- Listen to the deduction: Every **bird** has
wings. A **robin** is a bird. So a **robin** has
wings.

2. Your turn to say all three sentences.
- First sentence. (Signal.) *Every bird has
wings.*
- Next sentence. (Signal.) *A robin is a bird.*
- Conclusion. (Signal.) *So a robin has wings.*
- (Repeat step 2 until firm.)

3. Here's a different bird: a crow.

4. Say the whole thing with **a crow.**
- First sentence. (Signal.) *Every bird has
wings.*
- Next sentence. (Signal.) *A crow is a bird.*
- Conclusion. (Signal.) *So a crow has wings.*
- (Repeat step 4 until firm.)

5. Your turn to complete the deduction. Put
the name of any bird you want in the blank.
Then complete the last sentence. The
names of some birds are written below the
deduction. Raise your hand when you're
finished.
(Observe students and give feedback.)

6. (Call on individual students to read all three sentences. Praise students who have appropriate deductions.)

EXERCISE 6   Clarity

Pictures for Sentences

1. Everybody, take out a sheet of lined paper and write your name on the top line. Number your paper 1 through 4. Raise your hand when you're finished. ✔
- Everybody, pencils down. Open your textbook to lesson 77 and find part E. ✔
2. Look at the four pictures in part E. In each picture, a person held a container.
- Touch picture A.
  In that picture, Mark held a jar.
- Touch picture B.
  Everybody, what container did Ashley hold in that picture? (Signal.) *A jar.*
- Touch picture C.
  What container did Mark hold in that picture? (Signal.) *A pail.*
- Touch picture D.
  What container did Ashley hold in that picture? (Signal.) *A pail.*
- The four sentences below the pictures tell about the pictures.
3. I'll read sentence 1: Mark held a container. That sentence tells about two pictures. Find the two pictures. ✔
- Everybody, say the letters for the pictures that show: Mark held a container. (Signal.) *A and C.*
- Sentence 2: Ashley held a jar.
  Everybody, how many pictures show: Ashley held a jar? (Signal.) *One.*
- Yes, only one. Which picture shows: Ashley held a jar? (Signal.) *B.*
- Sentence 3: A person held a container. Look at the pictures carefully. Find the pictures that show: A person held a container. ✔
- Everybody, how many pictures show: A person held a container? (Signal.) *Four.*
- Yes, all four. Every picture shows that a person held a container-picture A, picture B, picture C and picture D.

- Sentence 4: Ashley held a container. Look at the pictures carefully. Find the pictures that show: Ashley held a container. ✔
- Everybody, how many pictures show: Ashley held a container? (Signal.) *Two.*
- Which pictures show: Ashley held a container? (Signal.) *B and D.*
- (Repeat step 3 until firm.)
4. I'll read the instructions: Read each sentence. Write the letter of each picture that shows what the sentence says. Do that now. Raise your hand when you're finished.
  (Observe students and give feedback.)
5. Let's check your work. Make an **X** next to any item you missed. I'll read the answers.
- Sentence 1: Mark held a container.
  The pictures are A and C.
- Sentence 2: Ashley held a jar.
  The picture is B.
- Sentence 3: A person held a container.
  The pictures are A, B, C and D.
- Sentence 4: Ashley held a container.
  The pictures are B and D.
6. Raise your hand if you made no mistakes. Great job.
- Everybody else, fix up any mistakes you made in part E.
  (Observe students and give feedback.)

EXERCISE 7   Main Idea

1. Skip a line on your paper. Then number your paper 1 through 3. Raise your hand when you're finished. ✔
- Everybody, pencils down. Find part F in your textbook. ✔
- You're going to say sentences that report on the main thing each picture shows. Remember, when you report, you can only tell what the picture shows.

2. Everybody, touch picture 1.
   Name the two people in that picture.
   (Signal.) *Fred and Bill.*
   - Say a sentence that reports on the main thing Fred and Bill did. (Call on a student. Praise sentences such as: *Fred and Bill watched television*. For each good sentence:) Everybody, say that sentence.
3. Everybody, touch picture 2.
   Name that animal. (Signal.) *A small dog.*
   - Get ready to say a sentence that reports on the main thing a small dog did. (Call on several students. Praise sentences such as: *A small dog jumped through a hoop*. For each good sentence:) Everybody, say that sentence.
4. Everybody, touch picture 3.
   Name that person. (Signal.) *A young woman.*
   - Get ready to say a sentence that reports on the main thing a young woman did. (Call on several students. Praise sentences such as: *A young woman kicked a soccer ball*. For each good sentence:) Everybody, say that sentence.
5. Touch the words in the vocabulary box as I read them: **hoop, through, television.** Be sure to spell those words correctly if you use them.
6. I'll read the instructions: Write a sentence for each picture. Each sentence should report on the main thing the picture shows. You have 4 minutes. Raise your hand when you're finished.
   (Observe students and give feedback.)
7. (After 4 minutes, say:) Stop writing. If you didn't finish, you can write the rest of the sentences at the end of the lesson.
8. I'll call on students to read their sentences. Listen to the sentences. Make sure they name what the picture shows and tell the main thing.
   (Call on individual students to read the sentences they wrote for pictures 1, 2 and 3. After each good sentence, tell the group:) Everybody, say that sentence.
9. Let's check your work. Make 3 check boxes below your last sentence. ✔
10. Everybody, touch the box for check 1. Here's check 1: Does each sentence begin with a capital and end with a period? Read your sentences. Fix up any sentences that don't have a capital and a period. Make a check in box 1 when your sentences check out. Raise your hand when you're finished.
    (Observe students and give feedback.)
11. Now touch the box for check 2. Here's check 2: Does each sentence tell the main thing the persons or animal did? Read over your sentences. Each sentence should start out by naming the persons or the animal. Then it should tell the main thing the persons or the animal did. When they all name and tell the main thing the persons or animal did, put a check in box 2. Raise your hand when you're finished. (Observe students and give feedback.)
12. Now touch the box for check 3. Here's the check: Did you spell words from the vocabulary box correctly? Look at each sentence. Make sure vocabulary words are spelled correctly. Fix up any mistakes and make a check in box 3. Raise your hand when you're finished.
    (Observe students and give feedback.)
13. Raise your hand if you think you'll get a **super** paper.
    - I'll read your sentences later and hand them back at the beginning of the next lesson. I'll mark any mistakes I find.

EXERCISE 8   Zelda The Artist

Storytelling

- I'll read the story titled, "Zelda the Artist." Let's see how well you can remember things that happened.

Zelda was an artist and a very good one. She could draw pictures that looked so real that you would think they were photographs. She could make wonderful designs, and she could even make statues that almost seemed to be alive. There wasn't anything she couldn't paint or draw.

But Zelda had one problem:

- What was that problem? (Call on a student. Idea: *She wasn't good at thinking*.)

She wasn't as good at **thinking** as she was at drawing or painting or making statues. So she sometimes made things that were pretty silly, like the time she illustrated Mrs. Hudson's book.

Mrs. Hudson wrote a book about some of the interesting things that happened to her. At least **she** thought they were interesting.

- Were they interesting? (Call on a student. *No.*)

Actually, they were very, very boring. She told about experiences she had when she grew up in the city. She told about her experiences when she moved to the farm. And she told about the many trips she had taken to all parts of the world.

- Why did Mrs. Hudson call Zelda? (Call on a student. Idea: *To ask Zelda to draw pictures for the book*.)

She loved her stories, but she felt they would be a lot better if the book had beautiful illustrations to show some of her experiences.

Mrs. Hudson had seen some of the fine work that Zelda had done, so she called Zelda on the phone and asked Zelda if she'd be interested in doing twenty illustrations for the book.

Zelda thought about it for a few moments. Then she said, "Yes, I'd like to do that."

Mrs. Hudson said, "Good. I'll bring over the book. I've marked parts of the book to let you know what you should illustrate."

Later that day, Mrs. Hudson drove over to Zelda's place and showed Zelda how she'd marked all the places in the story that gave Zelda information about illustrations.

Mrs. Hudson turned to the second page of the book and pointed to some sentences that were circled in red. Mrs. Hudson said, "Listen to this part." Then she read the circled sentence, "That spring, the apple trees were covered with white flowers, and their branches were black."

- Who remembers what Zelda thought she had to draw for this part of the story? (Call on a student. Idea: *Black branches on white flowers.*)

After Mrs. Hudson read that part, Zelda said, "That may be hard to illustrate."

"Why is that?"

"Well, it says that the tree was covered with white **flowers,** and their branches were black. But, how do you draw black branches on little tiny flowers?"

Mrs. Hudson looked at Zelda for a long moment. Mrs. Hudson blinked two times. Then she broke into laughter. "Ho, ho," she laughed. "That's very funny. I didn't catch the joke right away, but that's very funny—black branches on the flowers."

That spring, the apple trees were covered with white flowers, and **their** branches were black.

Mrs. Hudson went, "Ho, ho," but it wasn't really funny because Zelda was not joking. She didn't understand that the branches belonged to the trees, not to the flowers. So she said, "Well, I'll just do the best I can."

"Good for you, my dear," Mrs. Hudson said, and turned to the next part of the book that was circled.

Mrs. Hudson said, "Listen to this part: 'When we were on the farm, my brother and my sister had pet pigs. They just loved to roll around in the mud.'"

- Who remembers what Zelda drew for this part of the story? (Call on a student. Idea: *The children rolling around in the mud.*)

After Mrs. Hudson read, "They just loved to roll around in the mud," Zelda said, "They did?"

Mrs. Hudson said, "Oh, yes. They just loved it."

Zelda said, "Didn't they get their clothes all muddy?"

Mrs. Hudson looked at Zelda and blinked. Then she broke into laughter again: "Ho, ho, ho. My," she said, "you are very clever—'Didn't they get their clothes all muddy?' Very funny."

Mrs. Hudson flipped to the next part that was circled. "Here's one of my favorite parts," she said. "Listen to this: "Every day the children rode their horses through the valley. Their tails flew in the wind."

- What did Zelda draw for this part of the story? (Call on a student. Idea: *Children with tails.*)

After Mrs. Hudson read the part, "Their tails flew in the wind," Zelda shook her head and said, "They **all** had them?"

"Had what?"

"Tails."

"Well of course, long flowing tails."

"Golly," Zelda said.

"The youngest one had the longest tail. He was gray and white."

Zelda said, "Really?"

"Yes," Mrs. Hudson said. "He was just **covered** with gray and white spots."

"Poor boy," Zelda said.

Mrs. Hudson flipped to one more place that was marked in the book. She said, "This is a little different. This was something inside the farmhouse. Listen: 'We always kept a glass on top of the refrigerator. We kept it full of water.'"

- What did Zelda draw for this part of the story? (Call on a student. Idea: *A refrigerator filled with water.*)

Zelda shook her head.

After Mrs. Hudson read, "We kept it full of water," Zelda said, "Didn't it spill out when you opened the door?"

Blink, blink—"Ho, ho, ho, ho. Oh, my dear, you have such a clever wit."

Mrs. Hudson patted Zelda on the knee and handed her the book. She said, "Well, I'll leave this with you, my dear. You can read through it and see what to show for the other parts I've marked. If you have any questions, you can give me a call."

Zelda said, "I have one big question."

"What's that, my dear?"

"Is this book about very strange things?"

"Well," Mrs. Hudson said, "I suppose not many people have had the kinds of experiences I've had."

"You can say that again," Zelda said.

"All right," Mrs. Hudson said, "I suppose not many people have had the kinds of experiences I've had."

Note:

- Collect the students' workbooks and papers.
- Check the students' work before the next language period. Mark any mistakes.
- Write **super** on work that has all mistakes corrected. Write **good** or **pretty good** on work that has only 1 or 2 mistakes.

Objectives

- Change 2-word verbs in sentences to 1-word verbs. (Exercise 2)
- Indicate the subject of sentences in a paragraph. (Exercise 3)
- Replace the subject of a sentence with a pronoun (**he, she** or **it**). (Exercise 4)
- Write past-time verbs for irregular present-time verbs. (Exercise 5)
- Identify the set of pictures a sentence describes. (Exercise 6)
- Construct sentences that state the main thing that illustrated characters did. (Exercise 7)
- Listen to a familiar story and answer comprehension questions. (Exercise 8)

EXERCISE 1 Feedback On Lesson 77

- (Hand back the students' work from lesson 77.)
- Look at what I wrote on your lined paper. Raise your hand if I wrote **super.**
- If you didn't get a **super,** look at the mistakes you made and be more careful next time.

WORKBOOK

EXERCISE 2 Editing Sentences

Changing the Verb

1. Everybody, open your workbook to lesson 78 and find part A. ✔
- I'll read the instructions: Fix up the sentences so they tell what people did.
2. Fix up the sentences. Remember, you have to cross out two words. Raise your hand when you're finished.
(Observe students and give feedback.)
3. Let's check your work. Make an **X** next to any item you missed.
- Everybody, touch sentence 1. Miss Ross is digging holes for the fence posts. Say the sentence that tells what Miss Ross did. (Signal.) *Miss Ross dug holes for the fence posts.*
- What did you cross out? (Signal.) *Is digging.*
- Sentence 2: They are filling the box with sand. Say the sentence that tells what they did. (Signal.) *They filled the box with sand.*
- What did you cross out? (Signal.) *Are filling.*
- Sentence 3: My grandfather was starting his car. Say the sentence that tells what my grandfather did. (Signal.) *My grandfather started his car.*

- What did you cross out? (Signal.) *Was starting.*
- Sentence 4: She was having a party. Say the sentence that tells what she did. (Signal.) *She had a party.*
- What did you cross out? (Signal.) *Was having.*
- Sentence 5: Justin is buying milk. Say the sentence that tells what Justin did. (Signal.) *Justin bought milk.*
- What did you cross out? (Signal.) *Is buying.*
- Sentence 6: The children were cooking eggs. Say the sentence that tells what the children did. (Signal.) *The children cooked eggs.*
- What did you cross out? (Signal.) *Were cooking.*
4. Raise your hand if you got no items wrong. Great job.
- Everybody else, fix up any mistakes you made in part A.
(Observe students and give feedback.)

EXERCISE 3 Subject/Predicate

1. Everybody, find part B. ✔
You're going to circle the part of each sentence that names.
2. I'll read the paragraph: An old cowboy rode his horse to town. The cowboy wanted to buy a new hat. He rode his horse to the clothing store. He tied his horse to a post. The cowboy went in the store. He found a hat he liked.
3. Your turn: Read the paragraph. Circle the part of each sentence that names. Raise your hand when you're finished.
(Observe students and give feedback.)

4. Let's check your work. Make an **X** next to any sentence you missed.

- First sentence: An old cowboy rode his horse to town. Say that sentence. (Signal.) *An old cowboy rode his horse to town.*
  What part names? (Signal.) *An old cowboy.*

- What part tells more? (Signal.) *Rode his horse to town.*
  Make an **X** if you did not circle: **an old cowboy.**

- Next sentence: The cowboy wanted to buy a new hat. Say that sentence. (Signal.) *The cowboy wanted to buy a new hat.*
  What part names? (Signal.) *The cowboy.*
  What part tells more? (Signal.) *Wanted to buy a new hat.*

- Next sentence: He rode his horse to the clothing store. Say that sentence. (Signal.) *He rode his horse to the clothing store.*
  What part names? (Signal.) *He.*
  What part tells more? (Signal.) *Rode his horse to the clothing store.*

- Next sentence: He tied his horse to a post. Say that sentence. (Signal.) *He tied his horse to a post.*
  What part names? (Signal.) *He.*
  What part tells more? (Signal.) *Tied his horse to a post.*

- Next sentence: The cowboy went in the store. Say that sentence. (Signal.) *The cowboy went in the store.*
  What part names? (Signal.) *The cowboy.*
  What part tells more? (Signal.) *Went in the store.*

- Next sentence: He found a hat he liked. Say that sentence. (Signal.) *He found a hat he liked.*
  What part names? (Signal.) *He.*
  What part tells more? (Signal.) *Found a hat he liked.*

5. Raise your hand if you made no mistakes. Great job.

- Everybody else, fix up any mistakes you made in part B.
  (Observe students and give feedback.)

EXERCISE 4 Pronouns

He, She, It

1. Everybody, find part C. ✔
   The instructions say to fill in the blanks with **he, she** or **it.**
   What word can we use to refer to something that is not a person? (Signal.) *It.*

2. Fill in the blanks. Remember to start each sentence with a capital. Raise your hand when you're finished.
   (Observe students and give feedback.)

3. Let's check your work. Make an **X** next to any item you missed.

- Sentence 1: That red plate was broken. Say your sentence. (Signal.) *It was broken.*

- Sentence 2: Her brother fell down. Say your sentence. (Signal.) *He fell down.*

- Sentence 3: My sister had a cold. Say your sentence. (Signal.) *She had a cold.*

- Sentence 4: My father's hat was dirty. Say your sentence. (Signal.) *It was dirty.*

- Sentence 5: An airplane flew over the clouds. Say your sentence. (Signal.) *It flew over the clouds.*

- Sentence 6: Her window was open. Say your sentence. (Signal.) *It was open.*

4. Raise your hand if you got no items wrong. Great job.

- Everybody else, fix up any mistakes you made in part C.
  (Observe students and give feedback.)

LINED PAPER • TEXTBOOK

EXERCISE 5 Past Time

Irregular Verbs

1. Everybody, take out a sheet of lined paper and write your name on the top line. Number your paper 1 through 5. Raise your hand when you're finished. ✔

- Everybody, open your textbook to lesson 78 and find part D. ✔

2. The words in part D tell what people do. You're going to write the words that tell what they did.

- Word 1 is **see.** Everybody, what word tells what people did? (Signal.) *Saw.*

- Write **saw** for number 1. Then write the rest of the words for part D. Read each word that tells what people do and write the word that tells what they **did.** Raise your hand when you're finished.
  (Observe students and give feedback.)

3. Let's check your work. Make an **X** if you wrote the wrong word or did not spell the word correctly.

- Word 1: See. Say the word that tells what people did. (Signal.) *Saw.*
  Spell **saw.** (Signal.) *S-a-w.*
- Word 2: Go. Say the word that tells what people did. (Signal.) *Went.*
  Spell **went.** (Signal.) *W-e-n-t.*
- Word 3: Sit. Say the word that tells what people did. (Signal.) *Sat.*
  Spell **sat.** (Signal.) *S-a-t.*
- Word 4: Wear. Say the word that tells what people did. (Signal.) *Wore.*
  Spell **wore.** (Signal.) *W-o-r-e.*
- Word 5: Run. Say the word that tells what people did. (Signal.) *Ran.*
  Spell **ran.** (Signal.) *R-a-n.*
4. Raise your hand if you made no mistakes. Great job.
- Everybody else, fix up any mistakes you made in part D.
  (Observe students and give feedback.)

EXERCISE 6   Clarity

Pictures for Sentences

1. Skip a line on your paper. Then number your paper 1 through 4. Raise your hand when you're finished.
- Everybody, find part E in your textbook. ✔
2. I'll read the instructions: Read each sentence. Write the letter of each picture that shows what the sentence says. Do that now. Raise your hand when you're finished.
  (Observe students and give feedback.)
3. Let's check your work. Make an **X** next to any item you missed. I'll read the answers.
- Sentence 1: Brett ate fruit.
  The pictures are A and D.
- Sentence 2: A person ate fruit.
  The pictures are A, B, C and D.
- Sentence 3: Sandra ate an apple.
  The picture is C.
- Sentence 4: A person ate a banana.
  The pictures are B and D.
4. Raise your hand if you made no mistakes. Great job.
- Everybody else, fix up any mistakes you made in part E.
  (Observe students and give feedback.)

EXERCISE 7   Main Idea

1. Skip a line on your paper. Then number your paper 1 through 3. Raise your hand when you're finished. ✔
- Everybody, find part F in your textbook. ✔
  I'll read the instructions: Write a sentence for each picture. Each sentence should report on the main thing the picture shows.
2. Everybody, touch picture 1.
  Name that person. (Signal.) *Ramon.*
- Get ready to say a sentence that reports on the main thing Ramon did. (Call on several students. Praise sentences such as: *Ramon poured soup into a pot.* For each good sentence:) Everybody, say that sentence.
3. Everybody, touch picture 2.
  Name that person. (Signal.) *Yoshi.*
- Get ready to say a sentence that reports on the main thing Yoshi did. (Call on several students. Praise sentences such as: *Yoshi carried a log* . For each good sentence:) Everybody, say that sentence.
4. Everybody, touch picture 3.
  Name those persons. (Signal.) *Jerry and Ann.*
- Get ready to say a sentence that reports on the main thing Jerry and Ann did. (Call on several students. Praise sentences such as: *Jerry and Ann roasted marshmallows. Jerry and Ann cooked marshmallows over a campfire.* For each good sentence:) Everybody, say that sentence.
5. Touch the words in the vocabulary box as I read them: **poured, roasted, put, carried, soup, fire, marshmallows.** Be sure to spell those words correctly if you use them.
6. Next to each number on your lined paper, write a sentence that reports on what the picture shows. Tell the main thing the people did. Be sure each sentence starts with a capital and ends with a period. You have 4 minutes. Raise your hand when you're finished.
  (Observe students and give feedback.)

7. (After 4 minutes, say:) Stop writing.
8. I'll call on students to read their sentences. Listen to the sentences. Make sure they name what the picture shows and tell the main thing.
- (Call on individual students to read their sentences. After each good sentence, tell the group:) Everybody, say that sentence.
9. Let's check your work. Make 3 check boxes below your last sentence. ✔
10. Everybody, touch the box for check 1. Here's check 1: Does each sentence begin with a capital and end with a period? Read your sentences. Fix up any sentences that don't have a capital and a period. Make a check in box 1 when your sentences check out. Raise your hand when you're finished. (Observe students and give feedback.)
11. Now touch the box for check 2. Here's check 2: Does each sentence tell the main thing the persons did? Read over your sentences carefully.
Sentences should start out by naming. Then they should tell the main thing the persons did. When all your sentences name and tell the main thing, make a check in box 2. Raise your hand when you're finished.
(Observe students and give feedback.)
12. Now touch the box for check 3. Here's the check: Did you spell words from the vocabulary box correctly? Look at each sentence. Make sure vocabulary words are spelled correctly. Fix up any mistakes and make a check in box 3. Raise your hand when you're finished.
(Observe students and give feedback.)
13. Raise your hand if you think you'll get a **super** paper.
- I'll read your sentences later and hand them back at the beginning of the next lesson. I'll mark any mistakes I find.

EXERCISE 8   Zelda The Artist *Part 2*

Storytelling

- I'll read another part of the story about Zelda. Let's see how well you can remember things that happened.

Zelda read through Mrs. Hudson's book. Most of it was very, very boring. It told about things that were not very exciting—the rain falling in the springtime, chickens running around the barnyard, people going on long train trips—very boring.

Zelda did a couple of illustrations. The first one she did was for the part that said, "When we were on the farm, my brother and my sister had pet pigs. They just loved to roll around in the mud."

- What did Mrs. Hudson think Zelda would draw? (Call on a student. Idea: *Pigs rolling in the mud.*)
- What did Zelda draw? (Call on a student. Idea: *Children rolling in the mud*.)

Zelda made a beautiful picture of Mrs. Hudson's brother and sister rolling around in the mud next to the barn.

In the picture that Zelda drew, the pet pigs were standing there, looking at the students in the mud. When Zelda finished that picture, she said, "That woman must have a very strange family."

Then she did the next illustration. That one was for the part that said, "Every day the children rode their horses through the valley. Their tails flew in the wind."

- What did Mrs. Hudson think Zelda would draw? (Call on a student. Idea: *Horses running with their tails blown by the wind*.)
- What did Zelda draw? (Call on a student. Idea: *Children with tails.*)

Zelda didn't know how many students to draw or how long to make their "tails." But at last she decided to show three children riding horses. She gave each of the children a long tail. She gave the horses regular horse tails.

After she finished the illustration, she said, "That woman sure knows some very strange people."

Then she went on to the next part. It said: "We always kept a glass on top of the refrigerator. We kept it full of water."

- What did Mrs. Hudson think Zelda would draw? (Call on a student. Idea: *A glass full of water.*)
- What did Zelda draw? (Call on a student. Idea: *A refrigerator full of water.*)

Zelda decided to show a picture of somebody opening the refrigerator and water pouring out. She said to herself, "I don't know any other way to show that it was full of water."

Zelda didn't know what to put inside the glass. So she left the glass empty.

The part that was marked for the next illustration said this: "Our car stopped on top of the mountain. It was out of gas."

- What was out of gas? (Call on a student. *The car.*)
- What did Zelda think was out of gas? (Call on a student. *The mountain.*)

Zelda read that part again and again. At last she said, "How am I going to show that the mountain is out of gas? I can't illustrate this picture." Zelda called Mrs. Hudson and said, "I'm having trouble with one illustration. It's for the part that says, 'Our car stopped on top of the mountain. It was out of gas.' How am I going to show it was out of gas?"

"I see what you mean, my dear. Just looking at the picture, you wouldn't really know that it was out of gas, would you?"

"I sure wouldn't," Zelda said.

"Well, what if you sort of showed the inside of it, and we could see the gas gauge?"

"The gas gauge?"

"Yes, my dear. You could put us on top of the mountain, looking inside the window, and show the gas gauge."

"Looking inside **the window?**"

"Of course."

"It has a window?"

"Well, certainly. It has windows all the way around it."

"Wow," Zelda said. "I'll draw it, but I've never seen one with windows before."

"Well, the next time I go over to your place, I'll show you a picture of it."

Zelda said, "I'll take your word for it."

After Zelda hung up the phone, she did the illustration of a great mountain with a car parked on top.

- What strange things did she show in her picture? (Call on a student. Ideas: *A mountain with windows; A huge gas gauge inside one of the windows.*)

The mountain had windows all the way around, and inside one of the windows was a great huge gas gauge.

Zelda looked at the picture and said, "That woman has sure been to some strange places."

The next part of the book that was marked said this: "Our car went down the dirt road, leaving a dust cloud behind. Soon, it floated away on the breeze."

Zelda read the part to herself two times. Then she shook her head and made the illustration. It showed a car floating through the air over a dirt road. Zelda said to herself, "That woman sure has some strange vehicles, too."

Zelda worked on the illustrations week after week. And every week Mrs. Hudson would call Zelda and remind her that the book had to be finished soon.

"Remember, Zelda," she would say, "this book must go to the publisher by March. I certainly hope you'll be done with all the illustrations by then."

Every time Mrs. Hudson called to remind Zelda of getting the book ready for the publisher, Zelda would say, "I'm working as fast as I can, but some of these illustrations are not very easy."

Every week, Mrs. Hudson called and said the same thing. Every week, Zelda told her the same thing.

But then, in the middle of February, Mrs. Hudson called and started to say, "Remember, Zelda, this book must go to the publisher before . . . "

"I'm done with the illustrations," Zelda said.

"How perfectly wonderful!" Mrs. Hudson said. "How marvelous! Isn't this just grand?"

She told Zelda that she would be right over and she was. She was still talking about how wonderful everything was when she arrived at Zelda's place. "This is just perfect," she said. I can hardly wait to see your illustrations, my dear."

Then Mrs. Hudson saw Zelda's illustrations. She looked at the first one, and her eyes got wide, and her face became very serious and stiff. Her face stayed that way as she looked at the next illustration, and the next illustration, and the next illustration. She wasn't saying anything like, "How wonderful this is." She wasn't saying **anything.** She was just staring at those illustrations with wide eyes and a very stiff face.

At last, she dropped the illustrations on the floor and said to Zelda, "What have you done to my wonderful book? These illustrations are awful. They are terrible. They are unbelievable. They are . . . " (She had run out of bad words.)

Zelda said, "Well, I did the best I could. I had never seen any of the things your book told about. Like the picture of the students with their tails flying in the wind. I didn't know if they should have monkey tails, lion tails or short little bunny tails."

"Stop it," Mrs. Hudson said. "I do not find your wit one bit funny. And I find your illustrations terrible, awful, unbelievable, and simply . . . " (She'd run out of bad words again.)

"Well," Zelda said, "I'm sorry. I don't have time to redo them now, but I could . . . "

- What did Mrs. Hudson decide to do about the pictures? (Call on a student. Idea: *Send the book to the publisher with Zelda's illustrations.*)

"No, this book must be at the publisher by March. If it's not at the publisher by March, it doesn't get published."

"Well," Zelda said, "Maybe you can send it in without the illustrations."

"No," Mrs. Hudson said, "I promised the publisher that I would have twenty beautiful illustrations. I didn't know that I would have twenty illustrations that were unbelievable, terrible, awful, and just plain . . . "

So Mrs. Hudson picked up the illustrations, picked up her book and marched out of Zelda's place.

Nobody was very happy.

Objectives

- **Use appropriate pronouns in a short passage.** (Exercise 2)
- Indicate the subject of sentences in a paragraph. (Exercise 3)
- Change 2-word verbs in sentences to 1-word verbs. (Exercise 4)
- Write past-time verbs for irregular present-time verbs. (Exercise 5)
- Identify the set of pictures a sentence describes. (Exercise 6)
- Construct sentences that state the main thing that illustrated characters did. (Exercise 7)
- Listen to a familiar story and answer comprehension questions. (Exercise 8)

EXERCISE 1 Feedback On Lesson 78

- (Hand back the students' work from lesson 78.)
- Look at what I wrote on your lined paper. Raise your hand if I wrote **super.**
- If you didn't get a **super,** look at the mistakes you made and be more careful next time.

WORKBOOK

EXERCISE 2 Pronouns

He, She, It

1. Everybody, open your workbook to lesson 79 and find part A. ✔
- Each item tells what the same person or thing did. We don't want to start all the sentences with the same name. So we start the second sentence in each item with **he, she** or **it.**
2. Everybody, touch number 1.
   I'll read the first sentence: Robert spent all morning cleaning his room. Everybody, what part of that sentence names? (Signal.) *Robert.*
- The next sentence also tells about Robert. What other word can we use to refer to **Robert?** (Signal.) *He.*
- So here's the next sentence: He put his dirty clothes in the laundry basket.
3. Touch number 2.
   I'll read the first sentence: My sister went to the park. Everybody, what part of that sentence names? (Signal.) *My sister.*
- The next sentence also tells about my sister. What other word can we use to refer to **my sister?** (Signal.) *She.*

- So here's the next sentence: She played basketball with her friends for two hours.
4. Touch number 3.
   I'll read the first sentence: The boat held four people. Everybody, what part of that sentence names? (Signal.) *The boat.*
- The next sentence also tells about the boat. What other word can we use to refer to **the boat?** (Signal.) *It.*
- So here's the next sentence: It had three sails.
5. Fill in the blanks. Start the second sentence in each item with **he, she** or **it.** Remember to start each sentence with a capital. Raise your hand when you're finished.
   (Observe students and give feedback.)
6. Let's check your work. Make an **X** next to any item you missed.
- I'll read the sentences in item 1: Robert spent all morning cleaning his room. Capital **H, He** put his dirty clothes in the laundry basket.
- Item 2: My sister went to the park. Capital **S, She** played basketball with her friends for two hours.
- Item 3: The boat held four people. Capital **I, It** had three sails.
7. Raise your hand if you got no items wrong. Great job.
- Everybody else, fix up any mistakes you made in part A.
   (Observe students and give feedback.)

EXERCISE 3 Subject/Predicate

1. Everybody, find part B. ✔
   I'll read the instructions: Circle the part of each sentence that names.
2. I'll read the paragraph: A little boy found a small box in his yard. The box had three beans in it. The little boy showed the beans to his sister. She told him to plant the beans. Three plants grew from the beans. Those plants were made of gold.
3. Your turn: Read the sentences and circle the part of each sentence that names. Raise your hand when you're finished. (Observe students and give feedback.)
4. Let's check your work. Make an **X** next to item you missed.

- First sentence: A little boy found a small box in his yard. Say that sentence. (Signal.) *A little boy found a small box in his yard.*
  What part names? (Signal.) *A little boy.*
  What part tells more? (Signal.) *Found a small box in his yard.*
- Next sentence: The box had three beans in it. Say that sentence. (Signal.) *The box had three beans in it.*
  What part names? (Signal.) *The box.*
  What part tells more? (Signal.) *Had three beans in it.*
- Next sentence: The little boy showed the beans to his sister. Say that sentence. (Signal.) *The little boy showed the beans to his sister.*
  What part names? (Signal.) *The little boy.*
  What part tells more? (Signal.) *Showed the beans to his sister.*
- Next sentence: She told him to plant the beans. Say that sentence. (Signal.) *She told him to plant the beans.*
  What part names? (Signal.) *She.*
  What part tells more? (Signal.) *Told him to plant the beans.*
- Next sentence: Three plants grew from the beans. Say that sentence. (Signal.) *Three plants grew from the beans.*
  What part names? (Signal.) *Three plants.*
  What part tells more? (Signal.) *Grew from the beans.*
- Last sentence: Those plants were made of gold. Say that sentence. (Signal.) *Those plants were made of gold.*
  What part names? (Signal.) *Those plants.*
  What part tells more? (Signal.) *Were made of gold.*

5. Raise your hand if you made no mistakes. Great job.
- Everybody else, fix up any mistakes you made in part B.
  (Observe students and give feedback.)

EXERCISE 4 Editing Sentences

Changing the Verb

1. Everybody, find part C. ✔
   I'll read the instructions: Fix up the sentences so they tell what people did.
2. Your turn: Fix up the sentences. Remember, you have to cross out two words. Raise your hand when you're finished. (Observe students and give feedback.)
3. Let's check your work. Make an **X** next to any item you missed.

- Everybody, touch sentence 1.
  They were going to the store.
  Say the sentence that tells what they **did.** (Signal.) *They went to the store.*
- What did you cross out? (Signal.) *Were going.*
- Sentence 2: He is filling the sink with hot water. Say the sentence that tells what he did. (Signal.) *He filled the sink with hot water.*
- What did you cross out? (Signal.) *Is filling.*
- Sentence 3: My grandmother was fixing her car. Say the sentence that tells what my grandmother did. (Signal.) *My grandmother fixed her car.*
- What did you cross out? (Signal.) *Was fixing.*
- Sentence 4: She is having fun.
  Say the sentence that tells what she did. (Signal.) *She had fun.*
- What did you cross out? (Signal.) *Is having.*
- Sentence 5: Jane was buying a new shirt. Say the sentence that tells what Jane did. (Signal.) *Jane bought a new shirt.*
- What did you cross out? (Signal.) *Was buying.*
- Sentence 6: A boy is spelling a hard word. Say the sentence that tells what a boy did. (Signal.) *A boy spelled a hard word.*
- What did you cross out? (Signal.) *Is spelling.*

4. Raise your hand if you got no items wrong. Great job.
- Everybody else, fix up any mistakes you made in part C.
(Observe students and give feedback.)

LINED PAPER • TEXTBOOK

EXERCISE 5   Past Time

Irregular Verbs

1. Everybody, take out a sheet of lined paper and write your name on the top line. Number your paper 1 through 5. Raise your hand when you're finished.
- Everybody, open your textbook to lesson 79 and find part D. ✔
2. The words in part D tell what people do. You're going to write the words that tell what they did. Word 1 is **sit**.
Everybody, what word tells what people did? (Signal.) *Sat.*
- Write **sat** for number 1. Then write the rest of the words for part D. Read each word that tells what people do and write the word that tells what they did. Raise your hand when you're finished.
(Observe students and give feedback.)
3. Let's check your work. Make an **X** if you wrote the wrong word or did not spell the word correctly.
- Word 1: Sit. Say the word that tells what people did. (Signal.) *Sat.*
Spell **sat.** (Signal.) *S-a-t.*
- Word 2: Wear. Say the word that tells what people did. (Signal.) *Wore.*
Spell **wore.** (Signal.) *W-o-r-e.*
- Word 3: Run. Say the word that tells what people did. (Signal.) *Ran.*
Spell **ran.** (Signal.) *R-a-n.*
- Word 4: See. Say the word that tells what people did. (Signal.) *Saw.*
Spell **saw.** (Signal.) *S-a-w.*
- Word 5: Go. Say the word that tells what people did. (Signal.) *Went.*
Spell **went.** (Signal.) *W-e-n-t.*
4. Raise your hand if you made no mistakes. Great job.
- Everybody else, fix up any mistakes you made in part D.
(Observe students and give feedback.)

EXERCISE 6   Clarity

Pictures for Sentences

1. Everybody, skip a line on your paper. Then number your paper 1 through 4. Raise your hand when you're finished.
- Everybody, find part E in your textbook. ✔
2. I'll read the instructions: Read each sentence. Write the letter of each picture that shows what the sentence says. Do it now. Raise your hand when you're finished.
(Observe students and give feedback.)
3. Let's check your work. Make an **X** next to any item you missed.
- Sentence 1: An animal wore clothing. The pictures are A, B, C and D.
- Sentence 2: An animal wore a dress. The pictures are B and D.
- Sentence 3: A dog wore clothing. The pictures are A and B.
- Sentence 4: A cat wore a hat. The picture is C.
4. Raise your hand if you made no mistakes. Great job.
- Everybody else, fix up any mistakes you made in part E.
(Observe students and give feedback.)

EXERCISE 7   Main Idea

1. Skip a line on your paper. Then number your paper 1 through 3. Raise your hand when you're finished. ✔
- Everybody, find part F in your textbook. ✔
I'll read the instructions: Write a sentence for each picture. Each sentence should report on the main thing the picture shows.

2. Everybody, touch picture 1.
   Name that person. (Signal.) *That magician.*
   • Get ready to say a sentence that reports on the main thing the magician did. (Call on several students. Praise sentences such as: *That magician pulled a rabbit out of a hat.* For each good sentence:) Everybody, say that sentence.
3. Everybody, touch picture 2.
   Name those persons. (Signal.) *Hiro and his sister.*
   • Get ready to say a sentence that reports on the main thing Hiro and his sister did. (Call on several students. Praise sentences such as: *Hiro and his sister jumped over a fence.* For each good sentence:) Everybody, say that sentence.
4. Everybody, touch picture 3.
   Name that person. (Signal.) *The new carpenter.*
   • Get ready to say a sentence that reports on the main thing the new carpenter did. (Call on several students. Praise sentences such as: *The new carpenter carried three boards.* For each good sentence:) Everybody, say that sentence.
5. Touch the words in the vocabulary box as I read them: **jumped, carried, pulled, fence, boards, rabbit, over.** Be sure to spell those words correctly if you use them.
6. Next to each number on your lined paper, write a sentence that reports on what the picture shows. Tell the main thing the people did. Be sure each sentence starts with a capital and ends with a period. You have 4 minutes. Raise your hand when you're finished.
   (Observe students and give feedback.)
7. (After 4 minutes, say:) Stop writing. I'll call on students to read their sentences. Listen to the sentences. Make sure they name what the picture shows and tell the main thing.
   • (Call on individual students to read their sentences. After each good sentence, tell the group:) Everybody, say that sentence.
8. Let's check your work. Make 3 check boxes below your last sentence. ✔
9. Everybody, touch the box for check 1. Here's check 1: Does each sentence begin with a capital and end with a period? Read your sentences. Fix up any sentences that don't have a capital and a period. Make a check in box 1 when your sentences check out. Raise your hand when you're finished.
   (Observe students and give feedback.)

10. Now touch the box for check 2. Here's check 2: Does each sentence tell the main thing the persons did? Read over your sentences carefully. Sentences should start out by naming. Then they should tell the main thing the persons did. When all your sentences name and tell the main thing, make a check in box 2. Raise your hand when you're finished.
   (Observe students and give feedback.)
11. Now touch the box for check 3. Here's the check: Did you spell words from the vocabulary box correctly? Look at each sentence. Make sure vocabulary words are spelled correctly. Fix up any mistakes and make a check in box 3. Raise your hand when you're finished.
   (Observe students and give feedback.)
12. Raise your hand if you think you'll get a **super** paper. We'll see next time.

EXERCISE 8 Zelda the Artist *Part 3*

• I'll read another part of the Zelda story. Let's see how well you can remember things that happened.
• What happened at the end of the last part? (Call on a student. Praise reasonable responses.)

Mrs. Hudson sent her book and Zelda's illustrations to the publisher. Mrs. Hudson wrote a note. It said:

Dear Publisher,
   I am not completely pleased with the illustrations for this book, and I apologize for them. But I'm sure you'll find the writing very interesting. The book tells about one enjoyable experience after another.

She signed the note: Sincerely, Mrs. R. R. Hudson.

In the meantime, Zelda was trying to forget about that book. She was working on illustrations for an animal book. She tried to keep her mind on the animals she was drawing, but she couldn't help thinking about Mrs. Hudson's book.

"I worked a long time on that book," she told herself, "and I did the best job I could. I can't help it if I drew the wrong kind of windows on that mountain. And how do I know what kind of gas gauges mountains have? That Mrs. Hudson shouldn't have been so mean to me."

Weeks went by. Zelda heard nothing from Mrs. Hudson. Mrs. Hudson heard nothing from the publisher.

But things were very busy at the publisher.

- How did the publisher feel about the illustrations? (Call on a student. Idea: *The publisher thought the pictures were very funny.*)

The publisher read the book and laughed so hard that her ribs hurt for three days. She read about each of Mrs. Hudson's boring experiences. Then she looked at the picture and almost died from laughter.

She called in other people who worked at the publishing company to read the book, and they all had the same reaction. They all ended up with sore ribs for three days.

- Why did they have sore ribs? (Call on a student. Idea: *They laughed a lot.*)

One of the persons who read the book made a suggestion to the publisher. She said, "What you should do is make each of these illustrations two full pages big. Then underneath you could have the sentences from the book that tell about the illustration."

And that's just what the publisher did.

- In the book when it was published, how large were the pictures? (Call on a student. *Two full pages.*)

When the publishing company was finished with the book and it was ready to be printed, the picture of the children riding their horses was two full pages. Below the picture, it said: "Every day, the children rode their horses through the valley. Their tails flew in the wind."

The picture of the car on the mountain was two full pages. Below the picture is said: "Our car stopped on top of the mountain. It was out of gas."

And all the other pictures were also two pages, with Mrs. Hudson's sentences written below each picture.

Well, after the book was printed, the publisher sent copies to Mrs. Hudson and to Zelda. Mrs. Hudson didn't really like the book as much as she thought she would. She thought that the pictures were far, far too large. She said to herself, "Huh, they made the pictures more important than my wonderful experiences."

Zelda was very happy. She was even happier when she read the note the publisher sent to her.

- What did the note say? (Call on a student. Idea: *You have taken a boring book and made it exciting and funny.*)

The note said:

Dear Zelda,

I find your pictures superb. You have taken a very boring book and made it exciting and wonderfully funny. Thank you so much.

- How well did the book sell? (Call on a student. Idea: *It became the best selling book in the world.*)

And, when the bookstores got their copies of Mrs. Hudson's book, they didn't keep them very long. Within a few weeks, the bookstores sold thousands of copies of the book. Within three months, that book was the fastest-selling bestseller book in the world. Newspaper articles raved about the book. One report said this:

R. R. Hudson may be the greatest wit of the century. When you first read the book, you get the idea that she doesn't know how to write clearly. She makes up sentences that could have more than one meaning. And, as you read about her boring experiences, you begin to wonder: Does this woman have anything to say? But then, you come across an illustration that makes everything clear. The illustrations are so funny that they are hard to describe. The best way to appreciate them is to get the book and look at them. And that's just what **a lot** of people are doing.

After the book became so popular, Mrs. Hudson sort of pretended that she had planned it that way. She told reporters, "Yes, my good friend Zelda and I planned it that way. I selected the parts of the book she was to illustrate, and I might add that I selected them very carefully. Then Zelda did those quaint illustrations."

So Mrs. Hudson became very famous. And very rich.

And the book also made another person very rich and very popular.

- Did Zelda ever figure out why people thought her illustrations were funny? (Call on a student. *No.*)

But Zelda never really understood why people found the book so funny. She told reporters, "I just did the best I could with the sentences Mrs. Hudson gave me."

And the reporters would laugh so hard that their ribs hurt for three days.

Objectives

- Use appropriate pronouns in a short passage. (Exercise 2)
- Change 2-word verbs in sentences to 1-word verbs. (Exercise 3)
- Indicate the subject of sentences in a paragraph. (Exercise 4)
- **Select the appropriate name for a group.** (Exercise 5)
- Construct sentences that state the main thing that illustrated characters did. (Exercise 6)
- **Copy a paragraph.** (Exercise 7)
- Listen to a familiar story and answer comprehension questions. (Exercise 8)

EXERCISE 1   Feedback On Lesson 79

- (Hand back the students' work from lesson 79.)
- Look at what I wrote on your lined paper. Raise your hand if I wrote **super.**
- If you didn't get a **super,** look at the mistakes you made and be more careful next time.

WORKBOOK

EXERCISE 2   Pronouns

He, She, It

1. Everybody, open your workbook to lesson 80 and find part A. ✔
- Each item tells what the same person or thing did. We don't want to start all the sentences with the same name. So we start the second sentence in each item with **he, she** or **it.**
2. Complete all the sentences in part A. Remember to start each sentence with a capital. Raise your hand when you're finished.
(Observe students and give feedback.)
3. Let's check your work. Make an **X** next to any item you missed.
- I'll read the sentences in item 1: His mother liked to fix cars. Capital **S, She** worked in a car shop.
- Item 2: My father stayed home this morning. Capital **H, He** read a book.
- Item 3: The bus stopped. Capital **I, It** ran out of gas.
4. Raise your hand if you got no items wrong. Great job.

- Everybody else, fix up any mistakes you made in part A.
(Observe students and give feedback.)

EXERCISE 3   Editing Sentences

Changing the Verb

1. Everybody, find part B. ✔
I'll read the instructions: Fix up the sentences so they tell what people did. Some sentences tell what people did. Some sentences do **not** tell what people did.
2. I'll read the first sentence: Maria wanted a birthday party. That sentence tells what Maria did. So we don't change anything.
- I'll read sentence 2: She asked some boys and girls to the party. Everybody, does that sentence tell what she did? (Signal.) *Yes.* So we don't change it.
3. Sentence 3: The boys and girls were giving her some presents. That sentence tells what the boys and girls **were doing.** It should tell what the boys and girls **did.**
- Say the sentence so that it tells what the boys and girls did. (Signal.) *The boys and girls gave her some presents.*
- Cross out **were giving** and write **gave** above the crossed-out words.
(Observe students and give feedback.)
4. Read the rest of the sentences. Fix up any sentence that doesn't tell what somebody did. If a sentence already tells what somebody did, don't change it. Raise your hand when you're finished.
(Observe students and give feedback.)

5. Let's check your work. Make an **X** next to any item you missed.

- Touch sentence 4. ✔
Everybody was having fun. Does that sentence tell what everybody did? (Signal.) *No.*

- Say the sentence that tells what everybody did. (Signal.) *Everybody had fun.*

- Sentence 5: The children were playing games outside. Does that sentence tell what the children did? (Signal.) *No.*

- Say the sentence that tells what the children did. (Signal.) *The children played games outside.*

- Sentence 6: They ate cake and ice cream. Does that sentence tell what they did? (Signal.) *Yes.*

- So you shouldn't have changed anything.

6. Raise your hand if you got no items wrong. Great job.

- Everybody else, fix up any mistakes you made in part B.
(Observe students and give feedback.)

EXERCISE 4   Subject/Predicate

1. Everybody, find part C. ✔
I'll read the instructions: Circle the part of each sentence that names.

2. I'll read the paragraph: Alex taught his pet monkey to do many tricks. The monkey even learned how to ride a bicycle. Alex dressed his monkey in a costume one day. Alex and his monkey went to the circus. They showed a clown their tricks. The clown gave the monkey a job in the circus.

3. Your turn: Read the sentences and circle the part of each sentence that names. Raise your hand when you're finished.
(Observe students and give feedback.)

4. Let's check your work. Make an **X** next to any item you missed.

- First sentence: Alex taught his pet monkey to do many tricks. Say that sentence. (Signal.) *Alex taught his pet monkey to do many tricks.*
What part names? (Signal.) *Alex.*
What part tells more? (Signal.)
Taught his pet monkey to do many tricks.

- Next sentence: The monkey even learned how to ride a bicycle. Say that sentence. (Signal.) *The monkey even learned how to ride a bicycle.*

What part names? (Signal.) *The monkey.*
What part tells more? (Signal.)
Even learned how to ride a bicycle.

- Next sentence: Alex dressed his monkey in a costume one day. Say that sentence. (Signal.) *Alex dressed his monkey in a costume one day.*
What part names? (Signal.) *Alex.*
What part tells more? (Signal.) *Dressed his monkey in a costume one day.*

- Next sentence: Alex and his monkey went to the circus. Say that sentence. (Signal.) *Alex and his monkey went to the circus.*
What part names? (Signal.) *Alex and his monkey.*
What part tells more? (Signal.) *Went to the circus.*

- Next sentence: They showed a clown their tricks. Say that sentence. (Signal.) *They showed a clown their tricks.*
What part names? (Signal.) *They.*
What part tells more? (Signal.) *Showed a clown their tricks.*

- Next sentence: The clown gave the monkey a job in the circus. Say that sentence. (Signal.) *The clown gave the monkey a job in the circus.*
What part names? (Signal.) *The clown.*
What part tells more? (Signal.) *Gave the monkey a job in the circus.*

5. Raise your hand if you made no mistakes. Great job.

- Everybody else, fix up any mistakes you made in part C.
(Observe students and give feedback.)

LINED PAPER • TEXTBOOK

EXERCISE 5   Naming Groups

1. Everybody, take out a sheet of lined paper and write your name on the top line. Number your paper 1 through 5. Raise your hand when you're finished.

- Everybody, pencils down. Open your textbook to lesson 80 and find part D. ✔

2. In later lessons, you'll make up sentences that report on groups. The pictures in part D show some groups that you'll write about. The names of the groups are in the vocabulary box. Touch each name as I read it: **vehicles, children, firefighters, men, horses.**

3. Everybody, touch picture 1.
My turn to name group 1: Men.
4. Touch group 2.
Your turn: Name group 2. (Signal.) *Children.*
- Touch group 3.
Everybody, name group 3. (Signal.)
Vehicles.
- Touch group 4.
Name group 4. (Signal.) *Firefighters.*
- Touch group 5.
Name group 5. (Signal.) *Horses.*
- (Repeat step 4 until firm.)
5. Next to each number on your paper, write the name of the right group. Raise your hand when you're finished.
(Observe students and give feedback.)
6. Let's check your work. Make an **X** next to any item you missed.
- Everybody, name group 1. (Signal.) *Men.*
- Name group 2. (Signal.) *Children.*
- Name group 3. (Signal.) *Vehicles.*
- Name group 4. (Signal.) *Firefighters.*
- Name group 5. (Signal.) *Horses.*
7. Raise your hand if you made no mistakes. Great job.
- Everybody else, fix up any mistakes you made in part D.
(Observe students and give feedback.)

EXERCISE 6 Main Idea

1. A dog and a clown   2. The airplane

1. Skip a line on your paper. Then number your paper 1 and 2. Raise your hand when you're finished. ✔
- Everybody, find part E in your textbook. ✔
I'll read the instructions: Write a sentence for each picture. Each sentence should report on the main thing the picture shows.
2. Everybody, touch picture 1.
Who does that picture show? (Signal.) *A dog and a clown.*

- Get ready to say a sentence that reports on the main thing a dog and a clown did. (Call on several students. Praise sentences such as: *A clown and a dog walked across the tightrope.* For each good sentence:) Everybody, say that sentence.
3. Everybody, touch picture 2.
Name that object. (Signal.) *The airplane.*
- Get ready to say a sentence that reports on the main thing the airplane did. (Call on several students. Praise sentences such as: *The airplane flew under the bridge.* For each good sentence:) Everybody, say that sentence.
4. Touch the words in the vocabulary box as I read them: **flew, walked, tightrope, bridge, across, under.** Be sure to spell those words correctly if you use them.
5. Next to each number on your paper, write a sentence that reports on what the picture shows. Tell the main thing the person or thing did. You have 3 minutes. Raise your hand when you're finished.
(Observe students and give feedback.)
6. (After 3 minutes, say:) Stop writing. I'll call on students to read their sentences. Listen to the sentences. Make sure they name what the picture shows and tell the main thing.
- (Call on individual students to read their sentences. After each good sentence, tell the group:) Everybody, say that sentence.
7. Let's check your work. Make 3 check boxes below your last sentence. ✔
8. Here's check 1: Does each sentence begin with a capital and end with a period? Read your sentences. Fix up any sentences that don't have a capital and a period. Make a check in box 1 when your sentences check out. Raise your hand when you're finished.
(Observe students and give feedback.)
9. Here's check 2: Does each sentence tell the main thing the person or thing did? Read over your sentences carefully and fix up any mistakes. When all your sentences names and tell the main thing, put a check in box 2. Raise your hand when you're finished.
(Observe students and give feedback.)

10. Here's check 3: Did you spell words from the vocabulary box correctly? Look at each sentence. Make sure vocabulary words are spelled correctly. Fix up any mistakes and make a check in box 3. Raise your hand when you're finished.
(Observe students and give feedback.)

EXERCISE 7   Paragraph Copying

1. Everybody, pencils down. Find part F in your textbook. ✔

- You're going to copy a paragraph. A paragraph is a group of sentences that tell about the same topic. The paragraph you're going to copy tells what happened to a bird that fell out of a tree.

2. Listen: When you write a paragraph, you do not start at the margin. You must indent the first line. You indent by writing the first word two fingers from the margin. The picture shows you where to put your fingers.

- Touch the first word in the paragraph. ✔ Everybody, is the first word of the paragraph written next to the margin? (Signal.) *No.*

- The first word of a paragraph does not start at the margin. It is indented. It starts two fingers from the margin.

- Look at the second line in the paragraph. It starts right after the margin. (Call on a student:) Where do the rest of the lines start? (Idea: *Right after the margin.*)

- You only indent the first line. The other lines start right after the margin.

3. You're going to copy the first word of the paragraph. Put two fingers next to the margin on your paper, just like the two fingers in the picture. Don't draw your fingers. Just make a capital **A** right after your fingers.
(Observe students and give feedback.)

4. You wrote the first word of the paragraph. Now copy the rest of the first sentence. Then stop. Be sure to end the sentence with a period. Raise your hand when you're finished.
(Observe students and give feedback.)

5. Touch the period at the end of the first sentence you wrote.

- That's where you'll start writing the next sentence. Make a capital **I** just after the period. Then copy the rest of the paragraph. Remember to start each new sentence just after the period. And don't indent any more lines. Start them at the margin. You have 3 minutes. Raise your hand when you're finished.
(Observe students and give feedback.)

6. (After 3 minutes, say:) Everybody, stop. Raise your hand if you're finished. (Praise students who finished.)

- Let's check your work. Make 3 check boxes under your paragraph. ✔

7. Here's check 1: Does each sentence begin with a capital and end with a period? Read each sentence for check 1. Fix it up if it's not right. Then make a check in box 1. Raise your hand when you're finished.
(Observe students and give feedback.)

8. Here's check 2: Did you indent the first line? If you indented, make a check in box 2. If you didn't indent, fix up the first line. Then make a check in box 2. Raise your hand when you're finished.
(Observe students and give feedback.)

9. Here's check 3: Did you start all the other lines at the margin? Check each line after the first line and see if it starts at the margin. Make a check in box 3 when your paragraph is fixed up. Raise your hand when you're finished.
(Observe students and give feedback.)

10. Who thinks they'll get a **super** paper? We'll see next time.

EXERCISE 8   The Case Of The Missing Corn

Storytelling

- I'll read the story titled, "The Case of the Missing Corn." Let's see how well you can remember things that happened.

The gray rat worked at deductions until he could figure out an answer faster than any other rat in the pack. If somebody said, "Where's Martha the moth?" he'd say, "In the afternoon, all the moths are sleeping in the shed. Martha is a moth. So, in the afternoon, Martha is sleeping in the shed."

The gray rat was so good at deductions that he said, "Now I'm ready to be a detective. And I'll solve crimes."

- What did this gray rat use instead of a bloodhound? (Call on a student. *A beetle.*)

The gray rat looked through some books to learn more about detectives. He learned that some of them have hound dogs called bloodhounds that can follow the scent of people.

It didn't make much sense for a rat to have a great big bloodhound on a leash, but the gray rat knew a shy little beetle with a very good nose. Her name was Bertha. He went to Bertha and talked her into being his **blood**beetle.

Bertha didn't like wearing a leash very much, but the gray rat told her that, if she wanted to be a detective's bloodbeetle, she'd have to wear the leash.

- What was the last thing the rat needed to be a detective? (Call on a student. *A large magnifying glass.*)

Next, the gray rat got a large magnifying glass. The detectives in the books had large magnifying glasses, so the gray rat got one, too.

The rat's magnifying glass was so large that he could hardly lift it. So he didn't use it very much.

The only thing the rat needed to become a complete detective was a name.

- What did the rat name himself? (Call on a student. *Sherlock.*)

He thought and thought. One of the detectives in the books was named Sherlock. So the gray rat decided to name himself Sherlock.

So now he was ready to figure out the answers to puzzles. He knew how to work deductions; he had a bloodbeetle and a magnifying glass. And with the name of "Sherlock," everybody would know that he was a detective.

Just about the time that he was ready to start being a detective, a great problem came up in the rat pack.

- What was that problem? (Call on a student. Idea: *Corn from a special pile was missing.*)

There was a very special pile of corn in the corner of Goober's barn. This corn was in a place where none of the horses or cows could get it. The corn was special because all the rats agreed that the corn could be eaten as dessert.

- How much corn did each rat eat for dessert? (Call on a student. *Two kernels of corn.*)

Every day after dinner, each rat would go to the barn and have two kernels of corn—only two.

But lots of corn was missing from the pile, and the rats were getting mad at each other. The little black rat said to the rat with yellow teeth, "You ate that corn."

"I did not," the yellow-toothed rat said. "You ate it."

Some of the rats even said that the wise old rat was eating it.

This was the greatest argument that ever took place in the rat pack. Everybody was angry because, when that pile of corn was gone, nobody would have any dessert until next year. Boo-hoo.

Well, the gray rat said to himself, "This is a perfect spot for a detective." He put his bloodbeetle on her leash, stood up very straight and walked out to where the other rats were arguing. He decided to leave his magnifying glass at home.

"Calm down," he said loudly. "Listen to me. I have an announcement to make."

- Before the gray rat continued, what did five other rats say to him? (Call on a student. *You stole the corn.*)

Before the gray rat could continue, five rats pointed to him and said, "You stole that corn."

"No, no, I didn't steal any . . ."

Poor Sherlock wasn't able to finish what he was trying to say. "You're the corn stealer," the rats shouted. Nine or ten rats picked him up, carried him to the pond and threw him in. Splash.

- What did Sherlock's bloodbeetle do? (Call on a student. *Ran home.*)

Sherlock's bloodbeetle saw what happened to Sherlock and ran home the fast way.

While Bertha was running home, the rats were pointing their little paws at Sherlock and saying, "Don't you ever steal our dessert again."

Sherlock sputtered and said, "But I didn't steal any corn. You don't understand. I'm a detective, and I can help you find the thief."

"You can help us? How can you help us?"

As Sherlock waded out of the pond, he said, "I can use my skill at making deductions, and I can track anybody with my bloodbeetle."

- What would the rats do when they couldn't see the bloodbeetle? (Call on a student. Idea: *Say that Sherlock is lying.*)

"What bloodbeetle?"

Sherlock looked around, but there was no bloodbeetle in sight.

"You're just lying," the other rats said, and they started to throw Sherlock back into the pond. But just then the wise old rat said, "Stop. Listen to what he has to say. Maybe he can solve this mystery."

The other rats let go of Sherlock. He looked around and then said, "I do have a bloodbeetle, and, if you give me a chance, I'll solve this mystery for you.

But if I find the corn thief, you'll have to give me something for helping you.

- What did Sherlock think they should give him? (Call on a student. *Three times as much corn as another rat.*)

I think that I should get three times as much dessert as any other rat."

The rats argued about this offer for a while, and then they told Sherlock that, if he solved the mystery, he could get **two** times as much dessert as anybody else. And one rat said, "But if you don't solve this mystery pretty quick, nobody's going to have **any** dessert. That corn is disappearing fast."

Sherlock stood up straight again, and, with water dripping off the end of his nose, he said, "I will start solving this crime immediately."

Note:
- Collect the students' workbooks and papers.
- Check the students' work before the next language period. Mark any mistakes.
- Write **super** on work that has all mistakes corrected. Write **good** or **pretty good** on work that has only 1 or 2 mistakes.

Objectives

- Change 2-word verbs in a sentence to 1-word verbs. (Exercise 2)
- Indicate the subject of sentences in a paragraph. (Exercise 3)
- Use appropriate pronouns in a short passage. (Exercise 4)
- Copy a paragraph. (Exercise 5)
- Select the appropriate name for a group. (Exercise 6)
- Construct sentences that state the main thing that illustrated characters did. (Exercise 7)
- Listen to a familiar story and answer comprehension questions. (Exercise 8)

EXERCISE 1 Feedback On Lesson 80

- (Hand back the students' work from lesson 80.)
- Look at what I wrote on your lined paper. Raise your hand if I wrote **super.**
- If you didn't get a **super,** look at the mistakes you made and be more careful next time.

WORKBOOK

EXERCISE 2 Editing Sentences

Changing the Verb

1. Everybody, open your workbook to lesson 81 and find part A. ✔
- I'll read the instructions: Fix up the sentences so they tell what people did.
2. Read the sentences. Fix up any sentence that doesn't tell what somebody did. If a sentence already tells what somebody did, don't change it. Do the sentences now. Raise your hand when you're finished. (Observe students and give feedback.)
3. Let's check your work. Make an **X** next to any item you missed.
- Sentence 1: They were having fun at the party. Does that sentence tell what they did? (Signal.) *No.*
- Say the sentence that tells what they did. (Signal.) *They had fun at the party.*
- Sentence 2: Jessica is wearing a new dress. Does that sentence tell what Jessica did? (Signal.) *No.*
- Say the sentence that tells what Jessica did. (Signal.) *Jessica wore a new dress.*

- Sentence 3: My brother painted his room. Does that sentence tell what my brother did? (Signal.) *Yes.*
So you didn't cross out anything.
- Sentence 4: Tom and Alberto are going home. Does that sentence tell what Tom and Alberto did? (Signal.) *No.*
- Say the sentence that tells what Tom and Alberto did. (Signal.) *Tom and Alberto went home.*
- Sentence 5: She parked the car. Does that sentence tell what she did? (Signal.) *Yes.*
So you didn't cross out anything.
- Sentence 6: They were starting to run. Does that sentence tell what they did? (Signal.) *No.*
Say the sentence that tells what they did. (Signal.) *They started to run.*
4. Raise your hand if you got no items wrong. Great job.
- Everybody else, fix up any mistakes you made in part A.
(Observe students and give feedback.)

EXERCISE 3 Subject/Predicate

1. Everybody, find part B. ✔
I'll read the instructions: Circle the part of each sentence that names.
2. I'll read the paragraph: Wendy found a dirty old bicycle at the dump. She showed it to her brother. He told his sister that the bicycle was in very poor shape. Wendy worked on the bike every day for a month. It looked like a brand new bike when she was done. She gave it to her brother for his birthday. Wendy and her brother were very happy.

3. Your turn: Read the sentences and circle the part of each sentence that names. Raise your hand when you're finished. (Observe students and give feedback.)

4. Let's check your work. Make an **X** next to any item you missed.

• First sentence: Wendy found a dirty old bicycle at the dump. Say that sentence. (Signal.) *Wendy found a dirty old bicycle at the dump.*
What part names? (Signal.) *Wendy.*
What part tells more? (Signal.) *Found a dirty old bicycle at the dump.*

• Next sentence: She showed it to her brother. Say that sentence. (Signal.) *She showed it to her brother.*
What part names? (Signal.) *She.*
What part tells more? (Signal.) *Showed it to her brother.*

• Next sentence: He told his sister that the bicycle was in very poor shape. Say that sentence. (Signal.) *He told his sister that the bicycle was in very poor shape.*
What part names? (Signal.) *He.*
What part tells more? (Signal.) *Told his sister that the bicycle was in very poor shape.*

• Next sentence: Wendy worked on the bike every day for a month. Say that sentence. (Signal.) *Wendy worked on the bike every day for a month.*
What part names? (Signal.) *Wendy.*
What part tells more? (Signal.) *Worked on the bike every day for a month.*

• Next sentence: It looked like a brand new bike when she was done. Say that sentence. (Signal.) *It looked like a brand new bike when she was done.*
What part names? (Signal.) *It.*
What part tells more? (Signal.) *Looked like a brand new bike when she was done.*

• Next sentence: She gave it to her brother for his birthday. Say that sentence. (Signal.) *She gave it to her brother for his birthday.*
What part names? (Signal.) *She.*
What part tells more? (Signal.) *Gave it to her brother for his birthday.*

• Next sentence: Wendy and her brother were very happy. Say that sentence. (Signal.) *Wendy and her brother were very happy.*

What part names? (Signal.) *Wendy and her brother.*
What part tells more? (Signal.) *Were very happy.*

5. Raise your hand if you made no mistakes. Great job.

• Everybody else, fix up any mistakes you made in part B. (Observe students and give feedback.)

EXERCISE 4 Pronouns

He, She, It

1. Everybody, find part C. ✔
Each item tells what the same person or thing did. Start the second sentence in each item with **he, she** or **it**. Remember to start each sentence with a capital. Raise your hand when you're finished. (Observe students and give feedback.)

2. Let's check your work. Make an **X** next to any item you missed.

• I'll read the sentences in item 1: Jill went ice-skating. Capital **S, She** skated with her friends on the pond.

• Item 2: Her dad slept on the couch. Capital **H, He** snored loudly.

• Item 3: The motorcycle went by us quickly. Capital **I, It** made a lot of noise.

• Item 4: My kite was new. Capital **I, It** landed in a tree.

3. Raise your hand if you got no items wrong. Great job.

• Everybody else, fix up any mistakes you made in part C. (Observe students and give feedback.)

LINED PAPER • TEXTBOOK

EXERCISE 5 Paragraph Copying

1. Everybody, take out a sheet of lined paper and write your name on the top line. Raise your hand when you're finished.

• Everybody, pencils down. Open your textbook to lesson 81 and find part D. ✔

• You copied a paragraph in the last lesson. The rule box tells about paragraphs and how you write them. Touch the rule box in part D. ✔

2. I'll read the rule: A paragraph is a group of sentences that tell about the same topic.

You indent the first line of a paragraph. You start all the other lines right after the margin.

3. Everybody, touch the margin of the paragraph in part D. ✔
   Remember, you must indent the first line. You indent by writing the first word of that line two fingers from the margin. The picture shows you where to put your fingers.

4. Everybody, touch the first word in the paragraph. ✔
   • Is the first word of the paragraph written next to the margin? (Signal.) *No.*
   • The first word is indented. Look at the other lines in the paragraph. They start right after the margin.

5. You're going to copy the first word of the paragraph. Put two fingers next to the margin on your paper, just like the two fingers in the picture. Don't draw your fingers. Just make a capital **E** right after your fingers. Then complete the word **Ellen.** Raise your hand when you're finished with the word **Ellen.**
   (Observe students and give feedback.)

6. Now copy the rest of the first sentence. Then stop. Be sure to end the sentence with a period. Raise your hand when you're finished.
   (Observe students and give feedback.)

7. Touch the period at the end of the first sentence you wrote.
   • That's where you'll start writing the next sentence. Make a capital **S** just after the period. Then copy the rest of the paragraph. Remember to start each new sentence just after the period. And don't indent any more lines. Start them at the margin. You have 3 minutes. Raise your hand when you're finished.
   (Observe students and give feedback.)

8. (After 3 minutes, say:) Everybody, stop. Raise your hand if you're finished. If you didn't finish, you can finish later.
   (Praise students who finished.)
   • Let's check your work. Make 3 check boxes under your paragraph.

9. Here's check 1: Does each sentence begin with a capital and end with a period? Read each sentence for check 1. Fix it up if it's

not right. Then make a check in box 1. Raise your hand when you're finished.
(Observe students and give feedback.)

10. Here's check 2: Did you indent the first line? If you indented, make a check in box 2. If you didn't indent, fix up the first line. Then make a check in box 2. Raise your hand when you're finished.
    (Observe students and give feedback.)

11. Here's check 3: Did you start all the other lines at the margin? Check each line after the first line and see if it starts at the margin. Make a check in box 3 when your paragraph is fixed up. Raise your hand when you're finished.
    (Observe students and give feedback.)

EXERCISE 6   Naming Groups

1. Skip a line on your paper. Then number your paper 1 through 6.
   • Everybody, find part E in your textbook. ✔

2. In later lessons, you'll make up sentences that report on groups. The pictures in part E show some groups that you'll write about. The names of the groups are in the vocabulary box. Touch each name as I read it: **boys, girls, cars, women, police officers, dogs.**

3. Everybody, touch picture 1.
   Name group 1. (Signal.) *Cars.*

4. Next to each number on your paper, write the name of each group. Raise your hand when you're finished.
   (Observe students and give feedback.)

5. Let's check your work. Make an **X** next to any item you missed.
   • Everybody, name group 1. (Signal.) *Cars.*
   • Name group 2. (Signal.) *Boys.*
   • Name group 3. (Signal.) *Police officers.*
   • Name group 4. (Signal.) *Dogs.*
   • Name group 5. (Signal.) *Women.*
   • Name group 6. (Signal.) *Girls.*

6. Raise your hand if you made no mistakes. Great job.
   • Everybody else, fix up any mistakes you made in part E.
   (Observe students and give feedback.)

EXERCISE 7 Main Idea

1. Skip a line on your paper. Then number your paper 1 and 2. Raise your hand when you're finished.

- Everybody, find part F in your textbook. ✔ I'll read the instructions: Write a sentence for each picture. Each sentence should report on the main thing the picture shows.

2. Touch the words in the vocabulary box as I read them: **teeth, brushed, kicked, toothbrush, football.** Be sure to spell those words correctly if you use them.

3. Next to each number on your paper, write a sentence that reports on what the picture shows. Tell the main thing the person did. You have 3 minutes. Raise your hand when you're finished.
   (Observe students and give feedback.)

4. (After 3 minutes, say:) Stop writing. I'll call on students to read their sentences. Listen to each sentence. Make sure it names the right person and tells the main thing that person did.

- (Call on individual students to read their sentences. After each good sentence, tell the group:) Everybody, say that sentence.

5. Let's check your work. Make 3 check boxes below your last sentence. ✔

6. Here's check 1: Does each sentence begin with a capital and end with a period? Fix up any sentences that don't have a capital and a period. Make a check in box 1 when your sentences check out. Raise your hand when you're finished.
   (Observe students and give feedback.)

7. Here's check 2: Does each sentence tell the main thing the person did? Read over your sentences carefully and fix up any mistakes. When all your sentences name and tell the main thing the person did, make a check in box 2. Raise your hand when you're finished.
   (Observe students and give feedback.)

8. Here's check 3: Did you spell words from the vocabulary box correctly? Look at each sentence. Make sure vocabulary words are spelled correctly. Fix up any mistakes and make a check in box 3. Raise your hand when you're finished.
   (Observe students and give feedback.)

9. Raise your hand if you think you'll get a **super** paper. We'll see next time.

EXERCISE 8 The Case of the Missing Corn *Part 2*

Storytelling

- I'll read another part of the **The Case of the Missing Corn** story. Let's see how well you can remember things that happened.

- What was Sherlock planning to do at the end of the last part? (Call on a student. Idea: *Solve the mystery of the missing corn.*)

Sherlock was ready to solve the mystery of the missing corn in Goober's barn. But first, he had to talk his bloodbeetle into working for him again. He went to Bertha's home—which was a big hole in the ground.

- What did Bertha think the rats would do to her? (Call on a student. Idea: *Throw her in the pond.*)

He called to her, but she didn't want to come out. She kept saying, "I don't like this job. I saw what they did to you." She was talking about the other rats throwing Sherlock into the pond.

"That was a mistake," the gray rat said. "Everything is straightened out now. All the rats agreed to let me solve the mystery."

The beetle peeked out of her hole and said, "But I'm not sure I want to work for a gray rat, anyhow. And I don't like being on a leash."

"Please don't call me a gray rat," the gray rat said. "Call me Sherlock. I guess you don't have to wear a leash if you promise not to run home again."

Sherlock talked and talked. At last he agreed to give Bertha part of all the extra corn he'd get if he solved the mystery.

Now Sherlock and the bloodbeetle were ready to go to work.

- Where did they go? (Call on a student. *Goober's barn*.)

They went to Goober's barn. On the way, Sherlock explained the plan.

- What was his plan? (Call on a student. Idea: *Find someone who smells of oats*.)

"I have everything figured out," he said. "The corn thief went into the barn. So all we have to do is to find somebody who goes into the barn and we'll know who the corn thief is."

Bertha gave Sherlock a funny look. She said, "That doesn't sound right to me, but you're the detective."

"It's very hard for a beetle to understand," Sherlock said. "But you have to know how to make deductions. I'll try to explain how it works as we solve this crime. But, for my plan to work, we have to find out who went into the barn."

"That's easy," Bertha said. "Anyone who goes into the barn smells of oats. With one sniff I could tell if somebody went into that barn. Oat smell is very strong."

"Good," Sherlock said. "We'll find somebody who smells of oats, and we'll know who went into the barn."

Just as they were approaching the barn, Sherlock spotted a red chicken. "Look over there," he said to Bertha. "Go over and take a sniff of that chicken. See if she's been in the barn."

So Bertha scurried over near the chicken and then scurried back.

Sherlock asked, "Well? Has she been in the barn?"

Bertha said, "Yep."

Sherlock said, "There, you see? We've solved the mystery already. That chicken took the corn."

"How do you know that?" Bertha said.

"Listen carefully to this deduction: Anybody who goes into the barn smells of oats. The red chicken went into the barn. So the red chicken smells of oats."

"I know that," Bertha said. "I didn't need a deduction to figure that out. I could smell her a mile away."

"Don't interrupt," Sherlock said, "because that's only the **first** deduction. Here's the **next** deduction: The corn thief went into the barn. The red chicken went into the barn. So the red chicken is the corn thief.

- Is that deduction right? (Call on a student. *No*.)
- What's wrong with Sherlock's reasoning? (Call on a student. *Not everybody who goes in the barn is the corn thief*.)

Bertha didn't agree with that deduction. She couldn't shake her head the way you and I would do. So she rocked her little body from side to side as she said, "No, no, no. That still doesn't sound right to me."

Sherlock said, "You may not understand how I figured it out. But you can't question the deduction. I solved the crime, and now I'll be getting double corn. Good for me. I'm so smart."

- What did Bertha do when she tried to say, "No, no, no?" (Call on a student. Idea: *Rocked her body from side to side*.)

The beetle looked at him and rocked her body from side to side again.

Sherlock said, "Let's go back and tell the others." And they went back to the pack.

Then Sherlock jumped up on an old oak stump and said, "I have an announcement to make. Everybody, listen." The other rats gathered around.

Sherlock stood up very tall and pushed out his little chest as far as it would go. Then, in a very important-sounding voice, he said, "I have solved the mystery. I know who has been taking corn from the barn."

"Who? Who? Who?" all the rats shouted.

"Calm down, please," Sherlock said. When all the rats were very, very quiet, he said, "The red chicken on Goober's farm is the one who took the corn."

"How do you know that?" the wise old rat said.

"Simple," Sherlock said. Then he repeated his deductions. First the one about anybody who goes into the barn smells of oats.

- What's that deduction? (Call on a student. *Anybody who goes into the barn smells of oats. The red chicken went into the barn. So the real chicken smells of oats.*)

When Sherlock finished, some of the rats scratched their head. Some of them nodded yes-yes. Some of them shook their head no-no. Bertha just rocked from side to side.

At last a brown rat said, "I don't know. I've never heard so much talk to figure something out. Maybe he's right." Bertha rocked back and forth faster and harder.

The wise old rat smiled and said to Bertha, "You don't agree with the gray rat's deductions. Tell me why you don't agree."

"Well," Bertha said slowly, "I don't know much about deductions, but . . ."

She was getting embarrassed. She'd never talked before a large group of rats before.

"Go on," the wise old rat said.

She looked down and said, "Well, the gray rat—I mean Sherlock—said that the red chicken did it because she smelled of oats, which means she'd been in the barn. There's just one small problem."

- What was the problem? (Call on a student. Idea: *Every rat smells of oats*.)

"What's that? What's that?"

"Every single one of you rats smells of oats."

All the rats looked at each other. One of them said, "What does that mean? Does that mean we all stole the corn?"

Then the rats started pointing at each other and saying, "You're the one. You smell of oats. So you must have taken that corn."

"Not me. You smell of oats, too, you know. You're the one."

Fights started breaking out.

"Stop," the wise old rat said. He jumped up on the stump. "I don't know what's wrong with all of you. You must know that you've been in the barn. You've gone in there every evening after dinner. So of course you smell of oats."

"Yeah," one rat said. "We go in there every evening after dinner. Of course we smell of oats."

Then there was a long silence. At last the little black rat said, "If we all smell of oats and we've all been in the barn, how does that gray rat know that the red chicken is the one who took the corn? All he knows is that she went into the barn."

"Yeah, what does he know? All he does is talk a lot, come up with silly deductions and get all of us confused."

- What did the rats do next? (Call on a student. *Tossed Sherlock into the pond again*.)

> With that, nine or ten rats picked up the gray rat—I mean Sherlock—and tossed him into the pond again. By the time they reached the pond, the bloodbeetle was already home, and that's where she wanted to stay for a long time.

Objectives

- Use appropriate pronouns in a short passage. (Exercise 2)
- **Punctuate sentences (capitals and periods) and identify the subject of the sentences in a paragraph.** (Exercise 3)
- **Select sentences that state the main thing that illustrated groups did.** (Exercise 4)
- Copy a paragraph. (Exercise 5)
- Identify the set of pictures a sentence describes. (Exercise 6)
- Construct sentences that state the main thing that illustrated characters did. (Exercise 7)
- Listen to a familiar story and answer comprehension questions. (Exercise 8)

EXERCISE 1   Feedback On Lesson 81

- (Hand back the students' work from lesson 81.)
- Look at what I wrote on your lined paper. Raise your hand if I wrote **super.**
- If you didn't get a **super,** look at the mistakes you made and be more careful next time.

WORKBOOK

EXERCISE 2   Pronouns

He, She, It

1. Everybody, open our workbook to lesson 82 and find part A. ✔
- Each item tells what the same person or thing did.
  Start the second sentence in each item with **he, she** or **it.** Remember to start each sentence with a capital. Raise your hand when you're finished.
  (Observe students and give feedback.)
2. Let's check your work. Make an **X** next to any item you missed.
- I'll read the sentences in item 1: Jeff spent two hours doing his homework. Capital **H, He** worked hard.
- Item 2: Jane went to the park. Capital **S, She** sat and watched the ducks.
- Item 3: The cake tasted great. Capital **I, It** had whipped cream on top.
3. Raise your hand if you got no items wrong. Great job.

- Everybody else, fix up any mistakes you made in part A.
  (Observe students and give feedback.)

EXERCISE 3   Paragraph Editing

Capitals and Periods

1. Everybody, find part B. ✔
   Somebody forgot to put capitals and periods in the sentences.
2. Look at the first words in the paragraph and figure out what the first sentence names.
- Everybody, what does it name? (Signal.) *A red kite.*
  Circle **a red kite.** ✔
- The first sentence tells more about a red kite. (Call on a student:) Say the rest of the sentence that starts with **a red kite.** *Floated into the sky.*
- Everybody, put a period after the word **sky.** Start the next sentence with a capital **T.** ✔
3. Look at the first words in the second sentence and figure out what that sentence names.
- Everybody, what does it name? (Signal.) *The wind.*
  Circle the wind. ✔
- Everybody, say the words that tell more about the wind. (Signal.) *Blew the kite.*
- Put a period after the word **kite.** Start the next sentence with a capital **T.** ✔
4. Fix up the rest of this paragraph. Make sure each sentence begins with a capital and ends with a period. Circle the part of each sentence that names. Raise your hand when you're finished.
   (Observe students and give feedback.)

5. Let's check your work. Make an **X** over anything you missed.
- First sentence: You should have circled **a red kite.** A red kite floated into the sky, period.
- Next sentence: You should have circled **the wind.** Capital **T,** The wind blew the kite, period.
- Next sentence: You should have circled **three brown ducks.** Capital **T,** Three brown ducks flew near the kite, period.
- Next sentence: You should have circled **the kite.** Capital **T,** The kite went behind some clouds, period.
- Next sentence: You should have circled **it.** Capital **I,** It went so high that nobody could see it, period.
6. Raise your hand if you made no mistakes. Great job.
- Everybody else, fix up any mistakes you made in part B.
(Observe students and give feedback.)

EXERCISE 4   Main Idea

Groups

1. Everybody, pencils down. Find part C. ✔ These pictures show groups. You're going to circle the sentence that tells **the main thing** each group did. The sentence must do two things. First, it names the right group. Then it tells the main thing the group did. Remember, first it names. Then it tells the main thing.
2. Touch picture 1.
It shows cats. I'll read the sentences next to the picture.

3. First sentence: The cats had long tails. Everybody, does that sentence name the group and tell the main thing the group did? (Signal.) *No.*
- Next sentence: A cat chewed on a string. Everybody, does that sentence name the group and tell the main thing the group did? (Signal.) *No.*
- Next sentence: The cats played with string. Everybody, does that sentence name the group and tell the main thing the group did? (Signal.) *Yes.*
- Next sentence: The string was on the floor. Everybody, does that sentence name the group and tell the main thing the group did? (Signal.) *No.*
- (Repeat step 3 until firm.)
4. Circle the good sentence for picture 1.
- Everybody, read the sentence you circled. (Signal.) *The cats played with string.*
5. Everybody, touch picture 2.
Find the sentence that names the group and tells the main thing the group did. Circle that sentence and then stop. Raise your hand when you've circled the sentence.
(Observe students and give feedback.)
- Everybody, read the good sentence for picture 2. (Signal.) *The family worked in the yard.*
6. Everybody, touch picture 3.
Circle the sentence that names the group and tells the main thing the group did. Raise your hand when you've circled the sentence.
(Observe students and give feedback.)
- Everybody, read the good sentence for picture 3. (Signal.) *Three men walked through the snow.*
7. Raise your hand if you got everything right. Great job!
- Everybody else, fix up any mistakes you made in part C.
(Observe students and give feedback.)

LINED PAPER • TEXTBOOK

EXERCISE 5   Paragraph Copying

1. Everybody, take out a sheet of lined paper and write your name on the top line. Raise your hand when you're finished. ✔

- Everybody, pencils down. Open your textbook to lesson 82 and find part D. ✔
- You're going to copy the paragraph written in part D. Remember, the first word of a paragraph does not start at the margin. It is indented. It starts two fingers from the margin. The other lines in the paragraph start just after the margin.
2. Put two fingers next to the margin on your paper, and write the first word of the paragraph. Raise your hand when you're finished. ✔
- Now copy the rest of the paragraph. Remember to start each new sentence just after the period in the last sentence. And don't indent any more lines. You have 3 minutes. Raise your hand when you're finished.
   (Observe students and give feedback.)
3. (After 3 minutes, say:) Everybody, stop. Let's check your work. Make 3 check boxes under your paragraph.
4. Here's check 1: Does each sentence begin with a capital and end with a period? Read each sentence for check 1. Fix it up if it's not right. Then make a check in box 1. Raise your hand when you're finished.
   (Observe students and give feedback.)
5. Here's check 2: Did you indent the first line? If you indented, put a check in box 2. If you didn't indent, fix up the first line. Then make a check in box 2. Raise your hand when you're finished.
   (Observe students and give feedback.)
6. Here's check 3: Did you start all the other lines at the margin? Check each line after the first line and see if it starts at the margin. Put a check in box 3 when your paragraph is fixed up. Raise your hand when you're finished.
   (Observe students and give feedback.)
7. Who thinks they wrote a **super** paragraph?

EXERCISE 6   Clarity

Pictures for Sentences

1. Skip a line on your paper. Then number your paper 1 through 4. Raise your hand when you're finished. ✔
- Everybody, pencils down. Find part E in your textbook. ✔
- Some of the sentences for these pictures have the words **he** and **she.**

2. Touch sentence 1.
   He held a tool. Raise your hand when you know which pictures that sentence tells about.
- Everybody, which pictures? (Signal.) *B and C.*
- Touch sentence 2.
   She held a hammer. Raise your hand when you know which picture that sentence tells about.
- Everybody, which picture? (Signal.) *A.*
3. Your turn: Read each sentence carefully. Write the letter of each picture that shows what the sentence says. Raise your hand when you're finished.
   (Observe students and give feedback.)
4. Let's check your work. Make an **X** next to any item you missed. I'll read the answers for part E.
- Sentence 1: He held a tool.
   The pictures are B and C.
- Sentence 2: She held a hammer.
   The picture is A.
- Sentence 3: A person held a tool.
   The pictures are A, B, C and D.
- Sentence 4: She held a tool.
   The pictures are A and D.
5. Raise your hand if you made no mistakes. Great job.
- Everybody else, fix up any mistakes you made in part E.
   (Observe students and give feedback.)

EXERCISE 7   Main Idea

1. Skip a line on your paper. Then number your paper 1 and 2. Raise your hand when you're finished.
- Everybody, find part F in your textbook. ✔
- I'll read the instructions: Write a sentence for each picture. Each sentence should report on the main thing the person did.

2. Touch the words in the vocabulary box as I read them: **branch, water, sawed.** Be sure to spell those words correctly if you use them.

3. Next to each number on your paper, write a sentence that reports on what the picture shows. Tell the main thing the person did. You have 3 minutes. Raise your hand when you're finished.
(Observe students and give feedback.)

4. (After 3 minutes, say:) Stop writing. I'll call on students to read their sentences. Listen to each sentence and see if it names the right person and tells the main thing that person did.

• (Call on individual students to read their sentences. After each good sentence, tell the group:) Everybody, say that sentence.

5. Let's check your work. Make 3 check boxes below your last sentence. ✔

6. Here's check 1: Does each sentence begin with a capital and end with a period? Fix up any sentences that don't have a capital and a period. Make a check in box 1 when your sentences check out. Raise your hand when you're finished.
(Observe students and give feedback.)

7. Here's check 2: Does each sentence tell the main thing the person did? Read over your sentences carefully and fix up any mistakes. When all your sentences name and tell the main thing the person did, put a check in box 2. Raise your hand when you're finished.
(Observe students and give feedback.)

8. Here's check 3: Did you spell words from the vocabulary box correctly? Look at each sentence. Make sure vocabulary words are spelled correctly. Fix up any mistakes and make a check in box 3. Raise your hand when you're finished.
(Observe students and give feedback.)

9. Raise your hand if you think you'll get a **super** paper. We'll see next time.

EXERCISE 8   The Case of the Missing Corn *Part 3*

Storytelling

• I'll read another part of **The Case of the Missing Corn.** Let's see how well you can remember things that happened.

• In the last story, who did Sherlock say was the corn thief? (Call on a student. *The red chicken.*)

• Everybody, was the red chicken the corn thief? (Signal.) *No.*

• Sherlock had made up two deductions. The first one started out this way: Anybody who goes in the barn smells of oats. The red chicken went into the barn. So . . . What's the last sentence of that deduction? (Call on a student. *So, the red chicken smells of oats.*)

• What was the other deduction that Sherlock made? (Call on a student. *The corn thief went into the barn. The red chicken went into the barn. So the red chicken is the corn thief.*)

• What was the problem with that deduction? (Call on a student. Idea: *The red chicken was not the only animal that went into the barn. All the rats had gone into the barn.*)

• What did the rats do to Sherlock after they realized that he had made a bad deduction? (Call on a student. *Threw him into the pond.*)

The next day, the gray rat—I mean Sherlock—spent over half an hour bending over the entrance to Bertha's home, trying to talk her into coming out and working on the mystery again. He said, "We can't quit now. For some reason my deductions didn't work out the way they should have, but we can still solve this mystery if you'll come out and work with me."

"I don't think so," Bertha said. "Your deductions don't make a lot of sense to me."

"Of course they make sense. Just ask me where Benny the bluebird is right now, and I'll tell you the answer by using a deduction."

Bertha said, "I can tell you where he is right now without using a deduction."

"You can't either."

"I can too."

"Okay, let's see you do it."

Bertha peeked out of her hole and said, "He's in the berry bushes with the other bluebirds."

"Yeah, but how did you know that?" Sherlock asked.

"Well, that's simple: In the morning, all the bluebirds are in the berry bushes. Benny is a bluebird, so he's in the berry bushes."

"You used a **deduction,**" Sherlock shouted. He shouted so loudly that Bertha ducked back into her hole.

At last, she peeked out again and said, "I guess I did use a deduction, didn't I?"

"Of course you did. And that's all I was doing when I tried to solve the mystery of the missing corn. I just put a couple of deductions together."

Bertha crawled out of her hole and scratched her head with one of her very front legs. Then she said, "But there's something about the deductions you used that . . ."

"What about them?"

"They stink."

"Stink? They were great deductions."

"No," Bertha said. "They really stink."

"Why do you say a nasty thing like that?"

"Well, because you could use your deductions to show that everybody who went into the barn stole the corn."

"I still think that chicken did it," Sherlock said.

"Well," Bertha said. "I think **you** did it."

"How can you say anything as ridiculous as that?"

"I'll just say what **you** said." And Bertha did just that. First she said the deduction about the corn thief smelling of oats. Then she said, "The corn thief

went into the barn. Sherlock went into the barn. So. . ."

Bertha said, "So you must be the corn thief."

"No, no," Sherlock said. "I went into the barn, and I smell of oats, but I'm not the corn thief."

Bertha smiled and said, "That's why your deductions stink."

"You mean I spent all this time learning deductions and now I can't even use them?"

Bertha scratched her head again and then said, "I think I know the problem with your deductions. You want to figure out the **only** person who could have taken the corn. But **your** deductions tell you about a whole bunch of people."

"But how can I make a deduction that tells about the **only** person who could have taken the corn if I don't know who that person is?"

"Clues," Bertha said.

"What do you mean, clues?" Sherlock asked.

"I'm just a beetle," Bertha said. "But I think you need some clues that will tell about the **only** person who could have taken the corn."

"But I don't know how to make up good clues," Sherlock said. He was getting very nervous.

Bertha said, "Let me think about it. Come back in an hour. Maybe I'll have an idea by then."

So Sherlock went away and tried to think of a plan himself. But he didn't know much about how clues worked and how to get clues, so he didn't come up with any good plan.

An hour later, he went back to Bertha's place. She rushed up to him and said, "I've got it all worked out.

- What plan did she have? (Call on a student. Idea: *To make a circle of pine needles around the corn.*)

Tonight the rats won't go to the barn to get their dessert."

"Oh, no," Sherlock said. "They'll get very upset if they don't get their dessert."

"Stop interrupting," Bertha said. "They'll get their dessert. But you'll bring it to them so they won't have to go to the barn. Then we'll fix up the rest of the corn in the barn so that anybody who goes into the barn will not only smell of oats; that person will also smell of pine needles."

Sherlock shook his head. "I don't know how we could do that. There aren't any pine needles near that barn. And I . . ."

"Stop interrupting," Bertha said. "If you turn around, you'll see a large tree behind you."

Sherlock turned around and looked at the tree. "So?" he said.

"So, what do you see growing all over that tree?"

"Pine needles," he said.

"And what do you see all over the ground under that tree?"

"More pine needles."

"Well, all we need to do is gather up a few bags of those pine needles and take them to the barn. Then we'll make a circle of pine needles all the way around the corn. Anybody who goes after that corn will have to go through the pine needles. So we'll just find the person who has a strong smell of oats **and** a strong smell of pine needles. That's the one who's been stealing the corn."

"But. . ." Sherlock said. "But. . . won't **we** smell of oats and pine needles when we're all done?"

"Yes," said Bertha.

"So how will we know that **we** didn't steal the corn?"

Bertha looked at him and shook her little body from side to side. Then she said, "I'll watch you and you'll watch me. Then we'll know if we are guilty."

"This is getting pretty hard to understand," Sherlock said. "I'm not sure . . ."

"You don't have to be sure. I am. Let's get to work and solve this crime."

So they did.

Note:
- Collect the students' workbooks and papers.
- Check the students' work before the next language period. Mark any mistakes.
- Write **super** on work that has all mistakes corrected. Write **good** or **pretty good** on work that has only 1 or 2 mistakes.

Objectives

- Punctuate sentences (capitals and periods) and identify the subject of sentences in a paragraph. (Exercise 2)
- **Change 2-word verbs in a paragraph to 1-word past-time verbs.** (Exercise 3)
- Select sentences that state the main thing that illustrated groups did. (Exercise 4)
- Copy a paragraph. (Exercise 5)
- Select sentences that state the main thing that illustrated groups did. (Exercise 6)
- Listen to a familiar story and answer comprehension questions. (Exercise 7)

EXERCISE 1 **Feedback On Lesson 82**

- (Hand back the students' work from lesson 82.)
- Look at what I wrote on your lined paper. Raise your hand if I wrote **super.**
- If you didn't get a **super,** look at the mistakes you made and be more careful next time.

WORKBOOK

EXERCISE 2 **Paragraph Editing**

Capitals and Periods

1. Everybody, open your workbook to lesson 83 and find part A. ✔
- Somebody forgot to put capitals and periods in the sentences.
2. Look at the first words in the paragraph, and figure out who the first sentence names.
- Everybody, who does it name? (Signal.) *A woman.*
    Circle **a woman.** ✔
- The first sentence tells more about a woman. (Call on a student:) Say the rest of the sentence that starts with **a woman.** *Rode on a sled.*
- Everybody, put a period after the word **sled.** Start the next sentence with a capital **S.** ✔
3. Look at the first words in the second sentence, and figure out what that sentence names. Circle that part. Then figure out where the sentence ends and put a period there. Raise your hand when you've fixed up the second sentence. (Observe students and give feedback.)

- Everybody, say the part of the sentence that names. (Signal.) *Six dogs.*
- Say the part that tells more. (Signal.) *Pulled the sled.*
- You should have put a period after the word **sled.**
4. Start the next sentence with a capital **I.** Then fix up the rest of the paragraph. Make sure each sentence begins with a capital and ends with a period. Circle the part of each sentence that names. Do it now. Raise your hand when you're finished. (Observe students and give feedback.)
5. Let's check your work. Make an **X** over anything you missed.
- First sentence: You should have circled **A woman.** A woman rode on a sled, period.
- Next sentence: You should have circled **six dogs.** Capital **S,** Six dogs pulled the sled, period.
- Next sentence: You should have circled **it.** Capital **I,** It went through the deep snow, period.
- Next sentence: You should have circled **the woman.** Capital **T,** The woman was very cold, period.
- Next sentence: You should have circled **her dogs.** Capital **H,** Her dogs liked the snow, period.
- Next sentence: You should have circled **they.** Capital **T,** They slept in the snow, period.
6. Raise your hand if you made no mistakes. Great job.
- Everybody else, fix up any mistakes you made in part A.
    (Observe students and give feedback.)

EXERCISE 3 Paragraph Editing

Past Time

1. Everybody, find part B. ✔
   I'll read the instructions: Make each
   sentence tell what a person or thing did.
2. Touch the first sentence.
   Mark looked for a hidden treasure. That
   sentence tells what Mark did.
   - I'll read the next sentence: He is going into
     his backyard with a shovel.
     Everybody, does that sentence tell what he
     did? (Signal.) *No.*
   - Say the sentence so it tells what he did.
     (Signal.) *He went into his backyard with a
     shovel.*
   - Cross out **is going** and write **went** above
     the crossed-out words. ✔
3. Everybody, touch the check box below the
   paragraph.
   - I'll read the check: Does each sentence tell
     what a person or thing did?
     The **X**s in the box show how many
     mistakes there are in the paragraph. Count
     the **X**s and you'll know how many mistakes
     you should find. (Pause.)
   - Everybody, how many mistakes? (Signal.)
     Four.
   - Read the rest of the paragraph. Fix up
     any sentence that does not tell what Mark
     or his shovel did. Raise your hand when
     you're finished.
     (Observe students and give feedback.)
4. Let's check your work. Make an **X** next to
   any sentence you missed.
   - First sentence: Mark looked for a hidden
     treasure. That sentence is all right.
   - Next sentence: He is going into his
     backyard with a shovel. Does that
     sentence tell what he did? (Signal.) *No.*
   - Say the sentence that tells what he did.
     (Signal.) *He went into his backyard with a
     shovel.*
   - Next sentence: He was digging for a long
     time. Does that sentence tell what he did?
     (Signal.) *No.*
   - Say the sentence that tells what he did.
     (Signal.) *He dug for a long time.*
   - Next sentence: His shovel hit something
     hard. Does that sentence tell what his
     shovel did? (Signal.) *Yes.*
     So you didn't cross out anything.

- Next sentence: Mark was reaching into the
  hole. Does that sentence tell what Mark
  did? (Signal.) *No.*
- Say the sentence that tells what Mark did.
  (Signal.) *Mark reached into the hole.*
- Next sentence: He pulled something
  out. Does that sentence tell what he did?
  (Signal.) *Yes.*
  So you didn't cross out anything.
- Next sentence: He was finding a bone.
  Does that sentence tell what he did?
  (Signal.) *No.*
- Say the sentence that tells what he did.
  (Signal.) *He found a bone.*
5. Raise your hand if you made no mistakes.
   Great job.
   - Everybody else, fix up any mistakes you
     made in part B.
     (Observe students and give feedback.)

EXERCISE 4 Main Idea

Groups

1. Everybody, pencils down. Find part C. ✔
   These pictures show groups. You're going
   to circle the sentence that tells the main
   thing each group did. Remember, the
   sentence must do two things. First, it
   names the group. Then it tells the main
   thing the group did. Remember, first it
   names. Then it tells the main thing.
2. Touch picture 1.
   It shows a group of children. I'll read the
   sentences next to the picture.
   - First sentence: A boy swept the floor.
     Everybody, does that sentence name the
     group and tell the main thing the group
     did? (Signal.) *No.*
   - Next sentence: The room was dirty. Does
     that sentence name the group and tell the
     main thing the group did? (Signal.) *No.*
   - Next sentence: The children cleaned the
     room. Does that sentence name the group
     and tell the main thing the group did?
     (Signal.) *Yes.*
   - Next sentence: The children were standing.
     Does that sentence name the group and
     tell the main thing the group did? (Signal.)
     No.

3. Circle the good sentence for picture 1. ✔
   Everybody, read the sentence you circled.
   (Signal.) *The children cleaned the room.*
4. Everybody, touch picture 2.
   Circle the sentence that names the group
   and tells the main thing the group did.
   Raise your hand when you've circled the
   sentence.
   - Everybody, read the good sentence for
     picture 2. (Signal.) *The farmers fed the
     animals.*
5. Everybody, touch picture 3.
   Circle the sentence that names the group
   and tells the main thing the group did.
   Raise your hand when you've circled the
   sentence.
   - Everybody, read the good sentence for
     picture 3. (Signal.) *Four girls ate a meal.*
6. Raise your hand if you got everything right.
   Great job!
   - Everybody else, fix up any mistakes you
     made in part C.
     (Observe students and give feedback.)

LINED PAPER • TEXTBOOK

EXERCISE 5   Paragraph Copying

1. Everybody, take out a sheet of lined paper
   and write your name on the top line. Raise
   your hand when you're finished. ✔
   - Everybody, open your textbook to lesson
     83 and find part D. ✔
   - You're going to copy the paragraph written
     in part D. Remember, the first word of a
     paragraph does not start at the margin. It
     is indented. It starts two fingers from the
     margin. The other lines in the paragraph
     start just after the margin.
2. Copy the paragraph. You have 4 minutes.
   Raise your hand when you're finished.
   (Observe students and give feedback.)
3. (After 4 minutes, say:) Everybody, stop.
   Let's check your work. Make 3 check
   boxes under your paragraph. ✔
4. Here's check 1: Does each sentence begin
   with a capital and end with a period? Read
   each sentence for check 1. Fix it up if it's
   not right. Then make a check in box 1.
   Raise your hand when you're finished.
   (Observe students and give feedback.)

5. Here's check 2: Did you indent the first
   line? If you indented, make a check in box
   2. If you didn't indent, fix up the first line.
   Then make a check in box 2. Raise your
   hand when you're finished.
   (Observe students and give feedback.)
6. Here's check 3: Did you start all the other
   lines at the margin? Check each line
   after the first line and see if it starts at the
   margin. Make a check in box 3 when your
   paragraph is fixed up. Raise your hand
   when you're finished.
   (Observe students and give feedback.)
7. Who thinks they wrote a **super** paragraph?

EXERCISE 6   Main Idea

1. Skip a line on your paper. Then number
   your paper 1 through 3. Raise your hand
   when you're finished.
   - Everybody, find part E in your textbook. I'll
     read the instructions: Write a sentence for
     each picture. Each sentence should report
     on the main thing the animal did.
2. Touch the words in the vocabulary box
   as I read them: **walked, juggled, three,
   tightrope, across.** Be sure to spell those
   words correctly if you use them.
3. Next to each number on your paper, write
   a sentence that reports on what the picture
   shows. Tell the main thing the animal did.
   You have 3 minutes. Raise your hand when
   you're finished.
   (Observe students and give feedback.)
4. (After 3 minutes, say:) Stop writing. I'll call
   on students to read their sentences. Listen
   to each sentence and see if it names the
   right animal and tells the main thing the
   animal did.
   - (Call on individual students to read their
     sentences. After each good sentence, tell
     the group:) Everybody, say that sentence.
5. Let's check your work. Make 3 check
   boxes below your last sentence.

6. Here's check 1: Does each sentence begin with a capital and end with a period? Fix up any sentences that don't have a capital and a period. Make a check in box 1 when your sentences check out. Raise your hand when you're finished.

(Observe students and give feedback.)

7. Here's check 2: Does each sentence tell the main thing the animal did? Read over your sentences carefully and fix up any mistakes. When all your sentences name and tell the main thing the animal did, make a check in box 2. Raise your hand when you're finished.

(Observe students and give feedback.)

8. Here's check 3: Did you spell words from the vocabulary box correctly? Look at each sentence. Make sure vocabulary words are spelled correctly. Fix up any mistakes and make a check in box 3. Raise your hand when you're finished.

(Observe students and give feedback.)

9. Raise your hand if you think you'll get a **super** paper. We'll see next time.

EXERCISE 7 The Case of the Missing Corn *Part 4*

Storytelling

- I'll read another part of "The Case of the Missing Corn" story. Let's see how well you can remember things that happened.
- What plan did Bertha come up with for finding out who was stealing corn? (Call on a student. *Make a ring of pine needles around the corn.*)

The little beetle had a plan for figuring out who took the corn from the barn. That plan involved pine needles.

If the plan worked, somebody would have two smells. And any person who had both those smells must have gone into the barn **and** through the pine needles.

All afternoon, Sherlock and his bloodbeetle collected pine needles and carried them to the barn. Then they counted two kernels of corn for every rat in the pack. They put that corn outside the barn. Then they took the pine needles and made a great circle of pine needles around the pile of corn that was still in the barn.

When they were done, Bertha said, "Now we'll go back and tell the rats about our plan. Then we'll wait until tomorrow and go hunting for the person who smells of pine needles **and** oats."

They carried the corn that they had taken out of the barn back to the stump and called all the other rats.

- Why were they taking some corn out of the barn? (Call on a student. Idea: *So the rats wouldn't go into the barn.*)

Sherlock stood on the stump.

The rats looked at each other and asked, "What's all that corn doing out here?"

"Quiet please," Sherlock said. "Everybody quiet."

Sherlock cleared his throat—"ahem, ahem"—and stood up very straight. In his most important voice, he said, "I won't bother trying to tell you how we're going to find out who is stealing the corn, because it's very difficult to understand. But we've brought enough corn out here so every rat can have dessert tonight without going near the barn. We have very cleverly fixed the pile of corn that's still in the barn so that anybody who goes to the corn will give us a very good clue. But it's difficult to explain."

"What kind of clue?" one of the rats asked.

Bertha said, "We put pine needles all around the corn. So anybody who goes to the corn will smell of pine needles."

"Now that makes sense," one of the rats said. Then other rats agreed and nodded their head up and down. "Yeah, if somebody smells of oats **and** pine needles, that's the guilty person."

"Yeah, that's smart," the rats agreed.

So the rats had dinner and ate their dessert. Then they did what rats do in the evening—they went to sleep. Sherlock didn't sleep with the other rats. He had to sleep outside Bertha's place where she could keep an eye on him.

- Why did he have to stay close to Bertha? (Call on a student. Idea: *To make sure she didn't go into the barn*.)

The next morning, Bertha woke Sherlock up by tickling his nose with her little front legs. Then she said, "Let's go find the corn thief." And away they went.

They went all around, greeting every animal they saw and getting close enough for Bertha to get a good sniff.

After they greeted Cora the crow, Bertha said, "She smells of pine needles."

"She did it," Sherlock said.

"No, she didn't do it," Bertha said. "She doesn't smell of oats."

"Oh," Sherlock said. He wasn't really too good at figuring things out.

After they greeted the red chicken, Bertha said, "She smells of oats."

"She did it," Sherlock said.

"No, she didn't do it," Bertha said. And then she explained why.

At last they greeted Myron the mouse. Bertha took a good sniff. Then she walked away as Sherlock followed. Bertha stopped and whispered, "Myron smells of oats and he smells of pine needles."

Sherlock said, "Let's haul him back to the rat pack. He's the one who did it."

"I'm not really sure," Bertha said.

"Why not?" Sherlock asked.

"Something is missing," Bertha said. "Let's look around a little bit more."

- Was Myron guilty? (Call on a student. *No*.)
- Who had been stealing the corn? (Call on a student. *Cyrus*.)

So Sherlock and Bertha greeted frogs and toads and snakes and snails. They greeted chipmunks and skunks and sparrows and ducks. At last, they came to Cyrus the squirrel. He was leaning against a tree, yawning and stretching. After Sherlock and Bertha greeted him, they walked away. Then Bertha stopped and whispered, "Cyrus smells of oats and he smells of pine needles. He's the one who's been stealing the corn. Ask him."

"Okay," Sherlock said. He walked over and said, "Been near the barn lately?"

"Not me," Cyrus said and yawned again.

"Been stealing any corn from that barn?"

"Who me?" Cyrus asked. "I know that corn is for the rat pack. I wouldn't take any of that corn."

"So you didn't steal the corn from the barn?"

"Absolutely not," he said and yawned again.

Sherlock shrugged and went back to Bertha. "He said he didn't do it."

Bertha got so angry that she started to quiver all over. She said, "We will see about that."

She charged over to Cyrus and said, "If you didn't go into the barn, why is it that you smell of fresh pine needles?"

"I'm a squirrel," he said. "I climb pine trees all the time."

"Okay, if you didn't go into the barn, why do you smell of oats?"

"There's an oat field on the other side of the pond. I was walking around there early this morning."

- How did Bertha know that Cyrus was guilty? (Call on a student. *His breath smelled of oats*.)

"Oh yeah?" Bertha said. "Well if you didn't go into the barn, why does your breath smell of corn?"

"I, uh, I . . . well . . ."

Bertha said, "Your breath is so strong I could smell the corn every time you yawned. You're a liar and you stole the corn. Admit it."

"Well, I . . . uh . . . that is . . . I . . ."

"Stop trying to make excuses. You stole the corn. Admit it."

"Okay, okay. I admit it."

"Well, you'd better figure out some way of paying the pack back and you'd better think fast."

"I'm thinking. I'm thinking," Cyrus said.

- What did he do to pay the pack for the corn that he had stolen? (Call on a student. *Bring the rats hazelnuts for two weeks*.)

Later that day, Cyrus, Sherlock and Bertha went to the stump. Cyrus was carrying a large sack filled with something that would interest all the rats. Sherlock called the other rats. "Attention, attention," he said. "I have an announcement to make." He was talking in his important voice. "We have found the guilty party. It was Cyrus the squirrel, and he admitted it."

"Let's throw him into the pond."

"No, no," Sherlock said. "Cyrus has promised to bring us a special dessert every night for the next two weeks—that dessert is your very favorite nut."

The rats all stared at Sherlock. Then one of them said, "You don't mean hazelnuts, do you?"

"Yes, hazelnuts," Sherlock said. "Everybody gets a big hazelnut every night for two weeks."

Great cheers went up from the rat pack. "What a deal," they shouted. "Corn is good, but hazelnuts are the best!"

The rats crowded around Sherlock and patted him on the back. One of them said, "Yeah, Cyrus can steal all the corn he wants as long as he pays us back with hazelnuts."

Other rats told Sherlock how smart he was. "You did a great job," they said. "We didn't think you knew what you were doing, but you really figured it out."

They shook his hand, patted him on the back and gave him great hugs. Some of the pretty little girl rats even gave him a kiss. One of them said, "You're so big and smart. And you solved this crime all by yourself."

Sherlock said, "Oh, well, I had a little bit of help from Bertha."

Note:

- Collect the students' workbooks and papers.

- Check the students' work before the next language period. Mark any mistakes.

- Write **super** on work that has all mistakes corrected. Write **good** or **pretty good** on work that has only 1 or 2 mistakes.

Objectives

- Identify the subject and predicate of sentences. (Exercise 2)
- Punctuate sentences (capitals and periods) and identify the subject of sentences in a paragraph. (Exercise 3)
- Change 2-word verbs in a paragraph to 1-word past-time verbs. (Exercise 4)
- Select a sentence that states the main thing an illustrated group did. (Exercise 5)
- **Construct a paragraph that reports on what the members of an illustrated group did.** (Exercise 6)
- Listen to a familiar story and answer comprehension questions. (Exercise 7)

EXERCISE 1   Feedback On Lesson 83

- *(Hand back the students' work from lesson 83.)*
- Look at what I wrote on your lined paper. Raise your hand if I wrote **super.**
- If you didn't get a **super,** look at the mistakes you made and be more careful next time.

WORKBOOK

EXERCISE 2   Subject/Predicate

1. Everybody, open your workbook to lesson 84 and find part A. ✔
- I'll read the instructions: Circle the part that names. Underline the part that tells more.
2. Everybody, touch sentence 1.
   A horse and a goat were eating grass.
   Say the part of the sentence that names. (Signal.) *A horse and a goat.*
- Say the part of the sentence that tells more. (Signal.) *Were eating grass.*
- *(Repeat step 2 until firm.)*
3. Do part A. For each sentence, circle the part that names. Underline the part that tells more. Do it now. Raise your hand when you're finished.
   (Observe students and give feedback.)
4. Let's check your work. Make an **X** next to any item you missed.
- Sentence 1. A horse and a goat were eating grass. Say that sentence. (Signal.) *A horse and a goat were eating grass.*
   What part names? (Signal.) *A horse and a goat.*
   What part tells more? (Signal.) *Were eating grass.*
- Sentence 2. Those hungry animals ate all the grass. Say that sentence. (Signal.) *Those hungry animals ate all the grass.*
   What part names? (Signal.) *Those hungry animals.*
   What part tells more? (Signal.) *Ate all the grass.*
- Sentence 3. They drank water from a pond. Say that sentence. (Signal.) *They drank water from a pond.*
   What part names? (Signal.) *They.*
   What part tells more? (Signal.) *Drank water from a pond.*
- Sentence 4. A car and a truck went by a pond. Say that sentence. (Signal.) *A car and a truck went by a pond.*
   What part names? (Signal.) *A car and a truck.*
   What part tells more? (Signal.) *Went by a pond.*
- Sentence 5. They were very loud. Say that sentence. (Signal.) *They were very loud.*
   What part names? (Signal.) *They.*
   What part tells more? (Signal.) *Were very loud.*
5. Raise your hand if you got no items wrong. Great job.
- Everybody else, fix up any mistakes you made in part A.
   (Observe students and give feedback.)

EXERCISE 3   Paragraph Editing

Capitals and Periods

1. Everybody, find part B. ✔
   I'll read the instructions: Put in capitals and periods. Circle the part of each sentence that names.

2. Look at the first words in the paragraph, and figure out who the first sentence names.
- Everybody, who does it name? (Signal.) *Tom and his brother.*
  Circle **Tom and his brother.** ✔
- The first sentence tells more about Tom and his brother. (Call on a student:) Say the rest of the sentence that starts with **Tom and his brother.**
- Everybody, put a period after the word **food.** Start the next sentence with a capital **T.** ✔

3. Look at the first words in the second sentence, and figure out what that sentence names. Circle that part. Then figure out where the sentence ends and put a period there. Raise your hand when you've fixed up the second sentence. (Observe students and give feedback.)
- Everybody, say the part of the sentence that names. (Signal.) *They.*
- Say the part that tells more. (Signal.) *Bought four apples and six oranges.*
- You should have put a period after the word **oranges.**

4. Start the next sentence with a capital **T.** Then fix up the rest of the paragraph. Put in capitals and periods. Circle the part of each sentence that names. Do it now. Raise your hand when you're finished. (Observe students and give feedback.)

5. Let's check your work. Make an **X** next to any mistake you made.
- First sentence: You should have circled **Tom and his brother.** Tom and his brother went shopping for food, period.
- Next sentence: You should have circled **they.** Capital **T,** They bought four apples and six oranges, period.
- Next sentence: You should have circled **the food.** Capital **T,** The food cost less than five dollars, period.
- Next sentence: You should have circled **Tom.** Tom gave the clerk five dollars, period.
- Next sentence: You should have circled **the clerk.** Capital **T,** The clerk gave Tom change, period.

6. Raise your hand if you made no mistakes. Great job.

- Everybody else, fix up any mistakes you made in part B.
  (Observe students and give feedback.)

EXERCISE 4 Paragraph Editing

Past Time

1. Everybody, find part C. ✔
   Touch the check box below the paragraph. I'll read the check: Do the sentences tell what Mr. Walters did?
- The **X**s in the box show how many mistakes there are in the paragraph. Count the **X**s and you'll know how many mistakes you should find. Then read the paragraph. Fix up any sentence that does not tell what Mr. Walters did. Raise your hand when you're finished.
  (Observe students and give feedback.)

2. Let's check your work. Make an **X** next to any sentence you missed.
- First sentence: Mr. Walters was buying an apple tree. Does that sentence tell what Mr. Walters did? (Signal.) *No.*
- Say the sentence that tells what Mr. Walters did. (Signal.) *Mr. Walters bought an apple tree.*
- Next sentence: He dug a hole in his yard. Does that sentence tell what he did? (Signal.) *Yes.*
- Next sentence: He placed the tree in the hole. Does that sentence tell what he did? (Signal.) *Yes.*
- Next sentence: He is filling the hole with dirt. Does that sentence tell what he did? (Signal.) *No.*
- Say the sentence that tells what he did. (Signal.) *He filled the hole with dirt.*
- Next sentence: He is watering the tree. Does that sentence tell what he did? (Signal.) *No.*
- Say the sentence that tells what he did. (Signal.) *He watered the tree.*
- Next sentence: He took good care of the tree. Does that sentence tell what he did? (Signal.) *Yes.*

3. Raise your hand if you made no mistakes. Great job.
- Everybody else, fix up any mistakes you made in part C.
  (Observe students and give feedback.)

EXERCISE 5 Main Idea
Groups

1. Everybody, find part D. ✔
   These pictures show groups. You're going to circle the sentence that tells the main thing each group did. Remember, the sentence must do two things. First, it names the group. Then it tells the main thing the group did. Remember, first it names. Then it tells the main thing.

2. Everybody, circle the good sentence for picture 1. Raise your hand when you've circled the sentence.

 • Everybody, read the sentence you circled. (Signal.) *Three cowboys cooked supper.*

3. Circle the good sentence for picture 2. Raise your hand when you've circled the sentence.

 • Read the good sentence for picture 2. (Signal.) *The animals did tricks.*

4. Raise your hand if you got everything right. Great job.

 • Everybody else, fix up any mistakes you made in part D.
   (Observe students and give feedback.)

LINED PAPER • TEXTBOOK

EXERCISE 6 Paragraph Writing
Groups

1. Everybody, take out a sheet of lined paper and write your name on the top line. Raise your hand when you're finished.

 • Open your textbook to lesson 84 and find part E. ✔

2. Everybody, touch the words in the vocabulary box as I read them: **hammer, side, board, nail, saw, paint.** Be sure to spell those words correctly if you use them.

3. I'll read the instructions: Write a paragraph. Copy the sentence that tells the main thing the group did. Then write three more sentences. Write one sentence about each person. Tell the main thing each person did.

4. Everybody, touch Kay.

 • Raise your hand when you can say a sentence that reports on the main thing Kay did. (Call on several students. Praise sentences such as: *Kay hammered a nail into a board on the side of the house.* For each good sentence: Everybody, say that sentence.)

5. Everybody, touch Milly.

 • Raise your hand when you can say a sentence that reports on the main thing Milly did. (Call on several students. Praise sentences such as: *Milly sawed a board.* For each good sentence: Everybody, say that sentence.)

6. Everybody, touch Jean.

 • Raise your hand when you can say a sentence that reports on the main thing Jean did. (Call on several students. Praise sentences such as: *Jean painted the side of the house with a paintbrush.* For each good sentence: Everybody, say that sentence.)

7. The sentence that tells the main thing the group did is written under the picture. Everybody, read that sentence. (Signal.) *The women worked on the house.*

 • Everybody, copy that sentence. Remember to indent. Raise your hand when you're finished.
   (Observe students and give feedback.)

8. Now you're going to write a sentence about each of the women. Touch Kay.

 • Listen: Write a sentence that names Kay and tells the main thing she did. Start that sentence right after the period of the first sentence. Raise your hand when you're finished. (Observe students and give feedback.)

9. Touch Milly in the picture.

 • Write a sentence that names Milly and tells the main thing she did. Remember to start that sentence right after the period of the last sentence. Raise your hand when you're finished.
   (Observe students and give feedback.)

10. Now write a sentence that names Jean and tells the main thing she did. Remember to start that sentence right after the period. Raise your hand when you're finished. (Observe students and give feedback.)

11. I'm going to call on several students to read their paragraph. Let's see who the good listeners are. Each paragraph starts with the sentence about the group. Then it should have a sentence about Kay, a sentence about Milly, and a sentence about Jean. Each of these sentences should tell the main thing that person did.

   • If you hear a mistake, raise your hand. If a sentence is missing, raise your hand. If a sentence doesn't tell the main thing one of the women did, raise your hand. Listen carefully.

12. (Call on a student:) Read your paragraph. When you read it, stop at the end of each sentence so everybody can think about whether that sentence is right. (Praise the paragraph if it has no mistakes.)

13. (Call on several other students to read their paragraph. Praise good paragraphs.)

14. You're going to fix up your paragraph before you hand it in. Make 2 check boxes under your paragraph.

15. Here's check 1: Does each sentence begin with a capital and end with a period? Read each sentence you wrote and fix up any mistakes. Then make a check in box 1. Raise your hand when you're finished with check 1.
   (Observe students and give feedback.)

16. Here's check 2: Does each sentence tell the main thing the person did? Make sure you have a sentence for each person and it tells the main thing the person did. Then make a check in box 2. Raise your hand when you're finished with check 2.
   (Observe students and give feedback.)

17. Raise your hand if you think you'll get a **super** paper. We'll see next time.

Note: See *Language Arts Teacher's Guide* for details on marking the students' paragraphs.

Storytelling

• I'll read the story titled, **Mrs. Hudson Writes Another Book.** Let's see how well you can remember things that happened.

   Mrs. Hudson decided to write another book.

• What was this book about? (Call on a student. *Gardening*.)
• Was it interesting or boring? (Call on a student. *Boring*.)

   This book was about gardening. Mrs. Hudson loved to grow things in her garden, and she had lots of experiences to tell about. Of course, they were as boring as the experiences she told about in her first book.

   But, as Mrs. Hudson wrote her new book, she kept thinking about her first book and about Zelda.

   Mrs. Hudson knew that her first book was very popular and that people really liked it, but she was still a little upset because they thought the book was funny.

   She hadn't meant to write a funny book, but Zelda's illustrations made it funny.

   As Mrs. Hudson thought about that book, she decided that she didn't want Zelda to illustrate her new book.

   She said to herself, "I don't want people who read this book to see silly pictures and think the book is funny. I want them to enjoy my wonderful experiences and look at pictures that show those experiences."

   So, when Mrs. Hudson finished her book, she didn't take it to Zelda to be illustrated. She found another illustrator. His name was Henry.

Henry was a good illustrator, not as good as Zelda, but good. And Henry didn't misunderstand the parts of the stories that Mrs. Hudson marked for her illustrations.

One place that was marked for an illustration said this: "My two sisters pulled out the morning glories. They were climbing all over the fence."

- What would Zelda's picture show? (Call on a student. Idea: *The sisters climbing up the fence*.)
- What would Henry's picture show? (Call on a student. Idea: *The flowers growing on the fence*.)

If Zelda made an illustration for that part, she would get things mixed up. She would show something climbing all over the fence, but it wouldn't be morning glories.

Henry didn't have that problem. He knew that the morning glories were climbing all over the fence, and that's what his illustration showed.

It showed two sweet little girls pulling out morning glories. They were smiling.

Naturally, Mrs. Hudson went over every illustration with Henry before he drew anything. She wanted to make very sure that he understood what he would show in each picture.

Mrs. Hudson would turn to each part that was marked for an illustration. Then she'd read something like this: "Uncle George picked berries with my sisters. He liked them because they were so big and blue."

- What would Zelda's picture show? (Call on a student. Idea: *Girls that were big and blue*.)
- What would Henry's picture show? (Call on a student. *Berries that were big and blue*.)

Mrs. Hudson would ask questions because she didn't want the kind of picture that Zelda might make. We know what would be big and blue in Zelda's picture, and it wouldn't be the berries.

Henry would answer Mrs. Hudson's questions, and he'd explain how he planned to illustrate each part.

He'd say things like this: "Well, I thought I would show these wonderfully plump blue berries. The girls would be very close to them, smiling. Perhaps, one of the girls would have a slight blue line on her lower lip to show that she'd been eating berries as she picked them. Uncle George would be standing in the background, smiling at the girls and at the berries."

That's how every illustration went. Henry would always end up making a happy picture, with everybody smiling and everything just wonderful.

And that made Mrs. Hudson feel just wonderfully marvelous. She thought that Henry's illustrations were just what she needed to give her exciting stories even more excitement.

Henry worked on the illustrations for three months. At last, he was finished.

The next day, Mrs. Hudson called the publisher and said, "I'm sending you my latest book. I think it's wonderful. It's delightful. It's deliciously entertaining, and it's wonderfully educational. It's just superbly . . ." She had run out of **good** words this time.

The publisher said, "Well, I'll be looking forward to reading it. If it's half as good as your last book, you'll have another best seller."

"Oh," Mrs. Hudson said. "I'm sure you'll find this book perfectly delightful and absolutely marvelous and completely . . ." She'd run out of good words again.

She sent the book and the illustrations to the publisher and she waited for a phone call. She expected the publisher to call her and tell her how perfectly excited she was, how totally thrilled, how absolutely . . . But the call didn't come. Three weeks later, Mrs. Hudson received a large package from the publisher.

- Who remembers what was in the package? (Call on a student. *The book*.)
- We'll read about that next time.

TEST REMINDER

- On the next lesson, you'll have a test. Remember this rule: If you don't make any more than 2 mistakes, you'll get **super** on your test.

Note:

- Collect the students' workbooks and papers.
- Check the students' work before the next language period. Mark any mistakes.
- Write **super** on work that has all mistakes corrected. Write **good** or **pretty good** on work that has only 1 or 2 mistakes.

Objectives

- Construct a paragraph that reports on what the members of an illustrated group did. (Exercise 2)
- Listen to a familiar story and answer comprehension questions. (Exercise 3)
- Perform on a mastery test of skills presented in lessons 76–84. (Exercise 4)

Exercises 5–7 give instructions for marking the test, giving student feedback and providing remedies.

EXERCISE 1   Feedback On Lesson 84

- (Hand back the students' work from lesson 84.)
- Look at what I wrote on your lined paper. Raise your hand if I wrote **super.**
- If you didn't get a **super,** look at the mistakes you made and be more careful next time.

LINED PAPER • TEXTBOOK

EXERCISE 2   Paragraph Writing

Groups

1. Everybody, take out a sheet of lined paper and write your name on the top line. Raise your hand when you're finished. ✔
- Everybody, open your textbook to lesson 85 and find part A. ✔
2. Everybody, touch the words in the vocabulary box as I read them: **washed, floor, picked, swept, dirt, toys, rug, pile, scrubbed, under.** Be sure to spell those words correctly if you use them.
3. I'll read the instructions: Write a paragraph. Copy the sentence that tells the main thing the group did. Then write three more sentences. Write one sentence about each person. Tell the main thing each person did.
4. Everybody, touch Robert.

- Raise your hand when you can say a sentence that reports on the main thing Robert did. (Call on several students. Praise sentences such as: *Robert swept the floor with a broom.* For each good sentence: Everybody, say that sentence.)
5. Everybody, touch Alberto.
- Raise your hand when you can say a sentence that reports on the main thing Alberto did. (Call on several students. Praise sentences such as: *Alberto picked up toys from the floor.* For each good sentence: Everybody, say that sentence.)
6. Everybody, touch Steve.
- Raise your hand when you can say a sentence that reports on the main thing Steve did. (Call on several students. Praise sentences such as: *Steve washed the floor with a brush.* For each good sentence: Everybody, say that sentence.)
7. The sentence that tells the main thing the group did is written under the picture. Everybody, read that sentence. (Signal.) *The men cleaned the room.*
- Everybody, copy that sentence. Remember to indent. Raise your hand when you're finished. (Observe students and give feedback.)
8. Now you're going to write a sentence about each of the men. Touch Robert in the picture.
   Listen: Write a sentence that names Robert and tells the main thing he did. Start that sentence right after the period of the first sentence. Raise your hand when you're finished. (Observe students and give feedback.)

9. Touch Alberto in the picture.
Write a sentence that names Alberto and tells the main thing he did. Remember to start that sentence right after the period of the last sentence. Raise your hand when you're finished.
(Observe students and give feedback.)

10. Now write a sentence that names Steve and tells the main thing he did.
Remember to start that sentence right after the period. Raise your hand when you're finished.
(Observe students and give feedback.)

11. I'm going to call on several students to read their paragraph. Let's see who the good listeners are. Each paragraph starts with the sentence about the group. Then it should have a sentence about Robert, a sentence about Alberto, and a sentence about Steve. Each of these sentences should tell the main thing that person did.
• If you hear a mistake, raise your hand. If a sentence is missing, raise your hand. If a sentence doesn't tell the main thing one of the men did, raise your hand. Listen carefully.

12. (Call on a student:) Read your paragraph. When you read it, stop at the end of each sentence so everybody can think about whether that sentence is right. (Praise the paragraph if it has no mistakes.)

13. (Call on several other students to read their paragraph. Praise good paragraphs.)

14. You're going to fix up your paragraph before you hand it in. Make 2 check boxes under your paragraph.

15. Here's check 1: Does each sentence begin with a capital and end with a period? Read each sentence you wrote and fix up any mistakes. Then make a check in box 1. Raise your hand when you're finished with check 1.
(Observe students and give feedback.)

16. Here's check 2: Does each sentence tell the main thing the person did? Make sure you have a sentence for each person and make sure it tells the main thing the person did. Then make a check in box 2. Raise your hand when you're finished with check 2.
(Observe students and give feedback.)

17. Raise your hand if you think you'll get a **super** paper. We'll see next time.

Note:
• Collect **only** the students' papers.
• Check the students' work before the next language period. Mark any mistakes.
• Write **super** on work that has no mistakes. Write **good** or **pretty good** on work that has only 1 mistake.

EXERCISE 3   Mrs. Hudson Writes Another Book *Part 2*

Storytelling

• I'll read another part of the **Mrs. Hudson Writes Another Book** story. Let's see how well you can remember things that happened.

Last time, Mrs. Hudson sent her boring book to the publisher with Henry's illustrations. All of them were hap, hap, happy pictures showing nice things. They were as boring as the book.

Mrs. Hudson waited for a phone call from the publisher. But the call didn't come. Three weeks later, she received a large package from the publisher.

• What was in that package? (Call on a student. *Her book.*)
• Why was the publisher sending it back to Mrs. Hudson? (Call on a student. Idea: *The publisher felt the book was boring.*)

It was her book and the illustrations. There was also a note from the publisher. It said:

Dear Mrs. Hudson,

Thank you for sending us your latest book. Unfortunately, our company will not be able to publish it. We read it and we all agree that it doesn't have the same kind of spark and humor that your first book had. Frankly, Mrs. Hudson, this book is a little boring. And the illustrations are, frankly, a little boring too.

At the bottom of the letter was a note that said this: "Maybe the book would be more lively if Zelda did the illustrations."

Mrs. Hudson was crushed. She was completely saddened. She was so thoroughly disappointed that she cried.

She stopped crying by the next day. She had decided to take the publisher's advice. So she took the book to Zelda and said, "I've marked the places where you can make illustrations. Just do the pictures the way you think they should be."

Zelda read the book. After she read this part: "Uncle Rover's rosebush grew next to the garage. It was made of red brick," she said to herself, "That man sure has strange plants in his garden."

- What did she think was in his garden? (Call on a student. Idea: *Rose bushes made of bricks*.)

A few months later, Zelda finished the illustrations, and Mrs. Hudson sent them with her book to the publisher. This time, she didn't have to wait weeks to receive a letter from the publisher.

The publisher called two days later. She said, "It's great. It's just great. It's so funny and so humorous and so delightful and just so . . ." **She** had run out of good words.

And, of course, she was right. And Mrs. Hudson had a best-selling book again. But, when she looked through it, she still had trouble appreciating Zelda's illustrations.

Under each picture was the part of the story that was illustrated. Mrs. Hudson would read those parts and then shake her head sadly when she looked at the illustration that Zelda had drawn.

Here is what it said under one of the illustrations: "Donna and her mother watched the tiny spiders. They were upside down in their web."

- What did Henry's illustration for that part show? (Call on a student. *The spiders in the web*.)
- What did Zelda's illustration show? (Call on a student. Idea: *Donna and her mother in the web*.)

Mrs. Hudson did not like Zelda's picture at all.

Another picture made Mrs. Hudson particularly unhappy. That was the picture for this part: "Uncle George and Billy raked the leaves. The wind kept blowing them into the garage."

- What did Henry's illustration for that part show? (Call on a student. Idea: *Leaves blowing into the garage*.)
- What did Zelda's illustration show? (Call on a student. Idea: *Uncle George and Billy being blown into the garage*.)

"No, no, no, no," Mrs. Hudson would say to herself every time she looked at that picture.

But the picture that made Mrs. Hudson most unhappy was the picture for this part of the story: "The birds watched my sisters plant the new garden. They wore red sweaters and perky little caps."

- What did Henry's illustration for that part show? (Call on a student. Idea: *Her sisters dressed in red sweaters and little caps*.)
- What did Zelda's illustration show? (Call on a student. Idea: *The birds dressed in red sweaters and little caps*.)

"No, no, no, no," Mrs. Hudson would say to herself.

But the book sold a lot of copies and made lots of money. It also made Mrs. Hudson even more famous than her first book did.

And everybody thought that she was the funniest writer in the whole world.

EXERCISE 4 TEST

Editing—Capitals and Periods

1. The rest of the lesson is a test. You'll do the whole test and then we'll mark it. Open your workbook to lesson 85 and find part A. ✔

2. I'll read the instructions: Put in capitals and periods. Circle the part of each sentence that names. Do it. Raise your hand when you're finished.

Editing—Past Time

1. Everybody, find part B. ✔

2. Touch the check box below the paragraph. I'll read the check: Do the sentences tell what people did? The **X**s in the box show how many mistakes there are in the paragraph. Count the **X**s and you'll find how many mistakes there are. Then read the paragraph. Fix up any sentences that don't tell what people did. Do it. Raise your hand when you're finished.

Clarity

1. Everybody, find part C. ✔

2. I'll read the instructions: Write the letter of each picture that shows what the sentence says. Do it. Raise your hand when you're finished.

Pronouns—He, She, It

1. Everybody, find part D. ✔

2. I'll read the instructions: Fill in the blanks with **he, she** or **it.** Do it. Raise your hand when you're finished.

3. (When students finish the test, collect their workbooks.)

EXERCISE 5 MARKING THE TEST

1. (Mark the test before the next scheduled language lesson. Use the *Language Arts Workbook Answer Key* to determine acceptable responses.)

2. (Write the number of errors each student made in the test scorebox at the beginning of the test.)

3. (Enter the number of errors each student made on the Summary for Test 8. Reproducible Summary Sheets are at the back of the *Language Arts Teacher's Guide.*)

EXERCISE 6 FEEDBACK ON TEST 8

1. (Return the students' workbooks after they are marked.)

• Everybody, open your workbook to lesson 85.

2. The number I wrote in the scorebox tells how many items you got wrong on the whole test. Raise your hand if I wrote **0, 1** or **2** at the top of your test. **Those are super stars.**

• Raise your hand if I wrote **3** or **4.** Those are pretty good workers.

• If I wrote a number that's more than 4, you're going to have to work harder.

EXERCISE 7 TEST REMEDIES

• (Before beginning lesson 86, provide any necessary remedies. After students complete the exercises specified for a remedy, check their work and give feedback.)

Test Part A Editing—Capitals and Periods

If more than $\frac{1}{4}$ of the students made 2 or more errors in test part A, present the following exercises:

• (Direct students to part A on page 265 of the student workbook.)
  Put in capitals and periods. Circle the part of each sentence that names.

• (Direct students to part B on page 265 of the student workbook.)
  Put in capitals and periods. Circle the part of each sentence that names.

Test Part B Editing—Past Time

If more than $\frac{1}{4}$ of the students made 2 or more errors in test part B, present the following exercises:

• (Direct students to part C on page 265 of the student workbook.)
  Touch the check box at the end of the paragraph.
  I'll read the check: Do the sentences tell what people did?

The **X**s in the box show how many mistakes there are in the paragraph. Count the **X**s and you'll find how many mistakes there are. Then read the paragraph.

Fix up any sentences that do not tell what people did.

- (Direct students to part D on page 266 of the student workbook.)

  Touch the check box at the end of the paragraph.

  I'll read the check: Do the sentences tell what people did?

  The **X**s in the box show how many mistakes there are in the paragraph. Count the **X**s and you'll find how many mistakes there are. Then read the paragraph.

  Fix up any sentences that do not tell what people did.

Test Part C   Clarity

If more than $\frac{1}{4}$ of the students made any errors in test part C, present the following exercises:

- **Lesson 78, Exercise 6, Student Textbook Part E**
- **Lesson 79, Exercise 6, Student Textbook Part E**
- **Lesson 82, Exercise 6, Student Textbook Part E**

Test Part D   Pronouns—He, She, It

If more than $\frac{1}{4}$ of the students made any errors in test part D, present the following exercises:

- (Direct students to part E on page 266 of the student workbook.)

  Fill in the blanks with he, she or it.

- (Direct students to part F on page 266 of the student workbook.)

  Fill in the blanks with he, she or it.

Objectives

- Punctuate sentences (capitals and periods) and identify the subject of sentences in a paragraph. (Exercise 2)
- Indicate the subject and predicate of sentences. (Exercise 3)
- **Write past-time verbs for irregular present-time verbs.** (Exercise 4)
- Write a sentence that states the main thing an illustrated group did. (Exercise 5)
- Construct a paragraph that states the main thing that illustrated characters did. (Exercise 6)

EXERCISE 1 Feedback On Lesson 85

- (Hand back the students' paragraph-writing assignment from lesson 85.)
- Look at what I wrote on your lined paper. Raise your hand if I wrote **super.**
- If you didn't get a **super,** look at the mistakes you made and be more careful next time.

WORKBOOK

EXERCISE 2 Paragraph Editing

Capitals and Periods

1. Everybody, open your workbook to lesson 86 and find part A. ✔
- I'll read the instructions: Put in capitals and periods. Circle the part of each sentence that names. Do it. Raise your hand when you're finished.
  (Observe students and give feedback.)
2. Let's check your work. Make an **X** next to any mistake.
- First sentence: You should have circled **Sandy and her dog.** Sandy and her dog went for a walk, period.
- Next sentence: You should have circled **they.** Capital **T,** They went to the park, period.
- Next sentence: You should have circled **a cat.** Capital **A,** A cat ran in front of them, period.
- Next sentence: You should have circled **the dog.** Capital **T,** The dog started to chase the cat, period.
- Next sentence: You should have circled **the cat.** Capital **T,** The cat ran up a tree, period.
- Next sentence: You should have circled **Sandy.** Sandy took her dog home, period.
3. Raise your hand if you made no mistakes. Great job.
- Everybody else, fix up any mistakes you made in part A.
  (Observe students and give feedback.)

EXERCISE 3 Subject/Predicate

1. Everybody, find part B. ✔
   For each sentence in part B, you're going to circle the part that names and underline the part that tells more. Do it now. Raise your hand when you're finished.
   (Observe students and give feedback.)
2. Let's check your work. Make an **X** next to any item you missed.
- Sentence 1. My best friend and my sister helped me. Say that sentence. (Signal.) *My best friend and my sister helped me.*
  What part names? (Signal.) *My best friend and my sister.*
  What part tells more? (Signal.) *Helped me.*
- Sentence 2. She had two dollars. Say that sentence. (Signal.) *She had two dollars.*
  What part names? (Signal.) *She.*
  What part tells more? (Signal.) *Had two dollars.*
- Sentence 3. My little sister was sick. Say that sentence. (Signal.) *My little sister was sick.*
  What part names? (Signal.) *My little sister.*
  What part tells more? (Signal.) *Was sick.*
- Sentence 4. The horse fell over. Say that sentence. (Signal.) *The horse fell over.*

What part names? (Signal.) *The horse.*
What part tells more? (Signal.) *Fell over.*

- Sentence 5. He saw a big bird next to the house. Say that sentence. (Signal.) *He saw a big bird next to the house.*
What part names? (Signal.) *He.*
What part tells more? (Signal.) *Saw a big bird next to the house.*

- Sentence 6. A dog and a cat slept with James. Say that sentence. (Signal.) *A dog and a cat slept with James.*
What part names? (Signal.) *A dog and a cat.*
What part tells more? (Signal.) *Slept with James.*

3. Raise your hand if you made no mistakes. Great job.

- Everybody else, fix up any mistakes you made in part B.
(Observe students and give feedback.)

EXERCISE 4   Past Time

Irregular Verbs

1. Everybody, pencils down. Find part C. ✔
These are new words. They tell what somebody **does.** You're going to tell me what somebody **did.**

2. Everybody, touch number 1.
Gets tells what somebody does. What word tells what somebody did? (Signal.) *Got.*

- Rides. What word tells what somebody did? (Signal.) *Rode.*

- Drinks. What word tells what somebody did? (Signal.) *Drank.*

- Teaches. What word tells what somebody did? (Signal.) *Taught.*

- Holds. What word tells what somebody did? (Signal.) *Held.*

3. For words 6 through 10. I'll say the word that tells what somebody **does.** You'll say the word that tells what somebody **did.**

4. Rides. Everybody, tell me what somebody did. (Signal.) *Rode.*

- Teaches. Tell me what somebody did. (Signal.) *Taught.*

- Gets. Tell me what somebody did. (Signal.) *Got.*

- Holds. Tell me what somebody did. (Signal.) *Held.*

- Drinks. Tell me what somebody did. (Signal.) *Drank.*

- (Repeat step 4 until firm.)

5. Do words 6 through 10. Next to each word, write the word that tells what somebody did. Raise your hand when you're finished. (Observe students and give feedback.)

6. Check your work. Make an **X** for any mistake.

- Rides. What word tells what somebody did? (Signal.) *Rode.*

- Spell **rode.** (Signal.) *R-o-d-e.*

- Teaches. What word tells what somebody did? (Signal.) *Taught.*

- Spell **taught.** (Signal.) *T-a-u-g-h-t.*

- Gets. What word tells what somebody did? (Signal.) *Got.*

- Spell **got.** (Signal.) *G-o-t.*

- Holds. What word tells what somebody did? (Signal.) *Held.*

- Spell **held.** (Signal.) *H-e-l-d.*

- Drinks. What word tells what somebody did? (Signal.) *Drank.*

- Spell **drank.** (Signal.) *D-r-a-n-k.*

7. Raise your hand if you made no mistakes. Great job.

- Everybody else, fix up any mistakes you made in part C.
(Observe students and give feedback.)

LINED PAPER • TEXTBOOK

EXERCISE 5   Main Idea

Groups

1. Everybody, take out a sheet of lined paper and write your name on the top line. Number your paper 1 and 2. Raise your hand when you're finished.

- Everybody, pencils down. Open your textbook to lesson 21 and find part D. ✔

2. These pictures show groups. You're going to write a good sentence for each group. A good sentence does two things. First, it names the group. Then it tells the main thing the group did. Remember, first it names. Then it tells the main thing.

3. Everybody, touch picture 1.
   Name that group. (Signal.) *Girls.*
- Raise your hand when you can say a sentence that reports on the main thing the girls did. (Call on several students. Praise sentences such as: *The girls played basketball.* For each good sentence:) Everybody, say that sentence.
4. Everybody, touch picture 2.
   Name that group. (Signal.) *Clowns.*
- Raise your hand when you can say a sentence that reports on the main thing the clowns did. (Call on several students. Praise sentences such as: *The clowns cleaned an elephant; The clowns washed an elephant.* For each good sentence:) Everybody, say that sentence.
5. Touch the words in the vocabulary box as I read them: **cleaned, elephant, basketball, washed.** Be sure to spell those words correctly if you use them.
6. Write a good sentence for each picture. Remember, first name the group. Then tell the main thing the group did. You have 3 minutes. Raise your hand when you're finished.
   (Observe students and give feedback.)
7. (After 3 minutes, say:) Stop writing.
- (Call on several students to read their sentence for picture 1. Praise sentences such as: *The girls played basketball.*)
- (Call on several students to read their sentence for picture 2. Praise sentences such as: *The clowns washed the elephant.*)
8. Everybody, make 2 check boxes under your sentences.
9. Here's check 1: Does each sentence begin with a capital and end with a period? Read each sentence for check 1. Fix it up if it's not right. Then make a check in box 1. Raise your hand when you're finished. (Observe students and give feedback.)
10. Here's check 2: Does each sentence tell the main thing the group did? Read over each sentence for check 2. Fix it up if it's not right. Then make a check in box 2. Raise your hand when you're finished. (Observe students and give feedback.)
11. Pretty soon you'll be writing whole paragraphs about groups.

EXERCISE 6   Paragraph Writing

Groups

1. Everybody, find part E in your textbook. ✔
2. Touch the words in the vocabulary box as I read them: **fried, poured, potato, soup, pieces, hamburgers, pot, sliced, fire.** Be sure to spell those words correctly if you use them.
3. I'll read the instructions: Write a paragraph. Copy the sentence that tells the main thing the group did. Then write three more sentences. Write one sentence about each person. Tell the main thing each person did.
4. Everybody, touch Ramon.
- Raise your hand when you can say a sentence that reports on the main thing Ramon did. (Call on several students. Praise sentences such as: *Ramon cooked hamburgers in a pan.* For each good sentence:) Everybody, say that sentence.
5. Everybody, touch Carl.
- Raise your hand when you can say a sentence that reports on the main thing Carl did. (Call on several students. Praise sentences such as: *Carl poured soup from a can into a pot.* For each good sentence:) Everybody, say that sentence.
6. Everybody, touch Gary.
- Raise your hand when you can say a sentence that reports on the main thing Gary did. (Call on several students. Praise sentences such as: *Gary sliced potatoes with a knife.* For each good sentence:) Everybody, say that sentence.
7. The sentence that tells the main thing the group did is written under the picture. Everybody, read that sentence. (Signal.) *Three cowboys made dinner.*
- Everybody, copy that sentence. Remember to indent. Raise your hand when you're finished.
   (Observe students and give feedback.)

8. Now you're going to write a sentence about each of the cowboys. Touch Gary. Listen: Write a sentence that names Gary and tells the main thing he did. Start that sentence right after the period of the first sentence. Raise your hand when you're finished.
(Observe students and give feedback.)

9. Touch Carl in the picture.
Write a sentence that names Carl and tells the main thing he did. Remember to start that sentence right after the period of the last sentence. Raise your hand when you're finished.
(Observe students and give feedback.)

10. Now write a sentence that names Ramon and tells the main thing he did. Remember to start that sentence right after the period. Raise your hand when you're finished.
(Observe students and give feedback.)

11. I'm going to call on several students to read their paragraph. Let's see who the good listeners are. Each paragraph starts with the sentence about the group. Then it should have a sentence about each of the cowboys. Each of these sentences should tell the main thing that person did.
• If you hear a mistake, raise your hand. If a sentence is missing, raise your hand. If a sentence doesn't tell the main thing one of the cowboys did, raise your hand. Listen carefully.

12. (Call on a student:) Read your paragraph. When you read it, stop at the end of each sentence so everybody can think about whether that sentence is right. (Praise the paragraph if it has no mistakes.)

13. (Call on several other students to read their paragraph. Praise good paragraphs.)

14. You're going to fix up your paragraph before you hand it in. Make 2 check boxes under your paragraph. ✔

15. Here's check 1: Does each sentence begin with a capital and end with a period? Read each sentence you wrote and fix up any mistakes. Then make a check in box 1. Raise your hand when you're finished with check 1.
(Observe students and give feedback.)

16. Here's check 2: Does each sentence tell the main thing the person did? Make sure you have a sentence for each person and make sure it tells the main thing the person did. Then make a check in box 2. Raise your hand when you're finished with check 2.
(Observe students and give feedback.)

17. Raise your hand if you think you'll get a **super** paper. We'll see next time.

Note:

• Collect the students' workbooks and papers.

• Check the students' work before the next language period. Mark any mistakes.

• Write **super** on work that has all mistakes corrected. Write **good** or **pretty good** on work that has only 1 or 2 mistakes.

Objectives

- Punctuate sentences (capitals and periods) and identify the subject of sentences in a paragraph. (Exercise 2)
- Indicate the subject and predicate of sentences. (Exercise 3)
- Change 2-word verbs in a paragraph to 1-word past-time verbs. (Exercise 4)
- Write past-time verbs for irregular present-time verbs. (Exercise 5)
- Write a sentence that states the main thing an illustrated group did. (Exercise 6)
- Construct a paragraph that states the main thing that illustrated characters did. (Exercise 7)

EXERCISE 1   Feedback On Lesson 86

- (Hand back the students' work from lesson 86.)
- Look at what I wrote on your lined paper. Raise your hand if I wrote **super.**
- If you didn't get a **super,** look at the mistakes you made and be more careful next time.

WORKBOOK

EXERCISE 2   Paragraph Editing

Capitals and Periods

1. Everybody, open your workbook to lesson 87 and find part A. ✔
- I'll read the instructions: Put in capitals and periods. Circle the part of each sentence that names. Do it. Raise your hand when you're finished.
  (Observe students and give feedback.)
2. Let's check your work. Make an **X** next to any mistake.
- First sentence: You should have circled **a woman.** A woman bought a new bike for her son, period.
- Next sentence: You should have circled **it.** Capital **I,** It had big tires, period.
- Next sentence: You should have circled **the boy.** Capital **T,** The boy liked the bike, period.
- Next sentence: You should have circled **his mother.** Capital **H,** His mother showed him how to ride the bike, period.
- Next sentence: You should have circled **he.** Capital **H,** He rode it to school, period.

- Next sentence: You should have circled **his teacher.** Capital **H,** His teacher let him show the bike to the class, period.
3. Raise your hand if you made no mistakes. Great job.
- Everybody else, fix up any mistakes you made in part A.
  (Observe students and give feedback.)

EXERCISE 3   Subject

1. Pencils down. You're going to learn about the **subject** of a sentence. Listen: The **subject** of a sentence is the part of the sentence that names.
   Everybody, what do we call the part of the sentence that names? (Signal.) *The subject.*
2. Listen: Six little dogs barked loudly. Everybody, what's the part that names? (Signal.) *Six little dogs.*
- So what's the subject of that sentence? (Signal.) *Six little dogs.*
- Listen: A boy and a girl walked in the park. What's the subject of that sentence? (Signal.) *A boy and a girl.*
- Listen: They went home. What's the subject of that sentence? (Signal.) *They.*
- (Repeat step 2 until firm.)
3. Listen: That shirt is beautiful. What's the subject of that sentence? (Signal.) *That shirt.*
- Listen: My mother and her friend talked on the phone. What's the subject of that sentence? (Signal.) *My mother and her friend.*
- Listen: Her face and her hands got dirty. What's the subject of that sentence? (Signal.) *Her face and her hands.*
- (Repeat step 3 until firm.)

4. Find part B. ✔
   I'll read the instructions: Circle the subject. Underline the part that tells more. Do it now. Raise your hand when you're finished. (Observe students and give feedback.)

5. Let's check your work. Make an **X** next to any item you missed.

- Sentence 1. Three older boys went to the store. Say that sentence. (Signal.) *Three older boys went to the store.*
  What part names? (Signal.) *Three older boys.*
  What part tells more? (Signal.) *Went to the store.*

- Sentence 2. A horse and a dog went to a stream. Say that sentence. (Signal.) *A horse and a dog went to a stream.* (Signal.)
  What part names? (Signal.) *A horse and a dog.*
  What part tells more? (Signal.) *Went to a stream.*

- Sentence 3. A man sat on a log. Say that sentence. (Signal.) *A man sat on a log.*
  What part names? (Signal.) *A man.*
  What part tells more? (Signal.) *Sat on a log.*

- Sentence 4. They sat on a bench. Say that sentence. (Signal.) *They sat on a bench.*
  What part names? (Signal.) *They.*
  What part tells more? (Signal.) *Sat on a bench.*

- Sentence 5. My friend and his mother were hungry. Say that sentence. (Signal.) *My friend and his mother were hungry.*
  What part names? (Signal.) *My friend and his mother.*
  What part tells more? (Signal.) *Were hungry.*

- Sentence 6. My hands and my face got dirty. Say that sentence. (Signal.) *My hands and my face got dirty.*
  What part names? (Signal.) *My hands and my face.*
  What part tells more? (Signal.) *Got dirty.*

6. Raise your hand if you made no mistakes. Great job.

- Everybody else, fix up any mistakes you made in part B.
  (Observe students and give feedback.)

EXERCISE 4   Paragraph Editing

Past Time

1. Everybody, find part C. ✔
   Touch the check box below the paragraph.

2. I'll read the check: Does each sentence tell what someone or something did? The **X**s in the box show how many mistakes there are in the paragraph. Count the **X**s and you'll know how many mistakes you should find. Then read the paragraph. Fix up any sentence that does not tell what someone or something did. Raise your hand when you're finished.
   (Observe students and give feedback.)

3. Let's check your work. Make an **X** next to anything you missed.

- First sentence: Mr. Smith and his son are going to the circus. Does that sentence tell what they did? (Signal.) *No.*

- Say the sentence that tells what Mr. Smith and his son did. (Signal.) *Mr. Smith and his son went to the circus.*

- Next sentence: They looked at lions and tigers. Does that sentence tell what they did? (Signal.) *Yes.*
  So you didn't cross out anything.

- Next sentence: A lion tamer had a whip in his hand. Is that sentence correct? (Signal.) *Yes.*
  So you didn't cross out anything.

- Next sentence: His whip is making a big noise. Does that sentence tell what his whip did? (Signal.) *No.*

- Say the sentence that tells what his whip did. (Signal.) *His whip made a big noise.*

- Next sentence: One lion is jumping through a hoop. Does that sentence tell what one lion did? (Signal.) *No.*

- Say the sentence that tells what one lion did. (Signal.) *One lion jumped through a hoop.*

- Next sentence: Mr. Smith and his son are having a good time. Is that sentence correct? (Signal.) *No.*

- Say the correct sentence. (Signal.) *Mr. Smith and his son had a good time.*

4. Raise your hand if you made no mistakes. Great job.

- Everybody else, fix up any mistakes you made in part C.
  (Observe students and give feedback.)

EXERCISE 5   Past Time

Irregular Verbs

1. Everybody, pencils down. Find part D. ✔

2. Everybody, touch number 1.
   Rides tells what somebody does. **Rode** tells what somebody did.
- Holds. What word tells what somebody did? (Signal.) *Held.*
- Teaches. What word tells what somebody did? (Signal.) *Taught.*
- Drinks. What word tells what somebody did? (Signal.) *Drank.*
- Gets. What word tells what somebody did? (Signal.) *Got.*
3. Do words 6 through 10. Next to each word, write the word that tells what somebody did. Raise your hand when you're finished. (Observe students and give feedback.)
4. Let's check your work. Make an **X** for any mistake.
- Teaches. What word tells what somebody did? (Signal.) *Taught.*
- Spell **taught.** (Signal.) *T-a-u-g-h-t.*
- Holds. What word tells what somebody did? (Signal.) *Held.*
- Spell **held.** (Signal.) *H-e-l-d.*
- Gets. What word tells what somebody did? (Signal.) *Got.*
- Spell **got.** (Signal.) *G-o-t.*
- Rides. What word tells what somebody did? (Signal.) *Rode.*
- Spell **rode** (Signal.) *R-o-d-e.*
- Drinks. What word tells what somebody did? (Signal.) *Drank.*
- Spell **drank** (Signal.) *D-r-a-n-k.*
5. Raise your hand if you made no mistakes. Great job.
- Everybody else, fix up any mistakes you made in part D. (Observe students and give feedback.)

LINED PAPER • TEXTBOOK

EXERCISE 6   Main Idea

Groups

1. Everybody, take out a sheet of lined paper and write your name on the top line. Number your paper 1 and 2. Raise your hand when you're finished.
- Everybody, pencils down. Open your textbook to lesson 87 and find part E. ✔
2. These pictures show groups. You're going to write a good sentence for each group. I'll read what it says in the box: A good sentence does two things. First, it names the group. Then it tells the main thing the group did. Remember, first it names. Then it tells the main thing.
3. Everybody, touch picture 1.
   That picture shows a group of children.
- Raise your hand when you can say a sentence that reports on the main thing the children did. (Call on several students. Praise sentences such as: *The children cleaned the room.* For each good sentence:) Everybody, say that sentence.
4. Everybody, touch picture 2.
- Raise your hand when you can say a sentence that reports on the main thing the boys did. (Call on several students. Praise sentences such as: *The boys walked across the stream. The boys crossed the stream.* For each good sentence:) Everybody, say that sentence.
5. Touch the words in the vocabulary box as I read them: **stream, room, cleaned, crossed.** Be sure to spell those words correctly if you use them.
6. Write a good sentence for each picture. Remember, first name the group. Then tell the main thing the group did. You have 3 minutes. Raise your hand when you're finished. (Observe students and give feedback.)
7. (After 3 minutes, say:) Stop writing.
- (Call on several students to read their sentence for picture 1. Praise sentences such as: *The children cleaned the room.*)
- (Call on several students to read their sentence for picture 2. Praise sentences such as: *The boys crossed the stream.*)
8. Everybody, make 2 check boxes under your sentences. ✔
9. Here's check 1: Does each sentence begin with a capital and end with a period? Read each sentence for check 1. Fix it up if it's not right. Then make a check in box 1. Raise your hand when you're finished.

(Observe students and give feedback.)

10. Here's check 2: Does each sentence tell the main thing the group did? Read over each sentence for check 2. Fix it up if it's not right. Then make a check in box 2. Raise your hand when you're finished. (Observe students and give feedback.)

EXERCISE 7 Paragraph Writing

Groups

1. Everybody, find part F in your textbook. ✔
2. Everybody, touch the words in the vocabulary box as I read them: **bicycle, balanced, through, nose, its, ball.** Be sure to spell those words correctly if you use them.
3. I'll read the instructions: Write a paragraph. Copy the sentence that tells the main thing the group did. Then write three more sentences. Write one sentence about each animal. Tell the main thing each animal did.
- The sentence that is already written tells the main thing the group did. I'll read that sentence: Circus animals did tricks.
4. Everybody, touch the seal.
- Raise your hand when you can say a sentence that reports on the main thing a seal did. (Call on several students. Praise sentences such as: *A seal balanced a ball on its nose.* For each good sentence:) Everybody, say that sentence.
5. Everybody, touch the bear.
- Raise your hand when you can say a sentence that reports on the main thing a bear did. (Call on several students. Praise sentences such as: *A bear rode a bicycle.* For each good sentence:) Everybody, say that sentence.
6. Everybody, touch the poodle.
- Raise your hand when you can say a sentence that reports on the main thing a poodle did. (Call on several students. Praise sentences such as: *A poodle jumped through a hoop.* For each good sentence:) Everybody, say that sentence.

7. Your turn: Copy the sentence that tells the main thing the group did. Remember to indent. Then write three more sentences. Write one sentence about each animal. Tell the main thing each animal did. You have 5 minutes. Raise your hand when you're finished. (Observe students and give feedback.)
8. (After 5 minutes, say:) Stop writing. I'm going to call on several students to read their paragraph. If you hear a mistake, raise your hand. Listen carefully.
9. (Call on a student:) Read your paragraph. When you read it, stop at the end of each sentence so everybody can think about whether that sentence is right. (Praise the paragraph if it has no mistakes.)
10. (Call on several other students to read their paragraph. Praise good paragraphs.)
11. You're going to fix up your paragraph before you hand it in. Make 2 check boxes under your paragraph.
12. Here's check 1: Does each sentence begin with a capital and end with a period? Read each sentence you wrote and fix up any mistakes. Then make a check in box 1. Raise your hand when you're finished with check 1. (Observe students and give feedback.)
13. Here's check 2: Does each sentence you made up report on the main thing the animal did? Make sure you have a sentence for each animal and make sure it tells the main thing the animal did. Then make a check in box 2. Raise your hand when you're finished. (Observe students and give feedback.)
14. Who thinks they'll get a **super** paper? We'll see next time.

> **Note:**
> - Collect the students' workbooks and papers.
> - Check the students' work before the next language period. Mark any mistakes.
> - Write **super** on work that has all mistakes corrected. Write **good** or **pretty good** on work that has only 1 or 2 mistakes.

Objectives

- Indicate the subject and predicate of sentences. (Exercise 2)
- Punctuate sentences (capitals and periods) and identify the subject of sentences in a paragraph. (Exercise 3)
- Write past-time verbs for irregular present-time verbs. (Exercise 4)
- Write a sentence that states the main thing an illustrated group did. (Exercise 5)
- Construct a paragraph that states the main thing that illustrated characters did. (Exercise 6)
- **Identify sentences that tell about all of the pictures, two of the pictures and one of the pictures. (Exercise 7)**

EXERCISE 1 Feedback On Lesson 87

- (Hand back the students' work from lesson 87.)
- Look at what I wrote on your lined paper. Raise your hand if I wrote **super.**
- If you didn't get a **super,** look at the mistakes you made and be more careful next time.

WORKBOOK

EXERCISE 2 SUBJECT

1. Remember, the **subject** of a sentence is the part of the sentence that names. Everybody, what do we call the part of the sentence that names? (Signal.) *The subject.*
2. Listen: That train went very fast. Everybody, what's the subject of that sentence? (Signal.) *That train.*
   - Listen: They ate breakfast with Bill. What's the subject of that sentence? (Signal.) *They.*
   - Listen: She had a new coat. What's the subject of that sentence? (Signal.) *She.*
   - (Repeat step 2 until firm.)
3. Everybody, open your workbook to lesson 88 and find part A. ✔
   - I'll read the instructions: Circle the subject of each sentence. Underline the part that tells more. Do it now. Raise your hand when you're finished.
     (Observe students and give feedback.)
4. Let's check your work. Make an **X** next to any item you missed.
   - Sentence 1. What's the subject? (Signal.) *A jet airplane.*

- What part tells more? (Signal.) *Made a lot of noise.*
- Sentence 2. What's the subject? (Signal.) *A man and his dog.*
- What part tells more? (Signal.) *Went walking.*
- Sentence 3. What's the subject? (Signal.) *He.*
- What part tells more? (Signal.) *Ate lunch in the office.*
- Sentence 4. What's the subject? (Signal.) *My brother and his friend.*
- What part tells more? (Signal.) *Played in the park.*
- Sentence 5. What's the subject? (Signal.) *A little cat.*
- What part tells more? (Signal.) *Drank milk.*
5. Raise your hand if you made no mistakes. Great job.
- Everybody else, fix up any mistakes you made in part A.
  (Observe students and give feedback.)

EXERCISE 3 Paragraph Editing

Capitals and Periods

1. Everybody find part B. ✔
   I'll read the instructions: Put in capitals and periods. Circle the subject of each sentence. Do it. Raise your hand when you're finished.
   (Observe students and give feedback.)
2. Let's check your work. Make an **X** next to any mistake.
- First sentence: You should have circled **three workers.** Three workers built a dog house, period.

- Next sentence: You should have circled **a woman.** Capital **A,** A woman nailed boards together, period.
- Next sentence: You should have circled **she.** Capital **S,** She used a big hammer, period.
- Next sentence: You should have circled **a young man.** Capital **A,** A young man put a roof on the dog house, period.
- Next sentence: You should have circled **the workers.** Capital **T,** The workers finished the dog house in two hours, period.
3. Raise your hand if you made no mistakes. Great job.
- Everybody else, fix up any mistakes you made in part B.
  (Observe students and give feedback.)

EXERCISE 4 Past Time

Irregular Verbs

1. Everybody, find part C. ✔
   The words in part C tell what somebody does. You're going to write the words that tell what somebody did.
2. Word 1 is **drinks.** What word are you going to write? (Signal.) *Drank.*
- Write it. Spell it correctly. Then write the other words that tell what someone did. Raise your hand when you're finished.
  (Observe students and give feedback.)
3. Let's check your work. Make an **X** for any mistakes. I'll say the word that tells what somebody does. You'll say the word that tells what somebody did.
- Word 1: Drinks. Say the word that tells what somebody did. (Signal.) *Drank.*
- Spell **drank.** (Signal.) *D-r-a-n-k.*
- Word 2: Holds. Say the word that tells what somebody did. (Signal.) *Held.*
- Spell **held.** (Signal.) *H-e-l-d.*
- Word 3: Rides. Say the word that tells what somebody did. (Signal.) *Rode.*
- Spell **rode.** (Signal.) *R-o-d-e.*
- Word 4: Gets. Say the word that tells what somebody did. (Signal.) *Got.*
- Spell **got.** (Signal.) *G-o-t.*
- Word 5: Teaches. Say the word that tells what somebody did. (Signal.) *Taught.*
- Spell **taught.** (Signal.) *T-a-u-g-h-t.*
4. Raise your hand if you made no mistakes. Great job.

- Everybody else, fix up any mistakes you made in part C.
  (Observe students and give feedback.)

EXERCISE 5 Main Idea

Groups

1. Everybody, take out a sheet of lined paper and write your name on the top line. Number your paper 1 and 2. Raise your hand when you're finished.
- Everybody, pencils down. Open your textbook to lesson 88 and find part D. ✔
2. These pictures show groups. You're going to write a good sentence for each group.
3. Everybody, touch picture 1.
   Name that group. (Signal.) *Girls.*
- Raise your hand when you can say a sentence that reports on the main thing the girls did. (Call on several students. Praise sentences such as: *The girls played in the pool.* For each good sentence:) Everybody, say that sentence.
- Everybody, touch picture 2.
   Name that group. (Signal.) *Children.*
- Raise your hand when you can say a sentence that reports on the main thing the children did. (Call on several students. Praise sentences such as: *The children opened presents.* For each good sentence:) Everybody, say that sentence.
4. Touch the words in the vocabulary box as I read them: **opened, presents, water, pool, their.** Be sure to spell those words correctly if you use them.
5. Write a good sentence for each picture. Remember, first name the group. Then tell the main thing the group did. You have 3 minutes. Raise your hand when you're finished.
   (Observe students and give feedback.)

6. (After 3 minutes, say:) Stop writing.
- (Call on several students to read their sentence for picture 1. Praise sentences such as: *The girls played in the pool.*)
- (Call on several students to read their sentence for picture 2. Praise sentences such as: *The children opened their presents.*)
7. Everybody, make 2 check boxes under your sentences.
8. Here's check 1: Does each sentence begin with a capital and end with a period? Read each sentence for check 1. Fix it up if it's not right. Then make a check in box 1. Raise your hand when you're finished. (Observe students and give feedback.)
9. Here's check 2: Does each sentence tell the main thing the group did? Read over each sentence for check 2. Fix it up if it's not right. Then make a check in box 2. Raise your hand when you're finished. (Observe students and give feedback.)

EXERCISE 6 Paragraph Writing

Groups

1. Everybody, find part E in your textbook. ✔ I'll read the instructions: Write a paragraph that reports on the picture. Begin with a good sentence about the janitors. Then write one sentence about each person.
2. Everybody, touch Joe.
- Raise your hand when you can say a sentence that reports on the main thing Joe did. (Call on several students. Praise sentences such as: *Joe swept the floor.* For each good sentence:) Everybody, say that sentence.
3. Everybody, touch Ben.
- Raise your hand when you can say a sentence that reports on the main thing Ben did. (Call on several students. Praise sentences such as: *Ben put a chair on a desk.* For each good sentence:) Everybody, say that sentence.

4. Everybody, touch Pam.
- Raise your hand when you can say a sentence that reports on the main thing Pam did. (Call on several students. Praise sentences such as: *Pam cleaned the chalkboard.* For each good sentence:) Everybody, say that sentence.
5. Everybody, touch the words in the vocabulary box as I read them: **chalkboard, desk, chair, cleaned, classroom, janitors.** Be sure to spell those words correctly if you use them.
6. Start your paragraph. Write a good sentence about the group and then stop. Name the group and tell the main thing the group did. Raise your hand when you're finished.
(Observe students and give feedback.)
- (Call on several students to read their sentence. Praise sentences such as: *The janitors cleaned the classroom.*)
7. Everybody, now write the rest of your paragraph. Write one sentence about each janitor. Tell the main thing each janitor did. You have 5 minutes. Raise your hand when you're finished.
(Observe students and give feedback.)
8. (After 5 minutes, say:) Stop writing. I'm going to call on several students to read their paragraph. If you hear a mistake, raise your hand. Listen carefully.
9. (Call on a student:) Read your paragraph. When you read it, stop at the end of each sentence so everybody can think about whether that sentence is right. (Praise the paragraph if it has no mistakes.)
10. (Call on several other students to read their paragraph. Praise good paragraphs.)
11. Everybody, make 3 check boxes under your paragraph.
12. Here's check 1: Does each sentence begin with a capital and end with a period? Read each sentence you wrote and fix up any mistakes. Then make a check in box 1. Raise your hand when you're finished with check 1.
(Observe students and give feedback.)

13. Here's check 2: Does the first sentence tell the main thing the group did? Check your first sentence. When it tells the main thing the group did, make a check in box 2. Raise your hand when you're finished with check 2.
(Observe students and give feedback.)

14. Here's check 3: Does each of the other sentences report on the main thing a person did? Make sure you have a sentence for each person and make sure it tells the main thing that person did. Then make a check in box 3. Raise your hand when you're finished with check 3.
(Observe students and give feedback.)

EXERCISE 7 Clarity

1. Skip a line on your paper. Then number your paper 1 through 3. Raise your hand when you're finished.
- Everybody, pencils down. Find part F in your textbook. ✔

2. Under the pictures are sentences that tell about the pictures. Touch the sentences.
- I'll read the sentences.
  He pushed a vehicle.
  She pushed a vehicle.
  A person pushed a vehicle.

3. One sentence tells about **all** the pictures. Raise your hand when you know which sentence tells about **all** the pictures.
- Everybody, say the sentence that tells about all the pictures. (Signal.) *A person pushed a vehicle.*
- One sentence tells about **only one** picture. Raise your hand when you know which sentence tells about **only one** picture.
- Everybody, say the sentence that tells about only one picture. (Signal.) *She pushed a vehicle.*
- One of the sentences tells about **two** pictures. Raise your hand when you know which sentence tells about **two** pictures.
- Everybody, say the sentence that tells about two pictures. (Signal.) *He pushed a vehicle.*
- (Repeat step 3 until firm.)

4. You're going to copy the right sentence for each item above the pictures. I'll read the items.

- Touch item 1.
  Copy the sentence that tells about all the pictures.
- Touch item 2.
  Copy the sentence that tells about only one picture.
- Touch item 3.
  Copy the sentence that tells about two pictures.
- Copy the correct sentence for each item. Raise your hand when you're finished.
  (Observe students and give feedback.)

5. Let's check your work. Make an **X** next to any sentence you missed.
- Item 1: Copy the sentence that tells about all the pictures. Everybody, read that sentence. (Signal.) *A person pushed a vehicle.*
- Item 2: Copy the sentence that tells about only one picture. Everybody, read that sentence. (Signal.) *She pushed a vehicle.*
- Item 3: Copy the sentence that tells about two pictures. Everybody, read that sentence. (Signal.) *He pushed a vehicle.*

6. Raise your hand if you copied all the right sentences. Great job.
- Everybody else, fix up any mistakes you made in part F.
  (Observe students and give feedback.)

> **Note:**
> - Collect the students' workbooks and papers.
> - Check the students' work before the next language period. Mark any mistakes.
> - Write **super** on work that has all mistakes corrected. Write **good** or **pretty good** on work that has only 1 or 2 mistakes.

Objectives

- Punctuate sentences (capitals and periods) in a paragraph. (Exercise 2)
- Indicate the subject and predicate of sentences. (Exercise 3)
- Use appropriate pronouns in a short passage. (Exercise 4)
- Identify sentences that tell about all of the pictures, two of the pictures and one of the pictures. (Exercise 5)
- Construct a paragraph that states the main thing that illustrated characters did. (Exercise 6)
- Write a sentence that states the main thing an illustrated group did. (Exercise 7)

EXERCISE 1   Feedback On Lesson 88

- (Hand back the students' work from lesson 88.)
- Look at what I wrote on your lined paper. Raise your hand if I wrote **super.**
- If you didn't get a **super,** look at the mistakes you made and be more careful next time.

WORKBOOK

EXERCISE 2   Paragraph Editing

Capitals and Periods

1. Everybody, open your workbook to lesson 89 and find part A. ✔
- Some sentences in part A do not begin with a capital. Some sentences do not end with a period. You have to put in the missing capitals and periods.
2. I'll read the first sentence: Every student in the class read a book. Is anything wrong with that sentence? (Signal.) *Yes.*
- (Call on a student:) What's wrong with that sentence? (Idea: *The sentence doesn't start with a capital.*)
3. Everybody, fix up the first sentence. Then read the rest of the paragraph. Fix up any sentence that does not begin with a capital and end with a period. Raise your hand when you're finished.
(Observe students and give feedback.)
4. Let's check your work. Make an **X** next to any item you missed.
- First sentence: Capital **E,** Every student in the class read a book.

- Next sentence: Tom and Alice read a book about animals, period.
- Next sentence: Capital **T,** They learned about animals that live in different parts of the world.
- Next sentence: Two students read a book about roses, period.
- Next sentence: Capital **T,** That book told how to take care of roses.
5. Raise your hand if you made no mistakes. Great job.
- Everybody else, fix up any mistakes you made in part A.
(Observe students and give feedback.)

EXERCISE 3   Subject/Predicate

1. Everybody, pencils down. Find part B. ✔
2. You've learned about the part of a sentence that names. Everybody, what do we call the part that names? (Signal.) *The subject.*
- Listen: The part that tells more is the predicate. What's the part that tells more? (Signal.) *The predicate.*
Yes, the predicate.
3. I'll read sentence 1: Five cats were on the roof. What's the **subject** of that sentence? (Signal.) *Five cats.*
- Listen: Five cats were on the roof. What's the **predicate** of that sentence? (Signal.) *Were on the roof.*
Yes, were on the roof.
- Sentence 2: They read two funny books. What's the subject? (Signal.) *They.*
- What's the predicate? (Signal.) *Read two funny books.*
- (Repeat step 3 until firm.)

4. The instructions for part B say to circle the subject and underline the predicate for each sentence. Do it now. Raise your hand when you're finished.
(Observe students and give feedback.)

5. Let's check your work. Make an **X** next to any item you missed.
- Sentence 1: What's the subject? (Signal.) *Five cats.*
- What's the predicate? (Signal.) *Were on the roof.*
- Sentence 2. What's the subject? (Signal.) *They.*
- What's the predicate? (Signal.) *Read two funny books.*
- Sentence 3. What's the subject? (Signal.) *A red bird.*
- What's the predicate? (Signal.) *Landed on a roof.*
- Sentence 4. What's the subject? (Signal.) *A dog and a cat.*
- What's the predicate? (Signal.) *Played in their yard.*
- Sentence 5. What's the subject? (Signal.) *It.*
- What's the predicate? (Signal.) *Stopped.*

6. Raise your hand if you got no items wrong. Great job.
- Everybody else, fix up any mistakes you made in part B.
(Observe students and give feedback.)

EXERCISE 4 Pronouns

He, She, It

1. Everybody, find part C. ✔
Each item tells what the same person or thing did. Start the second sentence in each item with **he, she** or **it**. Remember to start each sentence with a capital. Raise your hand when you're finished.
(Observe students and give feedback.)

2. Let's check your work. Make an **X** next to any item you missed.
- I'll read the sentences in item 1: My grandmother loves to walk. Capital **S,** She walks five miles every day.
- I'll read the sentences for item 2: Her brother is ten years old. Capital **H,** He is in the fifth grade.
- I'll read the sentences in item 3: Our plane will leave at four o'clock. Capital **I,** It is going to China.

3. Raise your hand if you made no mistakes. Great job.
- Everybody else, fix up any mistakes you made in part C.
(Observe students and give feedback.)

LINED PAPER • TEXTBOOK

EXERCISE 5 Clarity

1. Everybody, take out a sheet of lined paper and write your name on the top line. Number your paper 1 through 3. Raise your hand when you're finished.
- Everybody, pencils down. Open your textbook to lesson 89 and find part D. ✔

2. Under the pictures are sentences that tell about the pictures. Touch the sentences.
- I'll read the sentences.
A person sat on an animal.
He sat on an animal.
Melissa sat on an animal.

3. You're going to copy the right sentence for each item above the pictures. I'll read the items.
- Touch item 1.
Copy the sentence that tells about two pictures.
- Touch item 2.
Copy the sentence that tells about all the pictures.
- Touch item 3.
Copy the sentence that tells about only one picture.
- Copy the correct sentence for each item. Raise your hand when you're finished.
(Observe students and give feedback.)

4. Let's check your work. Make an **X** next to any item you missed.
- Item 1: Copy the sentence that tells about two pictures. Everybody, read that sentence. (Signal.) *Melissa sat on an animal.*
- Item 2: Copy the sentence that tells about all the pictures. Everybody, read that sentence. (Signal.) *A person sat on an animal.*
- Item 3: Copy the sentence that tells about only one picture. Everybody, read that sentence. (Signal.) *He sat on an animal.*

5. Raise your hand if you copied all the right sentences. Great job.
- Everybody else, fix up any mistakes you made in part D.
(Observe students and give feedback.)

EXERCISE 6   Paragraph Writing

Groups

1. Everybody, find part E in your textbook. ✔
   I'll read the instructions: Write a paragraph
   that reports on the picture. Begin with a
   good sentence about the gardeners. Then
   write one sentence about each person.
2. Everybody, touch Raymond.
   - Raise your hand when you can say a
     sentence that reports on the main thing
     Raymond did. (Call on several students.
     Praise sentences such as: *Raymond
     sawed a branch on a tree.* For each good
     sentence:) Everybody, say that sentence.
3. Everybody, touch Sally.
   - Raise your hand when you can say a
     sentence that reports on the main thing
     Sally did. (Call on several students. Praise
     sentences such as: *Sally carried a plant.*
     For each good sentence:) Everybody, say
     that sentence.
4. Everybody, touch Jill.
   - Raise your hand when you can say a
     sentence that reports on the main thing
     Jill did. (Call on several students. Praise
     sentences such as: *Jill dug a hole with
     a shovel.* For each good sentence:)
     Everybody, say that sentence.
5. Everybody, touch the words in the
   vocabulary box as I read them: **gardeners,
   yard, carried, saw, plant, shovel, work,
   branch, hole.** Be sure to spell those words
   correctly if you use them.
6. Write a good sentence about the group
   and then stop. Name the group and tell the
   main thing the group did. Raise your hand
   when you're finished.
   (Observe students and give feedback.)
   - (Call on several students to read their
     sentence. Praise sentences such as: *The
     gardeners worked in the yard.*)

7. Now write the rest of your paragraph. Write
   one sentence about each gardener. Tell the
   main thing each gardener did. You have
   5 minutes. Raise your hand when you're
   finished.
   (Observe students and give feedback.)
8. (After 5 minutes, say:) Stop writing. I'm
   going to call on several students to read
   their paragraph. Remember, if you hear a
   mistake, raise your hand. Listen carefully.
9. (Call on a student:) Read your paragraph.
   When you read it, stop at the end of each
   sentence so everybody can think about
   whether that sentence is right. (Praise the
   paragraph if it has no mistakes.)
10. (Call on several other students to read their
    paragraph. Praise good paragraphs.)
11. Everybody, make 3 check boxes under
    your sentences.
12. Here's check 1: Does each sentence begin
    with a capital and end with a period? Read
    each sentence for check 1. Fix it up if it's
    not right. Then make a check in box 1.
    Raise your hand when you're finished.
    (Observe students and give feedback.)
13. Here's check 2: Does the first sentence
    tell the main thing the group did? Check
    your first sentence. When it tells the main
    thing the group did, make a check in box 2.
    Raise your hand when you're finished.
    (Observe students and give feedback.)
14. Here's check 3: Does each of the other
    sentences report on the main thing
    a person did? Make sure you have a
    sentence for each person, and make sure
    it tells the main thing that person did. Then
    make a check in box 3. Raise your hand
    when you're finished.
    (Observe students and give feedback.)

EXERCISE 7 Main Idea

Groups

1. Skip a line on your paper. Then number your paper 1 and 2. Raise your hand when you're finished.
- Everybody, find part F in your textbook. ✔
2. These pictures show groups. You're going to write a good sentence for each group.
3. Touch the words in the vocabulary box as I read them: **ate, through, snow, meal.** Be sure to spell those words correctly if you use them.
4. Write a good sentence for each picture. Remember, first name the group. Then tell the main thing the group did. You have 3 minutes. Raise your hand when you're finished.
(Observe students and give feedback.)

5. (After 3 minutes, say:) Stop writing.
- (Call on several students to read their sentence for picture 1. Praise sentences such as: *The girls ate a meal*.)
- (Call on several students to read their sentence for picture 2. Praise sentences such as: *The men walked through the snow.*)
6. Everybody, make 2 check boxes under your sentences.
7. Here's check 1: Does each sentence begin with a capital and end with a period? Read each sentence for check 1. Fix it up if it's not right. Then make a check in box 1. Raise your hand when you're finished. (Observe students and give feedback.)
8. Here's check 2: Does each sentence tell the main thing the group did? Read over each sentence for check 2. Fix it up if it's not right. Then make a check in box 2. Raise your hand when you're finished. (Observe students and give feedback.)

Note:

- Collect the students' workbooks and papers.
- Check the students' work before the next language period. Mark any mistakes.
- Write **super** on work that has all mistakes corrected. Write **good** or **pretty good** on work that has only 1 or 2 mistakes.

Objectives

- Punctuate sentences (capitals and periods) in a paragraph. (Exercise 2)
- **Use appropriate pronouns (he, she or it) in a paragraph.** (Exercise 3)
- Write past-time verbs for irregular present-time verbs. (Exercise 4)
- **Construct sentences by combining specified subjects and predicates.** (Exercise 5)
- Construct a paragraph that states the main thing that illustrated characters did. (Exercise 6)
- Identify sentences that tell about all the pictures, two of the pictures and one of the pictures. (Exercise 7)

EXERCISE 1 Feedback On Lesson 89

- (Hand back the students' work from lesson 89.)
- Look at what I wrote on your lined paper. Raise your hand if I wrote **super.**
- If you didn't get a **super,** look at the mistakes you made and be more careful next time.

WORKBOOK

EXERCISE 2 Paragraph Editing

Capitals and Periods

1. Everybody, open your workbook to lesson 90 and find part A. ✔
- Some sentences in part A do not begin with a capital. Some sentences do not end with a period. You have to put in the missing capitals and periods.
2. Read the paragraph. Fix up any sentence that does not begin with a capital and end with a period. Raise your hand when you're finished.
   (Observe students and give feedback.)
3. Let's check your work. Make an **X** next to anything you missed.
- My class had a picnic, period. Capital **E,** Everybody went on a bus. Our teacher brought apples and oranges. He also cooked a chicken, period. Capital **W,** We built a fire to cook the chicken, period.
4. Raise your hand if you made no mistakes. Great job.
- Everybody else, fix up any mistakes you made in part A.
   (Observe students and give feedback.)

EXERCISE 3 Pronouns

He, She, It

1. Everybody, pencils down. Find part B. ✔ You're going to change the part that names in some of the sentences to **he, she** or **it.**
2. I'll read the paragraph. Follow along. Susan loved birds. Susan wanted to build a bird house. Her grandfather gave Susan a book about bird houses. Her grandfather told Susan to read it carefully. The book was interesting. The book showed how to build a bird house.
3. Here's the rule for these sentences: If two sentences in a row name the same thing, we change the second sentence so it names **he, she** or **it.** Once more: If two sentences in a row name the same thing, we change the second sentence so it names **he, she** or **it.**
4. Sentence A names Susan. Look at sentence B. Everybody, who does sentence B name? (Signal.) *Susan.*
- Two sentences in a row name the same person, so we change the second sentence to **he, she** or **it.** Which of those words refers to Susan? (Signal.) *She.*
- Cross out **Susan** in sentence B. Write **she.** Remember to start with a capital. ✔
- Here are the first and second sentences: Susan loved birds. **She** wanted to build a bird house.
5. Now we look at the next sentence. Everybody, who does sentence C name? (Signal.) *Her grandfather.*
- Does that sentence name the same person sentence B names? (Signal.) *No.*

- So we **don't** change sentence C. We don't have two sentences in a row that name the same person. Sentence B refers to **Susan.** Sentence C refers to **her grandfather.**

6. Look at the next sentence—sentence D. Everybody, who does sentence D name? (Signal.) *Her grandfather.*
   - Does that sentence name the same person sentence C names? (Signal.) *Yes.*
   - So we have two sentences in a row that name the same person—sentence C and sentence D. Everybody, which sentence do you change? (Signal.) *Sentence D.*
   - You change **her grandfather** in sentence D to **he, she** or **it.** Which word refers to **her grandfather?** (Signal.) *He.* Change sentence D to **he.** ✔

7. Look at the next sentence—sentence E. Everybody, what does sentence E name? (Signal.) *The book.*
   - Does that sentence name the same thing sentence D names? (Signal.) *No.*
   - So we don't have to change sentence E. We don't have two sentences in a row that name the same thing.

8. Look at the last sentence—sentence F. Everybody, what does sentence F name? (Signal.) *The book.*
   - Does that sentence name the same thing sentence E names? (Signal.) *Yes.*
   - They both name the book. So we have two sentences in a row that name the same thing—sentence E and sentence F. Which sentence do you change? (Signal.) *Sentence F.*
   - You change **the book** in sentence F to **he, she** or **it.** Which word refers to **the book?** (Signal.) *It.*
   - Change sentence F to **it.** ✔

9. I'll read the fixed-up paragraph. Check your work. Susan loved birds. Capital **S, She** wanted to build a bird house. Her grandfather gave Susan a book about bird houses. Capital **H, He** told Susan to read it carefully. The book was interesting. Capital **I, It** showed how to build a bird house.

10. Fix up any mistakes you made in part B.
    (Observe students and give feedback.)

EXERCISE 4 PAST TIME

Irregular Verbs

1. Everybody, find part C. ✔
   The words in part C tell what somebody does. You're going to write the words that tell what somebody did. Spell the words correctly. Raise your hand when you're finished.
   (Observe students and give feedback.)

2. Let's check your work. Make an **X** for any mistake. I'll say the word that tells what somebody does. You'll say the word that tells what somebody did.
   - Word 1: Holds. Say the word that tells what somebody did. (Signal.) *Held.*
   - Spell **held.** (Signal.) *H-e-l-d.*
   - Word 2: Gets. Say the word that tells what somebody did. (Signal.) *Got.*
   - Spell **got.** (Signal.) *G-o-t.*
   - Word 3: Rides. Say the word that tells what somebody did. (Signal.) *Rode.*
   - Spell **rode.** (Signal.) *R-o-d-e.*
   - Word 4: Teaches. Say the word that tells what somebody did. (Signal.) *Taught.*
   - Spell **taught.** (Signal.) *T-a-u-g-h-t.*
   - Word 5: Drinks. Say the word that tells what somebody did. (Signal.) *Drank.*
   - Spell **drank.** (Signal.) *D-r-a-n-k.*

3. Raise your hand if you made no mistakes. Great job.
   - Everybody else, fix up any mistakes you made in part C.
   (Observe students and give feedback.)

LINED PAPER • TEXTBOOK

EXERCISE 5 Subject/Predicate

1. Everybody, take out a sheet of lined paper and write your name on the top line. Number your paper 1 through 3. Raise your hand when you're finished.
   - Everybody, pencils down. Open your textbook to lesson 90 and find part D. ✔

2. This part tells about the subject and predicate. I'll read what it says in the box: Sentences have two parts—the subject and the predicate. The **subject** is the part of the sentence that names. The **predicate** is the part of the sentence that tells more.

3. Everybody, what's the part of the sentence that names? (Signal.) *The subject.*
- What's the part of the sentence that tells more? (Signal.) *The predicate.*
- (Repeat step 3 until firm.)
4. I'll read the instructions below the box: Make up sentences by combining these subjects and predicates.
- Touch the column for the subjects. I'll read the subjects: two old men, my mother, they. Those are parts that name.
- Touch the column for the predicates. I'll read the predicates: went to the store, worked in the yard, had a good time. Those are parts that tell more.
5. You can make up three sentences by starting with one of the subjects and using each of the predicates. I'll say sentences that start with the subject **two old men.** Listen: Two old men went to the store. Two old men worked in the yard. Two old men had a good time.
6. Your turn: Say the three sentences that start with the subject two old men.
7. First sentence. (Signal.) *Two old men went to the store.*
- Next sentence. (Signal.) *Two old men worked in the yard.*
- Last sentence. (Signal.) *Two old men had a good time.*
- (Repeat step 7 until firm.)
8. Now say the three sentences that start with the subject **my mother.**
9. First sentence. (Signal.) *My mother went to the store.*
- Next sentence. (Signal.) *My mother worked in the yard.*
- Last sentence. (Signal.) *My mother had a good time.*
- (Repeat step 9 until firm.)
10. You're going to **write** three sentences that start with the subject **they.** The first sentence should start with **they** and have the first predicate. Write the first sentence and stop. Raise your hand when you're finished.
(Observe students and give feedback.)
- Check your work. Everybody, read the first sentence that starts with the subject **they.** (Signal.) *They went to the store.*

11. Now write the other sentences that start with the subject **they.** Raise your hand when you're finished.
(Observe students and give feedback.)
12. Check your work. Everybody, read the second sentence you wrote. (Signal.) *They worked in the yard.*
- Read the last sentence you wrote. (Signal.) *They had a good time.*
13. Your turn again: Circle the subject in the sentences you wrote and underline the predicate. Raise your hand when you're finished.
(Observe students and give feedback.)
14. Check your work. Make an **X** next to any mistake.
- Sentence 1: They went to the store. What's the subject? (Signal.) *They.*
- What's the predicate? (Signal.) *Went to the store.*
- Sentence 2: They worked in the yard. What's the subject? (Signal.) *They.*
- What's the predicate? (Signal.) *Worked in the yard.*
- Sentence 3: They had a good time. What's the subject? (Signal.) *They.*
- What's the predicate? (Signal.) *Had a good time.*
15. Raise your hand if you got everything right. Great job.
- Everybody else, fix up any mistakes you made in part D.
(Observe students and give feedback.)

EXERCISE 6   PARAGRAPH WRITING
Groups

1. Everybody, find part E in your textbook. ✔
- I'll read the instructions: Write a paragraph that reports on the picture. Begin with a good sentence about the group. Then write one sentence about each person. Remember to tell the main thing each person did.
2. Touch the words in the vocabulary box as I read them: **slide, yard, stood.** Be sure to spell those words correctly if you use them.

3. Skip a line on your paper. Then write your paragraph. Remember, the first sentence tells the main thing the group did. Then you write one sentence about each person. You have 5 minutes. Raise your hand when you're finished.
(Observe students and give feedback.)

4. (After 5 minutes, say:) Stop writing. I'm going to call on several students to read their paragraph. Remember, if you hear a mistake, raise your hand.

5. (Call on a student:) Read your paragraph. When you read it, stop at the end of each sentence so everybody can think about whether that sentence is right. (Praise the paragraph if it has no mistakes.)

6. (Call on several other students to read their paragraph. Praise good paragraphs.)

7. Now you're going to check your paragraph. Make 3 boxes under your paragraph.

8. Check 1: Does each sentence begin with a capital and end with a period? Everybody, read your paragraph for check 1. Fix it up if it's not right. Raise your hand when you're finished.
(Observe students and give feedback.)

9. Check 2: Does the first sentence tell the main thing the group did? Everybody, read your first sentence for check 2 and fix it up if it's not right. Raise your hand when you're finished.
(Observe students and give feedback.)

10. Check 3: Does each of the other sentences report on the main thing a person did? Raise your hand when you're finished with check 3.
(Observe students and give feedback.)

EXERCISE 7 CLARITY

1. Skip a line on your paper. Then number your paper 1 through 3. Raise your hand when you're finished.

• Everybody, pencils down. Find part F in your textbook. ✔

2. Next to the pictures are sentences that tell about the pictures. I'll read the sentences.
An animal sat on a bike.
A dog sat on a vehicle.
An animal sat on a vehicle.

3. Now I'll read the items.
• Item 1: Copy the sentence that tells about only one picture.
• Item 2: Copy the sentence that tells about all the pictures.
• Item 3: Copy the sentence that tells about two pictures.
• Listen: Copy the correct sentence for each item. Raise your hand when you're finished.
(Observe students and give feedback.)

4. Let's check your work. Make an **X** next to any item you missed.
• Item 1: Copy the sentence that tells about only one picture. Everybody, read that sentence. (Signal.) *An animal sat on a bike.*
• Item 2: Copy the sentence that tells about all the pictures. Everybody, read that sentence. (Signal.) *An animal sat on a vehicle.*
• Item 3: Copy the sentence that tells about two pictures. Everybody, read that sentence. (Signal.) *A dog sat on a vehicle.*

5. Raise your hand if you made no mistakes. Great job.
• Everybody else, fix up any mistakes you made in part F.
(Observe students and give feedback.)

Note:

• Collect the students' workbooks and papers.

• Check the students' work before the next language period. Mark any mistakes.

• Write **super** on work that has all mistakes corrected. Write **good** or **pretty good** on work that has only 1 or 2 mistakes.

Objectives

- Punctuate sentences (capitals and periods) in a paragraph. (Exercise 2)
- Write past-time verbs for irregular present-time verbs. (Exercise 3)
- Use appropriate pronouns in a paragraph. (Exercise 4)
- Construct a paragraph that states the main thing that illustrated characters did. (Exercise 5)
- Construct sentences by combining specified subjects and predicates. (Exercise 6)
- **Write two sentences about an illustrated character.** (Exercise 7)

EXERCISE 1 Feedback On Lesson 90

- (Hand back the students' work from lesson 90.)
- Look at what I wrote on your lined paper. Raise your hand if I wrote **super.**
- It you didn't get a **super,** look at the mistakes you made and be more careful next time.

WORKBOOK

EXERCISE 2 Paragraph Editing

Capitals and Periods

1. Everybody, open your workbook to lesson 91 and find part A. ✔
- Some sentences in part A do not begin with a capital. Some sentences do not end with a period. You have to put in the missing capitals and periods.
2. Read the paragraph. Fix up any sentence that does not begin with a capital and end with a period. Raise your hand when you're finished.
   (Observe students and give feedback.)
3. Let's check your work. Make an **X** next to anything you missed.
- A little bird fell out of a tree, period. Bill and his sister saw the little bird. Capital **I, It** was in a pile of leaves, period. Bill picked up the little bird, period. Capital **H,** His sister climbed up to the nest. Bill handed the bird to his sister, period. Capital **S,** She put the bird back in the nest.
4. Raise your hand if you made no mistakes. Great job.
- Everybody else, fix up any mistakes you made in part A.
   (Observe students and give feedback.)

EXERCISE 3 Past Time

Irregular Verbs

1. Everybody, pencils down. Find part B. ✔ These are new words. They tell what somebody **does.** You're going to tell me what somebody **did.**
2. Everybody, touch number 1.
   Thinks tells what somebody does. What word tells what somebody did? (Signal.) *Thought.*
- Flies. Everybody, what word tells what somebody did? (Signal.) *Flew.*
- Stands. What word tells what somebody did? (Signal.) *Stood.*
- Brings. What word tells what somebody did? (Signal.) *Brought.*
- Breaks. What word tells what somebody did? (Signal.) *Broke.*
3. Touch number 6.
   Stands. Everybody, tell me what somebody did. (Signal.) *Stood.*
- Brings. Tell me what somebody did. (Signal.) *Brought.*
- Thinks. Tell me what somebody did. (Signal.) *Thought.*
- Breaks. Tell me what somebody did. (Signal.) *Broke.*
- Flies. Tell me what somebody did. (Signal.) *Flew.*
- (Repeat step 3 until firm.)
4. Do words 6 through 10. Next to each word, write the word that tells what somebody did. Raise your hand when you're finished. (Observe students and give feedback.)
5. Check your work. Make an **X** next to any mistake.
- Stands. What word tells what somebody did? (Signal.) *Stood.*

- Spell **stood.** (Signal.) *S-t-o-o-d.*
- Brings. What word tells what somebody did? (Signal.) *Brought.*
- Spell **brought.** (Signal.) *B-r-o-u-g-h-t.*
- Thinks. What word tells what somebody did? (Signal.) *Thought.*
- Spell **thought.** (Signal.) *T-h-o-u-g-h-t.*
- Breaks. What word tells what somebody did? (Signal.) *Broke.*
- Spell **broke.** (Signal.) *B-r-o-k-e.*
- Flies. What word tells what somebody did? (Signal.) *Flew.*
- Spell **flew.** (Signal.) *F-l-e-w.*

6. Raise your hand if you made no mistakes. Great job.
- Everybody else, fix up any mistakes you made in part B.
  (Observe students and give feedback.)

EXERCISE 4   Pronouns

He, She, It

1. Everybody, pencils down. Find part C. ✔
   You're going to change the part that names in some of the sentences to **he, she** or **it.**
2. I'll read the paragraph. Follow along. The class was playing football during recess. Tom had the football. Tom threw the ball as far as he could. Alice jumped up and caught the ball. Alice scored a touchdown. The school bell rang. The school bell told the class that recess was over.
3. Remember the rule for these sentences: If two sentences in a row name the same thing, we change the second sentence so it names **he, she** or **it.** Once more: If two sentences in a row name the same thing, we change the second sentence so it names **he, she** or **it.**
4. Sentence A names **the class.** Look at sentence B. Everybody, who does sentence B name? (Signal.) *Tom.*
- Does that sentence name the same thing sentence A names? (Signal.) *No.*
- So we **don't** change sentence B because we don't have two sentences that name the same thing. Sentence A refers to **the class.** Sentence B refers to **Tom.**
5. Now look at the next sentence—sentence C. Everybody, who does sentence C name? (Signal.) *Tom.*

- Does that sentence name the same person sentence B names? (Signal.) *Yes.*
- Two sentences in a row name the same person, so we change the second sentence to **he, she** or **it.** Which of those words refers to Tom? (Signal.) *He.*
- Cross out **Tom** in sentence C. Write **he.** Remember to start with a capital. ✔
6. Look at the next sentence—sentence D. Everybody, who does sentence D name? (Signal.) *Alice.*
- Does that sentence name the same person sentence C names? (Signal.) *No.*
- So we don't have to change sentence D. We don't have two sentences in a row that name the same person.
7. Look at the next sentence—sentence E. Everybody, who does sentence E name? (Signal.) *Alice.*
- Does that sentence name the same person sentence D names? (Signal.) *Yes.*
- So we have two sentences in a row that name the same person—sentence D and sentence E. Which sentence do you change? (Signal.) *Sentence E.*
- You change **Alice** in sentence E to **he, she** or **it.** Which word refers to **Alice?** (Signal.) *She.*
- Change sentence E to **she.** ✔
8. Look at the next sentence—sentence F. Everybody, what does sentence F name? (Signal.) *The school bell.*
- Does that sentence name the same thing sentence E names? (Signal.) *No.*
- So we don't change sentence F.
9. Look at the last sentence—sentence G. Everybody, what does sentence G name? (Signal.) *The school bell.*
- Does that sentence name the same thing sentence F names? (Signal.) *Yes.*
- So we have two sentences in a row that name the same thing—sentence F and sentence G. Which sentence do you change? (Signal.) *Sentence G.*
- You change **the school bell** in sentence G to **he, she** or **it.** Which word refers to **the school bell?** (Signal.) *It.*
- Change sentence G to **it.** ✔

10. I'll read the fixed-up paragraph. Check your work. The class was playing football during recess. Tom had the football. Capital **H, He** threw the ball as far as he could. Alice jumped up and caught the ball. Capital **S, She** scored a touchdown. The school bell rang. Capital **I, It** told the class that recess was over.

11. Fix up any mistakes you made in part C. (Observe students and give feedback.)

LINED PAPER • TEXTBOOK

EXERCISE 5 Paragraph Writing
Groups

1. Everybody, take out a sheet of lined paper and write your name on the top line. Raise your hand when you're finished.
- Everybody, open your textbook to lesson 91 and find part D. ✔
- I'll read the instructions: Write a paragraph that reports on the picture. Begin with a good sentence about the group. Then write one sentence about each person. Remember to tell the main thing each person did.
2. Everybody, touch Doreen.
- Raise your hand when you can say a sentence that reports on the main thing Doreen did. (Call on several students. Praise sentences such as: *Doreen cut the string that was all around the box.* For each good sentence:) Everybody, say that sentence.
3. Everybody, touch Dwayne.
- Raise your hand when you can say a sentence that reports on the main thing Dwayne did. (Call on several students. Praise sentences such as: *Dwayne pulled wrapping paper off a new bike.* For each good sentence:) Everybody, say that sentence.

4. Everybody, touch Jerome.
- Raise your hand when you can say a sentence that reports on the main thing Jerome did. (Call on several students. Praise sentences such as: *Jerome pulled a teddy bear out of a box.* For each good sentence:) Everybody, say that sentence.
5. Touch the words in the vocabulary box as I read them: **Presents, string, opened, scissors, wrapping paper, teddy bear.** Be sure to spell those words correctly if you use them.
6. Write your paragraph. Remember, the first sentence tells the main thing the group did. Then you write one sentence about each person. You have 5 minutes. Raise your hand when you're finished.
(Observe students and give feedback.)
7. (After 5 minutes, say:) Stop writing. I'm going to call on several students to read their paragraph. Remember, if you hear a mistake, raise your hand.
8. (Call on a student:) Read your paragraph. When you read it, stop at the end of each sentence so everybody can think about whether that sentence is right. (Praise the paragraph if it has no mistakes.)
9. (Call on several other students to read their paragraph. Praise good paragraphs.)
10. Now you're going to check your paragraph. Make 3 check boxes under your paragraph.
11. Check 1: Does each sentence begin with a capital and end with a period? Everybody, read your paragraph for check 1. Fix it up if it's not right. Raise your hand when you're finished.
(Observe students and give feedback.)
12. Check 2: Does the first sentence tell the main thing the group did? Read your first sentence for check 2 and fix it up if it's not right. Raise your hand when you're finished.
(Observe students and give feedback.)
13. Check 3: Do the other sentences report on the main thing each person did? Raise your hand when you're finished with check 3.
(Observe students and give feedback.)

EXERCISE 6 Subject/Predicate
1. Skip a line on your paper. Then number your paper 1 through 3. Raise your hand when you're finished.

- Everybody, pencils down. Find part E in your textbook. ✔
2. You're going to make up sentences by combining subjects and predicates. Remember, a sentence has two parts. What's the part that names? (Signal.) *The subject.*
- What's the part that tells more? (Signal.) *The predicate.*
3. Touch the column for the subjects. I'll read the subjects: everybody, our teacher, she. Those are parts that name.
- Touch the column for the predicates. I'll read the predicates: drove to town, got sunburned, paddled a canoe. Those are parts that tell more.
4. You can make up three sentences by starting with one of the subjects and using each of the predicates. I'll say sentences that start with the subject **everybody.** Listen: Everybody drove to town. Everybody got sunburned. Everybody paddled a canoe.
5. Your turn: Say the three sentences that start with the subject **everybody.**
6. First sentence. (Signal.) *Everybody drove to town.*
- Next sentence. (Signal.) *Everybody got sunburned.*
- Last sentence. (Signal.) *Everybody paddled a canoe.*
- (Repeat step 6 until firm.)
7. Now say the three sentences that start with the subject **our teacher.**
8. First sentence. (Signal.) *Our teacher drove to town.*
- Next sentence. (Signal.) *Our teacher got sunburned.*
- Last sentence. (Signal.) *Our teacher paddled a canoe.*
- (Repeat step 8 until firm.)
9. You're going to **write** three sentences that start with the subject **she.** The first sentence should start with **she** and have the first predicate. Write the first sentence and stop. Raise your hand when you're finished.
   (Observe students and give feedback.)
- Check your work. Everybody, read the first sentence that starts with the subject **she.** (Signal.) *She drove to town.*

10. Now write the other sentences that start with the subject **she.** Raise your hand when you're finished.
    (Observe students and give feedback.)
11. Check your work. Everybody, read the second sentence you wrote. (Signal.) *She got sunburned.*
- Read the last sentence you wrote. (Signal.) *She paddled a canoe.*
12. Your turn again: Circle the subject in the sentences you wrote and underline the predicate. Raise your hand when you're finished.
    (Observe students and give feedback.)
13. Check your work. Make an **X** next to any mistake.
- Sentence 1: She drove to town. What's the subject? (Signal.) *She.*
- What's the predicate? (Signal.) *Drove to town.*
- Sentence 2: She got sunburned. What's the subject? (Signal.) *She.*
- What's the predicate? (Signal.) *Got sunburned.*
- Sentence 3: She paddled a canoe. What's the subject? (Signal.) *She.*
- What's the predicate? (Signal.) *Paddled a canoe.*
14. Raise your hand if you got everything right. Great job.
- Everybody else, fix up any mistakes you made in part E.
  (Observe students and give feedback.)

EXERCISE 7   Writing Sentences

Individuals

1. Everybody, find part F in your textbook. ✔ I'll read the instructions: Write two sentences that report on the person. The first sentence should tell the main thing the person did. The second sentence should tell something else about the person.
2. Name the person in the picture. (Signal.) *Mr. Harmon.*
- Raise your hand when you can say a sentence that reports on the main thing Mr. Harmon did. (Call on several students. Praise sentences such as: *Mr. Harmon mopped the floor.* For each good sentence:) Everybody, say that sentence.

- Raise your hand when you can say a sentence that tells something else about Mr. Harmon. You can tell what he wore. You can tell what he listened to. You can tell where he was. Begin your sentence with the word **he.** (Call on several students. Praise sentences such as: *He wore rubber boots. He smiled as he worked.* For each good sentence:) Everybody, say that sentence.

3. Touch the words in the vocabulary box as I read them: **radio, wore, mopped, listened, floor, kitchen, boots.** Be sure to spell those words correctly if you use them.

4. Touch the picture.
   Name the person in the picture. (Signal.) *Mr. Harmon.*

- Skip a line on your paper. Then write a sentence that tells the main thing Mr. Harmon did. Raise your hand when you're finished.
   (Observe students and give feedback.)

5. Now write a sentence that tells something else about Mr. Harmon. You'll have two sentences in a row that name the same person. So start the second sentence with the word **he.** Start the sentence right after the period for the first sentence. Raise your hand when you're finished.
   (Observe students and give feedback.)

6. (Call on several students to read both sentences. Praise sentences such as: *Mr. Harmon mopped the floor. He listened to the radio.*)

7. Look over your sentences. Make sure your first sentence starts with **Mr. Harmon** and tells the main thing. Make sure your second sentence starts with **he.** Raise your hand when you've checked over your sentences.

Note:

- Collect the students' workbooks and papers.

- Check the students' work before the next language period. Mark any mistakes.

- Write **super** on work that has all mistakes corrected. Write **good** or **pretty good** on work that has only 1 or 2 mistakes.

Objectives

- Indicate the subject and the predicate of sentences. (Exercise 2)
- Write past-time verbs for irregular present-time verbs. (Exercise 3)
- Use appropriate pronouns in a paragraph. (Exercise 4)
- Write two sentences about an illustrated character. (Exercise 5)
- Identify sentences that tell about all the pictures, two of the pictures and one of the pictures. (Exercise 6)
- Construct a paragraph that states the main thing that illustrated characters did. (Exercise 7)

EXERCISE 1   Feedback On Lesson 91

- (Hand back the students' work from lesson 91.)
- Look at what I wrote on your lined paper. Raise your hand if I wrote **super.**

WORKBOOK

EXERCISE 2   Subject/Predicate

1. Everybody, open your workbook to lesson 92 and find part A. ✔
2. Everybody, what's the part of a sentence that names? (Signal.) *The subject.*
- What's the part of a sentence that tells more? (Signal.) *The predicate.*
- (Repeat step 2 until firm.)
3. For each sentence, circle the subject and underline the predicate. Do it now. Raise your hand when you're finished. (Observe students and give feedback.)
4. Let's check your work. Make an **X** next to any item you missed.
- Sentence 1. What's the subject? (Signal.) *Sara and Rodney.*
- What's the predicate? (Signal.) *Painted the kitchen blue.*
- Sentence 2. What's the subject? (Signal.) *Sara.*
- What's the predicate? (Signal.) *Had a paintbrush.*
- Sentence 3. What's the subject? (Signal.) *Rodney.*
- What's the predicate? (Signal.) *Used a roller.*
- Sentence 4. What's the subject? (Signal.) *They.*
- What's the predicate? (Signal.) *Stopped to eat lunch.*
- Sentence 5. What's the subject? (Signal.) *She.*

- What's the predicate? (Signal.) *Laughed.*
- Sentence 6. What's the subject? (Signal.) *The windows.*
- What's the predicate? (Signal.) *Were blue.*
5. Raise your hand if you made no mistakes. Great job.
- Everybody else, fix up any mistakes you made in part A.

EXERCISE 3   Past Time

Irregular Verbs

1. Everybody, pencils down. Find part B. ✔
2. Everybody, touch number 1.
- **Stands** tells what somebody does. Everybody, what word tells what somebody did? (Signal.) *Stood.*
- Thinks. What word tells what somebody did? (Signal.) *Thought.*
- Breaks. What word tells what somebody did? (Signal.) *Broke.*
- Flies. What word tells what somebody did? (Signal.) *Flew.*
- Brings. What word tells what somebody did? (Signal.) *Brought.*
3. Do words 6 through 10. Write the words that tell what somebody did. Raise your hand when you're finished. (Observe students and give feedback.)
4. Check your work. Make an **X** next to any mistake.
- Breaks. What word tells what somebody did? (Signal.) *Broke.*
- Spell **broke.** (Signal.) *B-r-o-k-e.*
- Brings. What word tells what somebody did? (Signal.) *Brought.*
- Spell **brought.** (Signal.) *B-r-o-u-g-h-t.*
- Flies. What word tells what somebody did? (Signal.) *Flew.*

- Spell **flew.** (Signal.) *F-l-e-w.*
- Stands. What word tells what somebody did? (Signal.) *Stood.*
- Spell **stood.** (Signal.) *S-t-o-o-d.*
- Thinks. What word tells what somebody did? (Signal.) *Thought.*
- Spell **thought.** (Signal.) *T-h-o-u-g-h-t.*

5. Raise your hand if you made no mistakes. Great job.

- Everybody else, fix up any mistakes you made in part B.

EXERCISE 4   **Pronouns**

He, She, It

1. Everybody, pencils down. Find part C. ✔
2. I'll read the paragraph: John wanted to have a party for his birthday. John was going to be ten years old. His mother planned a big party. His mother called all John's friends. His mother bought lots of party things. The party started right after school. The party was a lot of fun.
3. You're going to change the subject of some sentences to **he, she** or **it.** Remember the rule: If two sentences in a row name the same thing, you change the second sentence so it names **he, she** or **it.**
4. Look at sentence A and sentence B to see if they name the same thing. ✔

- Everybody, do those sentences name the same thing? (Signal.) *Yes.*
  So you'll change sentence B.
- Now look at sentence B and sentence C to see if they name the same thing. ✔
- Everybody, do those sentences name the same thing? (Signal.) *No.*
  So you don't change sentence C.
- Now look at sentence C and sentence D to see if they name the same thing. ✔
- Everybody, do those sentences name the same thing? (Signal.) *Yes.*
- So which sentence do you change? (Signal.) *Sentence D.*
- Yes, you'll change sentence D so it names **he, she** or **it.**

5. Your turn: Fix up any sentences in the paragraph that should name **he, she** or **it.** Raise your hand when you're finished. (Observe students and give feedback.)

6. Let's check your work. I'll read the passage. Make an **X** over anything you missed. John wanted to have a party for his birthday. Capital **H, He** was going to be ten years old. His mother planned a big party. Capital **S, She** called all John's friends. Capital **S, She** bought lots of party things. The party started right after school. Capital **I, It** was a lot of fun.

7. Raise your hand if you made no mistakes. Great job.

- Everybody else, fix up any mistakes you made in part C.

LINED PAPER • TEXTBOOK

EXERCISE 5   **Writing Sentences**

Individuals

1. A girl   2. Arthur

1. Everybody, take out a sheet of lined paper and write your name on the top line. Then write the number 1. Raise your hand when you're finished.

- Everybody, pencils down. Open your textbook to lesson 92 and find part D. ✔
- I'll read the instructions: Write two sentences that report on each person. The first sentence should tell the main thing the person did. The second sentence should tell something else about the person.

2. Touch picture 1.
   Name the person in the picture. (Signal.) *A girl.*

- Raise your hand when you can say a sentence that reports on the main thing a girl did. (Call on several students. Praise sentences such as: *A girl caught a baseball.* For each good sentence:) Everybody, say that sentence.

- Raise your hand when you can say a sentence that tells something else about the girl. You can tell something else she did, where she was or what she wore. Begin your sentence with the word **she.** (Call on several students. Praise sentences such as: *She stood in front of the fence. She lifted her hands up high. She wore a red, white and blue uniform.* For each good sentence:) Everybody, say that sentence.
3. Touch picture 2.
   Name the person in the picture. (Signal.) *Arthur.*
- Raise your hand when you can say a sentence that reports on the main thing Arthur did. (Call on several students. Praise sentences such as: *Arthur chopped down a tree with an ax.* For each good sentence:) Everybody, say that sentence.
- Raise your hand when you can say a sentence that tells something else about Arthur. You can tell something else he did, where he was, what he wore or what he had. Begin your sentence with the word **he.** (Call on several students. Praise sentences such as: *He had big muscles. He wore a helmet and big boots.* For each good sentence:) Everybody, say that sentence.
4. Touch the words in the vocabulary box as I read them: **baseball, caught, stood, glove, muscles, chopped, ax, uniform, fence.** Be sure to spell those words correctly if you use them.
5. Touch picture 1.
   Name the person in that picture. (Signal.) *A girl.*
- Write a sentence that tells the main thing the girl did. Raise your hand when you're finished.
   (Observe students and give feedback.)
6. Now you'll write a sentence that tells something else about the girl. You can tell something else she did, where she was, or what she wore. You'll have two sentences in a row that name the same person. So start the second sentence with the word **she.** Start the sentence right after the period for the first sentence. Raise your hand when you're finished.
   (Observe students and give feedback.)

- (Call on several students to read both sentences for picture 1. Praise sentences such as: *A girl caught a baseball. She stood in front of the fence* or *A girl caught a baseball. She had a baseball glove.*)
7. Write the number 2 on your paper. Then touch picture 2.
   Name the person in that picture. (Signal.) *Arthur.*
- Write a sentence that tells the main thing that person did. Then write a sentence that tells something else about him. Begin the second sentence with the word **he.** Raise your hand when you're finished.
   (Observe students and give feedback.)
- (Call on several students to read both sentences for picture 2. Praise sentences such as: *Arthur chopped down a tree with an ax. He had big muscles.*)

EXERCISE 6   Clarity
1. Skip a line on your paper. Then number your paper 1 through 3. Raise your hand when you're finished.
- Everybody, pencils down. Find part E in your textbook. ✔
2. Under the pictures are sentences that tell about the pictures. I'll read the sentences.
   He pushed a truck.
   A person pushed a vehicle.
   A person pushed a car.
3. Now I'll read the items above the pictures.
   Item 1: Copy the sentence that tells about two pictures.
   Item 2: Copy the sentence that tells about all the pictures.
   Item 3: Copy the sentence that tells about only one picture.
- Write the correct sentence for each item. Raise your hand when you're finished.
   (Observe students and give feedback.)
4. Let's check your work. Make an **X** next to any item you missed.
- Item 1: Copy the sentence that tells about two pictures. Everybody, read that sentence. (Signal.) *A person pushed a car.*
- Item 2: Copy the sentence that tells about all the pictures. Everybody, read that sentence. (Signal.) *A person pushed a vehicle.*

- Item 3: Copy the sentence that tells about only one picture. Everybody, read that sentence. (Signal.) *He pushed a truck.*
5. Raise your hand if you made no mistakes. Great job.
- Everybody else, fix up any mistakes you made in part E.

EXERCISE 7 Paragraph Writing

Groups

1. Everybody, find part F. ✔
- I'll read the instructions: Write a paragraph that reports on the picture. Begin with a good sentence about the group. Then write one sentence about each person. Remember to tell the main thing each person did.
2. Everybody, touch Glenda.
- Raise your hand when you can say a sentence that reports on the main thing Glenda did. (Call on several students. Praise sentences such as: *Glenda poured water over a bulldog.* For each good sentence:) Everybody, say that sentence.
3. Everybody, touch Linda.
- Raise your hand when you can say a sentence that reports on the main thing Linda did. (Call on several students. Praise sentences such as: *Linda scrubbed the back of a police dog with a brush.* For each good sentence:) Everybody, say that sentence.
4. Everybody, touch Tina.
- Raise your hand when you can say a sentence that reports on the main thing Tina did. (Call on several students. Praise sentences such as: *Tina dried the poodle with a towel.* For each good sentence:) Everybody, say that sentence.
5. Touch the words in the vocabulary box as I read them: **cleaned, water, brush, scrubbed, washed, towel, dried off, poured, their, women.** Be sure to spell those words correctly if you use them.

6. Skip a line on your paper. Then write your paragraph. Remember, the first sentence tells the main thing the group did. Then you write one sentence about each person. You have 5 minutes. Raise your hand when you're finished.
(Observe students and give feedback.)
7. (After 5 minutes, say:) Stop writing. I'm going to call on several students to read their paragraph. Remember, if you hear a mistake, raise your hand.
8. (Call on a student:) Read your paragraph. (Praise the paragraph if it has no mistakes.)
9. (Call on several other students to read their paragraph. Praise good paragraphs.)
10. Now you're going to check your paragraph. Make 3 check boxes under your paragraph. ✔
11. Check 1: Does each sentence begin with a capital and end with a period? Everybody, read your paragraph for check 1. Fix it up if it's not right. Then make a check in box 1. Raise your hand when you're finished. (Observe students and give feedback.)
12. Check 2: Does the first sentence tell the main thing the group did? Read your first sentence for check 2 and fix it up if it's not right. Then make a check in box 2. Raise your hand when you're finished. (Observe students and give feedback.)
13. Check 3: Do the other sentences report on the main thing each person did? Read the rest of your sentences for check 3 and fix up any mistakes. Then make a check in box 3. Raise your hand when you're finished.
(Observe students and give feedback.)

Note:

- Collect the students' workbooks and papers.
- Check the students' work before the next language period. Mark any mistakes.
- Write **super** on work that has all mistakes corrected. Write **good** or **pretty good** on work that has only 1 or 2 mistakes.

Objectives

- Punctuate sentences (capitals and periods) in a paragraph. (Exercise 2)
- Indicate the subject and the predicate of sentences. (Exercise 3)
- Use appropriate pronouns in a paragraph. (Exercise 4)
- Write past-time verbs for irregular present-time verbs. (Exercise 5)
- **Complete similar sentences so they tell about only one picture.** (Exercise 6)
- **Construct a paragraph that includes one sentence about an illustrated group and two sentences about each illustrated character.** (Exercise 7)

EXERCISE 1 Feedback On Lesson 92

- (Hand back the students' work from lesson 92.)
- Look at what I wrote on your lined paper. Raise your hand if I wrote **super.**

WORKBOOK

EXERCISE 2 Paragraph Editing

Capitals and Periods

1. Everybody, open your workbook to lesson 93 and find part A. ✔
- Some sentences in part A do not begin with a capital. Some sentences do not end with a period. You're going to put in the missing capitals and periods.
2. Fix up the paragraph so each sentence begins with a capital and ends with a period. Raise your hand when you're finished.
   (Observe students and give feedback.)
3. Let's check your work. Make an **X** next to anything you missed.
- Tom threw a rock at a tree, period. Capital **H,** His rock hit a beehive. Capital **T,** The bees got very mad, period. Capital **T,** They flew out of the nest. Tom ran away from the bees. Capital **M,** Many bees chased him, period. Capital **T,** Tom jumped into the lake. Capital **H,** He never threw rocks at trees again, period.
4. Raise your hand if you made no mistakes. Great job.
- Everybody else, fix up any mistakes you made in part A.

EXERCISE 3 Subject/Predicate

1. Everybody, find part B. ✔
2. Everybody, what's the part of a sentence that names? (Signal.) *The subject.*
- What's the part of a sentence that tells more? (Signal.) *The predicate.*
- (Repeat step 2 until firm.)
3. For each sentence, circle the subject and underline the predicate. Do it now. Raise your hand when you're finished. (Observe students and give feedback.)
4. Let's check your work. Make an **X** next to any item you missed.
- Sentence 1. What's the subject? (Signal.) *Mr. Dunn and his son.*
- What's the predicate? (Signal.) *Went to the store.*
- Sentence 2. What's the subject? (Signal.) *Mrs. Iverson.*
- What's the predicate? (Signal.) *Met Mrs. Lopez and her son.*
- Sentence 3. What's the subject? (Signal.) *Two dogs.*
- What's the predicate? (Signal.) *Started to run around the store.*
- Sentence 4. What's the subject? (Signal.) *Mr. Jones.*
- What's the predicate? (Signal.) *Was happy.*
- Sentence 5. What's the subject? (Signal.) *They.*
- What's the predicate? (Signal.) *Sat in a rocking chair.*
5. Raise your hand if you got no items wrong. Great job.
- Everybody else, fix up any mistakes you made in part B.

EXERCISE 4   Pronouns

He, She, It

1. Everybody, pencils down. Find part C. ✔
I'll read the instructions: Fix up any sentences in the paragraph that should name **he, she** or **it**. The sentences in part C don't have letters, but remember the rule: If two sentences in a row name the same thing, change the second sentence so it names **he, she** or **it**.

2. Look at the first sentence of the paragraph. Everybody, who does the first sentence name? (Signal.) *Greg.*

• Does the second sentence also name Greg? (Signal.) *Yes.*

• What are you going to write instead of **Greg** in the second sentence? (Signal.) *He.*

• Cross out **Greg** at the beginning of the second sentence and write **he**. Then fix up the names in the rest of the paragraph. Raise your hand when you're finished. (Observe students and give feedback.)

3. Let's check your work. Make an **X** next to anything you missed. I'll read the fixed-up paragraph.
Greg cleaned up his room last week. Capital **H, He** put all his toys in the closet. His grandmother was very happy. Capital **S, She** gave him a big hug.

4. Raise your hand if you made no mistakes. Great job.

• Everybody else, fix up any mistakes you made in part C.

EXERCISE 5   Part Time

Irregular Verbs

1. Everybody, find part D. ✔
The words in part D tell what somebody does. In the blank next to each word, write the word that tells what somebody did. Raise your hand when you're finished. (Observe students and give feedback.)

2. Let's check your work. Make an **X** next to any mistake.

• Word 1: Flies. Say the word that tells what somebody did. (Signal.) *Flew.*

• Spell **flew.** (Signal.) *F-l-e-w.*

• Word 2: Brings. Say the word that tells what somebody did. (Signal.) *Brought.*

• Spell **brought.** (Signal.) *B-r-o-u-g-h-t.*

• Word 3: Breaks. Say the word that tells what somebody did. (Signal.) *Broke.*

• Spell **broke.** (Signal.) *B-r-o-k-e.*

• Word 4: Thinks. Say the word that tells what somebody did. (Signal.) *Thought.*

• Spell **thought.** (Signal.) *T-h-o-u-g-h-t.*

• Word 5: Stands. Say the word that tells what somebody did. (Signal.) *Stood.*

• Spell **stood.** (Signal.) *S-t-o-o-d.*

3. Raise your hand if you made no mistakes. Great job.

• Everybody else, fix up any mistakes you made in part D.

EXERCISE 6   Clarity

1. Everybody, pencils down. Find part E. ✔
Each of these pictures shows what a cat did. You're going to make up a sentence that tells about all the pictures. Then you're going to make up sentences that tell about each picture.

2. Look at all the pictures, and raise your hand when you can say a sentence that tells about **all** the pictures. Start your sentence with **a cat.**

• (Call on a student. Praise sentences such as: *A cat sat on a chair.*)

3. Here are the rules about the sentences you're going to fix up: Sentence 1 should tell only about picture 1. Sentence 2 should tell only about picture 2. And sentence 3 should tell only about picture 3.

4. Touch sentence 1.
You're going to fix up that sentence so it tells only about picture 1. You can do that by telling what kind of cat **and** what kind of chair.

• (Call on a student:) What kind of cat is that in picture 1? *A black cat.*

• (Call on another student:) What kind of chair is that in picture 1? *A big chair.*

• Everybody, fix up sentence 1 by putting words in the blanks. Raise your hand when you're finished. (Observe students and give feedback.)

• (Call on a student:) Read the sentence that tells only about picture 1. (Praise sentences such as: *A black cat sat on a big chair.*)

5. Everybody, look at the cat and the chair in picture 2.
- (Call on a student:) What kind of cat is that in picture 2? *A white cat.*
- (Call on another student:) What kind of chair is that in picture 2? *A small chair.*
- Everybody, fix up sentence 2 by putting words in the blanks. Raise your hand when you're finished.
(Observe students and give feedback.)
- (Call on a student:) Read the sentence that tells only about picture 2. *A white cat sat on a small chair.*
6. Everybody, fix up sentence 3 by putting words in the blanks. Raise your hand when you're finished.
(Observe students and give feedback.)
- (Call on a student:) Read the sentence that tells only about picture 3. *A white cat sat on a big chair.*
7. Let's see if we did the right sentences. If a sentence is right, it tells about only one picture. I'll read the fixed-up sentences. See if you can find the right picture.
- Listen: A white cat sat on a small chair. Everybody, which picture does that sentence tell about? (Signal.) *Picture 2.*
- That's a good sentence because it tells only about picture 2.
- Listen: A black cat sat on a big chair. Everybody, which picture does that sentence tell about? (Signal.) *Picture 1.*
- That's a good sentence because it tells only about picture 1.
8. Listen: A white cat sat on a big chair. Everybody, is that a good sentence? (Signal.) *Yes.*
- (Call on a student:) Why? (Idea: *Because it tells only about picture 3.*)
- Listen: A cat sat on a big chair. Everybody, is that a good sentence? (Signal.) *No.*
- (Call on a student:) Why not? (Idea: *Because it tells about picture 1 and picture 3.*)

EXERCISE 7 Paragraph Writing

Pairs

1. Everybody, take out a sheet of lined paper and write your name on the top line. Raise your hand when you're finished.
- Everybody, open your textbook to lesson 93 and find part F. ✔
- I'll read the instructions: Write a paragraph that reports on the picture. Begin with a good sentence that tells what the painters did. Then write two sentences about each person. The first sentence should tell the main thing the person did. The second sentence should tell something else about the person.
2. Touch the words in the vocabulary box as I read them: **room, ceiling, painted, bottom, roller, kneeled, knees, brushed, ladder, used.** Be sure to spell those words correctly if you use them.
3. Write a good sentence that tells the main thing the painters did. Raise your hand when you're finished.
(Observe students and give feedback.)
- (Call on several students to read their sentence. Praise sentences such as: *The painters painted the room.*)
4. Touch Jim.
- Raise your hand when you can say a sentence that reports on the main thing Jim did. (Call on several students. Praise sentences such as: *Jim painted the bottom of a wall.* For each good sentence:) Everybody, say that sentence.

152   *Lesson 93*

- Raise your hand when you can say a sentence that tells something else about Jim. Begin your sentence with the word **he.** (Call on several students. Praise sentences such as:) *He used a brush. He sat on his knees.* For each good sentence:) Everybody, say that sentence.

5. Now write two sentences about Jim. Remember, the first sentence names Jim. The second sentence starts with he. Raise your hand when you're finished. (Observe students and give feedback.)

6. Touch Susan.

- Raise your hand when you can say a sentence that reports on the main thing Susan did. (Call on several students. Praise sentences such as: *Susan painted the ceiling.* For each good sentence:) Everybody, say that sentence.

- Raise your hand when you can say a sentence that tells something else about Susan. Begin your sentence with the word **she.** (Call on several students. Praise sentences such as: *She used a roller. She stood on a ladder.* For each good sentence:) Everybody, say that sentence.

7. Everybody, write two sentences about Susan. What word will the second sentence about Susan start with? (Signal.) *She.*

- Write your sentences about Susan. Raise your hand when you're finished. (Observe students and give feedback.)

8. I'm going to call on several students to read their paragraphs. Let's see who the good listeners are. Remember, the first sentence should tell the main thing the painters did. Then there should be two sentences that tell about Jim. The first sentence tells the main thing Jim did. Then there should be two sentences that tell about Susan. The first sentence should tell the main thing Susan did. Listen carefully and raise your hand if a sentence is wrong or if it doesn't use the right word to name the person.

- (Call on several students to read their paragraph. Praise good paragraphs.)

9. Now you're going to check your paragraph. Make 3 check boxes under your paragraph.

10. I'll read check 1: Does each sentence begin with a capital and end with a period? Check your paragraph. Fix up any mistakes. Then make a check in box 1. Raise your hand when you're finished. (Observe students and give feedback.)

11. I'll read check 2: Did you write two sentences about each person? Read your paragraph. If you wrote two sentences about Jim and two sentences about Susan, make a check in box 2. Fix up any mistakes. Raise your hand when you're finished. (Observe students and give feedback.)

12. I'll read check 3: Does the second sentence about each person begin with **he** or **she?** Check your paragraph. Fix up any mistakes. Then make a check in box 3. Raise your hand when you're finished. (Observe students and give feedback.)

13. Raise your hand if you think you'll get a super paper.

Note:

- Collect the students' workbooks and papers.

- Check the students' work before the next language period. Mark any mistakes.

- Write **super** on work that has all mistakes corrected. Write **good** or **pretty good** on work that has only 1 or 2 mistakes.

Objectives

- Punctuate sentences (capitals and periods) in a paragraph. (Exercise 2)
- Use appropriate pronouns in a paragraph. (Exercise 3)
- **Capitalize the name of a person.** (Exercise 4)
- Complete similar sentences so they tell about only one picture. (Exercise 5)
- Write past-time verbs for irregular present-time verbs. (Exercise 6)
- Construct a paragraph that includes one sentence about an illustrated group and two sentences about each illustrated character. (Exercise 7)

EXERCISE 1 Feedback On Lesson 93

- (Hand back the students' work from lesson 93.)
- Look at what I wrote on your lined paper. Raise your hand if I wrote **super.**

WORKBOOK

EXERCISE 2 Paragraph Editing

Capitals and Periods

1. Everybody, open your workbook to lesson 94 and find part A. ✔
- Read the paragraph. Fix up any sentence that does not begin with a capital and end with a period. Raise your hand when you're finished.
(Observe students and give feedback.)
2. Let's check your work. Make an **X** next to anything you missed.
- Snow fell all night long. Doris got up and looked outside, period. Capital **E,** Everything was white. Doris thought about things to do in the snow, period. Capital **S,** She wanted to throw snowballs. She wanted to roll in the snow. Capital **H,** Her mother handed her a snow shovel. Doris went out in the snow, period. She did not have a lot of fun, period.
3. Raise your hand if you made no mistakes. Great job.
- Everybody else, fix up any mistakes you made in part A.

EXERCISE 3 Pronouns

He, She, It

1. Everybody, find part B. ✔
I'll read the instructions: Fix up any sentences in the paragraph that should name **he, she** or **it.** If two sentences in a row name the same thing, change the second sentence so it names **he, she** or **it.** Fix up the paragraph. Raise your hand when you're finished.
(Observe students and give feedback.)
2. Let's check your work. Make an **X** next to anything you missed. I'll read the fixed-up paragraph.
- Sandra wanted to play baseball. Capital **S, She** looked for her ball and bat. Her brother also wanted to play baseball. Capital **H, He** helped her look for the ball and bat. Sandra looked in the yard. Capital **S, She** found the ball and bat near the doghouse. The ball was in bad shape. Capital **I, It** was all chewed up.
3. Raise your hand if you made no mistakes. Great job.
- Everybody else, fix up any mistakes you made in part B.

EXERCISE 4 Capitalizing

Names

1. Everybody, find part C. ✔
Names of people in sentences should begin with a capital letter, even if the name is not the first word in the sentence.
2. The first word in part C is **nancy.** Everybody, is that somebody's name? (Signal.) *Yes.*

- Fix it up so it begins with a capital letter. ✔
3. The next word is **he.** Is that somebody's name? (Signal.) *No.*
   Don't change it.
4. The next word is **truck.** Is that somebody's name? (Signal.) *No.*
   Don't change it.
5. The next word is **tammy.** Is that somebody's name? (Signal.) *Yes.*
- Fix it up. ✔
6. The next word is **james.** Is that somebody's name? (Signal.) *Yes.*
- Fix it up. ✔
7. Do the rest of the words in part C. Remember, if a word is somebody's name, begin the word with a capital letter. Raise your hand when you're finished. (Observe students and give feedback.)
8. Let's check your work. I'll read each word. You say **capital** if the word begins with a capital. Say **no capital** if the word does not begin with a capital. Start with the word **they** in the second row. Listen: They. (Signal.) *No capital.*
- Linda. (Signal.) *Capital.*
- Ann. (Signal.) *Capital.*
- Jack. (Signal.) *Capital.*
- My. (Signal.) *No capital.*
- Sam. (Signal.) *Capital.*
- Tina. (Signal.) *Capital.*
- She. (Signal.) *No capital.*
- Window. (Signal.) *No capital.*
- Tim. (Signal.) *Capital.*
- It. (Signal.) *No capital.*
9. Raise your hand if you got no words wrong. Great job.
- Everybody else, fix up any mistakes you made in part C.

EXERCISE 5   **Clarity**

1. Everybody, pencils down. Find part D. ✔
   Each of these pictures shows what a woman did. You're going to make up a sentence that tells about all the pictures. Then you're going to make up sentences that tell about each picture.
2. Look at all the pictures, and raise your hand when you can say a sentence that tells about all the pictures. Start your sentence with **a woman.**

- (Call on a student. Praise sentences such as: *A woman held a ball.*)
3. You may not know what kind of ball each woman is holding. Who knows what that big ball in picture 1 is called?
   (Call on a student.) *A beach ball.*
- That little ball in picture 2 is a tennis ball.
4. Touch sentence 1.
   You're going to fix up that sentence so it tells only about picture 1. You can do that by telling what kind of woman **and** what kind of ball.
- (Call on a student:) What kind of woman is that in picture 1? *An old woman.*
- (Call on another student:) What kind of ball is that in picture 1? *A beach ball.*
- Everybody, fix up sentence 1 by putting words in the blanks. Raise your hand when you're finished.
   (Observe students and give feedback.)
- (Call on a student:) Read the sentence that tells only about picture 1.
   (Praise sentences such as: *An old woman held a beach ball.*)
5. Everybody, look at the woman and the ball in picture 2.
- Everybody, fix up sentence 2 by putting words in the blanks. Raise your hand when you're finished.
   (Observe students and give feedback.)
- (Call on a student:) Read the sentence that tells only about picture 2.
   A young woman held a tennis ball.
6. Everybody, fix up sentence 3 by putting words in the blanks. Raise your hand when you're finished.
   (Observe students and give feedback.)
- (Call on a student:) Read the sentence that tells only about picture 3.
   An old woman held a tennis ball.
7. Let's see if we did the right sentences. Remember, if a sentence is right, it tells only about one picture. I'll read the fixed-up sentences. See if you can find the right picture.
- Listen: A young woman held a tennis ball. Everybody, which picture does that sentence tell about? (Signal.) *Picture 2.*
- That's a good sentence because it tells only about picture 2.

- Listen: An old woman held a beach ball. Everybody, which picture does that sentence tell about? (Signal.) *Picture 1.*
- That's a good sentence because it tells only about picture 1.

8. Listen: An old woman held a tennis ball. Everybody, is that a good sentence? (Signal.) *Yes.*
- (Call on a student:) Why? (Idea: *Because it tells only about picture 3.*)
- Listen: A woman held a tennis ball. Everybody, is that a good sentence? (Signal.) *No.*
- (Call on a student:) Why not? (Idea: *Because it tells about picture 2 and picture 3.*)

EXERCISE 6 Past Time

Irregular Verbs

1. Everybody, find part E. ✔
   The words in part E tell what somebody does. In the blank next to each word, write the word that tells what somebody did. Raise your hand when you're finished. (Observe students and give feedback.)
2. Let's check your work. Make an **X** next to any mistake.
- Word 1: Stands. Say the word that tells what somebody did. (Signal.) *Stood.*
- Spell **stood.** (Signal.) *S-t-o-o-d.*
- Word 2: Breaks. Say the word that tells what somebody did. (Signal.) *Broke.*
- Spell **broke.** (Signal.) *B-r-o-k-e.*
- Word 3: Thinks. Say the word that tells what somebody did. (Signal.) *Thought.*
- Spell **thought.** (Signal.) *T-h-o-u-g-h-t.*
- Word 4: Brings. Say the word that tells what somebody did. (Signal.) *Brought.*
- Spell **brought.** (Signal.) *B-r-o-u-g-h-t.*
- Word 5: Flies. Say the word that tells what somebody did. (Signal.) *Flew.*
- Spell **flew.** (Signal.) *F-l-e-w.*
3. Raise your hand if you made no mistakes. Great job.
- Everybody else, fix up any mistakes you made in part E.

EXERCISE 7 Paragraph Writing

Pairs

1. Everybody, take out a sheet of lined paper and write your name on the top line. Raise your hand when you're finished.
- Everybody, open your textbook to lesson 94 and find part F. ✔
- I'll read the instructions: Write a paragraph that reports on the picture. Begin with a good sentence that tells what the waiters did. Then write two sentences about each person. The first sentence should tell the main thing the person did. The second sentence should tell something else about the person.
2. Touch the words in the vocabulary box as I read them: **silverware, plates, table, placed, put, waiters, stack, set, held.** Be sure to spell those words correctly if you use them.
3. Write a good sentence that tells the main thing the waiters did. Raise your hand when you're finished. (Observe students and give feedback.)
- (Call on several students to read their sentence. Praise sentences such as: *The waiters set the table.*)
4. Touch James.
- Raise your hand when you can say a sentence that reports on the main thing James did. (Call on several students. Praise sentences such as: *James put silverware on the table. James put a knife on the table.* For each good sentence:) Everybody, say that sentence.

- Raise your hand when you can say a sentence that tells something else about James. Begin your sentence with the word **he.** (Call on several students. Praise sentences such as: *He held a cup filled with forks, knives, and spoons. He wore a brown vest and a black bowtie.* For each good sentence:) Everybody, say that sentence.

5. Now write two sentences about James. Remember, the first sentence names James. The second sentence starts with **he.** Raise your hand when you're finished. (Observe students and give feedback.)

6. Touch Joe.

- Raise your hand when you can say a sentence that reports on the main thing Joe did. (Call on several students. Praise sentences such as: *Joe put a plate on the table.* For each good sentence:) Everybody, say that sentence.

- Raise your hand when you can say a sentence that tells something else about Joe. Begin your sentence with the word **he.** (Call on several students. Praise sentences such as: *He held a pile of plates in one hand. He wore a brown vest and a black bowtie.* For each good sentence:) Everybody, say that sentence.

7. Everybody, now you're going to write two sentences about Joe. What word will the second sentence about Joe start with? (Signal.) *He.*

- Write your sentences about Joe. Raise your hand when you're finished. (Observe students and give feedback.)

8. I'm going to call on several students to read their paragraphs. Listen carefully and raise your hand if a sentence is wrong or if it doesn't use the right word to name the person.

- (Call on several students to read their paragraph. Praise good paragraphs.)

9. Now you're going to check your paragraph. Make 3 check boxes under your paragraph.

10. I'll read check 1: Does each sentence begin with a capital and end with a period? Check your paragraph. Fix up any mistakes. Then make a check in box 1. Raise your hand when you're finished. (Observe students and give feedback.)

11. I'll read check 2: Did you write two sentences about each person? Read your paragraph. If you wrote two sentences about James and two sentences about Joe, make a check in box 2. Fix up any mistakes. Raise your hand when you're finished.
    (Observe students and give feedback.)

12. I'll read check 3: Does the second sentence about each person begin with **he?** Check your paragraph. Fix up any mistakes. Then make a check in box 3. Raise your hand when you're finished. (Observe students and give feedback.)

13. Raise your hand if you think you'll get a **super** paper.

Note:

- Collect the students' workbooks and papers.

- Check the students' work before the next language period. Mark any mistakes.

- Write **super** on work that has all mistakes corrected. Write **good** or **pretty good** on work that has only 1 or 2 mistakes.

Objectives

- Complete similar sentences so they tell about only one picture. (Exercise 2)
- **Edit sentences for irregular past-time verbs.** (Exercise 3)
- Perform on a mastery test of skills presented in lesson 86–94. (Exercise 4)
  Exercises 5–7 give instructions for marking the test, giving student feedback and providing remedies.

EXERCISE 1   Feedback On Lesson 94

- (Hand back the students' work from lesson 94.)
- Look at what I wrote on your lined paper. Raise your hand if I wrote **super.**

WORKBOOK

EXERCISE 2   Clarity

1. Everybody, open your workbook to lesson 95 and find part A. ✔
- Look at all the pictures and raise your hand when you can say a sentence that tells about all the pictures.
- (Call on a student:) Say a sentence that tells about all the pictures. (Praise sentences such as: *A cat sat on a chair.*)
2. You're going to fix up the sentences so they tell only about one picture. You can do that by telling **where** the cat was on the chair.
- (Call on a student:) Tell me the part of the chair the cat is on in picture 1. *The arm.*
- Fix up sentence 1 by putting words in the blank. Tell what part of the chair the cat sat on. Raise your hand when you're finished. (Observe students and give feedback.)
- (Call on a student:) Read the sentence that tells only about picture 1. *A cat sat on the arm of a chair.*
3. I'll read the words in the vocabulary box. They tell about different parts of chairs. Follow along: **seat, leg, back, arm.**
4. Your turn: Fix up the rest of the sentences. Remember, sentence 2 should tell only about picture 2. Sentence 3 should tell only about picture 3. Raise your hand when you're finished.
   (Observe students and give feedback.)

5. Everybody, check your work. Make an **X** next to any item you miss.
- (Call on a student:) Read the sentence that tells only about picture 2.
  A cat sat on the seat of a chair.
- Everybody, raise your hand if you got it right.
- (Call on a student:) Read the sentence that tells only about picture 3.
  A cat sat on the back of a chair.
- Everybody, raise your hand if you got it right. Good thinking.
6. Let's see if we did the right sentences. Remember, if a sentence is right, it tells only about one picture. I'll read the fixed-up sentences. See if you can find the right picture.
- Listen: A cat sat on the back of a chair. Everybody, which picture does that sentence tell about? (Signal.) *Picture 3.*
- That's a good sentence because it tells only about picture 3.
- Listen: A cat sat on the arm of a chair. Everybody, which picture does that sentence tell about? (Signal.) *Picture 1.*
- That's a good sentence because it tells only about picture 1.
7. Listen: A cat sat on the seat of a chair. Everybody, is that a good sentence? (Signal.) *Yes.*
- (Call on a student:) Why? (Idea: *Because it tells only about picture 2.*)

EXERCISE 3 Past Time

Irregular Verbs

1. Everybody, find part B. ✔
   Each sentence in part B uses the wrong word to tell what somebody did. You're going to cross out the wrong word and write the correct word above it.
2. Sentence 1: Tyrell gets a new dog. What word is wrong? (Signal.) *Gets.*
- What word should be in place of **gets?** (Signal.) *Got.*
- Cross out **gets** and write **got.** ✔
3. Sentence 2: His sister teached him to ride a bike. What word is wrong? (Signal.) *Teached.*
- Fix up sentence 2.
  (Observe students and give feedback.)
- Everybody, what word did you write in place of **teached?** (Signal.) *Taught.*
4. Sentence 3: The airplane flied over the mountain. What word is wrong? (Signal.) *Flied.*
- Fix up sentence 3.
  (Observe students and give feedback.)
- Everybody, what word did you write in place of **flied?** (Signal.) *Flew.*
5. Sentence 4: Vanessa standed on a table. What word is wrong? (Signal.) *Standed.*
- Fix up sentence 4.
  (Observe students and give feedback.)
- Everybody, what word did you write in place of **standed?** (Signal.) *Stood.*
6. Sentence 5: We seen an elephant at the circus. What word is wrong? (Signal.) *Seen.*
- Fix up sentence 5.
  (Observe students and give feedback.)
- Everybody, what word did you write in place of **seen?** (Signal.) *Saw.*
7. (Call on a student:) Read all the sentences with the right words.
   She got a new dog.
   His sister taught him to ride a bike.
   The airplane flew over the mountain.
   She stood on a table.
   We saw an elephant at the circus.
8. Fix up any mistakes you made in part B.

EXERCISE 4 Test

Subject/Predicate

1. The rest of the lesson is a test. Find part A of test 3. ✔
2. The instructions say to circle the subject and underline the predicate. Do it. Raise your hand when you're finished.

Paragraph Editing—Capitals and Periods

1. Everybody, find part B. ✔
2. I'll read the instructions: Fix up the paragraph so each sentence begins with a capital and ends with a period. Do it. Raise your hand when you're finished.

Pronouns—He, She, It

1. Everybody, find part C. ✔
2. I'll read the instructions: Fix up any sentences that should name **he, she** or **it.** Do it. Raise your hand when you're finished.

Clarity

1. Everybody, find part D. ✔
2. Copy the correct sentence for each item. Do it. Raise your hand when you're finished.
3. (When students finish the test, collect their workbooks.)

EXERCISE 5 Marking The Test

1. (Mark the workbooks before the next scheduled language lesson. Use the *Language Arts Workbook Answer Key* to determine acceptable responses for the test.)
2. (Write the number of errors each student made on the test in the test scorebox at the beginning of the test.)
3. (Enter the number of errors each student made on the Summary for Test 9. Reproducible Summary Sheets are at the back of the *Language Arts Teacher's Guide.*)

EXERCISE 6　Feedback On Test 9

1. (Return the students' workbooks after they are marked.)
- Everybody, open your workbook to lesson 95.
2. The number I wrote in the test scorebox tells how many items you got wrong on the whole test. Raise your hand if I wrote **0, 1** or **2** at the top of your test. **Those are super stars.**
- Raise your hand if I wrote **3** or **4.** Those are pretty good workers.
- If I wrote a number that's more than 4, you're going to have to work harder.

EXERCISE 7　Test Remedies

- (Before beginning lesson 96, provide any necessary remedies. After students complete the exercises specified for a remedy, check their work and give feedback.)

Test Part A　Subject/Predicate

If more than $\frac{1}{4}$ of the students made 2 or more errors in test part A, present the following exercises:

- (Direct students to part A on page 267 of the student workbook.)
  For each sentence, circle the subject and underline the predicate.
- (Direct students to part B on page 267 of the student workbook.)
  For each sentence, circle the subject and underline the predicate.

Test Part B　Paragraph Editing— Capitals and Periods

If more than $\frac{1}{4}$ of the students made 2 or more errors in test part B, present the following exercises:

- (Direct students to part C on page 267 of the student workbook.)
  Fix up the paragraph so each sentence begins with a capital and ends with a period.
- (Direct students to part D on page 268 of the student workbook.)
  Fix up the paragraph so each sentence begins with a capital and ends with a period.

Test Part C　Pronouns—He, She, It

If more than $\frac{1}{4}$ of the students made any errors in test part C, present the following exercises:

- (Direct students to part E on page 268 of the student workbook.)
  Fix up any sentences in the paragraph that should name **he, she** or **it.**
- (Direct students to part F on page 268 of the student workbook.)
  Fix up any sentences in the paragraph that should name **he, she** or **it.**

Test Part D　Clarity

If more than $\frac{1}{4}$ of the students made any errors in test part D, present the following exercises:

- **Lesson 88, Exercise 7, Student Textbook Part F**
- **Lesson 91, Exercise 7, Student Textbook Part F**
- **Lesson 92, Exercise 7, Student Textbook Part E**

Objectives

- **Capitalize all parts of a person's name.** (Exercise 1)
- Punctuate sentences (capitals and periods) in a paragraph. (Exercise 2)
- Edit sentences for irregular past-time verbs. (Exercise 3)
- Complete similar sentences so they tell about only one picture. (Exercise 4)
- Indicate the subject and the predicate of sentences. (Exercise 5)
- Construct a paragraph that includes one sentence about an illustrated group and two sentences about each illustrated character. (Exercise 6)

WORKBOOK

EXERCISE 1   Capitalizing

Names

1. Everybody, open your workbook to lesson 96 and find part A. ✔
   - I'll read the instructions: Begin all parts of a person's name with a capital letter.
2. Item 1 is **bill jones.** Is that somebody's name? (Signal.) *Yes.*
   - So we have to make **bill** and **jones** begin with capitals. Fix up **bill jones.** Make the **b** in **bill** a capital. Make the **j** in **jones** a capital. Raise your hand when you're finished.
   (Observe students and give feedback.)
3. Item 2 is **mrs. williams.** Is that somebody's name? (Signal.) *Yes.*
   - Make the **m** in **mrs.** a capital. Make the **w** in **williams** a capital. ✔
4. Item 3 is **the doctor.** Is that somebody's name? (Signal.) *No.*
   - Don't capitalize anything in those words. ✔
5. Item 4 is **his brother.** Is that somebody's name? (Signal.) *No.*
   - Don't capitalize anything.
6. Item 5 is **anita.** Is that somebody's name? (Signal.) *Yes.*
   - Fix it up. ✔
7. Item 6 is **sam miller.** Is that somebody's name? (Signal.) *Yes.*
   - Fix up both parts of the name. ✔
8. Finish part A. Make sure each part of a person's name begins with a capital. Raise your hand when you're finished.
   (Observe students and give feedback.)

9. Let's check your work. I'll read each item. You say **capital** if it's a person's name. Say **no capital** if it's not a person's name.
   - Item 7: this boy. (Signal.) *No capital.*
   - Item 8: Mr. Adams. (Signal.) *Capital.*
   - Item 9: the girl. (Signal.) *No capital.*
   - Item 10: Ted. (Signal.) *Capital.*
   - Item 11: the nurse. (Signal.) *No capital.*
   - Item 12: Mrs. Cash. (Signal.) *Capital.*
10. Raise your hand if you got all the items right. Great job.
    - Everybody else, fix up any mistakes you made in part A.

EXERCISE 2   Capitals and Periods

Editing Sentences with And

1. Everybody, pencils down. Find part B. ✔
   There are no capitals or periods in this paragraph. A lot of the sentences have the word **and.**
   Listen: A sentence won't start with the word **and.** So read past the word **and** to find out where the sentence ends.
2. Your turn: Figure out where the first sentence ends. Don't write anything. Just put your finger where the first sentence ends. Raise your hand when you've got it.
   - (Call on a student:) Read the first sentence. *A strong wind blew down a tree and a fence.*
3. The next sentence begins with **a boy.** Read and figure out where that sentence ends. Put your finger there. Raise your hand when you've got it.
   - (Call on a student:) Read the sentence that starts with **a boy.** *A boy and a girl saw the broken fence.*

4. The next sentence begins with **the boy.** Read and figure out where that sentence ends. Raise your hand when you've got it.

•   (Call on a student:) Read the sentence that starts with **the boy.** *The boy got a can of paint.*

5. The next sentence begins with **the girl.** Read and figure out where that sentence ends. Raise your hand when you've got it.

•   (Call on a student:) Read the sentence that starts with **the girl.** *The girl got a hammer and nails.*

6. Everybody, what word does the next sentence begin with? (Signal.) *They.*

•   I'll read that sentence: They worked very hard to fix the fence.

7. Your turn: Fix up the paragraph so that each sentence begins with a capital and ends with a period. Raise your hand when you're finished.
    (Observe students and give feedback.)

8. Check your work.

•   Capital **A,** A strong wind blew down a tree and a fence, period. Capital **A,** A boy and a girl saw the broken fence, period. Capital **T,** The boy got a can of paint, period. Capital **T,** The girl got a hammer and nails, period. Capital **T,** They worked very hard to fix the fence, period.

9. Raise your hand if you made no mistakes. Great job.

•   Everybody else, fix up any mistakes you made in part B.

EXERCISE 3   Past Time

Irregular Verbs

1. Everybody, find part C. ✔
    Each sentence in part C uses the wrong word to tell what somebody did. You're going to cross out the wrong word and write the correct word above it.

2. Sentence 1: Lee bringed home a new dog. What word is wrong? (Signal.) *Bringed.*

•   What word should be in place of **bringed?** (Signal.) *Brought.*

•   Cross out **bringed** and write **brought.** ✔

3. Sentence 2: We thinked about it all night. What word is wrong? (Signal.) *Thinked.*

•   Fix up sentence 2. Raise your hand when you're finished.

•   Everybody, what word did you write in place of **thinked?** (Signal.) *Thought.*

4. Sentence 3: He standed on the corner. What word is wrong? (Signal.) *Standed.*

•   Fix up sentence 3. Raise your hand when you're finished.

•   Everybody, what word did you write in place of **standed?** (Signal.) *Stood.*

5. Sentence 4: Carlos gots new gloves for his birthday. What word is wrong? (Signal.) *Gots.*

•   Fix up sentence 4. Raise your hand when you're finished.

•   Everybody, what word did you write in place of **gots?** (Signal.) *Got.*

6. Sentence 5: My mom teached me to ride a bike. What word is wrong? (Signal.) *Teached.*

•   Fix up sentence 5. Raise your hand when you're finished.

•   Everybody, what word did you write in place of **teached?** (Signal.) *Taught.*

7. (Call on a student:) Read all the sentences with the right words.
    Lee brought home a new dog.
    We thought about it all night.
    He stood on the corner.
    Carlos got new gloves for his birthday.
    My mom taught me to ride a bike.

8. Fix up any mistakes you made in part C.

EXERCISE 4   Clarity

1. Everybody, pencils down. Find part D. ✔
    Look at all the pictures and raise your hand when you can say a sentence that tells about all the pictures.

•   (Call on a student:) Say a sentence that tells about all the pictures. (Praise sentences such as: *A monkey sat on a car.*)

2. You're going to fix up the sentences so they tell only about one picture.

•   Touch picture 1.
    (Call on a student:) What part of the car is the monkey sitting on? *The hood.*

•   Everybody, touch picture 2.
    (Call on a student:) What part of the car is the monkey sitting on? *The roof.*

•   Everybody, touch picture 3.
    (Call on a student:) What part of the car is the monkey sitting on? *The trunk.*

3. I'll read the words in the vocabulary box: **roof, tire, hood, trunk, headlight.**

4. Your turn: Fix up the sentences. Remember, sentence 1 should tell only about picture 1. Sentence 2 should tell only about picture 2. Sentence 3 should tell only about picture 3. Raise your hand when you're finished. (Observe students and give feedback.)

5. Everybody, check your work.
   - (Call on a student:) Read the sentence that tells only about picture 1.
     A monkey sat on the hood of a car.
   - Everybody, raise your hand if you got it right.
   - (Call on a student:) Read the sentence that tells only about picture 2.
     A monkey sat on the roof of a car.
   - Everybody, raise your hand if you got it right.
   - (Call on a student:) Read the sentence that tells only about picture 3.
     A monkey sat on the trunk of a car.
   - Everybody, raise your hand if you got it right. Good thinking.

6. I'll say some sentences. You're going to tell me if each sentence is **good** or **not good.** Remember, it's a good sentence if it tells about only one picture.
   - Listen: A monkey sat on a car. Is that a good sentence? (Signal.) *No.*
   - (Call on a student:) Why not? (Idea: *It tells about more than one picture.*)
   - Listen: A monkey sat on a part of a car. Everybody, is that a good sentence? (Signal.) *No.*
   - (Call on a student:) Why not? (Idea: *It tells about more than one picture.*)
   - Listen: A monkey sat on the roof of a car. Everybody, is that a good sentence? (Signal.) *Yes.*
   - (Call on a student:) Why? (Idea: *It tells about only one picture.*)
   - Listen: A dog sat on the roof of a car. Everybody, is that a good sentence? (Signal.) *No.*

- (Call on a student:) Why not? (Idea: *It doesn't tell about any of the pictures.*)
- Right, that sentence doesn't tell about any of the pictures, so it's really bad.

EXERCISE 5 Subject/Predicate

1. Everybody, find part E. ✔
   For each sentence, circle the subject and underline the predicate. Do it now. Raise your hand when you're finished. (Observe students and give feedback.)

2. Check your work.
   - Sentence 1: That old house fell down. What's the subject? (Signal.) *That old house.*
   - What's the predicate? (Signal.) *Fell down.*
   - Sentence 2: A new flower came up in the garden. What's the subject? (Signal.) *A new flower.*
   - What's the predicate? (Signal.) *Came up in the garden.*
   - Sentence 3: Marcus laughed at the joke. What's the subject? (Signal.) *Marcus.*
   - What's the predicate? (Signal.) *Laughed at the joke.*
   - Sentence 4: The box was full of money. What's the subject? (Signal.) *The box.*
   - What's the predicate? (Signal.) *Was full of money.*
   - Sentence 5: His room was clean. What's the subject? (Signal.) *His room.*
   - What's the predicate? (Signal.) *Was clean.*
   - Sentence 6: Three cows and two horses were in the barn. What's the subject? (Signal.) *Three cows and two horses.*
   - What's the predicate? (Signal.) *Were in the barn.*

3. Raise your hand if you made no mistakes. Great job.
   - Everybody else, fix up any mistakes you made in part E.

EXERCISE 6   Paragraph Writing

Pairs

1. Everybody, take out a sheet of lined paper and write your name on the top line. Raise your hand when you're finished.
- Everybody, open your textbook to lesson 96 and find part F. ✔
- I'll read the instructions: Write a paragraph that reports on the picture. Begin with a good sentence that tells what the girls did. Then write two sentences about each person.

2. Touch the words in the vocabulary box as I read them: **stood, surfboard, swimming pool, played, cap, wore, girls, water, jumped, nose.**

3. Write a good sentence that tells the main thing the girls did. Then stop. Raise your hand when you're finished.
   (Observe students and give feedback.)
- (Call on several students to read their sentences. Praise sentences such as: *The girls played at the swimming pool.* For each good sentence:) Everybody, say that sentence.

4. Now write two sentences about Linda. Remember, the first sentence names Linda and tells the main thing Linda did. The second sentence starts with **she.** Raise your hand when you're finished.
   (Observe students and give feedback.)
- (Call on several students to read their sentences about Linda. Praise sentences such as: *Linda jumped into the water. She held her nose.*)

5. Everybody, now you're going to write two sentences about Bonnie. What word will the second sentence start with? (Signal.) *She.*
- Write your sentences about Bonnie. Raise your hand when you're finished.
  (Observe students and give feedback.)

6. I'm going to call on several students to read their paragraphs. Listen carefully and raise your hand if a sentence is wrong or if it doesn't use the right word to name the person.
- (Call on several students to read their paragraphs. Praise good paragraphs.)

7. Now you're going to check your paragraph. Make 3 check boxes under your paragraph.

8. Here's check 1: Does each sentence begin with a capital and end with a period? Check your paragraph. Fix up any mistakes. Then make a check in box 1. Raise your hand when you're finished.
   (Observe students and give feedback.)

9. Here's check 2: Did you write two sentences about each person? Read your paragraph. If you wrote two sentences about Linda and two sentences about Bonnie, make a check in box 2. Fix up any mistakes. Raise your hand when you're finished.
   (Observe students and give feedback.)

10. Here's check 3: Does the second sentence about each person begin with **she?** Check your paragraph. Fix up any mistakes. Then make a check in box 3. Raise your hand when you're finished.
    (Observe students and give feedback.)

Note:

- Collect the students' workbooks and papers.

- Check the students' work before the next language period. Mark any mistakes.

- Write **super** on work that has all mistakes corrected. Write **good** or **pretty good** on work that has only 1 or 2 mistakes.

Objectives

- Capitalize all parts of a person's name. (Exercise 2)
- **Replace the subject of a sentence with a pronoun (he, she, it or they).** (Exercise 3)
- Punctuate sentences (capitals and periods) in a paragraph. (Exercise 4)
- **Rewrite a paragraph to correct unclear parts.** (Exercise 5)
- Construct sentences by combining specified subjects and predicates. (Exercise 6)

EXERCISE 1 Feedback On Lesson 96

- (Hand back the students' work from lesson 96.)
- Look at what I wrote on your lined paper. Raise your hand if I wrote **super.**

WORKBOOK

EXERCISE 2 Capitalizing

Names

1. Everybody, open your workbook to lesson 97 and find part A. ✔
- I'll read the instructions: Begin all parts of a person's name with a capital letter.
2. Item 1: **mrs. robinson.** Is that somebody's name? (Signal.) *Yes.*
- So we have to make **mrs.** and **robinson** begin with capitals. Fix up **mrs. robinson.** Raise your hand when you're finished. (Observe students and give feedback.)
3. Item 2: **her sister.** Is that somebody's name? (Signal.) *No.*
- So don't capitalize anything.
4. Your turn: Look at the rest of the items in part A. Fix up each person's name so all parts of the name begin with a capital. Raise your hand when you're finished. (Observe students and give feedback.)
5. Let's check your work. I'll read each item. You say **capital** if it's a person's name. Say **no capital** if it's not a person's name.
- Item 3: Steve Crosby. (Signal.) *Capital.*
- Item 4: a police officer. (Signal.) *No capital.*
- Item 5: my teacher. (Signal.) *No capital.*
- Item 6: tigers. (Signal.) *No capital.*
- Item 7: Debbie. (Signal.) *Capital.*
- Item 8: Mr. James. (Signal.) *Capital.*
- Item 9: a clown. (Signal.) *No capital.*

6. Raise your hand if you got all the items right. Great job.
- Everybody else, fix up any mistakes you made in part A.

EXERCISE 3 Pronouns

He, She, It and They

1. Everybody, pencils down. Find part B. ✔ I'll read the instructions: Fill in the blanks with **he, she, it** or **they.**
- Some of the sentences name more than one person or thing. The word you use to refer to more than one person or thing is **they.** What word refers to more than one person or thing? (Signal.) *They.*
2. Sentence 1: A man and a woman ate dinner. What word refers to **a man and a woman?** (Signal.) *They.*
- Say the sentence with **they.** (Signal.) *They ate dinner.*
- Sentence 2: Two boys walked on the sand. Who does that sentence name? (Signal.) *Two boys.*
- What word refers to **two boys?** (Signal.) *They.*
- Say the sentence with **they.** (Signal.) *They walked on the sand.*
- Sentence 3: Our bus had a flat tire. What does that sentence name? (Signal.) *Our bus.*
- What word refers to **our bus?** (Signal.) *It.*
- Say the sentence with **it.** (Signal.) *It had a flat tire.*
3. Your turn: Fill in the blanks. Write **he, she, it** or **they.** Remember to begin each sentence with a capital letter. Raise your hand when you're finished. (Observe students and give feedback.)

4. Let's check your work. I'll read each sentence. You say the sentence you wrote.
  • Sentence 1: A man and a woman ate dinner. (Signal.) *They ate dinner.*
  • Sentence 2: Two boys walked on the sand. (Signal.) *They walked on the sand.*
  • Sentence 3: Our bus had a flat tire. (Signal.) *It had a flat tire.*
  • Sentence 4: Bananas cost 68 cents. (Signal.) *They cost 68 cents.*
  • Sentence 5: The men wore red jackets. (Signal.) *They wore red jackets.*
  • Sentence 6: That old car went fast. (Signal.) *It went fast.*
5. Raise your hand if you got no items wrong. Great job.
  • Everybody else, fix up any mistakes you made in part B.

EXERCISE 4   Capitals and Periods

Editing Sentences with And

1. Everybody, pencils down. Find part C. ✔ There are no capitals or periods in this paragraph. A lot of the sentences have the word **and**. Remember, sentences won't start with the word **and**. So read past the word **and** to find out where the sentence ends.
2. Your turn: Figure out where the first sentence ends. Put your finger there. Raise your hand when you've got it.
  • (Call on a student:) Read the first sentence. *A dog ran after a cat.*
3. The next sentence begins with **the animals.** Read and figure out where that sentence ends. Put your finger there. Raise your hand when you've got it.
  • (Call on a student:) Read the sentence that starts with **the animals.** *The animals ran through the kitchen and the living room.*
4. Your turn: Fix up the paragraph so that each sentence begins with a capital and ends with a period. Remember, if a sentence has the word **and,** you just keep reading until you find the end of the sentence. Raise your hand when you've fixed up the whole paragraph with capitals and periods.
  (Observe students and give feedback.)

5. Check your work.
  • Capital **A,** A dog ran after a cat, period. Capital **T,** The animals ran through the kitchen and the living room, period. Capital **T,** They ran up the stairs and down the stairs, period. Capital **T,** The dog ran slower and slower, period. Capital **T,** The cat kept going faster, period. Capital **T,** The dog stopped and fell over, period. Capital **T,** The cat was not even tired, period.
6. Raise your hand if you made no mistakes. Great job.
  • Everybody else, fix up any mistakes you made in part C.

EXERCISE 5   Paragraph Clarity

1. Everybody, pencils down. Find part D. ✔ Here's a rule about good writing: Good writing tells about things so that you can get a clear picture of what happened. The paragraph in part D has words that are unclear because they don't give us a good picture. The unclear words are underlined.
2. I'll read the first sentence: An animal fell out of a large old tree. The unclear words are **an animal.** We don't know what kind of animal to get a picture of. So we could all get different pictures.
  • What kind of animal do you think fell out of a large old tree? (Call on several students. After each suggested animal, say:) Yes, that's an animal. So that's one of the pictures you could get from the first sentence.
3. Next sentence: It landed on the soft ground. We can get a picture of the soft ground.
4. Next sentence: A person picked it up. The words **a person** are underlined. (Call on a student:) Why? (Praise a response that expresses the idea: *We don't know what kind of person.*)
  • We can get pictures of different persons. I could get a picture of an old man with a long beard.
  • What other kind of person could you picture? (Call on several students. After each suggested person, say:) Yes, that's a person. So that's one of the pictures you could get from that sentence.

5. Last sentence: The person put it in a container and took it home. You could get pictures of a lot of different persons and a lot of different containers.
   - What are some containers the person might have used? (Call on several students. After each suggested container, say:) Yes, that's a container. So that's one of the pictures you could get from that sentence.

LINED PAPER • TEXTBOOK

6. Everybody, take out a sheet of lined paper and write your name on the top line. Raise your hand when you're finished. ✔
   - Pencils down. Open your textbook to lesson 97 and find part D. ✔

7. The picture shows what happened. You can see what kind of animal fell out of a tree. You can see the person who picked it up. You can see what kind of container the person put it in.
   - You're going to rewrite the paragraph so it lets anybody reading the paragraph get a clear picture of what happened. When you rewrite it, you don't want to call the snake just **a snake.** Call it a **big** snake or **striped** snake.
   - You don't want to call the person who picked it up just **a girl.** What could you call that person so somebody could get a clear picture of her? (Call on several students. Ideas: *A young girl; a girl wearing cowgirl clothes.*)
   - What are you going to call the container? (Call on several students. Ideas: *A wooden basket.*)
8. I'll read the words in the vocabulary box. Follow along: **snake, striped, large, wooden, cowgirl, wearing, boots, outfit, young, basket.**

9. Who can say the first sentence with the underlined part changed so it gives a clear picture of the animal? (Call on several students. Praise sentences such as: *A huge striped snake fell out of a large old tree.* For each good sentence:) Everybody, say that sentence.
   - The next sentence says, "It landed on the soft ground." No part is underlined.
   - Next sentence. A person picked it up. Who can say that sentence with the underlined part changed so the sentence gives a clear picture of the person? (Call on several students. Praise sentences such as: *A young girl in a cowgirl suit picked it up.* For each good sentence:) Everybody, say that sentence.
   - Next sentence. The person put it in a container and took it home. Who can say that sentence with the underlined parts changed so the sentence gives a clear picture of the person and the container? (Call on several students. Praise sentences such as: *The girl put it in a wooden basket and took it home.* For each good sentence:) Everybody, say that sentence.
10. Your turn: Rewrite the paragraph on your lined paper. Remember, change the underlined parts so they give a clear picture. Copy the rest of each sentence. You have 7 minutes. Raise your hand when you're finished.
    (Observe students and give feedback.)
11. (After 7 minutes, say:) Stop writing. I'm going to call on several students to read their paragraphs. Remember, the only parts of the sentences that should be changed are the underlined parts. The new parts should give a clear picture of what happened. Listen carefully and raise your hand if a sentence is wrong or if it doesn't give a clear picture.
    - (Call on several students to read their paragraphs. After each paragraph is read, ask the students:) Does that paragraph give a clear picture? (Praise paragraphs that have clear replacements for the underlined words.)
12. Now you're going to check your paragraph. Make 2 check boxes under your paragraph.

13. Check 1: Does each sentence begin with a capital and end with a period? Check your paragraph. Fix up any mistakes. Then make a check in box 1. Raise your hand when you're finished.

14. Check 2: Does each sentence give a clear picture of what happened? Read your paragraph. Make sure each sentence gives a clear picture. Fix up any mistakes. Then make a check in box 2. Raise your hand when you're finished.

15. Next time, I'll read some of the **super** paragraphs to you.

EXERCISE 6   Subject/Predicate

1. Skip a line on your paper. Then number your paper 1 through 3. Raise your hand when you're finished.
   - Everybody, pencils down. Find part E in your textbook.
   - The parts in the first column are subjects. The parts in the second column are predicates. I'll read the subjects: Mrs. Jones, Fran and Jill, my uncle. I'll read the predicates: ate breakfast, had new shoes, ran every morning.

2. Listen: You're going to say the three sentences that have the predicate **ran every morning.** Start the first sentence with the first subject.
   - First sentence. (Signal.) *Mrs. Jones ran every morning.*
   - Second sentence. (Signal.) *Fran and Jill ran every morning.*
   - Third sentence. (Signal.) *My uncle ran every morning.*

3. Now you're going to say the three sentences that have the predicate **ate breakfast.** Start the first sentence with the first subject.
   - First sentence. (Signal.) *Mrs. Jones ate breakfast.*
   - Second sentence. (Signal.) *Fran and Jill ate breakfast.*
   - Third sentence. (Signal.) *My uncle ate breakfast.*

4. Your turn: Write the three sentences that have the predicate **had new shoes.** Once more: Write the three sentences that have the predicate **had new shoes.** Raise your hand when you're finished.
   (Observe students and give feedback.)

5. Check your work. You're going to read the three sentences that have the predicate **had new shoes.**
   - First sentence. (Signal.) *Mrs. Jones had new shoes.*
   - Second sentence. (Signal.) *Fran and Jill had new shoes.*
   - Third sentence. (Signal.) *My uncle had new shoes.*

6. Raise your hand if you got all of them right. (Praise students who raise their hand.)

> *Note:*
> - Collect the students' workbooks and papers.
> - Check the students' work before the next language period. Mark any mistakes.
> - Write **super** on work that has all mistakes corrected. Write **good** or **pretty good** on work that has only 1 or 2 mistakes.

Objectives

- **Listen to well-written paragraphs.** (Exercise 1)
- Capitalize all parts of a person's name. (Exercise 2)
- Replace the subject of a sentence with a pronoun (**he, she**, **it** or **they**). (Exercise 3)
- **Edit a paragraph for capitals, periods and past-time verbs.** (Exercise 4)
- **Identify sentence parts as subjects or predicates.** (Exercise 5)
- Edit sentences for irregular past-time verbs. (Exercise 6)
- Rewrite a paragraph to correct unclear parts. (Exercise 7)

EXERCISE 1 Feedback On Lesson 97

- (Before returning the students' papers and workbooks, read some of the better paragraphs for part D of lesson 97.)

- (Hand back the students' work from lesson 97.)
- Look at what I wrote on your lined paper. Raise your hand if I wrote **super.**

WORKBOOK

EXERCISE 2 Capitalizing

Names

1. Everybody, open your workbook to lesson 98 and find part A. ✔
- I'll read the instructions: Begin all parts of a person's name with a capital letter.
2. Look at the items in part A. Fix up each person's name so all parts of the name begin with a capital. Raise your hand when you're finished.
   (Observe students and give feedback.)
3. Let's check your work. I'll read the items. You say **capital** if it's a person's name. Say **no capital** if it's not a person's name.
- Item 1: Greg. (Signal.) *Capital.*
- Item 2: Mrs. Abbott. (Signal.) *Capital.*
- Item 3: my sister. (Signal.) *No capital.*
- Item 4: cowboys. (Signal.) *No capital.*
- Item 5: Ronnie Lee. (Signal.) *Capital.*
- Item 6: a little poodle. (Signal.) *No capital.*
- Item 7: Jerry Adams. (Signal.) *Capital.*
- Item 8: Mr. Sanders. (Signal.) *Capital.*
- Item 9: cats. (Signal.) *No capital.*
- Item 10: the fireman. (Signal.) *No capital.*
- Item 11: Peggy. (Signal.) *Capital.*

- Item 12: Mrs. Jackson. (Signal.) *Capital.*
4. Raise your hand if you got all the items right. Great job.
- Everybody else, fix up any mistakes you made in part A.

EXERCISE 3 Pronouns

He, She, It and They

1. Everybody, find part B. ✔
   I'll read the instructions: Fill in the blanks with **he, she, it** or **they.**
2. Do it. Remember to begin each sentence with a capital. Raise your hand when you're finished.
   (Observe students and give feedback.)
3. Let's check your work. I'll read each sentence. You say the sentence you wrote.
- Sentence 1: A cow and a horse drank water. (Signal.) *They drank water.*
- Sentence 2: My shoes were wet. (Signal.) *They were wet.*
- Sentence 3: Anna played baseball. (Signal.) *She played baseball.*
- Sentence 4: A boy shouted. (Signal.) *He shouted.*
- Sentence 5: His sister stood in line. (Signal.) *She stood in line.*
- Sentence 6: A bottle fell off the table. (Signal.) *It fell off the table.*
4. Raise your hand if you got all the items right. Great job.
- Everybody else, fix up any mistakes you made in part B.

EXERCISE 4 Paragraph Editing

1. Everybody, find part C. ✔
   You're going to edit the paragraph in part C for two different things.
2. I'll read the checks. Follow along.
   - Check 1: Does each sentence begin with a capital and end with a period?
   - Check 2: Does each sentence tell what somebody or something did?
3. Listen: First check the paragraph to make sure each sentence begins with a capital and ends with a period. Do it now. Then make a check in box 1. Raise your hand when you're finished.
   (Observe students and give feedback.)
4. (After students complete check 1, say:)
   Now go through the paragraph again for check 2. Fix up the paragraph so all the sentences tell what somebody or something did. Then make a check in box 2 to show that all the sentences tell what somebody or something did. Raise your hand when you're finished.
   (Observe students and give feedback.)
5. Let's check your work. I'll read the fixed-up paragraph.
   - A woman drove an old car, period. Capital **S,** She **had** the car for many years. She took good care of her car. She even **painted** the car. Her car looked as good as new, period. Capital **E,** Everybody **liked** that wonderful old car, period.
6. Raise your hand if you fixed up all the mistakes. Great job.
   - Everybody else, fix up any mistakes you missed.

EXERCISE 5 Subject/Predicate

1. Everybody, pencils down. Find part D. ✔
   The items are not sentences. They are parts of sentences. Some parts are subjects. Some parts are predicates. Remember, the subject is the part that names. The predicate is the part that tells what the person or thing did.
2. Part 1: ran to the store. Is that a subject or a predicate? (Signal.) *A predicate.*
   - Yes, that part tells what somebody did.
   - Part 2: had a long tail. Is that a subject or a predicate? (Signal.) *A predicate.*
   - Yes, that part tells what somebody did.

- Part 3: my dog. Is that a subject or a predicate? (Signal.) *A subject.*
- Yes, that part names.
- Part 4: Troy and Chris. Is that a subject or a predicate? (Signal.) *A subject.*
- Yes, that part names.
3. Your turn: Write **S** in front of each part that is a subject. Write **P** in front of each part that is a predicate. Raise your hand when you're finished.
   (Observe students and give feedback.)
4. Check your work. I'll read each part. Tell me whether the part is a subject or a predicate.
   - Part 1: ran to the store. (Signal.) *A predicate.*
   - Part 2: had a long tail. (Signal.) *A predicate.*
   - Part 3: my dog. (Signal.) *A subject.*
   - Part 4: Troy and Chris. (Signal.) *A subject.*
   - Part 5: had four new tires. (Signal.) *A predicate.*
   - Part 6: she. (Signal.) *A subject.*
   - Part 7: my sister. (Signal.) *A subject.*
   - Part 8: was on the table. (Signal.) *A predicate.*
   - Part 9: two dogs and three cats. (Signal.) *A subject.*
   - Part 10: bought a yellow dress. (Signal.) *A predicate.*
5. Raise your hand if you got everything right.
   (Praise students who raise their hand.)

EXERCISE 6 Past Time

Irregular Verbs

1. Everybody, find part E. ✔
   Each sentence in part E uses the wrong word to tell what somebody did. You're going to cross out the wrong word and write the correct word above it.
2. Sentence 1: He breaked his leg. What word is wrong? (Signal.) *Breaked.*
   - What word should be in place of **breaked?** (Signal.) *Broke.*
   - Cross out **breaked** and write **broke.** ✔
3. Sentence 2: They rided a horse. What word is wrong? (Signal.) *Rided.*
   - Fix up sentence 2. Raise your hand when you're finished.
   - Everybody, what word did you write in place of **rided?** (Signal.) *Rode.*
4. Sentence 3: I seen my brother in the park. What word is wrong? (Signal.) *Seen.*

- Fix up sentence 3: Raise your hand when you're finished.
- Everybody, what word did you write in place of **seen?** (Signal.) *Saw.*
5. Sentence 4: Tamika gots an A on the test. What word is wrong? (Signal.) *Gots.*
- Fix up sentence 4. Raise your hand when you're finished.
- Everybody, what word did you write in place of **gots?** (Signal.) *Got.*
6. Sentence 5: Tyrell drinked a glass of water. What word is wrong? (Signal.) *Drinked.*
- Fix up sentence 5. Raise your hand when you're finished.
- Everybody, what word did you write in place of **drinked?** (Signal.) *Drank.*
7. (Call on a student:) Read all the sentences with the right words.
   He broke his leg.
   They rode a horse.
   I saw my brother in the park.
   Tamika got an A on the test.
   Tyrell drank a glass of water.
8. Fix up any mistakes you made in part E.

EXERCISE 7 Paragraph Clarity

1. Everybody, pencils down. Find part F. ✔
- Remember the rule about good writing. Good writing tells about things so that you can get a clear picture of what happened. The paragraph in part F has words that are unclear because they don't give us a good picture. The unclear words are underlined.
2. I'll read the first sentence: A man sat on an object. The first unclear part is a **man.** We don't know what the man looks like, so we could all get different pictures.
- What kind of man do you think is in the picture? (Call on several students. After each suggested man, say:) Yes, that's a man. So that's one of the pictures you could get.
- Listen to the first sentence again: A man sat on an object. What's the other unclear part in that sentence? (Signal.) *An object.*
- (Call on a student:) Why is **an object** unclear?
   (Praise a response that expresses the idea: *We don't know what kind of object.*)
   Right, we could picture different kinds of objects.

3. Next sentence: A bird sat on him. We can get pictures of different kinds of birds.
- What kind of bird do you picture? (Call on several students. After each suggested bird, say:) Yes, that's a bird. So that's one picture you could get.
- Listen to the sentence again: A bird sat on him. The word **him** is underlined because you can get a picture of the bird sitting on different parts of him. Where could the bird be sitting? (Call on several students. After each suggested part, say:) Yes, that's part of a person, so that's one picture you could get.
4. I'll read the rest of the paragraph: He held it in one hand. He tossed food with the other hand. Three animals picked up the food.
- We can get a lot of different pictures from that paragraph.

LINED PAPER • TEXTBOOK

5. Take out a sheet of lined paper and write your name on the top line. Raise your hand when you're finished. ✔
- Pencils down. Open your textbook to lesson 98 and find part F. ✔

6. The picture shows what happened. You can see what kind of man, what kind of object he sat on, what kind of bird sat on him and where the bird sat.
- Look at the man. You could call that man a **bald** man. That would give a clear picture.
- How could you give an even clearer picture of that man? (Call on several students. Praise descriptions such as: *An old bald man with a beard.*)

- Who can say the first sentence with the underlined parts changed so they give a clear picture of the man and the object he sat on? (Call on several students. Praise sentences such as: *An old bald man with a beard sat on a large log.* For each good sentence:) Everybody, say that sentence.

7. Next sentence. <u>A bird</u> sat on <u>him</u>. Who can say that sentence with the underlined parts changed so the sentence gives a clear picture of what kind of bird and on what part of the man the bird sat? (Call on several students. Praise sentences such as: *A parrot sat on his shoulder.* For each good sentence:) Everybody, say that sentence.

- Next sentence. He held <u>it</u> in one hand. Who can say that sentence with the underlined part changed so the sentence gives a clear picture of what he held? (Call on several students. Praise sentences such as: *He held a bag of peanuts in one hand.* For each good sentence:) Everybody, say that sentence.

8. I'll read the words in the vocabulary box. Follow along: **beard, sailor suits, parrot, his shoulder, three, bald.**

9. Your turn: Rewrite the paragraph on your lined paper. Remember, change the underlined parts so they give a clear picture. Copy the rest of each sentence. You have 7 minutes. Raise your hand when you're finished.
   (Observe students and give feedback.)

10. (After 7 minutes say:) Stop writing. I'm going to call on several students to read their paragraphs. Remember, the only parts of the sentences that should be changed are the underlined parts. The new parts should give a clear picture of what happened. Listen carefully and raise your hand if a sentence is wrong or if it doesn't give a clear picture.

- (Call on several students to read their paragraphs. After each paragraph is read, ask the group:) Does that paragraph give a clear picture? (Praise paragraphs that have clear replacements for the underlined words.)

11. Now you're going to check your paragraph. Make 2 check boxes under your paragraph.

12. Check 1: Does each sentence begin with a capital and end with a period? Check your paragraph. Fix up any mistakes. Then make a check in box 1. Raise your hand when you're finished.

13. Check 2: Does each sentence give a clear picture of what happened? Read your paragraph. Make sure each sentence gives a clear picture. Fix up any mistakes. Then make a check in box 2. Raise your hand when you're finished.

14. Next time, I'll read some of the **super** paragraphs to you.

Note:

- Collect the students' workbooks and papers.

- Check the students' work before the next language period. Mark any mistakes.

- Write **super** on work that has all mistakes corrected. Write **good** or **pretty good** on work that has only 1 or 2 mistakes.

Objectives

- Identify sentence parts as subjects or predicates. (Exercise 2)
- Edit a paragraph for capitals, periods and past-time verbs. (Exercise 3)
- Replace the subject of a sentence with a pronoun (**he, she, it** or **they**). (Exercise 4)
- Capitalize all parts of a person's name. (Exercise 5)
- Rewrite a paragraph to correct unclear parts. (Exercise 6)
- **Write a sentence that tells about only one of two similar pictures.** (Exercise 7)

EXERCISE 1   Feedback On Lesson 98

- (Before returning the students' papers and workbooks, read some of the better paragraphs for part F of lesson 98.)
- (Hand back the students' work from lesson 98.)
- Look at what I wrote on your lined paper. Raise your hand if I wrote **super.**

WORKBOOK

EXERCISE 2   Subject/Predicate

1. Everybody, open your workbook to lesson 99 and find part A. ✔
- For each part, you're going to write **S** or **P.** You'll write **S** in front of each part that is a subject and **P** in front of each part that is a predicate. Do it now. Raise your hand when you're finished.
   (Observe students and give feedback.)
2. Let's check your work. I'll read each part. Tell me whether the part is a subject or a predicate.
- Part 1: Jerry and Tom. (Signal.) *A subject.*
- Part 2: walked to the store. (Signal.) *A predicate.*
- Part 3: played cards with Jill. (Signal.) *A predicate.*
- Part 4: my brother and I. (Signal.) *A subject.*
- Part 5: three eggs. (Signal.) *A subject.*
- Part 6: went to the movies. (Signal.) *A predicate.*
- Part 7: they. (Signal.) *A subject.*
- Part 8: she. (Signal.) *A subject.*
- Part 9: talked to the doctor. (Signal.) *A predicate.*

- Part 10: had fun with his friend. (Signal.) *A predicate.*
3. Raise your hand if you got everything right. Great job.

EXERCISE 3   Paragraph Editing

1. Everybody, find part B. ✔
   You're going to edit the paragraph in part B for two different things.
2. I'll read the checks. Follow along.
- Check 1: Does each sentence begin with a capital and end with a period?
- Check 2: Does each sentence tell what somebody or something did?
3. Listen: First check the paragraph to make sure each sentence begins with a capital and ends with a period. Do it now. Then make a check in box 1. Raise your hand when you're finished.
   (Observe students and give feedback.)
4. (After students complete check 1, say:) Now go through the paragraph again for check 2. Fix up the paragraph so all the sentences tell what somebody or something did. Then make a check in box 2 to show that all the sentences tell what somebody or something did. Raise your hand when you're finished.
   (Observe students and give feedback.)
5. Let's check your work. I'll read the fixed-up paragraph.
- A car went past our house. It **had** old tires, period. Capital **I,** It had four broken doors. The car **made** lots of noise, period. Capital **S,** Smoke came out of the hood. The driver **got** out of the car, period. Capital **H,** He **kicked** the car, period. Capital **H,** His car fell apart.

6. Raise your hand if you fixed up all the mistakes. Great job.
- Everybody else, fix up any mistakes you missed.

EXERCISE 4 Pronouns

He, She, It and They

1. Everybody, find part C. ✔
   I'll read the instructions: Fill in the blanks with **he, she, it** or **they.**
2. Fill in the blanks for part C. Remember to begin each sentence with a capital. Raise your hand when you're finished.
   (Observe students and give feedback.)
3. Let's check your work. I'll read each sentence. You say the sentence you wrote.
- Sentence 1: Two women fixed the car. (Signal.) *They fixed the car.*
- Sentence 2: My father bought a new tie. (Signal.) *He bought a new tie.*
- Sentence 3: The boys and girls played baseball. (Signal.) *They played baseball.*
- Sentence 4: Jill found ten dollars. (Signal.) *She found ten dollars.*
- Sentence 5: His bag was full of apples. (Signal.) *It was full of apples.*
- Sentence 6: Those apples were not ripe. (Signal.) *They were not ripe.*
- Sentence 7: Her sisters painted Jim's room. (Signal.) *They painted Jim's room.*
- Sentence 8: David fed the dog. (Signal.) *He fed the dog.*
4. Raise your hand if you got all the items right. Great job.
- Everybody else, fix up any mistakes you made in part C.

EXERCISE 5 Capitalizing

Names

1. Everybody, find part D. ✔
   I'll read the instructions: Begin all parts of a person's name with a capital letter.
2. Look at the items in part D. Fix up each person's name so all parts of the name begin with a capital. Raise your hand when you're finished.
   (Observe students and give feedback.)
3. Let's check your work. I'll read the items. You say **capital** if it's a person's name. Say **no capital** if it's not a person's name.

- Item 1: Alice. (Signal.) *Capital.*
- Item 2: Mr. Martinez. (Signal.) *Capital.*
- Item 3: my brother. (Signal.) *No capital.*
- Item 4: the doctor. (Signal.) *No capital.*
- Item 5: the new boss. (Signal.) *No capital.*
- Item 6: Robert. (Signal.) *Capital.*
- Item 7: Mrs. Adams. (Signal.) *Capital.*
- Item 8: a big fish. (Signal.) *No capital.*
- Item 9: a fire fighter. (Signal.) *No capital.*
- Item 10: Sally. (Signal.) *Capital.*
- Item 11: Carl Sanders. (Signal.) *Capital.*
- Item 12: that teacher. (Signal.) *No capital.*
4. Raise your hand if you got all the items right. Great job.
- Everybody else, fix up any mistakes you made in part D.

EXERCISE 6 Paragraph Clarity

1. Everybody, pencils down. Find part E. ✔
   The paragraph in part E has words that are unclear because they don't give us a clear picture of what happened. The unclear words are underlined.
2. I'll read the first sentence: **A man** was carrying **some food.** We can't get a clear picture of the man or the food he was carrying.
3. Next sentence: He saw **some animals.** We don't know how many animals there were or what kind of animals they were. I can picture 12 elephants.
- What kind of animals can you picture? (Call on several students. After each appropriate suggestion, say:) Yes, you told about some animals, so that's one of the pictures you could get.
4. Next sentence: He dropped **it** and climbed up **a plant.** We're not really sure what he dropped and we don't know what kind of plant he climbed.
5. Next sentence: **Some of the animals** ate **it.** We don't know how many animals ate it, or what they ate.
6. Last sentence: **Some of the animals** looked up at the man. What's underlined in that sentence? (Signal.) *Some of the animals.*
- (Call on a student:) Why is **some of the animals** underlined? (Praise a response that expresses the idea: *We don't know how many animals or what kind of animals.*)

7. Take out a sheet of lined paper and write your name. Raise your hand when you're finished. ✔
• Pencils down. Open your textbook to lesson 99 and find part F. ✔

8. The picture shows what happened. You can see what the man looked like, what he was carrying before he climbed the plant and what kind of plant he climbed. You can also see **how many** animals there were and **what kind** of animals they were.
• Look at the man. You could call that man a **large** man. That would give a clear picture. What could you call him to give a picture that's even clearer? (Call on several students. Praise descriptions such as: *A large man with a tattoo on his arm; a large man with a tattoo and curly hair.*)
• Look at the first sentence in part E of your workbook. Who can say the first sentence with the underlined parts changed so they give a clear picture of the man and the food? (Call on several students. Praise sentences such as: *A large man with big muscles was carrying a cherry pie.* For each good sentence:) Everybody, say that sentence.
9. Next sentence. He saw <u>some animals.</u> Who can say that sentence with the underlined part changed so the sentence gives a clear picture of the animals? (Call on several students. Praise sentences such as: *He saw four skunks. He saw two big skunks and two little skunks.* For each good sentence:) Everybody, say that sentence.
• Next sentence. He dropped <u>it</u> and climbed up <u>a plant.</u> Who can say that sentence

with the underlined parts changed so the sentence gives a clear picture of what he dropped and what he climbed? (Call on several students. Praise sentences such as: *He dropped the cherry pie and climbed up a big tree.* For each good sentence:) Everybody, say that sentence.
• Next sentence. <u>Some of the animals</u> ate <u>it.</u> Who can say that sentence with the underlined parts changed so the sentence gives a clear picture of the animals and what they ate? (Call on several students. Praise sentences such as: *The two baby skunks ate a piece of the pie.* For each good sentence:) Everybody, say that sentence.
10. I'll read the words in the vocabulary box. Follow along: **skunks, muscles, tattoo, pie, piece.**
11. Your turn: Rewrite the paragraph on your lined paper. Remember, change the underlined parts so they give a clear picture. Copy the rest of each sentence. You have 7 minutes. Raise your hand when you're finished.
(Observe students and give feedback.)
12. (After 7 minutes, say:) Stop writing. I'm going to call on several students to read their paragraphs. Remember, the only parts of the sentences that should be changed are the underlined parts. The new parts should give a clear picture of what happened. Listen carefully and raise your hand if a sentence is wrong or if it doesn't give a clear picture.
(Call on several students to read their paragraphs. After each paragraph is read, ask the group:) Does that paragraph give a clear picture? (Praise paragraphs that have clear replacements for the underlined parts.)
13. Now you're going to check your paragraph. Make 2 check boxes under your paragraph.
14. Check 1: Does each sentence begin with a capital and end with a period? Check your paragraph. Fix up any mistakes. Then make a check in box 1. Raise your hand when you're finished.
(Observe students and give feedback.)

15. Check 2: Does each sentence give a clear picture of what happened? Read your paragraph. Make sure each sentence gives a clear picture. Fix up any mistakes. Then make a check in box 2. Raise your hand when you're finished.
(Observe students and give feedback.)

16. Next time, I'll read some of the **super** paragraphs to you.

EXERCISE 7 Clarity

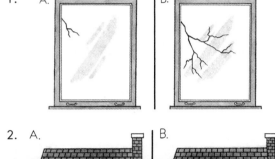

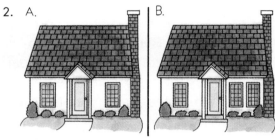

1. Skip a line on your paper. Then number your paper 1 and 2. Raise your hand when you're finished.

- Pencils down. Find part G in your textbook. ✔

- For each item, you're going to write a sentence that tells only about picture A, not picture B.

2. Look at the pictures for item 1. They are different in some way. Raise your hand when you can make up a sentence that tells **only** about picture A, not picture B. Your sentence should start with **the window.**

- (Call on a student. Praise a sentence such as: *The window had a small crack in it.*)

3. Everybody, look at the pictures for item 2. Raise your hand when you can make up a sentence that tells only about picture A, not picture B. Your sentence should start with **the house.** (Call on a student. Praise a sentence such as: *The house had one window on each side of the door; The house had two windows.*)

4. Your turn: Write the sentence for each item on your lined paper. Sentence 1 should tell only about picture A in item 1. Sentence 2 should tell only about picture A in item 2. Raise your hand when you're finished. (Observe students and give feedback.)

5. I'm going to call on several students to read their sentences. Listen carefully and make sure that each sentence tells only about picture A.

- (Call on several students to read their sentences. Praise good sentences.)

6. Check your work. Read your sentences. Make sure they begin with a capital and end with a period. Also, make sure they begin with the right words. Sentence 1 should begin with the words **the window.** Sentence 2 should begin with the words **the house.** Raise your hand when you're finished.

Note:

- Collect the students' workbooks and papers.

- Check the students' work before the next language period. Mark any mistakes.

- Write **super** on work that has all mistakes corrected. Write **good** or **pretty good** on work that has only 1 or 2 mistakes.

Objectives

- **Capitalize people's names in a paragraph.** (Exercise 2)
- **Edit a paragraph for he, she, it and they.** (Exercise 3)
- Write past-time verbs for irregular present-time verbs. (Exercise 4)
- Identify sentence parts as subjects or predicates. (Exercise 5)
- Rewrite a paragraph to correct unclear parts. (Exercise 6)
- Write a sentence that tells about only one of two similar pictures. (Exercise 7)

EXERCISE 1 **Feedback On Lesson 99**

- (Before returning the students' papers and workbooks, read some of the better paragraphs for part E of lesson 99.)
- (Hand back the students' work from lesson 99.)
- Look at what I wrote on your lined paper. Raise your hand if I wrote **super.**

WORKBOOK

EXERCISE 2 **Capitalizing**

Names

1. Everybody, open your workbook to lesson 100 and find part A. ✔
- You've learned that all parts of a person's name are capitalized. They are capitalized even if they are not the first words of a sentence.
2. Find the check box for part A. ✔
   I'll read the check: Does each part of a person's name begin with a capital?
- The number after the check question is **9.** That means the passage has 9 mistakes. There are 9 words that are not properly capitalized.
3. Your turn: Read the paragraph. Make sure that each part of someone's name begins with a capital letter. Find all 9 words that are not capitalized and fix them up. Raise your hand when you're finished. (Observe students and give feedback.)

4. Let's check your work. I'll read the paragraph and tell you the words you should have fixed up.
- James had two good friends. Their names were capital **J,** Jill capital **A,** Adams and capital **R,** Robert capital **G,** Gomez, period. Capital **J,** Jill and capital **R,** Robert went to the same school that capital **J,** James went to. Their teacher was capital **M,** Mr. capital **R,** Ray.
5. Raise your hand if you fixed up all the words. Great job.
- Everybody else, fix up any mistakes you made in part A.

EXERCISE 3 **Paragraph Editing**

Pronouns

1. Everybody, find part B. ✔
   I'll read the instructions: Cross out some of the names and write **he, she, it** or **they.**
- Remember the rule for using the words **he, she** and **it** in paragraphs: If two sentences in a row name the same person or thing, change the second sentence. That same rule works for **they.**
2. Here's the first sentence: Tom and Mary went to the airport. Who does that sentence name? (Signal.) *Tom and Mary.*
- Look at the next sentence. Does that sentence also name Tom and Mary? (Signal.) *Yes.*

- What are you going to write instead of **Tom and Mary** in the second sentence? (Signal.) *They.*
- Cross out **Tom and Mary** in the second sentence and write **they.**
  (Observe students and give feedback.)
3. Fix up the rest of the paragraph. Remember, if two sentences in a row name the same people, cross out the names in the second sentence and write **they.** Raise your hand when you're finished.
  (Observe students and give feedback.)
4. Let's check your work. I'll read the fixed-up paragraph.
- Tom and Mary went to the airport. **They** were going to meet their dad in San Francisco. Tom had never been on a plane before. **He** was very frightened. Tom and Mary sat together on the plane. **They** had fun after Tom stopped worrying.
5. Raise your hand if you made no mistakes. Great job.
- Everybody else, fix up any mistakes you made in part B.

EXERCISE 4   Past Time

Irregular Verbs

1. Everybody, pencils down. Find part C. ✔
   These are new words.
2. Touch word 1.
   The word that tells what somebody does is **swims.** What word tells what somebody did? (Signal.) *Swam.*
- Begins. What word tells what somebody did? (Signal.) *Began.*
- Comes. What word tells what somebody did? (Signal.) *Came.*
- Draws. What word tells what somebody did? (Signal.) *Drew.*
- Takes. What word tells what somebody did? (Signal.) *Took.*
3. Do words 6 through 10. Next to each word, write the word that tells what somebody did. Raise your hand when you're finished.
   (Observe students and give feedback.)
4. Let's check your work.
- Draws. What word tells what somebody did? (Signal.) *Drew.*
- Spell **drew.** (Signal.) *D-r-e-w.*
- Takes. What word tells what somebody did? (Signal.) *Took.*

- Spell **took.** (Signal.) *T-o-o-k.*
- Begins. What word tells what somebody did? (Signal.) *Began.*
- Spell **began.** (Signal.) *B-e-g-a-n.*
- Comes. What word tells what somebody did? (Signal.) *Came.*
- Spell **came.** (Signal.) *C-a-m-e.*
- Swims. What word tells what somebody did? (Signal.) *Swam.*
- Spell swam. (Signal.) *S-w-a-m.*
5. Raise your hand if you made no mistakes. Great job.
- Everybody else, fix up any mistakes you made in part C.

EXERCISE 5   Subject/Predicate

1. Everybody, find part D. ✔
   For each part, you're going to write **S** or **P.** You'll write **S** in front of each part that is a subject and **P** in front of each part that is a predicate. Do it now. Raise your hand when you're finished.
   (Observe students and give feedback.)
2. Let's check your work. I'll read each part. Tell me whether the part is a subject or a predicate.
- Part 1: went to the circus. (Signal.) *A predicate.*
- Part 2: our family. (Signal.) *A subject.*
- Part 3: laughed at the clowns. (Signal.) *A predicate.*
- Part 4: was very exciting. (Signal.) *A predicate.*
- Part 5: lions and tigers. (Signal.) *A subject.*
- Part 6: my sister. (Signal.) *A subject.*
- Part 7: sat under a large tree. (Signal.) *A predicate.*
- Part 8: Tom and his sister. (Signal.) *A subject.*
- Part 9: ate dinner with us. (Signal.) *A predicate.*
- Part 10: they. (Signal.) *A subject.*
3. Raise your hand if you got everything right. Great job.

EXERCISE 6   Paragraph Clarity

1. Everybody, find part E. ✔
   The paragraph has words that are unclear because they don't give us a good picture.
2. I'll read the first sentence: She was riding a vehicle. The underlined parts are **she** and **vehicle.**

- (Call on a student:) Why is **she** underlined? (Praise a response that expresses the idea: *We don't know what kind of woman.*)
- (Call on a student:) Why is **vehicle** underlined? (Praise a response that expresses the idea: *We don't know what kind of vehicle.*)
- What kind of vehicle do you picture? (Call on several students. After each appropriate suggestion, say:) Yes, you told about a vehicle, so that's one of the pictures you could get.

3. Next sentence: She was in the middle of it. We don't know what **it** is. She could be in the middle of a city or the middle of a forest.
- Next sentence: An animal jumped in front of it. We don't know what kind of **animal** or what the animal jumped in front of.
- Listen to the rest of the passage: She turned sharply. The vehicle ran into a plant. The plant damaged it. We could get a lot of different pictures from that passage.

LINED PAPER • TEXTBOOK

4. Take out a sheet of lined paper and write your name. Raise your hand when you're finished.
- Pencils down. Open your textbook to lesson 100 and find part E. ✔

5. The picture shows what happened. You can see what the woman looked like and what kind of vehicle she was riding. She was in the middle of something.
- (Call on a student:) What was she in the middle of? *A desert.*
  Yes, she was in the middle of a great desert.

- You can see the animal that jumped out in front of her. (Call on a student:) What kind of animal is that? *A mountain lion.*
- Who knows what kind of plant she ran into? (Call on a student:) *A cactus.*
- Look at the motorcycle. The passage says the plant damaged it. Who can tell me what **it** is so we can get a clear picture of what got damaged? (Call on a student:) *The front wheel of the motorcycle.*

6. I'll read the words in the vocabulary box: **woman, cactus, motorcycle, young, desert, wheel, mountain lion.**

7. Your turn: Rewrite the paragraph on your lined paper. Remember, change the underlined parts so they give a clear picture. Copy the rest of each sentence. You have 7 minutes. Raise your hand when you're finished.
   (Observe students and give feedback.)

8. (After 7 minutes, say:) Stop writing. I'm going to call on several students to read their paragraphs. Remember, the only parts of the sentences that should be changed are the underlined parts. The new parts should give a clear picture of what happened. Listen carefully and raise your hand if a sentence is wrong or if it doesn't give a clear picture.
- (Call on several students to read their paragraphs. After each paragraph is read, ask the group:) Does that paragraph give a clear picture?
   (Praise paragraphs that have clear replacements for the underlined parts.)

9. Now you're going to check your paragraph. Make 2 check boxes under your paragraph.

10. Check 1: Does each sentence begin with a capital and end with a period? Check your paragraph. Fix up any mistakes. Then make a check in box 1. Raise your hand when you're finished.
    (Observe students and give feedback.)

11. Check 2: Does each sentence give a clear picture of what happened? Read your paragraph. Make sure each sentence gives a clear picture. Fix up any mistakes. Then make a check in box 2. Raise your hand when you're finished.
    (Observe students and give feedback.)

12. Next time, I'll read some of the **super** paragraphs to you.

EXERCISE 7 Clarity

1.

 A.    B.

2.

 A.    B.

1. Skip a line on your paper. Then number your paper 1 and 2. Raise your hand when you're finished.
- Everybody, find part F in your textbook.
- For each item, you're going to write a sentence that tells only about picture A, not picture B.
2. Look at the pictures for item 1. Write a sentence that tells only about picture A. Start your sentence with **a boy.** Remember, write just one sentence. And that sentence should tell only about picture A, not picture B. Raise your hand when you're finished.
(Observe students and give feedback.)
- (Call on several students to read their sentence for item 1. Praise sentences such as: *A boy had a big bandage on his chin.*)

3. Look at the pictures for item 2. Write a sentence that tells only about picture A. Start your sentence with **a painter.** Remember, write just one sentence. And that sentence should tell only about picture A, not picture B. Raise your hand when you're finished.
(Observe students and give feedback.)
- (Call on several students to read their sentence for item 2. Praise sentences such as: *A painter stood on top of a little ladder.*)
4. Check your work. Read your sentences. Make sure they begin with a capital and end with a period. Also, make sure they begin with the right words. Sentence 1 should begin with the words **a boy.** Sentence 2 should begin with the words **a painter.**

Note:

- Collect the students' workbooks and papers.

- Check the students' work before the next language period. Mark any mistakes.

- Write **super** on work that has all mistakes corrected. Write **good** or **pretty good** on work that has only 1 or 2 mistakes.

Objectives

- **Edit a paragraph for sentences that begin with and or and then.** (Exercise 2)
- Write past-time verbs for irregular present-time verbs. (Exercise 3)
- Edit a paragraph to correct unclear parts. (Exercise 4)
- Write a paragraph that reports on an illustrated action sequence. (Exercise 5)

EXERCISE 1   Feedback On Lesson 100

- (Before returning the students' papers and workbooks, read some of the better paragraphs for part E of lesson 100.)
- (Hand back the students' work from lesson 100.)
- Look at what I wrote on your lined paper. Raise your hand if I wrote **super.**

WORKBOOK

EXERCISE 2   Paragraph Editing

And, And Then

1. Everybody, open your workbook to lesson 101 and find part A. ✔
- Some sentences in this paragraph begin with the words **and then.** Other sentences begin with the word **and.** Sometimes a sentence **can** begin with **and** or **and then,** but most of the time these beginnings are not good. You're going to fix up the paragraph so that none of the sentences begin with **and** or **and then.**
2. I'll read the first sentence: Morgan threw a Frisbee to his dad. That sentence is all right.
- Next sentence: **And** it went over his dad's head. (Call on a student.) What's wrong with that sentence? (Praise a response such as: *It starts with and.*)
- Everybody, cross out the word **and.** Make the **i** in the word **it** a capital **I.** ✔
3. Next sentence: And then his dad ran after the Frisbee. (Call on a student.) What's wrong with that sentence? (Praise a response such as: *It starts with and then.*)
- Everybody, cross out the words **and then.** Make the **h** in **his** a capital **H.** ✔

4. Listen: Read the rest of the sentences in the paragraph. If any sentence begins with **and** or **and then,** cross out those words and make the next word begin with a capital. Raise your hand when you're finished.
   (Observe students and give feedback.)
5. Let's check your work. I'll read the fixed-up paragraph.
- Morgan threw a Frisbee to his dad. Capital **I,** It went over his dad's head. Capital **H,** His dad ran after the Frisbee. Capital **H,** He tripped in the mud. Morgan started to run after the Frisbee. Capital **A,** A big dog picked it up before Morgan could grab it. Capital **T,** The dog ran away with it. Morgan chased after the dog. His dad went in the house to clean up.
6. Raise your hand if you made no mistakes. Great job.
- Everybody else, fix up any mistakes you made in part A.

EXERCISE 3   Past Time

Irregular Verbs

1. Everybody, pencils down. Find part B. ✔
2. Touch word 1. ✔
   The word that tells what somebody does is **draws.** What word tells what somebody did? (Signal.) *Drew.*
- Swims. What word tells what somebody did? (Signal.) *Swam.*
- Begins. What word tells what somebody did? (Signal.) *Began.*
- Takes. What word tells what somebody did? (Signal.) *Took.*
- Comes. What word tells what somebody did? (Signal.) *Came.*

3. Do words 6 through 10. Next to each word, write the word that tells what somebody did. Raise your hand when you're finished. (Observe students and give feedback.)

4. Let's check your work.
- Begins. What word tells what somebody did? (Signal.) *Began.*
- Spell **began.** (Signal.) *B-e-g-a-n.*
- Comes. What word tells what somebody did? (Signal.) *Came.*
- Spell **came.** (Signal.) *C-a-m-e.*
- Draws. What word tells what somebody did? (Signal.) *Drew.*
- Spell **drew.** (Signal.) *D-r-e-w.*
- Swims. What word tells what somebody did? (Signal.) *Swam.*
- Spell **swam.** (Signal.) *S-w-a-m.*
- Takes. What word tells what somebody did? (Signal.) *Took.*
- Spell **took.** (Signal.) *T-o-o-k.*

5. Raise your hand if you made no mistakes. Great job.
- Everybody else, fix up any mistakes you made in part B.

EXERCISE 4 Edit For Clarity

1. You've learned the rule that if two sentences in a row name the same person or thing, you use **he, she, it** or **they** in the second sentence. But when you use **he, she, it** or **they** in the first sentence, the reader can't get a clear picture of what happened.

2. Everybody, find part C. ✔
The writer of this passage made mistakes by using **he, she, it** or **they** before giving us a clear picture of the persons or things.

3. I'll read the first sentence: They cleaned the animal. Two words are unclear. What's the first unclear word? (Signal.) *They.*
- What's the other unclear word? (Signal.) *Animal.*
- Underline the word **they** and the word **animal.** ✔
- Next sentence: She wore great big shoes and dark glasses. One word is unclear. What's that word? (Signal.) *She.*
- Underline **she.** ✔

4. Next sentence: She squirted the animal with a hose. I'll tell you a secret. The **she** in this sentence is the same **she** that's in the last sentence. So if we fix up the last

sentence, the word **she** won't be unclear in this sentence. But the word **animal** is unclear. Underline the word **animal.** ✔
- Next sentence: He wore a cowboy hat. One word is unclear. What's that word? (Signal.) *He.*
- Underline **he.** ✔
- Next sentence: He sat on the animal and scrubbed its back. The word **he** won't be unclear if we fix up the last sentence. The word **animal** is unclear. Underline **animal.**

5. Next sentence: She wore a funny suit and a tiny hat. One word is unclear. What's that word? (Signal.) *She.*
- Underline **she.** ✔
- Next sentence: She stood on a ladder. That's the same **she** that was in the last sentence. Think big. Everybody, if we fixed up the last sentence, would there be any unclear words in this sentence? (Signal.) *No.*
- Next sentence: She poured it on the animal. The word **she** is not unclear. But two other words are unclear. What's the first unclear word? (Signal.) *It.*
- What's the other unclear word? (Signal.) *Animal.*
- Underline **it** and **animal.** ✔

6. This passage could give us a lot of different pictures. You're going to fix it up.
- Open your textbook to lesson 101 and find part C. ✔

- Look at the picture. The first sentence is: They cleaned the animal. To give a clear picture of **they,** you could name the group. Everybody, what's a good name for the group? (Signal.) *The clowns.*

- Everybody, what kind of animal is in that picture? (Signal.) *An elephant.*
7. Your turn: Fix up the paragraph in your workbook. Above each word that you underlined, write words that give a clear picture. For some words, you can give a clearer picture just by naming the person. Fix up the whole passage. Then read it to yourself to make sure it gives a pretty clear picture of what happened. Raise your hand when you're finished.
(Observe students and give feedback.)
8. I'll read a paragraph that's pretty clear.
- The clowns cleaned the elephant. Sally wore great big shoes and dark glasses. She squirted the elephant with a hose. Pete wore a cowboy hat. He sat on the elephant and scrubbed its back. Jessica wore a funny suit and a tiny hat. She stood on a ladder. She poured water on the elephant.
9. I'm going to call on several students to read their fixed-up paragraphs. Listen and make sure that each paragraph gives a pretty clear picture. Raise your hand if you hear a mistake.
- (Call on several students to read their paragraphs. Praise paragraphs that have good descriptions for the underlined words.)

LINED PAPER

EXERCISE 5 Paragraph Writing

1. Everybody, take out a sheet of lined paper. Write your name on the top line. ✔
- Everybody, pencils down. Find part D in your textbook. ✔
I'll read the instructions: Write a paragraph that reports on what happened. Write a sentence for each name shown in the pictures.

2. Everybody, touch number 1. ✔
Name that animal. (Signal.) *A bluebird.*
- Raise your hand when you can say a sentence that reports on the main thing a bluebird did in that picture. (Call on several students. Praise sentences such as: *A bluebird sat on a branch of a tree.* For each good sentence:) Everybody, say that sentence.
3. Everybody, touch number 2. ✔
Name that animal. (Signal.) *A striped cat.*
- Raise your hand when you can say a sentence that reports on the main thing a striped cat did in that picture. (Call on several students. Praise sentences such as: *A striped cat ran up the trunk of the tree.* For each good sentence:) Everybody, say that sentence.
4. Everybody, touch number 3. ✔
Name that animal. (Signal.) *The cat.*
- Raise your hand when you can say a sentence that reports on the main thing the cat did in that picture. (Call on several students. Praise sentences such as: *The cat walked out on the branch toward the bird.* For each good sentence:) Everybody, say that sentence.
5. Everybody, touch number 4. ✔
Name that animal. (Signal.) *The bird.*
- Raise your hand when you can say a sentence that reports on the main thing the bird did in that picture. (Call on several students. Praise sentences such as: *The bird flew into the air.* For each good sentence:) Everybody, say that sentence.
6. Everybody, touch number 5. ✔
Name that object. (Signal.) *The branch.*
- Raise your hand when you can say a sentence that reports on the main thing the branch did in that picture. (Call on several students. Praise sentences such as: *The branch broke.* For each good sentence:) Everybody, say that sentence.
7. Everybody, touch number 6. ✔
Name that animal. (Signal.) *The cat.*
- Raise your hand when you can say a sentence that reports on the main thing the cat did in that picture. (Call on several students. Praise sentences such as: *The cat fell toward the ground.* For each good sentence:) Everybody, say that sentence.

8. I'll read a passage that reports on what happened: A bluebird sat on a branch of a tree. A striped cat ran up the trunk of the tree. The cat walked out on the branch toward the bird. The bird flew into the air. The branch broke. The cat fell toward the ground.

9. I'll say those sentences again.
   • A bluebird sat on the branch of a tree. Say that sentence. (Signal.) *A bluebird sat on the branch of a tree.*
   • A striped cat ran up the trunk of the tree. Say that sentence. (Signal.) *A striped cat ran up the trunk of the tree.*
   • The cat walked out on the branch toward the bird. Say that sentence. (Signal.) *The cat walked out on the branch toward the bird.*
   • The bird flew into the air. Say that sentence. (Signal.) *The bird flew into the air.*
   • The branch broke. Say that sentence. (Signal.) *The branch broke.*
   • The cat fell toward the ground. Say that sentence. (Signal.) *The cat fell toward the ground.*

10. Touch the words in the vocabulary box as I read them: ground, climbed, flew, jumped, landed, broke, trunk, branch.

11. Touch number 1 in the first picture. Name that animal. (Signal.) *A bluebird.*
    • Write a sentence that tells the main thing a bluebird did in the picture. This sentence is the first one in your paragraph, so be sure to indent. Raise your hand when you're finished.
    (Observe students and give feedback.)

12. Touch number 2.
    Name that animal. (Signal.) *A striped cat.*
    • Write a sentence that tells the main thing a striped cat did in the picture. Don't write any numbers. Start writing the sentence about the striped cat just after the period. Raise your hand when you're finished.
    (Observe students and give feedback.)

13. Touch number 3.
    Name that animal. (Signal.) *The cat.*
    • Write a sentence that tells the main thing the cat did in that picture. Raise your hand when you're finished.
    (Observe students and give feedback.)

14. Touch number 4.
    Name that animal. (Signal.) *The bird.*

• Finish your paragraph. Write a clear sentence for each of the names in the pictures. You'll write sentences for names 4, 5 and 6. Raise your hand when you're finished.
(Observe students and give feedback.)

15. I'm going to call on several students to read their paragraphs. Listen carefully. Make sure each sentence tells the main thing. Make sure no sentences are missing. And make sure each sentence tells what somebody or something did. Raise your hand if you hear a mistake.
    • (Call on several students to read their paragraphs. Praise good paragraphs.)

16. Now you're going to check your paragraph. Make 3 check boxes under your paragraph. ✔

17. Check 1: Does each sentence begin with a capital and end with a period? Check your paragraph. Fix up any mistakes. Then make a check in box 1. Raise your hand when you're finished.
    (Observe students and give feedback.)

18. Check 2: Does each sentence tell the main thing? Read your paragraph. Make sure each sentence tells the main thing. Fix up any mistakes. Then make a check in box 2. Raise your hand when you're finished.
    (Observe students and give feedback.)

19. Check 3: Does each sentence tell what somebody or something **did?** Remember, you can't tell what somebody or something was doing. You have to tell what they did. Fix up any mistakes. Then make a check in box 3. Raise your hand when you're finished.
    (Observe students and give feedback.)

20. Next time, I'll read some of the **super** paragraphs to you.

Note:
• Collect the students' workbooks and papers.
• Check the students' work before the next language period. Mark any mistakes.
• Write **super** on work that has all mistakes corrected. Write **good** or **pretty good** on work that has only 1 or 2 mistakes.

Objectives

- **Edit a paragraph for periods and capitals, including people's names.** (Exercise 2)
- Edit a paragraph for sentences that begin with **and** or **and then.** (Exercise 3)
- Edit a paragraph to correct unclear parts. (Exercise 4)
- Write past-time verbs for irregular present-time verbs. (Exercise 5)
- Write a paragraph that reports on an illustrated action sequence. (Exercise 6)

EXERCISE 1 Feedback On Lesson 101

- (Before returning the students' papers and workbooks, read some of the better paragraphs for part D of lesson 101.)
- (Hand back the students' work from lesson 101.)
- Look at what I wrote on your lined paper. Raise your hand if I wrote **super.**

WORKBOOK

EXERCISE 2 Paragraph Editing

1. Everybody, open your workbook to lesson 102 and find part A. ✔
- You're going to edit the paragraph in part A for two different things.
2. I'll read the checks. Follow along.
- Check 1: Does each sentence begin with a capital and end with a period?
- Check 2: Does each part of a person's name begin with a capital letter?
3. Listen: First check the paragraph to make sure each sentence begins with a capital and ends with a period. Do it now. Then make a check in box 1. Raise your hand when you're finished.
(Observe students and give feedback.)
4. (After students complete check 1, say:) Now go through the paragraph again for check 2. Fix up the paragraph so all parts of a person's name begin with a capital letter. Then make a check in box 2. Raise your hand when you're finished.
(Observe students and give feedback.)
5. Let's check your work. I'll read the fixed-up paragraph.

- We had a good time at the park, period. Tom played basketball with capital **B,** Bob. Alice and capital **J,** Jane went jogging. I listened to capital **M,** Mr. capital **A,** Anderson read from a book, period. Capital **M,** My sister went swimming, period. Capital **W,** We got home just in time for dinner, period.
6. Raise your hand if you fixed up all the mistakes. Great job.
- Everybody else, fix up any mistakes you missed in part A.

EXERCISE 3 Paragraph Editing

And, And Then

1. Everybody, pencils down. Find part B. ✔ Some sentences in this paragraph begin with the words **and then.** Other sentences begin with the word **and.** You're going to fix up the paragraph so that none of the sentences begin with **and** or **and then.**
2. I'll read the first sentence: Sandra went to the zoo yesterday. That sentence is all right.
- Next sentence: And then she met her friends near the monkey house. (Call on a student.) What's wrong with that sentence? (Praise a response such as: *It starts with and then.*)
- Everybody, cross out the words **and then.** Make the **s** in **she** a capital **S.** ✔
3. Next sentence: And the monkeys were doing tricks. (Call on a student.) What's wrong with that sentence? (Praise a response such as: *It starts with and.*)
- Everybody, cross out the word **and.** Make the **t** in **the** a capital **T.** ✔

4. Listen: Read the rest of the sentences in the paragraph. If any sentence begins with **and** or **and then,** cross out those words and make the next word begin with a capital. Raise your hand when you're finished.
   (Observe students and give feedback.)

5. Let's check your work. I'll read the fixed-up paragraph.
   - Sandra went to the zoo yesterday. Capital **S,** She met her friends near the monkey house. Capital **T,** The monkeys were doing tricks. Two monkeys were swinging by their tails. Capital **O,** One monkey was doing flips. Sandra and her friends went to the snack bar. Capital **T,** They bought peanuts for the monkeys.

6. Raise your hand if you made no mistakes. Great job.
   - Everybody else, fix up any mistakes you made in part B.

EXERCISE 4 Edit For Clarity

1. You've learned the rule that if two sentences in a row name the same person or thing, you use **he, she, it** or **they** in the second sentence. But when you use **he, she, it** or **they** in the first sentence, the reader can't get a clear picture of what happened.

2. Everybody, find part C. ✔
   - The writer of this passage made mistakes by using **he, she, it** or **they** before giving us a clear picture of the persons or things.

3. I'll read the first sentence: They were in a corral. One word is unclear. What's the unclear word? (Signal.) *They.*
   - Underline the word **they.** ✔
   - Next sentence: It drove up. One word is unclear. What's the word? (Signal.) *It.*
   - Underline **it.** ✔

4. Next sentence: It started to make a loud noise. That's the same **it** that was in the last sentence. Think big. If we fixed up the last sentence, would there be any unclear words in this sentence? (Signal.) *No.*
   - Next sentence: They were in it. Two words are unclear. What's the first unclear word? (Signal.) *They.* What's the other unclear word? (Signal.) *It.*
   - Underline **they** and **it.** ✔

5. Next sentence: He grabbed a rope and jumped out of it. Two words are unclear. What's the first unclear word? (Signal.) *He.*
   - What's the other unclear word? (Signal.) *It.*
   - Underline **he** and **it.** ✔

- Last sentence: They stayed in it.
- Underline **they** and **it** in the last sentence. ✔

TEXTBOOK

6. You're going to fix up this paragraph. Open your textbook to lesson 102 and find part C. ✔

- Look at the picture. The first sentence is: They were in a corral. To give a clear picture, you could tell how many and what kind of group was in the corral. How could you describe the group inside the corral clearly? (Call on several students. Praise descriptions such as: *Three horses.*)
- The next sentences are: It drove up. It started to make a loud noise. You can see what it is. And you can see that it made a loud noise.
- Listen to the next sentence: They were in it. To give a clear picture of who **they** were, you could tell how many and what kind of group was in the jeep when it drove up. How could you describe the group clearly? (Call on several students. Praise descriptions such as: *Three cowboys.*)
- Next sentence: He grabbed a rope and jumped out of it. How could you describe the cowboy who jumped out? (Call on several students. Praise descriptions such as: *An old cowboy.*)
- Last sentence: They stayed in it. You could tell how many cowboys and what kind of cowboys stayed in the jeep. How are those cowboys different from the cowboy who jumped out? (Call on several students. Praise descriptions such as: *Two young cowboys.*)

7. Your turn: Fix up the paragraph in your workbook. Above each word that you underlined, write words that give a clear picture. Fix up the whole passage. Then read it to yourself to make sure it gives a pretty clear picture of what happened. Raise your hand when you're finished. (Observe students and give feedback.)

8. I'll read a paragraph that's pretty clear. Three horses were in a corral. A jeep drove up. It started to make a loud noise. Three cowboys were in the jeep. An old cowboy grabbed a rope and jumped out of the jeep. Two young cowboys stayed in the jeep.

9. I'm going to call on several students to read their fixed-up paragraphs. Listen and make sure that each paragraph gives a pretty clear picture. Raise your hand if you hear a mistake.

• (Call on several students to read their paragraphs. Praise paragraphs that have good descriptions for the underlined words.)

LINED PAPER

EXERCISE 5 Past Time

Irregular Verbs

1. Everybody, take out a sheet of lined paper and write your name on the top line. Number your paper 1 through 5. Raise your hand when you're finished. ✔

• Everybody, find part D in your textbook. ✔

2. The words in part D tell what somebody does. For each number, you'll write the word that tells what somebody did. Do it now. Raise your hand when you're finished. (Observe students and give feedback.)

3. Let's check your work.

• Word 1: draws. Say the word that tells what somebody did. (Signal.) *Drew.*

• Spell **drew.** (Signal.) *D-r-e-w.*

• Word 2: takes. Say the word that tells what somebody did. (Signal.) *Took.*

• Spell **took.** (Signal.) *T-o-o-k.*

• Word 3: comes. Say the word that tells what somebody did. (Signal.) *Came.*

• Spell **came.** (Signal.) *C-a-m-e.*

• Word 4: begins. Say the word that tells what somebody did. (Signal.) *Began.*

• Spell **began.** (Signal.) *B-e-g-a-n.*

• Word 5: swims. Say the word that tells what somebody did. (Signal.) *Swam.*

• Spell **swam.** (Signal.) *S-w-a-m.*

4. Raise your hand if you made no mistakes. Great job.

• Everybody else, fix up any mistakes you made in part D.

EXERCISE 6 Paragraph Writing

1. Everybody, pencils down. Find part E in your textbook. ✔
I'll read the instructions: Write a paragraph that reports on what happened. Write a sentence for each name shown in the pictures.

2. I'll read the words in the vocabulary box: grabbed, window sill, started, yelled, ate, piece, pie, answered, phone, scolded.

3. Look at the first picture.
Hector put a pie somewhere. (Call on a student:) Where did he put it? *On the window sill.*

• (Call on a student:) Why did he put the pie on the window sill? *To cool.*

• Who can make up a good sentence about what Hector did in the first picture? (Call on several students. Praise sentences such as: *Hector put a hot pie on the window sill to cool.* For each good sentence:) Everybody, say that sentence.

4. Everybody, touch number 2.
Number 2 is Hector again.

• Raise your hand when you can say a sentence that reports on the main thing Hector did in that picture. Start your sentence with **he.** (Call on several students. Praise sentences such as: *He went inside the room to answer the telephone.* For each good sentence:) Everybody, say that sentence.

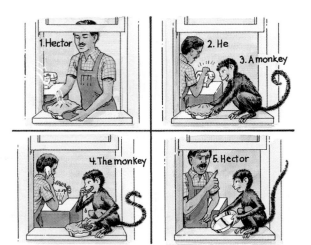

5. Everybody, touch number 3.
   Name that animal. (Signal.) *A monkey.*
- Raise your hand when you can say a
  sentence that reports on the main thing
  a monkey did in that picture. Start your
  sentence with **he.** (Call on several students.
  Praise sentences such as: *A monkey
  grabbed the pie.* For each good sentence:)
  Everybody, say that sentence.
6. Everybody, touch number 4.
   Name that animal. (Signal.) *The monkey.*
- Raise your hand when you can say a
  sentence that reports on the main thing
  the monkey did in that picture. (Call on
  several students. Praise sentences such
  as: *The monkey ate the pie.* For each good
  sentence:) Everybody, say that sentence.
7. Everybody, touch number 5.
   Name that person. (Signal.) *Hector.*
- Raise your hand when you can say a
  sentence that reports on the main thing
  Hector did in that picture. (Call on several
  students. Praise sentences such as:
  Hector scolded the monkey. For each good
  sentence:) Everybody, say that sentence.
8. I'll read a passage that reports on what
   happened: Hector put a hot pie on the
   windowsill. He went inside the room to
   answer the telephone. A monkey grabbed
   the pie. The monkey ate the pie. Hector
   scolded the monkey.
9. I'll say those sentences again.
- Hector put a hot pie on the windowsill. Say
  that sentence. (Signal.) *Hector put a hot pie
  on the windowsill.*
- He went inside the room to answer the
  telephone. Say that sentence. (Signal.)
  *He went inside the room to answer the
  telephone.*
- A monkey grabbed the pie. Say that
  sentence. (Signal.) *A monkey grabbed
  the pie.*

- The monkey ate the pie. Say that sentence.
  (Signal.) *The monkey ate the pie.*
- Hector scolded the monkey. Say that
  sentence. (Signal.) *Hector scolded the
  monkey.*
10. Your turn: Write your paragraph.
    Remember, write a clear sentence for each
    number. Indent your first sentence. You
    have 8 minutes to write your paragraph.
    Raise your hand when you're finished.
    (Observe students and give feedback.)
11. (After 8 minutes, say:) Stop writing. I'm
    going to call on several students to read
    their paragraphs. Listen carefully. Make
    sure each sentence tells the main thing.
    Make sure no sentences are missing.
    And make sure each sentence tells what
    somebody or something did. Raise your
    hand if you hear a mistake.
- (Call on several students to read their
  paragraphs. Praise good paragraphs.)
12. Now you're going to check your paragraph.
    Make 3 check boxes under your paragraph.
13. Check 1: Does each sentence begin with
    a capital and end with a period? Check
    your paragraph. Fix up any mistakes. Then
    make a check in box 1. Raise your hand
    when you're finished.
    (Observe students and give feedback.)
14. Check 2: Does each sentence tell the main
    thing? Read your paragraph. Make sure
    each sentence tells the main thing. Fix up
    any mistakes. Then make a check in box 2.
    Raise your hand when you're finished.
    (Observe students and give feedback.)
15. Check 3: Does each sentence tell what
    somebody or something **did?** Remember,
    you can't tell what somebody or something
    was doing. You have to tell what they did.
    Fix up any mistakes. Then make a check
    in box 3. Raise your hand when you're
    finished.
    (Observe students and give feedback.)
16. Next time, I'll read some of the **super**
    paragraphs to you.

> *Note:*
> - Collect the students' workbooks and papers.
> - Check the students' work before the next language
>   period. Mark any mistakes.
> - Write **super** on work that has all mistakes corrected.
>   Write **good** or **pretty good** on work that has only 1 or
>   2 mistakes.

Objectives

- Identify the subject and predicate of sentences. (Exercise 2)
- **Edit a paragraph for sentences that begin with *and* and for names that are not capitalized.** (Exercise 3)
- Write past-time verbs for irregular present-time verbs. (Exercise 4)
- **Write a sentence that tells about only one of three similar pictures.** (Exercise 5)
- Write a paragraph that reports on an illustrated action sequence. (Exercise 6)

EXERCISE 1 Feedback On Lesson 102

- (Before returning the students' papers and workbooks, read some of the better paragraphs for part E of lesson 102.)
- (Hand back the students' work from lesson 102.)
- Look at what I wrote on your lined paper. Raise your hand if I wrote **super.**

WORKBOOK

EXERCISE 2 Subject/Predicate

1. Everybody, open your workbook to lesson 103 and find part A. ✔
- For each sentence, you're going to circle the subject and underline the predicate.
2. What's the part of the sentence that names? (Signal.) *The subject.*
- What's the part of the sentence that tells more? (Signal.) *The predicate.*
3. For each sentence, circle the subject and underline the predicate. Do it now. Raise your hand when you're finished.
(Observe students and give feedback.)
4. Let's check your work.
- Sentence 1. What's the subject? (Signal.) *Carlos.*
- What's the predicate? (Signal.) *Built a fire.*
- Sentence 2. What's the subject? (Signal.) *Susan and Vanessa.*
- What's the predicate? (Signal.) *Are planning a party.*
- Sentence 3. What's the subject? (Signal.) *My old clock.*
- What's the predicate? (Signal.) *Was broken.*
- Sentence 4. What's the subject? (Signal.) *It.*
- What's the predicate? (Signal.) *Is very cold.*

- Sentence 5. What's the subject? (Signal.) *The horses and cows.*
- What's the predicate? (Signal.) *Stood in the barn.*
- Sentence 6. What's the subject? (Signal.) *They.*
- What's the predicate? (Signal.) *Gave a prize to every child.*
5. Raise your hand if you got no items wrong. Great job.
- Everybody else, fix up any mistakes you made in part A.

EXERCISE 3 Paragraph Editing

1. Everybody, find part B. ✔
You're going to edit the paragraph in part B for two different things.
2. I'll read the checks. Follow along.
- Check 1: Did you fix each sentence that started with **and** or **and then?**
- Check 2: Does each part of a person's name begin with a capital letter?
3. Listen: First check the paragraph for sentences that begin with **and** or **and then.** Fix up those sentences. Then make a check in box 1. Raise your hand when you're finished.
(Observe students and give feedback.)
4. (After students complete check 1, say:) Now go through the paragraph again for check 2. Make sure that each part of a person's name begins with a capital. Then make a check in box 2. Raise your hand when you're finished.
(Observe students and give feedback.)
5. Let's check your work. I'll read the fixed-up paragraph.

- Everybody went to the beach. Jerry and capital **A,** Alice built a fire on the sand. Tom and capital **B,** Bill roasted hot dogs and marshmallows. Mr. capital **J,** Jones and capital **S,** Sammy played ball.
6. Raise your hand if you fixed up all the mistakes. Great job.
- Everybody else, fix up any mistakes you missed in part B.

EXERCISE 4 Past Time

Irregular Verbs

1. Everybody, find part C. ✔
   The words in part C tell what somebody does. For each word, write the word that tells what somebody did. Raise your hand when you're finished.
   (Observe students and give feedback.)
2. Let's check your work.
- Word 1: comes. Say the word that tells what somebody did. (Signal.) *Came.*
- Spell **came.** (Signal.) *C-a-m-e.*
- Word 2: swims. Say the word that tells what somebody did. (Signal.) *Swam.*
- Spell **swam.** (Signal.) *S-w-a-m.*
- Word 3: draws. Say the word that tells what somebody did. (Signal.) *Drew.*
- Spell **drew.** (Signal.) *D-r-e-w.*
- Word 4: takes. Say the word that tells what somebody did. (Signal.) *Took.*
- Spell **took.** (Signal.) *T-o-o-k.*
- Word 5: begins. Say the word that tells what somebody did. (Signal.) *Began.*
- Spell **began.** (Signal.) *B-e-g-a-n.*
- Word 6: thinks. Say the word that tells what somebody did. (Signal.) *Thought.*
- Spell **thought.** (Signal.) *T-h-o-u-g-h-t.*
3. Raise your hand if you made no mistakes. Great job.
- Everybody else, fix up any mistakes you made in part C.

LINED PAPER • TEXTBOOK

EXERCISE 5 Clarity

1.

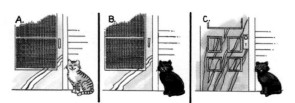

2.

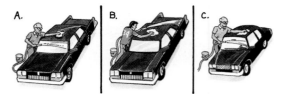

1. Take out a sheet of lined paper and write your name on the top line. Then number your paper 1 and 2. Raise your hand when you're finished.
- Everybody, pencils down. Find part D in your textbook.
- For each item, you're going to write a sentence that tells only about the first picture, not the second **or** the third picture. These are really hard.
2. Look at the pictures for item 1.
   Raise your hand when you can say a sentence that tells only about picture A. Your sentence should start by naming the kind of cat that is in picture A. Then the sentence should tell what kind of door is in picture A.
- (Call on a student. Praise a sentence such as: *A striped cat sat next to the screen door.*)
3. Look at the pictures for item 2.
   Raise your hand when you can say a sentence that tells only about picture A. Your sentence should start by naming the kind of man that is in picture A. Then the sentence should tell what kind of car is in that picture.
- (Call on a student. Praise a sentence such as: *An old man washed a long black car.*)
4. Everybody, write your sentences. Raise your hand when you're finished.
   (Observe students and give feedback.)
5. I'm going to call on several students to read their sentences. Listen carefully and make sure each sentence tells only about picture A.
- (Call on several students to read their sentences. Praise good sentences.)
6. Check your work. Make sure your sentences tell only about picture A in each item. Raise your hand when you're sure your sentences are clear.

EXERCISE 6   Paragraph Writing

1. Everybody, pencils down. Find part E in your textbook. ✔
   I'll read the instructions: Write a paragraph that reports on what happened. Write a sentence for each name shown in the pictures.

2. Everybody, touch number 1. ✔
   Name that person. (Signal.) *Jill.*

- Raise your hand when you can say a sentence that reports on the main thing Jill did in that picture. (Call on several students. Praise sentences such as: *Jill threw a ball to Robert.* For each good sentence:) Everybody, say that sentence.

3. Everybody, touch number 2. ✔
   Name that person. (Signal.) *Robert.*

- Raise your hand when you can say a sentence that reports on what Robert did in that picture. (Call on several students. Praise sentences such as: *Robert jumped up to catch the ball.* For each good sentence:) Everybody, say that sentence.

4. Everybody, touch number 3. ✔
   Name that object. (Signal.) *The ball.*

- Raise your hand when you can say a sentence that reports on the main thing the ball did in that picture. (Call on several students. Praise sentences such as: *The ball went over Robert.* For each good sentence:) Everybody, say that sentence.

5. Everybody, touch number 4. ✔
   That sentence will also tell about the ball. What word will you use to name the ball? (Signal.) *It.*

- We can see the ball rolled down the hill. Who did the ball roll towards? (Signal.) *A skunk.*

- Raise your hand when you can say a sentence that reports where the ball rolled in that picture. Begin your sentence with **it**. (Call on several students. Praise sentences such as: *It rolled down the hill toward a skunk.* For each good sentence:) Everybody, say that sentence.

6. Everybody, touch number 5. ✔
   Name that animal. (Signal.) *Rover.*

- Raise your hand when you can say a sentence that reports on the main thing Rover did in that picture. (Call on several students. Praise sentences such as: *Rover chased the ball down the hill.* For each good sentence:) Everybody, say that sentence.

7. Everybody, touch number 6. ✔
   Name that animal. (Signal.) *The skunk.*

- Raise your hand when you can say a sentence that reports on the main thing the skunk did in that picture. (Call on several students. Praise sentences such as: *The skunk made a big stink.* For each good sentence:) Everybody, say that sentence.

8. Everybody, touch number 7. ✔
   Name those persons. (Signal.) *Robert and Jill.*

- Raise your hand when you can say a sentence that reports on the main thing Robert and Jill did in that picture. (Call on several students. Praise sentences such as: *Robert and Jill held their noses.* For each good sentence:) Everybody, say that sentence.

9. I'll read a passage that reports on what happened: Jill threw a ball to Robert. Robert jumped up to catch the ball. The ball went over Robert. It rolled down a hill toward a skunk. Rover chased the ball down the hill. The skunk made a big stink. Robert and Jill held their noses.

10. I'll say those sentences again.

- Jill threw a ball to Robert. Say that sentence. (Signal.) *Jill threw a ball to Robert.*

- Robert jumped up to catch the ball. Say that sentence. (Signal.) *Robert jumped up to catch the ball.*

- The ball went over Robert. Say that sentence. (Signal.) *The ball went over Robert.*

- It rolled down a hill toward a skunk. Say that sentence. (Signal.) *It rolled down a hill toward a skunk.*
- Rover chased the ball down the hill. Say that sentence. (Signal.) *Rover chased the ball down the hill.*
- The skunk made a big stink. Say that sentence. (Signal.) *The skunk made a big stink.*
- Robert and Jill held their noses. Say that sentence. (Signal.) *Robert and Jill held their noses.*

11. I'll read the words in the vocabulary box: **because, missed, head, threw, held, smelled, their.**

12. Your turn: Write your paragraph. Remember, write a clear sentence for each number. Indent your first sentence. You have 8 minutes to write your paragraph. Raise your hand when you're finished. (Observe students and give feedback.)

13. (After 8 minutes, say:) Stop writing. I'm going to call on several students to read their paragraphs. Listen carefully. Make sure each sentence tells the main thing. Make sure no sentences are missing. And make sure each sentence tells what somebody or something did. Raise your hand if you hear a mistake.
- (Call on several students to read their paragraphs. Praise good paragraphs.)

14. Now you're going to check your paragraph. Make 3 check boxes under your paragraph.

15. Here's check 1: Does each sentence begin with a capital and end with a period? Check your paragraph. Fix up any mistakes. Then make a check in box 1. Raise your hand when you're finished. (Observe students and give feedback.)

16. Here's check 2: Does each sentence tell the main thing? Read your paragraph. Make sure each sentence tells the main thing. Fix up any mistakes. Then make a check in box 2. Raise your hand when you're finished. (Observe students and give feedback.)

17. Here's check 3: Does each sentence tell what somebody or something **did?** Remember, you can't tell what somebody or something was doing. You have to tell what they did. Fix up any mistakes. Then make a check in box 3. Raise your hand when you're finished. (Observe students and give feedback.)

18. Next time, I'll read some of the **super** paragraphs to you.

Note:

- Collect the students' workbooks and papers.

- Check the students' work before the next language period. Mark any mistakes.

- Write **super** on work that has all mistakes corrected. Write **good** or **pretty good** on work that has only 1 or 2 mistakes.

Objectives

- Edit a paragraph for capitals, periods and past-time verbs. (Exercise 2)
- **Edit run-on sentences.** (Exercise 3)
- Edit a paragraph to correct unclear parts. (Exercise 4)
- Write a sentence that tells about only one of three similar pictures. (Exercise 5)
- Write a paragraph that reports on an illustrated action sequence. (Exercise 6)

EXERCISE 1 **Feedback On Lesson 103**

- (Before returning the students' papers and workbooks, read some of the better paragraphs for part E of lesson 103.)
- (Hand back the students' work from lesson 103.)
- Look at what I wrote on your lined paper. Raise your hand if I wrote **super.**

WORKBOOK

EXERCISE 2 **Paragraph Editing**

1. Everybody, open your workbook to lesson 104 and find part A. ✔
- You're going to edit the paragraph in part A for two different things.
2. I'll read the checks. Follow along.
- Check 1: Does each sentence begin with a capital and end with a period?
- Check 2: Does each sentence tell what somebody or something did?
3. Listen: First check the paragraph for capitals and periods and fix up any mistakes. Do it now. Make a check in box 1 to show you've checked for capitals and periods. Raise your hand when you're finished.
(Observe students and give feedback.)
4. (After students complete check 1, say:) Now go through the paragraph again for check 2. Fix up the paragraph so all the sentences tell what somebody or something did. Then make a check in box 2 to show that all the sentences tell what somebody or something did. Raise your hand when you're finished.
(Observe students and give feedback.)

5. Let's check your work. I'll read the fixed-up paragraph.
- Sam and Ellen **cooked** supper for their family. Ellen made hamburgers, period. Capital **S,** She cooked them over a fire. Sam **made** corn, period. Capital **H,** He **put** butter and salt on each piece. Everyone **liked** the meal.
6. Raise your hand if you fixed up all the mistakes. Great job.
- Everybody else, fix up any mistakes you missed in part A.

EXERCISE 3 **Run-On Sentences**

1. Everybody, pencils down. Find part B. ✔ Each item is a run-on sentence. They are called run-ons because they are really more than one sentence.
2. I'll read the first run-on: Two girls played football and their dad watched them and then they asked him if he wanted to play.
- Let's fix the run-on by getting rid of the **ands** and **and thens.** Then we'll put in capitals and periods. We have to figure out where the first sentence should end. We'll find the subject and the predicate of that sentence. The run-on starts by naming **two girls.** What words tell more about two girls? (Signal.) *Played football.*
- So the first sentence should say: **Two girls played football.** Put a period after **football.** Cross out the word **and.** Make the word **their** begin with a capital **T.** Raise your hand when you're finished.
(Observe students and give feedback.)
3. The next part of the run-on begins by naming **their dad.** What words tell more about their dad? (Signal.) *Watched them.*

- So the second sentence should say: **Their dad watched them.** Put a period after the word **them.** Cross out the words **and then.** Make the word **they** begin with a capital **T.** Raise your hand when you're finished. (Observe students and give feedback.)

4. The next part of the run-on uses the word **they** to name **the girls.** What words tell more about the girls? (Signal.) *Asked him if he wanted to play.*
  - So here's the last sentence: **They asked him if he wanted to play.**

5. Check your work. I'll read the three sentences we made: Two girls played football, period. Capital **T,** Their dad watched them, period. Capital **T,** They asked him if he wanted to play.

6. I'll read item 2: A boy asked his mother for some food and then she gave him an apple and he asked if he could also have some cheese and his mother gave him a piece of cheese.
  - Fix up that run-on. Make four sentences. Remember to put in periods, make capitals and cross out the words **and** and **and then.** Raise your hand when you're finished. (Observe students and give feedback.)
  - Check your work. I'll read the four sentences you should have made for item 2. Fix up any mistakes.
  - A boy asked his mother for some food, period. Capital **S,** She gave him an apple, period. Capital **H,** He asked if he could also have some cheese, period. Capital **H,** His mother gave him a piece of cheese.

7. Raise your hand if you didn't make any mistakes. Great job.

EXERCISE 4 Edit For Clarity

1. Everybody, find part C. ✔
  The writer of this passage made mistakes by using **he, she, it** or **they** before giving us a clear picture of the persons or things.

2. I'll read the first sentence: They came out of the building. Two words are unclear in that sentence. What's the first unclear word? (Signal.) *They.*
  - What's the other unclear word? (Signal.) *Building.*
  - Underline the word **they** and the word **building.**

3. Next sentence: They walked toward it. Everybody, would the word **they** be unclear if it is fixed up in the first sentence? (Signal.) *No.*
  - What's the unclear word in that sentence? (Signal.) *It.*
  - Underline the word **it.**

4. Next sentence: She carried it. There are two unclear words. Underline them. ✔
  - Listen: She carried it. Everybody, what's the first unclear word? (Signal.) *She.*
  - What's the other unclear word? (Signal.) *It.*

5. Next sentence: He carried them. There are two unclear words. Underline them. ✔
  - Everybody, what's the first unclear word? (Signal.) *He.*
  - What's the other unclear word? (Signal.) *Them.*

6. Last sentence: She waved to them. The words **she** and **them** are unclear in that sentence. Underline those words.

TEXTBOOK

7. Open your textbook to lesson 104 and find part C. ✔

  - Look at the picture.
  The first sentence is: They came out of the building. To give a clear picture of **they,** you could name the group, or you could tell the names of the people.
  - You can see what kind of building they came out of. It even has a name. And you can see who waved at them.

8. Your turn: Fix up the sentences in part C. Above each word that you underlined, write words that give a clear picture. For some words, you can give a clearer picture just by naming the person. Fix up the whole passage. Then read it to yourself to make sure it gives a pretty clear picture of what happened. Raise your hand when you're finished. (Observe students and give feedback.)

9. I'll read a paragraph that's pretty clear. Follow along. **Tina and Henry** came out of the **grocery store.** They walked toward **a pickup truck. Tina** carried **a bottle of milk. Henry** carried **two large bags. A girl on a bicycle** waved to **Tina and Henry.**

10. I'm going to call on several students to read their fixed-up paragraphs. Listen and make sure that each paragraph gives a pretty clear picture. Raise your hand if you hear a mistake.

• (Call on several students to read their paragraphs. Praise paragraphs that have good descriptions.)

LINED PAPER

EXERCISE 5 Clarity

1. Everybody, find part D in your textbook. ✔ You're going to write a sentence that tells about only the first picture, not the second or the third picture.

2. Look at the pictures.
Write a sentence that tells about only the first picture. Your sentence should name the kind of woman that is in the first picture and tell what she did. The sentence should also tell what kind of tree is in the first picture.

3. Skip a line on your paper and then write your sentence. Raise your hand when you're finished.
(Observe students and give feedback.)

4. I'm going to call on several students to read their sentences. Listen and make sure each sentence tells only about the first picture.

• (Call on several students to read their sentences. Praise good sentences, such as: *A young woman sat under a small tree.*)

5. Check your work. Make sure your sentence tells about only the first picture. Raise your hand when you're sure your sentence is clear.

EXERCISE 6 Paragraph Writing

1. Everybody, pencils down. Find part E in your textbook. ✔

• I'll read the instructions: Write a paragraph that reports on what happened. Write a sentence for each name shown in the pictures.

2. I'll read the words in the vocabulary box: **carried, broke, pieces, brought, tripped, another.**

3. Everybody, touch number 1 in the first picture. ✔
Name that person. (Signal.) *James.*

• Raise your hand when you can say a sentence that reports on the main thing James did in that picture. (Call on several students. Praise sentences such as: *James carried a bottle of juice out of a store.* For each good sentence:) Everybody, say that sentence.

4. Everybody, touch number 2. ✔
You'll write another sentence about James. You'll start that sentence with **he.**

• Raise your hand when you can say a sentence that reports on what James did in that picture. Start your sentence with **he.** (Call on several students. Praise sentences such as: *He tripped over a rock. He tripped over a rock and dropped the bottle.* For each good sentence:) Everybody, say that sentence.

5. Everybody, touch number 3. ✔
Name that object. (Signal.) *The bottle.*

• Raise your hand when you can say a sentence that reports on the main thing the bottle did in that picture. (Call on several students. Praise sentences such as: *The bottle fell out of his hands. The bottle fell to the ground.* For each good sentence:) Everybody, say that sentence.

6. Everybody, touch number 4. ✔
   You'll write another sentence about the bottle.

- Raise your hand when you can say a sentence that reports on the main thing the bottle did in that picture. Begin your sentence with **It.** (Call on several students. Praise sentences such as: *It broke when it hit the ground.* For each good sentence:) Everybody, say that sentence.

7. Everybody, touch number 5. ✔
   Name that person. (Signal.) *James.*

- Raise your hand when you can say a sentence that reports on the main thing James did in that picture. (Call on several students. Praise sentences such as: *James swept up the pieces of the bottle.* For each good sentence:) Everybody, say that sentence.

8. Everybody, touch number 6. ✔
   Name that person. (Signal.) *The store owner.*

- Raise your hand when you can say a sentence that reports on the main thing the store owner did in that picture. (Call on several students. Praise sentences such as: *The store owner brought out another bottle of juice.* For each good sentence:) Everybody, say that sentence.

9. I'll read a passage that reports on what happened: James carried a bottle of juice out of a store. He tripped over a rock. The bottle fell out of his hands. It landed on the ground and broke into pieces. James swept up the pieces of the bottle. The store owner brought out another bottle of juice.

10. I'll say those sentences again.

- James carried a bottle of juice out of a store. Say that sentence. (Signal.) *James carried a bottle of juice out of a store.*

- He tripped over a rock. Say that sentence. (Signal.) *He tripped over a rock.*

- The bottle fell out of his hands. Say that sentence. (Signal.) *The bottle fell out of his hands.*

- It landed on the ground and broke into pieces. Say that sentence. (Signal.) *It landed on the ground and broke into pieces.*

- James swept up the pieces of the bottle. Say that sentence. (Signal.) *James swept up the pieces of the bottle.*

- The store owner brought out another bottle of juice. Say that sentence. (Signal.) *The store owner brought out another bottle of juice.*

11. Your turn: Write your paragraph. Remember, write a clear sentence for each number. Indent your first sentence. You have 8 minutes to write your paragraph. Raise your hand when you're finished. (Observe students and give feedback.)

12. (After 8 minutes, say:) Stop writing. I'm going to call on several students to read their paragraphs. Listen carefully. Make sure each sentence tells the main thing. Make sure no sentences are missing. And make sure each sentence tells what somebody or something did. Raise your hand if you hear a mistake.

- (Call on several students to read their paragraphs. Praise good paragraphs.)

13. Now you're going to check your paragraph. Make 3 check boxes under your paragraph.

14. Here's check 1: Does each sentence begin with a capital and end with a period? Check your paragraph. Fix up any mistakes. Then make a check in box 1. (Observe students and give feedback.)

15. Here's check 2: Does each sentence tell the main thing? Read your paragraph. Make sure each sentence tells the main thing. Fix up any mistakes. Then make a check in box 2.
   (Observe students and give feedback.)

16. Here's check 3: Does each sentence tell what somebody or something **did?** Remember, you can't tell what somebody or something was doing. You have to tell what they did. Fix up any mistakes. Then make a check in box 3.
   (Observe students and give feedback.)

17. Next time, I'll read some of the super paragraphs to you.

Note:

- Collect the students' workbooks and papers.

- Check the students' work before the next language period. Mark any mistakes.

- Write **super** on work that has all mistakes corrected. Write **good** or **pretty good** on work that has only 1 or 2 mistakes.

Objectives

- Edit run-on sentences. (Exercise 2)
- **Identify the verbs in sentences.** (Exercise 3)
- Perform on a mastery test of skills presented in lessons 96–104. (Exercise 4)
  Exercises 5–7 give instructions for marking the test, giving student feedback and providing remedies.

EXERCISE 1 Feedback On Lesson 104

- (Before returning the students' papers and workbooks, read some of the better paragraphs for part E of lesson 104.)
- (Hand back the students' work from lesson 104.)
- Look at what I wrote on your lined paper. Raise your hand if I wrote **super.**

WORKBOOK

EXERCISE 2 Run-On Sentences

1. Everybody, open your workbook to lesson 105 and find part A. ✔
- Each item is a run-on sentence. Remember, they are called run-ons because they are really more than one sentence. We're going to find these sentences and fix them up.
2. I'll read the first run-on: Mr. Clark went for a ride in the country and then his car ran out of gas and then he had to walk three miles to a gas station.
- Listen: Make three sentences out of that run-on. Remember the capitals and periods. And remember to cross out **and** or **and then.** Raise your hand when you're finished.
  (Observe students and give feedback.)
- Let's check your work. Fix up any mistakes. I'll read the three sentences for run-on 1.
- Mr. Clark went for a ride in the country, period. Capital **H,** His car ran out of gas, period. Capital **H,** He had to walk three miles to a gas station.
3. I'll read the next run-on: Kathy liked to read books and her favorite book was about horses and her brother gave her that book.

- Listen: Make three sentences out of that run-on. Raise your hand when you're finished.
  (Observe students and give feedback.)
- Check your work. Fix up any mistakes. I'll read the three sentences for run-on 2.
- Kathy liked to read books, period. Capital **H,** Her favorite book was about horses, period. Capital **H,** Her brother gave her that book.
4. I'll read the last run-on: Pam's mother asked Pam to mow the lawn and then Pam started to cut the grass and it was too wet.
- Listen: Make three sentences out of that run-on. Raise your hand when you're finished.
  (Observe students and give feedback.)
- Check your work. Fix up any mistakes. I'll read the three sentences for run-on 3.
- Pam's mother asked Pam to mow the lawn, period. Pam started to cut the grass, period. Capital **I,** It was too wet.
5. Raise your hand if you got everything right. Great job.

EXERCISE 3 Predicate

Verbs

1. Everybody, pencils down.
- You're going to learn about verbs. Listen: Every sentence has a verb. The verb is usually in **the first part** of the predicate. In what part of the predicate is the verb? (Signal.) *The first part.*

2. I'm going to say some sentences. Listen: The young boy ate ice cream. Say it. (Signal.) *The young boy ate ice cream.*
   • What's the subject? (Signal.) *The young boy.*
     What's the predicate? (Signal.) *Ate ice cream.*
   • Listen: What's the **first word** in the predicate? (Signal.) *Ate.*
   • That's a verb.
   • Listen: Boys and girls ran to the store. Say it. (Signal.) *Boys and girls ran to the store.*
   • What's the subject? (Signal.) *Boys and girls.*
     What's the predicate? (Signal.) *Ran to the store.*
   • What's the **first word** in the predicate? (Signal.) *Ran.*
   • Yes, **ran.** That's a verb.
   • Listen: A frog had long legs. Say it. (Signal.) *A frog had long legs.*
   • What's the subject? (Signal.) *A frog.*
     What's the predicate? (Signal.) *Had long legs.*
   • What's the first word in the predicate? (Signal.) *Had.*
   • Yes, **had.** That's a verb.
   • (Repeat step 2 until firm.)
3. Listen: Those girls were tall. Say it. (Signal.) *Those girls were tall.*
   • What's the subject? (Signal.) *Those girls.*
     What's the predicate? (Signal.) *Were tall.*
     What's the verb? (Signal.) *Were.*
     Yes, **were.**
   • Listen: A fish swam. Say it. (Signal.) *A fish swam.*
   • What's the subject? (Signal.) *A fish.*
     What's the predicate? (Signal.) *Swam.*
     What's the verb? (Signal.) *Swam.*
     Yes, **swam.** There's only one word in the predicate, so that word has to be the verb.
   • Listen: His new bike was green. Say it. (Signal.) *His new bike was green.*
   • What's the subject? (Signal.) *His new bike.*
     What's the predicate? (Signal.) *Was green.*
     What's the verb? (Signal.) *Was.*
     Yes, **was.**
   • Listen: Bill cut the grass. Say it. (Signal.) *Bill cut the grass.*
   • What's the subject? (Signal.) *Bill.*
     What's the predicate? (Signal.) *Cut the grass.*
     What's the verb? (Signal.) *Cut.*
     Yes, **cut.**
   • (Repeat step 3 until firm.)
4. Remember, the verb is usually the first word of the predicate.

EXERCISE 4 Test

Capitalizing—Names

1. The rest of the lesson is a test. You'll do the whole test and then I'll mark it. Find part A of test 10.
2. I'll read the instructions: Fix up each person's name so all parts of the name begin with a capital. Do it. Raise your hand when you're finished.

Pronouns-He, She, It, They

1. Everybody, find part B. ✔
2. I'll read the instructions: Fill in the blanks with **he, she, it** or **they.** Do it. Raise your hand when you're finished.

Subject/Predicate

1. Everybody, find part C. ✔
2. I'll read the instructions: Circle the subject. Underline the predicate. Do it. Raise your hand when you're finished.

EXERCISE 5 Marking The Test

1. (Mark the workbooks before the next scheduled language lesson. Use the *Language Arts Workbook Answer* Key to determine acceptable responses for the test.)
2. (Write the number of errors each student made on the test in the test scorebox at the beginning of the test.)
3. (Enter the number of errors each student made on the Summary for Test 10. Reproducible Summary Sheets are at the back of the *Language Arts Teacher's Guide.*)

EXERCISE 6 Feedback On Test 10

1. (Return the students' workbooks after they are marked.)
   • Everybody, open your workbook to lesson 105.
2. The number I wrote in the test scorebox tells how many items you got wrong on the whole test. Raise your hand if I wrote **0, 1** or **2** at the top of your test. **Those are super stars.**
   • Raise your hand if I wrote **3** or **4.** Those are pretty good workers.
   • If I wrote a number that's more than 4, you're going to have to work harder.

EXERCISE 7 Test Remedies

- (Before beginning lesson 106, provide any necessary remedies. After students complete the exercises specified for a remedy, check their work and give feedback.)

Test Part A Capitalizing—Names

If more than $\frac{1}{4}$ of the students made 2 or more errors in test part A, present the following exercises:

- (Direct students to part A on page 269 of the student workbook.)
  Fix up each person's name so all parts of the name begin with a capital.
- (Direct students to part B on page 269 of the student workbook.)
  Fix up each person's name so all parts of the name begin with a capital.

Test Part B Pronouns—He, She, It, They

If more than $\frac{1}{4}$ of the students made 2 or more errors in test part B, present the following exercises:

- (Direct students to part C on page 270 of the student workbook.)
  Fill in the blanks with **he, she, it** or **they.**
- (Direct students to part D on page 270 of the student workbook.)
  Fill in the blanks with **he, she, it** or **they.**

Test Part C Subject/Predicate

If more than $\frac{1}{4}$ of the students made 2 or more errors in test part C, present the following exercises:

- (Direct students to part E on page 271 of the student workbook.)
  For each sentence, circle the subject and underline the predicate.
- (Direct students to part F on page 271 of the student workbook.)
  For each sentence, circle the subject and underline the predicate.

Objectives

- **Determine whether a pronoun is appropriate for the subject of a sentence.** (Exercise 1)
- Edit run-on sentences. (Exercise 2)
- **Identify the subject, predicate and verb in sentences.** (Exercise 3 and 4)
- Edit a paragraph for capitals, periods and names that are not capitalized. (Exercise 5)
- Construct a paragraph that includes one sentence about an illustrated group and two sentences about each illustrated character. (Exercise 6)

WORKBOOK

EXERCISE 1 Clarity

Pronouns

1. Everybody, open your workbook to lesson 106 and find part A. ✔
- The paragraph reports on the picture. You'll write the correct words for each missing subject.
2. Here's the rule: If two sentences in a row name the same person or group, you can use **he, she, it** or **they** for the **second** sentence. But you can't use **he, she, it** or **they** for the first sentence. If you do that, your paragraph will be unclear. Remember, for two sentences in a row that have the same subject, you name the person or group in the first sentence. Then you can use **he, she, it** or **they** in the second sentence.
3. Look at the picture.
Here's the first sentence: Three women worked on a house. Remember, if the next sentence names the same group, you can use **he, she, it** or **they.**
- Here's the next sentence: Blank wore work clothes. That sentence tells about all the women. So what word goes in the blank? (Signal.) *They.*
- Write **they** in the blank. ✔
4. Next sentence: Blank cut a board. Are we still talking about all the women? (Signal.) *No.*
- So we'll have to name the new person or group. Blank cut a board. What word goes in the blank? (Signal.) *Milly.*
- Write **Milly.** ✔

5. Next sentence: Blank used a saw. Think big: What word goes in the blank? (Signal.) *She.*
- Milly was already named in the last sentence, so we can use the word **she.** Write **she.**
6. Remember, if you introduce somebody or something for the first time, use the name. If the next sentence refers to the same person or thing, use **he, she, it** or **they.**
- Fill in the rest of the words on your own. Raise your hand when you're finished. (Observe students and give feedback.)
7. Let's check your work. I'll read the paragraph.
- Three women worked on a house. **They** wore work clothes. **Milly** cut a board. **She** used a saw. **Kay** carried three pieces of wood. **She** carried the boards on her shoulder. **Jean** hammered nails into the wood.
That paragraph is pretty clear now.
8. Raise your hand if you made no mistakes. Great job.
- Everybody else, fix up any mistakes you made in part A.

EXERCISE 2 Run-On Sentences

1. Everybody, pencils down. Find part B. ✔
- I'll read the instructions: Fix up the run-on sentences. The number at the end of each run-on tells how many sentences you should make.
2. Touch the number at the end of run-on 1. ✔
- What number is at the end of run-on 1? (Signal.) *Three.*
- That means you make three sentences out of that run-on.

- Look at run-on 2.
  How many sentences are you going to make out of that run-on? (Signal.) *Four.*
- Look at run-on 3.
  How many sentences are you going to make out of that run-on? (Signal.) *Three.*
3. Fix up the run-ons. Do it now. Raise your hand when you're finished.
   (Observe students and give feedback.)
4. Let's check your work.
- Run-on 1: Miss Wilson saw a used bike at a store, period. Capital **T,** The bike was red and blue, period. Miss Wilson bought it for her sister.
- Run-on 2: Richard and his sister went to a movie, period. Capital **I,** It was very funny, period. Richard and his sister ate popcorn, period. Capital **T,** Their mother picked them up after the movie.
- Run-on 3: Tina built a doghouse for her dog, period. Capital **S,** She looked in the doghouse, period. Capital **F,** Four cats were in the doghouse with her dog.
5. Raise your hand if you made no mistakes. Great job.
- Everybody else, fix up any mistakes you made in part B.

EXERCISE 3 Parts Of Speech

Verbs

1. Everybody, pencils down. Remember, every sentence has a verb. The verb is usually in the first part of the predicate.
- I'm going to say some sentences.
2. Listen: A dog ate lots of food. Say it. (Signal.) *A dog ate lots of food.*
- What's the subject? (Signal.) *A dog.*
  What's the predicate? (Signal.) *Ate lots of food.*
  What's the first word in the predicate? (Signal.) *Ate.*
- That's the verb.
- Listen: The girl threw a ball. Say it. (Signal.) *The girl threw a ball.*
- What's the subject? (Signal.) *The girl.*
  What's the predicate? (Signal.) *Threw a ball.*
  What's the first word in the predicate? (Signal.) *Threw.*
- That's the verb.
- (Repeat step 2 until firm.)

3. Listen: Boys and girls were in school. Say it. (Signal.) *Boys and girls were in school.*
- What's the subject? (Signal.) *Boys and girls.*
  What's the predicate? (Signal.) *Were in school.*
  What's the verb? (Signal.) *Were.*
- Listen: A bird flew. Say it. (Signal.) *A bird flew.*
- What's the subject? (Signal.) *A bird.*
  What's the predicate? (Signal.) *Flew.*
  What's the verb? (Signal.) *Flew.*
- Yes, **flew.** There's only one word in the predicate, so that word has to be the verb.
- (Repeat step 3 until firm.)

EXERCISE 4 Verbs

1. Everybody, find part C. ✔
2. I'll read sentence 1: Six bottles were on the table. What's the subject? (Signal.) *Six bottles.*
- What's the predicate? (Signal.) *Were on the table.*
- What's the verb? (Signal.) *Were.*
- Sentence 2: An old lion chased the rabbit. What's the subject? (Signal.) *An old lion.*
- What's the predicate? (Signal.) *Chased the rabbit.*
- What's the verb? (Signal.) *Chased.*
3. Here are the instructions for part C: Circle the subject of each sentence. Underline the predicate. Then make a **V** above the verb. Remember, the verb is the first word of the predicate. Do the sentences now. Raise your hand when you're finished.
   (Observe students and give feedback.)
4. Let's check your work.
- Sentence 1. What's the subject? (Signal.) *Six bottles.*
- What's the predicate? (Signal.) *Were on the table.*
- What's the verb? (Signal.) *Were.*
- You should have written **V** above the word **were.** Raise your hand if you got it right.
- Sentence 2. What's the subject? (Signal.) *An old lion.*
- What's the predicate? (Signal.) *Chased the rabbit.*
- What's the verb? (Signal.) *Chased.*
- Sentence 3. What's the subject? (Signal.) *Jane and Sue.*

- What's the predicate? (Signal.) *Sat under a tree.*
- What's the verb? (Signal.) *Sat.*
- Sentence 4. What's the subject? (Signal.) *His brother.*
- What's the predicate? (Signal.) *Had a candy bar.*
- What's the verb? (Signal.) *Had.*

5. Raise your hand if you made no mistakes. Great job.
- Everybody else, fix up any mistakes you made in part C.

EXERCISE 5   Paragraph Editing

1. Everybody, pencils down. Find part D. ✔
- You're going to edit the paragraph in part D for two different things.
2. I'll read the checks. Follow along.
- Check 1: Does each sentence begin with a capital and end with a period?
- Check 2: Does each part of a person's name begin with a capital letter?
3. Listen: First check to make sure each sentence starts with a capital and ends with a period. Make a check in box 1 to show you've checked the sentences. Raise your hand when you're finished.
   (Observe students and give feedback.)
4. (After students complete check 1, say:) Now go through the paragraph again for check 2. Fix up the paragraph so all the parts of a person's name begin with a capital letter. Then make a check in box 2. Raise your hand when you're finished.
   (Observe students and give feedback.)
5. Let's check your work. I'll read the fixed-up paragraph.
- A woman lived near our school, period. Her name was capital **M,** Mrs. capital **J,** Jones, period. Capital **S,** She was an airplane pilot. She told us many stories about flying planes, period.
6. Raise your hand if you fixed up all the mistakes. Great job.
- Everybody else, fix up any mistakes you missed in part D.

EXERCISE 6   Paragraph Writing
Pairs

1. Everybody, take out a sheet of lined paper and write your name on the top line. Raise your hand when you're finished.
- Everybody, pencils down. Open your textbook to lesson 106 and find part E. ✔
- I'll read the instructions: Write a paragraph that reports on the picture. Begin with a good sentence that tells what the women did. Then write two sentences about each person. The first sentence should tell the main thing the person did. Listen: For that sentence, tell how the person got across the stream. The second sentence should tell something else about the person.
2. Touch the words in the vocabulary box as I read them: **stream, canoe, backpack, crossed, carried.**
3. Write a good sentence that tells the main thing the women did. Raise your hand when you're finished.
   (Observe students and give feedback.)
- (Call on several students to read their sentences. Praise sentences such as: *The women crossed the stream.*)
4. Touch Lisa.
- Raise your hand when you can say a sentence that reports on the main thing Lisa did. (Call on several students. Praise sentences such as: *Lisa walked on a tree trunk that went from one side of the stream to the other side.* For each good sentence:) Everybody, say that sentence.

- Raise your hand when you can say a sentence that tells something else about Lisa. Begin your sentence with the word **she.** (Call on several students. Praise sentences such as: *She carried canoe paddles. She wore a backpack.* For each good sentence:) Everybody, say that sentence.
- Write your sentences about Lisa. First tell how Lisa got across the stream. Raise your hand when you're finished.
  (Observe students and give feedback.)

5. Everybody, now you're going to write two sentences about Tina. What word will the second sentence start with? (Signal.) *She.*
- Write your sentences about Tina. Raise your hand when you're finished.
  (Observe students and give feedback.)

6. I'm going to call on several students to read their paragraphs. Listen carefully and raise your hand if a sentence is wrong or if it doesn't use the right word to name the person.
- (Call on several students to read their paragraphs. Praise paragraphs that give a clear picture.)

7. Now you can check your paragraph and fix it up before you hand it in. Make 3 check boxes under your paragraph.

8. Here's check 1: Does each sentence begin with a capital and end with a period? Check your paragraph. Fix up any mistakes. Then make a check in box 1. Raise your hand when you're finished. (Observe students and give feedback.)

9. Here's check 2: Did you write two sentences about each person? Read your paragraph. If you wrote two sentences about Lisa and two sentences about Tina, make a check in box 2. Fix up any mistakes. Raise your hand when you're finished.
(Observe students and give feedback.)

10. Here's check 3: Does the second sentence about each person begin with **she?** Check your paragraph. Fix up any mistakes. Then make a check in box 3. Raise your hand when you're finished.
(Observe students and give feedback.)

11. Next time, I'll read some of the **super** paragraphs to you.

Note:

- Collect the students' workbooks and papers.
- Check the students' work before the next language period. Mark any mistakes.
- Write **super** on work that has all mistakes corrected. Write **good** or **pretty good** on work that has only 1 or 2 mistakes.

LESSON 107

Objectives

- Identify the subject, predicate and verb in sentences. (Exercise 2)
- **Edit a paragraph for run-on sentences.** (Exercise 3)
- Write past-time verbs for irregular present-time verbs. (Exercise 4)
- Determine whether a pronoun is appropriate for the subject of a sentence. (Exercise 5)
- **Write a paragraph that tells about one of two similar pictures.** (Exercise 6)

EXERCISE 1 Feedback On Lesson 106

- (Before returning the students' papers and workbooks, read some of the better paragraphs for part E of lesson 106.)
- (Hand back the students' work from lesson 106.)
- Look at what I wrote on your lined paper. Raise your hand if I wrote **super.**

WORKBOOK

EXERCISE 2 Subject/Predicate Verbs

1. I'm going to say some sentences. You're going to tell me the subject, the predicate and the verb of each sentence. Remember, the verb is usually in the first part of the predicate.

2. Listen: She sat on the table. What's the subject? (Signal.) *She.*
   - What's the predicate? (Signal.) *Sat on the table.*
     What's the verb? (Signal.) *Sat.*
   - Listen: My dad had a headache.
     What's the subject? (Signal.) *My dad.*
   - What's the predicate? (Signal.) *Had a headache.*
     What's the verb? (Signal.) *Had.*
   - Listen: Three dogs and two cats played in the yard. What's the subject? (Signal.) *Three dogs and two cats.*
   - What's the predicate? (Signal.) *Played in the yard.*
     What's the verb? (Signal.) *Played.*
   - (Repeat step 2 until firm.)

3. Open your workbook to lesson 107 and find part A. ✔

- Here's what you'll do: Circle the subject of each sentence. Underline the predicate. Then make a **V** above each verb. Do it now. Raise your hand when you're finished. (Observe students and give feedback.)

4. Let's check your work.
   - Sentence 1. What's the subject? (Signal.) *A black pencil.*
   - What's the predicate? (Signal.) *Fell off the table.*
     What's the verb? (Signal.) *Fell.*
     You should have written **V** above the word **fell.**
   - Sentence 2. What's the subject? (Signal.) *My sister.*
   - What's the predicate? (Signal.) *Was sick.*
     What's the verb? (Signal.) *Was.*
   - Sentence 3. What's the subject? (Signal.) *A dog and a cat.*
   - What's the predicate? (Signal.) *Played in the park.*
   - What's the verb? (Signal.) *Played.*
   - Sentence 4. What's the subject? (Signal.) *They.*
   - What's the predicate? (Signal.) *Smiled.*
   - What's the verb? (Signal.) *Smiled.*
   - Sentence 5. What's the subject? (Signal.) *Ana.*
   - What's the predicate? (Signal.) *Sang softly.*
   - What's the verb? (Signal.) *Sang.*
   - Sentence 6. What's the subject? (Signal.) *An old horse.*
   - What's the predicate? (Signal.) *Drank from a bucket.*
   - What's the verb? (Signal.) *Drank.*

5. Raise your hand if you made no mistakes. Great job.
   - Everybody else, fix up any mistakes you made in part A.

EXERCISE 3   Editing Paragraphs

Run-On Sentences

1. Everybody, pencils down. Find part B. ✔
- I'll read the instructions: Fix up the run-on sentences in this paragraph. Not all of the sentences are run-ons.
2. I'll read the first sentence: Don found a lost dog and the dog had a collar around its neck. Everybody, is that a run-on sentence? (Signal.) *Yes.*
- So we'll find where the first sentence should end by finding the subject and the predicate. The subject is **Don.** Everybody, what words tell more about Don? (Signal.) *Found a lost dog.*
- That's the predicate, and that's where the sentence should end. Put a period after **dog.** Cross out **and.** Then make the next word begin with a capital. Raise your hand when you're finished.
3. Next sentence: The dog had a collar around its neck. Everybody, is that a run-on sentence? (Signal.) *No.*
4. Next sentence: The collar had a phone number on it and then Don called the phone number and the dog's owner answered the telephone. Is that a run-on sentence? (Signal.) *Yes.*
- Fix it up. Raise your hand when you're finished.
- Check your work. You should have three sentences for that run-on. Here they are: The collar had a phone number on it, period. Don called the phone number, period. Capital **T,** The dog's owner answered the telephone.
5. Read the rest of the paragraph. If there are any more run-on sentences, fix them up. Raise your hand when you're finished. (Observe students and give feedback.)
6. Check your work. The last sentence was a run-on sentence. I'll read that sentence: He went to Don's house and then Don gave the dog to the owner.
- Here's what you should have: He went to Don's house, period. Don gave the dog to the owner.

7. Check your paragraph to make sure you have all the sentences right and each sentence begins with a capital and ends with a period. Raise your hand when you're finished checking your paragraph.

EXERCISE 4   Irregular Verbs

1. Everybody, find part C. ✔
- These are words that tell what somebody **does.**
2. Listen: All these words are verbs. You're going to write words that tell what somebody **did.** Listen: All the words you'll write are also verbs. Words that tell what somebody does are verbs. Words that tell what somebody did are verbs.
3. I'll read the instructions: For each verb that tells what somebody does, write the verb that tells what somebody did. Do it. Write the verbs. Raise your hand when you're finished.
(Observe students and give feedback.)
4. Let's check your work.
- Verb 1: begins. What verb tells what somebody did? (Signal.) *Began.*
- Brings. What verb tells what somebody did? (Signal.) *Brought.*
- Flies. What verb tells what somebody did? (Signal.) *Flew.*
- Swims. What verb tells what somebody did? (Signal.) *Swam.*
- Takes. What verb tells what somebody did? (Signal.) *Took.*
- Comes. What verb tells what somebody did? (Signal.) *Came.*
5. Raise your hand if you made no mistakes. Great job.
- Everybody else, fix up any mistakes you made in part C.

EXERCISE 5   Clarity

Pronouns

1. Everybody, find part D. ✔
- You'll write the correct words for each subject. Remember, if two sentences in a row have the same subject, you name the person or group in the first sentence. Then you can use **he, she, it** or **they** in the second sentence.

2. Look at the picture.
   Here's the first sentence: Blank sat in the wheelchair. We're naming a person for the first time. What word goes in the blank? (Signal.) *Ben.*
   • Write **Ben** in the blank. ✔
3. Next sentence: Blank wore pajamas. What word goes in the blank? (Signal.) *He.*
   • Write **he** in the blank. ✔
   • I'll read the rest of the paragraph: The blank had big wheels and little wheels. Blank had a seat, a back and two handles. Blank held a purse. Blank wore a skirt and a sweater. Blank was behind the wheelchair. Blank pushed the wheelchair.
   • Fill in the rest of the words on your own. Raise your hand when you're finished. (Observe students and give feedback.)
4. Let's check your work. I'll read the paragraph.
   • **Ben** sat in the wheelchair. **He** wore pajamas. The **wheelchair** had big wheels and little wheels. **It** had a seat, a back and two handles. **Dora** held a purse. **She** wore a skirt and a sweater. **Ruth** was behind the wheelchair. **She** pushed the wheelchair.
5. Raise your hand if you made no mistakes. Great job.
   • Everybody else, fix up any mistakes you made in part D.

LINED PAPER • TEXTBOOK

EXERCISE 6 Paragraph Writing

Clarity

1. Everybody, take out a sheet of lined paper and write your name on the top line. Raise your hand when you're finished. ✔
   • Pencils down. Open your textbook to lesson 107 and find part E.
   • You're going to write a whole paragraph that tells about the first picture. Your paragraph will begin with a sentence that tells the main thing the group did.

Remember, name the group and tell the main thing the group did.
   • Make up a sentence that tells the main thing the group did in the pictures. (Call on a student. Praise sentences such as: *The girl scouts cleaned the car.* For each good sentence:) Everybody, say that sentence.
2. Now you're going to make up sentences that tell what each girl scout did. But you have to make sure that you tell about the first picture and not the second picture.
   • Make up a sentence that tells about Jenny in the first picture. (Call on a student. Praise sentences such as: *Jenny washed the windows with a big sponge.* For each good sentence:) Everybody, say that sentence.
   • Make up a sentence that tells about Alicia in the first picture. (Call on a student. Praise sentences such as: *Alicia scrubbed the wheels with a brush.* For each good sentence:) Everybody, say that sentence.
   • Make up a sentence that tells about Pam in the first picture. (Call on a student. Praise sentences such as: *Pam waxed the roof of the car.* For each good sentence:) Everybody, say that sentence.
3. I'll read the words in the vocabulary box: **scrubbed, roof, sponge, wheels.**
4. Your turn: Write your paragraph. Remember, start with a sentence that tells the main thing the group did. Then write a sentence about each person in the first picture. You have 6 minutes. Raise your hand when you're finished. (Observe students and give feedback.)
5. (After 6 minutes, say:) Stop writing. I'm going to call on several students to read their paragraphs. Listen carefully. Make sure each sentence is clear. If it's clear, it will tell about the first picture, but not the second picture. So if you hear a sentence like **Alicia used a scrub brush,** that sentence would not be clear, because it could tell about either picture. Listen carefully and raise your hand if you hear a mistake.
6. (Call on several students to read their paragraphs. Praise paragraphs that give a clear picture.)
7. Now you're going to check your paragraph. Make 3 check boxes under your paragraph.

8. Here's check 1: Does each sentence begin with a capital and end with a period? Check your paragraph. Fix up any mistakes. Then make a check in box 1. Raise your hand when you're finished. (Observe students and give feedback.)

9. Here's check 2: Does each sentence tell the main thing? Read your paragraph. Make sure each sentence tells the main thing. The first sentence should tell the main thing the group did. Each of the other sentences should tell the main thing a person did. Fix up any mistakes. Then make a check in box 2. Raise your hand when you're finished. (Observe students and give feedback.)

10. Here's check 3: Do the sentences give a clear picture of what the persons did? The sentences about each girl should tell about the first picture, not the second picture. Fix up any mistakes. Then make a check in box 3. Raise your hand when you're finished. (Observe students and give feedback.)

11. Next time I'll read some of the **super** paragraphs to you.

Note:

- Collect the students' workbooks and papers.

- Check the students' work before the next language period. Mark any mistakes.

- Write **super** on work that has all mistakes corrected. Write **good** or **pretty good** on work that has only 1 or 2 mistakes.

Objectives

- Indicate the subject, predicate and verb in sentences. (Exercise 2)
- Edit a paragraph for run-on sentences. (Exercise 3)
- **Determine whether a pronoun is appropriate for the subject of a sentence.** (Exercise 4)
- **Write two sentences that tell about one of two similar pictures.** (Exercise 5)
- Write a paragraph that tells about one of two similar pictures. (Exercise 6)

EXERCISE 1   Feedback On Lesson 107

- (Before returning the students' papers and workbooks, read some of the better paragraphs for part E of lesson 107.)
- (Hand back the students' work from lesson 107.)
- Look at what I wrote on your lined paper. Raise your hand if I wrote **super.**

WORKBOOK

EXERCISE 2   Subject/Predicate

Verbs

1. Everybody, open your workbook to lesson 108 and find part A. ✔
- Here's what you'll do: Circle the subject of each sentence. Underline the predicate. Then make a **V** above each verb. Do it now. Raise your hand when you're finished. (Observe students and give feedback.)
2. Let's check your work.
- Sentence 1. What's the subject? (Signal.) *She.*
- What's the predicate? (Signal.) *Jumped into the pool.*
- What's the verb? (Signal.) *Jumped.*
- You should have written **V** above the word **jumped.**
- Sentence 2. What's the subject? (Signal.) *A young woman.*
- What's the predicate? (Signal.) *Read a book about dinosaurs.*
- What's the verb? (Signal.) *Read.*
- Sentence 3. What's the subject? (Signal.) *My mother.*
- What's the predicate? (Signal.) *Had a new car.*
- What's the verb? (Signal.) *Had.*

- Sentence 4. What's the subject? (Signal.) *They.*
- What's the predicate? (Signal.) *Laughed.*
- What's the verb? (Signal.) *Laughed.*
- Sentence 5. What's the subject? (Signal.) *My brother and my sister.*
- What's the predicate? (Signal.) *Ate cookies and ice cream.*
- What's the verb? (Signal.) *Ate.*
3. Raise your hand if you made no mistakes. Great job.
- Everybody else, fix up any mistakes you made in part A.

EXERCISE 3   Editing Paragraphs

Run-On Sentences

1. Everybody, find part B. ✔
- I'll read the paragraph: Serena went on an airplane and she had never been on an airplane before. She sat in a seat next to the window and the plane took off. She fell asleep for an hour and she woke up and the plane landed. Her grandmother was waiting for her.
2. Fix up the run-on sentences. Raise your hand when you're finished. (Observe students and give feedback.)
3. Check your paragraph. I'll read the fixed-up paragraph.
- Linda went on an airplane, period. Capital **S,** She had never been on an airplane before. She sat in a seat next to the window, period. Capital **T,** The plane took off. She fell asleep for an hour, period. Capital **S,** She woke up, period. Capital **T,** The plane landed. Her grandmother was waiting for her.

4. Raise your hand if you fixed up all the sentences. Great job.

- Everybody else, fix up any run-ons you missed.

EXERCISE 4 Clarity

Pronouns

1. Everybody, find part C. ✔

- You'll write the correct words for each subject. Remember, if two sentences in a row have the same subject, you name the person or group in the first sentence. Then you can use **he, she, it** or **they** in the next sentence.

2. Look at the picture.
Here's the first sentence: Blank and blank worked in the garden.

- (Call on a student:) Who worked in the garden? *James and Alice.*

- Everybody, write **James** and **Alice** in the first two blanks. ✔

3. I'll read the rest of the paragraph: Blank wore work clothes. Blank dug a hole. Blank pushed the shovel down with her foot. Blank sawed a branch. Blank held the branch with one hand.

- Fill in the rest of the words on your own. Raise your hand when you're finished. (Observe students and give feedback.)

4. Let's check your work. I'll read the paragraph.

- **James** and **Alice** worked in the garden. **They** wore work clothes. **Alice** dug a hole. **She** pushed the shovel down with her foot. **James** sawed a branch. **He** held the branch with one hand.

5. Raise your hand if you made no mistakes. Great job.

- Everybody else, fix up any mistakes you made in part C.

EXERCISE 5 Clarity

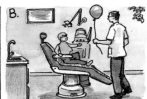

1. Everybody, take out a sheet of lined paper and write your name on the top line. Then write the number **1.** Raise your hand when you're finished. ✔

- Pencils down. Open your textbook to lesson 108 and find part D. ✔

2. Touch item 1.
Picture A is different from picture B. You're going to write two sentences about picture A. Listen: Your first sentence will tell what's **different** about the dentist in picture A. It won't tell the main thing the dentist did. Your second sentence about the dentist will tell the **main thing** he did. That sentence will start with **he.**

3. Let's do the first sentence. Raise your hand when you can say a sentence that tells what's different about picture A. Start your sentence with **the dentist.** (Call on a student. Praise sentences such as: *The dentist sat on a stool.* For each good sentence:) Everybody, say that sentence.

- Now make up a sentence that tells the main thing the dentist did. Start your sentence with **he.** (Call on a student. Praise sentences such as: *He gave the boy a balloon.* For each good sentence:) Everybody, say that sentence.

4. Everybody, write two sentences about picture A. Remember, the first sentence tells what's different in picture A. The second sentence starts with **he** and tells the main thing the dentist did. Raise your hand when you're finished. (Observe students and give feedback.)

5. (Call on several students to read their sentences. Praise sentence pairs such as: *The dentist sat on a stool. He gave the boy a balloon.*)

6. Check over your sentences. Make sure the first sentence tells what's different in picture A. Make sure the second sentence tells the main thing the dentist did. Fix up any mistakes. Raise your hand when you're finished.

7. Touch item 2.
   This is another pair of pictures. You're going to write two sentences.

   • I'll read the instructions: Write two sentences about picture A. Begin your first sentence with **the man.** That sentence should tell what's **different** in picture A. Begin your second sentence with **he.** That sentence should tell the **main thing** the man did. Write the number **2.** Then write your sentences for item 2. Raise your hand when you're finished.
   (Observe students and give feedback.)

8. (Call on several students to read their sentences. Praise sentence pairs such as: *The man had a curly beard. He fed a baby with a spoon.*)

9. Check over your sentences. Make sure the first sentence tells what's different in picture A. Make sure the second sentence tells the main thing the man did. Fix up any mistakes. Raise your hand when you're finished. ✔

EXERCISE 6 Paragraph Writing

Clarity

1. Everybody, pencils down. Find part E in your textbook. ✔

• You're going to write a whole paragraph that tells about the first picture. Your paragraph will begin with a sentence that tells the main thing the group did. Remember, name the group and tell the main thing the group did.

• Say a sentence that tells the main thing the group did in the pictures. (Call on a student. Praise sentences such as: *The clowns did tricks.* For each good sentence:) Everybody, say that sentence.

2. Now you're going to make up sentences that tell what each clown did. But you have to make sure that you tell about the first picture and not the second picture.

• Make up a sentence that tells about Harpo in the first picture. (Call on a student. Praise sentences such as: *Harpo juggled four large bananas.* For each good sentence:) Everybody, say that sentence.

• Make up a sentence that tells about Zeppo in the first picture. (Call on a student. Praise sentences such as: *Zeppo rode a bike with a big front wheel.* For each good sentence:) Everybody, say that sentence.

• Make up a sentence that tells about Elmo in the first picture. (Call on a student. Praise sentences such as: *Elmo walked across a high wire on his hands* For each good sentence:) Everybody, say that sentence.

3. I'll read the words in the vocabulary box: **high wire, juggled, wheel, bananas.**

4. Your turn: Write your paragraph. Remember, start with a sentence that tells the main thing the group did. Then write a sentence about each person in the first picture. You have 6 minutes. Raise your hand when you're finished.
   (Observe students and give feedback.)

5. (After 6 minutes, say:) Stop writing. I'm going to call on several students to read their paragraphs. Listen carefully. Make sure each sentence is clear. If it's clear, it will tell about the first picture, but not the second picture. So if you hear a sentence like **Harpo juggled bananas,** that sentence would not be clear, because it could tell about either picture. Listen carefully and raise your hand if you hear a mistake.

• (Call on several students to read their paragraphs. Praise paragraphs that give a clear picture.)

6. Now you're going to check your paragraph. Make 3 check boxes under your paragraph.
7. Here's check 1: Does each sentence begin with a capital and end with a period? Check your paragraph. Fix up any mistakes. Then make a check in box 1. Raise your hand when you're finished. (Observe students and give feedback.)
8. Here's check 2: Does each sentence tell the main thing? Read your paragraph. Make sure each sentence tells the main thing. The first sentence should tell the main thing the group did. Each of the other sentences should tell the main thing a person did. Fix up any mistakes. Then make a check in box 2. Raise your hand when you're finished.
(Observe students and give feedback.)
9. Here's check 3: Do the sentences give a clear picture of what the clowns did? The sentences about each clown should tell about the first picture, not the second picture. Fix up any mistakes. Then make a check in box 3. Raise your hand when you're finished.
(Observe students and give feedback.)
10. Next time, I'll read some of the **super** paragraphs to you.

Note:

- Collect the students' workbooks and papers.

- Check the students' work before the next language period. Mark any mistakes.

- Write **super** on work that has all mistakes corrected. Write **good** or **pretty good** on work that has only 1 or 2 mistakes.

Objectives

- Edit a paragraph for run-on sentences. (Exercise 2)
- **Identify 2-word verbs.** (Exercise 3)
- **Rewrite expressions so that a word is written with an apostrophe (the dress that belongs to the girl becomes the girl's dress).** (Exercise 4)
- Write two sentences that tell about one of two similar pictures. (Exercise 5)
- Write a paragraph that tells about one of two similar pictures. (Exercise 6)

EXERCISE 1   Feedback On Lesson 108

- (Before returning the student's papers and workbooks, read some of the better paragraphs for part E of lesson 108.)
- (Hand back the students' work from lesson 108.)
- Look at what I wrote on your lined paper. Raise your hand if I wrote **super.**

WORKBOOK

EXERCISE 2   Editing Paragraphs

Run-On Sentences

1. Everybody, open your workbook to lesson 109 and find part A. ✔
- The instructions say to fix up the run-on sentences in the paragraph.
2. I'll read the paragraph: Jessica and Mark bought a pumpkin for Halloween and the pumpkin was so big that they could not carry it home. They started to roll it home. They pushed the pumpkin up a steep hill and then Mark slipped. The pumpkin rolled down the hill. It smashed into a tree and Jessica and Mark had lots of pumpkin pie the next day.
3. Fix up the run-on sentences. Raise your hand when you're finished.
   (Observe students and give feedback.)
4. Check your paragraph. I'll read the fixed-up paragraph.
- Jessica and Mark bought a pumpkin for Halloween, period. Capital **T,** The pumpkin was so big that they could not carry it home. They started to roll it home. They pushed the pumpkin up a steep hill, period. Mark slipped. The pumpkin rolled down the

hill. It smashed into a tree, period. Jessica and Mark had lots of pumpkin pie the next day.
5. Raise your hand if you made no mistakes. Great job.
- Everybody else, fix up any mistakes you made in part A.

EXERCISE 3   Two-Word Verbs

1. Everybody, pencils down. Find part B. ✔
2. Item 1 has two verbs that tell about the same thing. The top verb has only one word. The bottom verb tells about the same thing, but it has two words.
- The one-word verb is **walked.** The two-word verb is **was walking.** Everybody, what's the one-word verb? (Signal.) *Walked.*
- What's the two-word verb? (Signal.) *Was walking.*
3. Item 2. Only the one-word verb is shown. Everybody, what's the one-word verb? (Signal.) *Smiled.*
- What's the two-word verb? (Signal.) *Was smiling.*
- Item 3. What's the one-word verb? (Signal.) *Picked.*
- What's the two-word verb? (Signal.) *Was picking.*
- Item 4. What's the one-word verb? (Signal.) *Cried.*
- What's the two-word verb? (Signal.) *Was crying.*
- (Repeat step 3 until firm.)

EXERCISE 4   Possessive

Apostrophe + S

1. Everybody, find part C. ✔

- Some words tell that something belongs to something else. Those words have a punctuation mark called an apostrophe.
2. Touch item 1: the hat that belongs to the boy. Here's what we write: The **boy's** hat. We write the word **boy** and then put an apostrophe before the **s.**
- I'll spell **boy's:** b-o-y-apostrophe-s. Your turn: Spell **boy's.** (Signal.) *B-o-y-apostrophe-s.*
- Touch item 2: the bone that belongs to the dog. We write the **dog's** bone. I'll spell **dog's:** d-o-g-apostrophe-s. Your turn: Spell **dog's.** (Signal.) *D-o-g-apostrophe-s.*
3. Touch item 3: the car that belongs to her father. What do we write? (Signal.) *Her father's car.*
- Spell **father's.** (Signal.) *F-a-t-h-e-r-apostrophe-s.*
- Touch item 4: the arm that belongs to the girl. What do we write? (Signal.) *The girl's arm.*
- Spell **girl's.** (Signal.) *G-i-r-l-apostrophe-s.*
- (Repeat step 3 until firm.)
4. Your turn: Write the missing word in each item. Raise your hand when you're finished. (Observe students and give feedback.)
5. Check your work.
- Item 2: the dog's bone. Spell **dog's.** (Signal.) *D-o-g-apostrophe-s.*
- Item 3: her father's car. Spell **father's.** (Signal.) *F-a-t-h-e-r-apostrophe-s.*
- Item 4: the girl's arm. Spell **girl's.** (Signal.) *G-i-r-l-apostrophe-s.*
- Item 5: my friend's book. Spell **friend's.** (Signal.) *F-r-i-e-n-d-apostrophe-s.*
- Item 6: the cat's toy. Spell **cat's.** (Signal.) *C-a-t-apostrophe-s.*
6. Raise your hand if you made no mistakes. Great job.
- Everybody else, fix up any mistakes you made in part C.

LINED PAPER • TEXTBOOK

EXERCISE 5 Clarity

I.

1. Everybody, take out a sheet of lined paper and write your name on the top line. Then write the number **1.** Raise your hand when you're finished. ✔
- Pencils down. Open your textbook to lesson 109 and find part D. ✔
2. Touch item 1.
Picture A is different from picture B. You're going to write two sentences about picture A. Listen: Your first sentence will tell what's different about the woman in picture A. It won't tell the main thing the woman did. Your second sentence about the woman will tell the main thing she did. That sentence will start with **she.**
3. Let's do the first sentence. Raise your hand when you can say a sentence that tells what's different about picture A. Start your sentence with **the woman.** (Call on a student. Praise sentences such as: *The woman wore dark glasses.* For each good sentence:) Everybody, say that sentence.
- Now make up a sentence that tells the main thing the woman did. Start your sentence with **she.** (Call on a student. Praise sentences such as: *She drank a glass of lemonade.* For each good sentence:) Everybody, say that sentence.
4. Your turn: Write two sentences about picture A. Remember, the first sentence tells what's different in picture A. The second sentence starts with **she** and tells the main thing the woman did. Raise your hand when you're finished. (Observe students and give feedback.)
5. (Call on several students to read their sentences. Praise sentence pairs such as: *The woman wore sunglasses. She drank a glass of lemonade.*)
6. Check over your sentences. Make sure the first sentence tells what's different in picture A. Make sure the second sentence tells the main thing the woman did. Fix up any mistakes. Raise your hand when you're finished.

2.

A.  | B.

7. Touch item 2.
   This is another pair of pictures. You're going to write two sentences.

• I'll read the instructions: Write two sentences about picture A. Begin your first sentence with **the boy.** That sentence should tell what's **different** in picture A. Begin your second sentence with **he.** That sentence should tell the **main thing** the boy did. Write the number **2.** Then write your sentences for item 2. Raise your hand when you're finished.
   (Observe students and give feedback.)

8. (Call on several students to read their sentences. Praise sentence pairs such as: *The boy had a cast on his arm. He jumped over a fence.*)

9. Check over your sentences. Make sure the first sentence tells what's different in picture A. Make sure the second sentence tells the main thing the man did. Fix up any mistakes. Raise your hand when you're finished.

EXERCISE 6 Paragraph Writing

Clarity

1. Everybody, find part E in your textbook. ✔
• You're going to write a whole paragraph that tells about the first picture, but not about the second picture.

2. I'll read the words in the vocabulary box: fire fighters, window, through, chopped, hose, climbed.

3. You'll begin with a sentence that tells what the group did. Raise your hand when you can say a sentence that reports on the main thing the group did. (Call on several students. Praise sentences such as: *The firefighters tried to put out the fire.* For each good sentence:) Everybody, say that sentence.

4. Touch Carlos.
• Raise your hand when you can say a sentence that reports on the main thing Carlos did. (Call on several students. Praise sentences such as: *Carlos put water on the fire with a short hose. Carlos used a small hose to put water on the fire.* For each good sentence:) Everybody, say that sentence.

5. Touch Marcus.
• Raise your hand when you can say a sentence that reports on the main thing Marcus did. (Call on several students. Praise sentences such as: *Marcus swung his ax against the top of the front door.* For each good sentence:) Everybody, say that sentence.

6. Touch Cindy.
• Raise your hand when you can say a sentence that reports on the main thing Cindy did in the first picture. (Call on several students. Praise sentences such as: *Cindy climbed through a window next to the front door.* For each good sentence:) Everybody, say that sentence.

7. Your turn: Write your paragraph. Start with a sentence that tells the main thing the group did. Then write a sentence about each person in the first picture. You have 6 minutes. Raise your hand when you're finished.
   (Observe students and give feedback.)

8. (After 6 minutes, say:) Stop writing. I'm going to call on several students to read their paragraphs. Listen carefully. Make sure each sentence is clear. If it's clear, it will tell about the first picture, but not the second picture. Raise your hand if you hear a mistake.
• (Call on several students to read their paragraphs. Praise paragraphs that give a clear picture.)

9. Now you're going to check your paragraph. Make 3 check boxes under your paragraph.

10. Here's check 1: Does each sentence begin with a capital and end with a period? Check your paragraph. Fix up any mistakes. Then make a check in box 1. Raise your hand when you're finished. (Observe students and give feedback.)

11. Here's check 2: Does each sentence tell the main thing? Read your paragraph. Make sure each sentence tells the main thing. The first sentence should tell the main thing the group did. Each of the other sentences should tell the main thing a person did. Fix up any mistakes. Then make a check in box 2. Raise your hand when you're finished. (Observe students and give feedback.)

12. Here's check 3: Do the sentences give a clear picture of what the fire fighters did? The sentences about each fire fighter should tell about the first picture, not the second picture. Fix up any mistakes. Then make a check in box 3. Raise your hand when you're finished. (Observe students and give feedback.)

13. Next time, I'll read some of the **super** paragraphs to you.

Note:

• Collect the students' workbooks and papers.

• Check the students' work before the next language period. Mark any mistakes.

• Write **super** on work that has all mistakes corrected. Write **good** or **pretty good** on work that has only 1 or 2 mistakes.

Objectives

- Edit a paragraph for run-on sentences. (Exercise 2)
- **Identify the verb in sentences that have 1-word verbs and in similar sentences that have 2-word verbs.** (Exercise 3)
- Rewrite expressions so that a word is written with an apostrophe. (Exercise 4)
- Write two sentences that tell about one of two similar pictures. (Exercise 5)
- **Identify the two actions specified in a sentence.** (Exercise 6)
- Write a paragraph that tells about one of two similar pictures. (Exercise 7)

EXERCISE 1   Feedback On Lesson 109

- (Before returning the students' papers and workbooks, read some of the better paragraphs for part E of lesson 109.)
- (Hand back the students' work from lesson 109.)
- Look at what I wrote on your lined paper. Raise your hand if I wrote **super.**

WORKBOOK

EXERCISE 2   Editing Paragraphs
Run-On Sentences

1. Everybody, open your workbook to lesson 110 and find part A. ✔
- The instructions say to fix up the run-on sentences in the paragraph.
2. I'll read the paragraph: Ronald put his finger in a bottle and his finger got stuck in the bottle and then he asked his sister to help him. His sister got some butter and then she rubbed the butter around the top of the bottle. She pulled on the bottle and then his finger came out.
3. Fix up the run-on sentences. Raise your hand when you're finished.
(Observe students and give feedback.)
4. Check your paragraph. I'll read the fixed-up paragraph.
- Ronald put his finger in a bottle, period. Capital **H,** His finger got stuck in the bottle, period. Capital **H,** He asked his sister to help him. His sister got some butter, period. Capital **S,** She rubbed the butter around the top of the bottle. She pulled on the bottle, period. Capital **H,** His finger came out.

5. Raise your hand if you made no mistakes. Great job.
- Everybody else, fix up any mistakes you made in part A.

EXERCISE 3   Two-Word Verbs

1. Everybody, find part B. ✔
2. Listen: You're going to fix up the first sentence in item 1-just the first sentence. Circle the subject and underline the predicate. Then make a **V** above the verb. Raise your hand when you're finished. (Observe students and give feedback.)
- Check your work. Everybody, what's the subject of the sentence? (Signal.) *The boy.*
- What's the predicate? (Signal.) *Walked to the store.*
- What's the verb? (Signal.) *Walked.*
3. I'll read the other sentence in item 1: The boy was walking to the store. That sentence is almost like the first sentence, except the verb has two words. Listen: Circle the subject. Underline the predicate. Write two **V**s, one V above **each word** of the verb. Raise your hand when you're finished.
(Observe students and give feedback.)
- Check your work. Everybody, what's the subject of the sentence? (Signal.) *The boy.*
- What's the predicate? (Signal.) *Was walking to the store.*
- What's the verb? (Signal.) *Was walking.*
- You should have written a **V** over **was** and a **V** over **walking.**

4. I'll read the sentences in item 2: Two girls ate candy. Two girls were eating candy. Those sentences are almost the same, except the second sentence has a two-word verb. Circle the subjects, underline the predicates and write **V** above each verb. Raise your hand when you're finished.
   (Observe students and give feedback.)
5. Check your work.
   - Two girls ate candy. What's the subject? (Signal.) *Two girls.*
   - What's the predicate? (Signal.) *Ate candy.* What's the verb? (Signal.) *Ate.*
   - Two girls were eating candy. What's the subject? (Signal.) *Two girls.*
   - What's the predicate? (Signal.) *Were eating candy.*
   - What's the verb? (Signal.) *Were eating.*
   - Everybody, what's the verb in the **first** sentence? (Signal.) *Ate.*
   - What's the verb in the **second** sentence? (Signal.) *Were eating.*
6. Your turn: Work item 3. Raise your hand when you're finished.
   (Observe students and give feedback.)
7. Check your work.
   - A fish swam in the bathtub. What's the subject? (Signal.) *A fish.*
   - What's the predicate? (Signal.) *Swam in the bathtub.*
   - What's the verb? (Signal.) *Swam.*
   - A fish was swimming in the bathtub. What's the subject? (Signal.) *A fish.*
   - What's the predicate? (Signal.) *Was swimming in the bathtub.*
   - What's the verb? (Signal.) *Was swimming.*
8. Raise your hand if you did everything right. Great job.
   - Everybody else, fix up any mistakes you made in part B.

EXERCISE 4   Possessisve

Apostrophe + S

1. Everybody, pencils down. Find part C. ✔
   - Some words tell that something belongs to something else. Those words have a punctuation mark called an apostrophe.
2. Touch item 1: the dress that belongs to the girl. Here's what we write: the **girl's** dress. We write the word **girl,** then put an apostrophe before the **s.**

- I'll spell **girl's:** g-i-r-l-apostrophe-s. Your turn: Spell **girl's.** (Signal.) *G-i-r-l-apostrophe-s.*
3. Touch item 2: the tent that belongs to her friend. What do we write? (Signal.) *Her friend's tent.*
   - I'll spell **friend's:** f-r-i-e-n-d-apostrophe-s. Your turn: Spell **friend's.** (Signal.) *F-r-i-e-n-d-apostrophe-s.*
   - Touch item 3: the toy that belongs to my cat. What do we write? (Signal.) *My cat's toy.*
   - Spell **cat's.** (Signal.) *C-a-t-apostrophe-s.*
   - Touch item 4: the watch that belongs to that boy. What do we write? (Signal.) *That boy's watch.*
     Spell **boy's.** (Signal.) *B-o-y-apostrophe-s.*
   - (Repeat step 3 until firm.)
4. Your turn: Write the missing word in each item. Raise your hand when you're finished.
   (Observe students and give feedback.)
5. Check your work.
   - Item 2: her friend's tent. Spell **friend's.** (Signal.) *F-r-i-e-n-d-apostrophe-s.*
   - Item 3: my cat's toy. Spell cat's. (Signal.) *C-a-t-apostrophe-s.*
   - Item 4: that boy's watch. Spell **boy's.** (Signal.) *B-o-y-apostrophe-s.*
   - Item 5: his mother's hammer. Spell **mother's.** (Signal.) *M-o-t-h-e-r-apostrophe-s.*
   - Item 6: my father's leg. Spell **father's.** (Signal.) *F-a-t-h-e-r-apostrophe-s.*
6. Raise your hand if you made no mistakes. Great job.
   - Everybody else, fix up any mistakes you made in part C.

EXERCISE 5   Clarity

I.

2.

1. Everybody, take out a sheet of lined paper and write your name on the top line. Then write the number **1.** Raise your hand when you're finished.

• Pencils down. Open your textbook to lesson 110 and find part D. ✔

2. Touch item 1.
   Picture A is different from picture B. You're going to write two sentences about picture A. Listen: Your first sentence will tell what's **different** about the girl in picture A. It won't tell the main thing the girl did. Your second sentence about the girl will tell the **main thing** she did. That sentence will start with **she.**

3. Let's do the first sentence. Raise your hand when you can say a sentence that tells what's different about picture A. Start your sentence with **the girl.** (Call on a student. Praise sentences such as: *The girl wore a fancy dress.* For each good sentence:) Everybody, say that sentence.

• Now make up a sentence that tells the main thing the girl did. Start your sentence with **she.** (Call on a student. Praise sentences such as: *She climbed a tree.* For each good sentence:) Everybody, say that sentence.

4. Your turn: Write two sentences about picture A. Remember the first sentence tells what's different in picture A. The second sentence starts with **she** and tells the main thing the girl did. Raise your hand when you're finished.
   (Observe students and give feedback.)

5. (Call on several students to read their sentences. Praise sentence pairs such as: *The girl wore a fancy dress. She climbed a tree.*)

6. Check over your sentences. Make sure the first sentence tells what's different in picture A. Make sure the second sentence tells the main thing the girl did. Fix up any mistakes. Raise your hand when you're finished.

7. Touch item 2.
   This is another pair of pictures. You're going to write two sentences.

• I'll read the instructions: Write two sentences about picture A. Begin your first sentence with **the woman.** That sentence should tell what's **different** in picture A. Begin your second sentence with **she.** That sentence should tell the **main thing** the woman did. Write the number **2.** Then write your sentences for item 2. Raise your hand when you're finished.
   (Observe students and give feedback.)

8. (Call on several students to read their sentences. Praise sentence pairs such as: *The woman wore a blindfold. She walked across a high wire.*)

9. Check over your sentences. Make sure the first sentence tells what's different in picture A. Make sure the second sentence tells the main thing the woman did. Fix up any mistakes. Raise your hand when you're finished.

EXERCISE 6   Sentences

Double Predicate

1. Everybody, pencils down. Find part E in your textbook. ✔

• Not all sentences that have the word **and** are run-ons. Some sentences tell about two things a person did. That kind of sentence is not a run-on and the **and** is all right. The sentences in part E tell two things that people did, so they are not run-ons.

2. Sentence 1: Steve bent down and picked up a pencil. What's the first thing Steve did? (Signal.) *Bent down.*

• What's the other thing he did? (Signal.) *Picked up a pencil.*

• (Repeat step 2 until firm.)

3. Sentence 2: Three girls watched a movie and ate popcorn. What's the first thing three girls did? (Signal.) *Watched a movie.*

• What was the other thing three girls did? (Signal.) *Ate popcorn.*

• (Repeat step 3 until firm.)

4. Sentence 3: He brushed his teeth and washed his face. What was the first thing he did? (Signal.) *Brushed his teeth.*
- What was the other thing he did? (Signal.) *Washed his face.*
- (Repeat step 4 until firm.)

EXERCISE 7   Paragraph Writing

Clarity

1. Everybody, find part F in your textbook. ✔
- You're going to write a whole paragraph that tells about the first picture, but not about the second picture.
2. I'll read the words in the vocabulary box: salad, sliced, meal, sprinkled, tomatoes, hamburgers.
3. Your turn: Write your paragraph. Start with a sentence that tells the main thing the group did. Then write a sentence about each person in the first picture. You have 6 minutes. Raise your hand when you're finished.
   (Observe students and give feedback.)
4. (After 6 minutes, say:) Stop writing. I'm going to call on several students to read their paragraphs. Listen carefully. Make sure each sentence is clear. If it's clear, it will tell about the first picture, but not the second picture. Raise your hand if you hear a mistake.
- (Call on several students to read their paragraphs. Praise paragraphs that give a clear picture.)
5. Now you're going to check your paragraph. Make 3 check boxes under your paragraph.
6. Here's check 1: Does each sentence begin with a capital and end with a period? Check your paragraph. Fix up any mistakes. Then make a check in box 1. Raise your hand when you're finished.
   (Observe students and give feedback.)

7. Here's check 2: Does each sentence tell the main thing? Read your paragraph. Make sure each sentence tells the main thing. The first sentence should tell the main thing the group did. Each of the other sentences should tell the main thing a person did. Fix up any mistakes. Then make a check in box 2. Raise your hand when you're finished.
   (Observe students and give feedback.)
8. Here's check 3: Do the sentences give a clear picture of what the cooks did? The sentences about each cook should tell about the first picture, not the second picture. Fix up any mistakes. Then make a check in box 3. Raise your hand when you're finished.
   (Observe students and give feedback.)

Note:
- Collect the students' workbooks and papers.
- Check the students' work before the next language period. Mark any mistakes.
- Write **super** on work that has all mistakes corrected. Write **good** or **pretty good** on work that has only 1 or 2 mistakes.

Note:
For second grade teachers who complete the grade 2 language arts program early in the school year and plan to proceed to the grade 3 language arts:
- The first 14 lessons of grade 3 language present a review of the content from grade 2.
- If students are firm on the skills taught in grade 2, second grade teachers can begin the grade 3 language arts program at lesson 15.

Scope and Sequence

Scope and Sequence Chart

	Phonics/ Vocabulary	Comprehension	Grammar/ Usage/ Mechanics	Writing/ Composition/ Speaking	Study Skills
Lesson 1	Left, right: 2	Classification: 3, 4 Sequence: 5 Listening comprehension: 7 Recalling details: 8		Sentences: 6	
Lesson 2	Left, right: 2	True, false: 3, 7 Sequence: 4 Classification: 5 Listening comprehension: 6 Recalling details: 8		Sentences: 1	
Lesson 3	Left, right: 1	True, false: 2 Classification: 3 Listening comprehension: 5 Recalling details: 6		Sentences: 4	
Lesson 4		True, false: 2 Classification: 3 Listening comprehension: 4 Recalling details: 5		Sentences: 1	
Lesson 5	Left, right: 5	True, false: 3 Classification: 4 Listening comprehension: 6 Recalling details: 7		Sentences: 1	Cardinal directions: 2
Lesson 6		Classification: 3 Listening comprehension: 4	Correcting word usage errors: 5, 6	Sentences: 2	Cardinal directions: 1
Lesson 7		Classification: 2 Listening comprehension: 4	Correcting word usage errors: 5	Sentences: 3	Cardinal directions: 1
Lesson 8		If-then reasoning: 3 Deduction: 5 Listening comprehension: 6 Recalling details: 7	Correcting word usage errors: 4	Sentences: 2	Cardinal directions: 1
Lesson 9	Left, right: 4	If-then reasoning: 3 Deduction: 5 Listening comprehension: 6 Recalling details: 7		Sentences: 2	Cardinal directions: 1
Lesson 10	Left, right: 2	Listening comprehension: 3		Sentences: 1	
Lesson 11	Seasons: 4	Deduction: 2 Listening comprehension: 5 Recalling details: 6		Sentences: 3	Cardinal directions: 1
Lesson 12	Seasons: 1	Deduction: 3 Listening comprehension: 5	Correcting word usage errors: 6	Sentences: 4	Maps: 2
Lesson 13	Seasons: 1	Deduction: 3 Listening comprehension: 5	Correcting word usage errors: 6	Sentences: 4	Maps: 2
Lesson 14		Deduction: 4 Listening comprehension: 5 Recalling details: 6		Sentences: 1	Cardinal directions: 2 Maps: 3
Lesson 15	Initial letter substitution: 5	Deduction: 2 Listening comprehension: 4		Sentences: 3	Maps: 1

Lesson 16		Listening comprehension: 4 True, false: 5		Sentences: 1	Cardinal directions: 2 Maps: 3
Lesson 17		Deduction: 2 Listening comprehension: 3 Comparisons: 4		Sentences: 1	
Lesson 18		Listening comprehension: 3 Comparisons: 4		Sentences: 1	Mazes directions: 2
Lesson 19		Listening comprehension: 3 Comparisons: 4		Sentences: 1	Maze directions: 2
Lesson 20		Listening directions: 3		Sentences: 1	Maps: 2
Lesson 21				Story sentences: 1	
Lesson 22	To, from: 2	Classification: 3 Deduction: 4 Listening comprehension: 5		Sentences: 1	
Lesson 23	To, from: 1	Classification: 3 Listening comprehension: 4		Sentences: 5	Maps: 2
Lesson 24		Classification, subclass: 2 Listening comprehension: 3	Correcting word usage errors: 4	Sentences: 1	
Lesson 25	To, from: 1	Listening comprehension: 2 Deduction: 3			Maps: 1
Lesson 26				Story sentences: 1	
Lesson 27	To, from: 1	Sequencing: 2 Classification, subclass: 3 Listening comprehension: 4		Fictional story: 5	Maps: 1
Lesson 28		Sequencing: 1 Deduction: 2		Fictional story: 3 Story presentation: 3	
Lesson 29		Deduction: 1 Listening comprehension: 3		Writing deductions: 1	Maps: 2, 4
Lesson 30	To, from: 2	Deduction: 2 Listening comprehension: 3		Sentences: 1	Maps: 2
Lesson 31				Story sentences: 1	
Lesson 32		Classification: 3 Listening comprehension: 4			Alphabetical order: 1 Maps: 2, 5
Lesson 33		Classification: 3 Listening comprehension: 4			Alphabetical order: 1 Maps: 2
Lesson 34		Classification: 1 Sequencing: 3 Listening comprehension: 4	Pronoun referents: 5	Sentences: 6	Maps: 2
Lesson 35		Classification: 3 Listening comprehension: 4	Pronoun referents: 5		Alphabetical order: 1 Maps: 2
Lesson 36		Following written directions: 3 Listening comprehension: 4	Pronoun referents: 5		Alphabetical order: 1 Maps: 2, 3
Lesson 37		Following written directions: 2 Deduction: 3 Listening comprehension: 5	Pronoun referents: 4	Story sentences: 1	

Lesson					
Lesson 38		Listening comprehension: 4 Deduction: 5	Pronoun referents: 3		Alphabetical order: 1 Maps: 2
Lesson 39		Deduction: 2, 5 Listening comprehension: 4	Pronoun referents: 3		Alphabetical order: 1
Lesson 40		Sequencing: 2 Classification: 2 Listening comprehension: 3		Sentences: 1	Maps: 2
Lesson 41		Listening comprehension: 4 Recalling details: 5	Pronoun referents: 3	Sentences: 1	Maps: 2
Lesson 42		Listening comprehension: 3 Recalling details: 4	Pronoun referents: 2	Sentences: 1	
Lesson 43		Listening comprehension: 3	Pronoun referents: 4	Story sentences: 1	Maps: 2
Lesson 44		Deduction: 2 Listening comprehension: 3 Recalling Details: 4		Sentences: 1	
Lesson 45		Deduction: 4 Listening comprehension: 5	Pronoun referents: 3	Sentences: 1, 2	
Lesson 46		Listening comprehension: 4 Sequencing: 5		Story sentences: 1, 3	Maps: 2
Lesson 47		Listening comprehension: 4	Pronoun referents: 3	Sentences: 2 Dramatic activity: 5	Maps: 1
Lesson 48		Listening comprehension: 3	Correcting word usage errors: 4	Sentences: 1, 2	
Lesson 49		Listening comprehension: 2	Correcting word usage errors: 3	Sentences: 1 Story sentences: 4	
Lesson 50		Listening comprehension: 3		Sentences: 1	Maps: 2
Lesson 51		Sequencing: 2 Listening comprehension: 4 Deduction: 5	Pronoun referents: 3	Sentences: 1, 2 Deductive sentences: 5	
Lesson 52		Sequencing: 1 Listening comprehension: 2 Deduction: 3		Sentences: 1 Deductive sentences: 3	
Lesson 53		Sequencing: 2 Deduction: 3 Listening comprehension: 4 Recalling details: 5		Letter writing: 1 Sentences: 2 Deductive writing: 3	
Lesson 54		Listening comprehension: 4	Pronoun referents: 3	Letter writing: 1 Dramatic activity: 5	Maps: 2
Lesson 55		Deduction: 3 Listening comprehension: 4 Character extrapolation: 5		Letter writing: 1	Maps: 2
Lesson 56		Deduction: 1 Main idea: 2 Listening comprehension: 3	Pronoun referents: 4		
Lesson 57		Main idea: 1, 2 Listening comprehension: 3 Deduction: 5		Sentences: 2 Write an ending to a story: 4	
Lesson 58		Main idea: 1		Sentences: 1 Write an ending to a story: 2	

Lesson					
Lesson 59		Main idea: 1 Listening comprehension: 2		Sentences: 1 Write an ending to a story: 2	
Lesson 60		Main idea: 1 Deduction: 2	Correcting word usage errors: 2	Sentences: 1 Write an ending to a story: 3	
Lesson 61		Listening comprehension: 3	Pronoun referents: 4	Sentences: 2	Maps: 1
Lesson 62		Listening comprehension: 4	Pronoun referents: 5	Sentences: 1	Maps: 2, 3
Lesson 63	After: 1	Sequencing: 1 Listening comprehension: 3		Sentences: 2	Maps: 4
Lesson 64		Main idea: 1 Listening comprehension: 2 Recalling details: 3		Sentences: 1 Letter writing: 4	Maps: 3
Lesson 65		Main idea: 1 Listening comprehension: 2 Recalling details: 3		Sentences: 1 Letter writing: 4	
Lesson 66		Main idea: 1 Deductions: 5 Listening Comprehension: 6	Subject of sentence: 2, 4 Capitalization: 3 Sentence punctuation: 3		
Lesson 67		Deduction: 6 Listening Comprehension: 7	Subject of sentence: 2, 3, 5		
Lesson 68		Deduction: 4 Main idea: 6 Listening Comprehension: 7	Subject of sentence: 2, 3, 5 Capitalization: 4		
Lesson 69	Suffix –ed: 2	Deduction: 3 Main idea: 5 Listening Comprehension: 7	Subject of sentence: 4, 6 Punctuation: 5		
Lesson 70	Suffix-ed: 2	Deduction: 4 Listening Comprehension: 7	Predicate of sentence: 5 Subject of sentence: 6 Irregular Verbs: 3		
Lesson 71		Deduction: 5 Main idea: 6, 7 Listening Comprehension: 8	Irregular verbs: 2 Verb tense: 3 Subject/predicate: 4	Editing: 3	
Lesson 72		Main idea: 5, 6 Listening Comprehension: 7	Subject/predicate: 2 Verb tense: 3 Pronouns: 4	Editing: 3	
Lesson 73		Deduction: 5 Main idea: 7 Listening Comprehension: 8	Subject/predicate: 2 Pronouns: 3 Verb tense: 4 Irregular verb: 6	Editing: 4	
Lesson 74		Main idea: 5 Listening Comprehension: 6	Pronouns: 2 Verb tense: 3 Subject/predicate: 4	Editing: 3	
Lesson 75		Main idea: 2 Listening Comprehension: 3	Irregular verbs: 4 Subject/predicate: 4 Verb tense: 4	Editing: 4	
Lesson 76		Main idea: 6, 7 Listening Comprehension: 8	Irregular verbs: 2 Subject/predicate: 3 Pronouns: 4 Verb tense: 5	Editing: 5	
Lesson 77		Deduction: 5 Main idea: 6, 7 Listening Comprehension: 8	Subject/predicate: 2 Irregular verbs: 3 Pronouns: 4		

Lesson 78		Main idea: 6, 7 Listening Comprehension: 8	Verb tense: 2 Subject/predicate: 3 Pronouns: 4 Irregular verbs: 5	Editing: 2	
Lesson 79		Main idea: 6, 7 Listening Comprehension: 8	Pronouns: 2 Subject/predicate: 3 Verb tense: 4 Irregular verbs: 5	Editing: 4	
Lesson 80		Classification: 5 Main idea: 6 Listening Comprehension: 8	Pronouns: 2 Verb tense: 3 Subject/predicate: 4	Editing: 3 Paragraph copying: 7	
Lesson 81		Classification: 6 Main idea: 7 Listening Comprehension: 8	Verb tense: 2 Subject/predicate: 3 Pronouns: 4 Capitalization: 5 Punctuation: 5	Editing: 2 Paragraph copying: 5	
Lesson 82		Classification: 4 Main Idea: 6, 7 Listening Comprehension: 8	Pronouns: 2 Subject/Predicate: 3 Capitalization: 3, 5 Punctuation: 3, 5	Editing: 3 Paragraph copying: 5	
Lesson 83		Classification: 4 Main idea: 4, 6	Subject/Predicate: 2 Capitalization: 2 Punctuation: 2 Verb tense: 3	Editing: 2, 3 Paragraph copying: 5	
Lesson 84		Main idea: 5 Classification: 5 Listening Comprehension: 7	Subject/predicate: 2 Capitalization: 3, 6 Punctuation: 3, 6 Verb tense: 4	Editing: 3, 4 Paragraph writing: 6	
Lesson 85		Main idea: 3 Listening Comprehension: 3	Capitalization: 2, 3 Punctuation: 2, 3 Pronouns: 3 Past Time: 3 Clarity: 3	Paragraph writing: 2 Editing: 3	
Lesson 86		Main idea: 5	Capitalization: 2, 6 Punctuation: 2, 6 Subject/predicate: 3 Verb tense: 4 Irregular verbs: 4	Editing: 2 Paragraph writing: 6	
Lesson 87		Main idea: 6	Capitalization: 2, 7 Punctuation: 2, 7 Subject/Predicate: 3 Verb tense: 4 Irregular verbs: 5	Editing: 2, 4 Paragraph writing: 7	
Lesson 88		Main idea: 5, 7	Subject/Predicate: 2 Capitalization: 3, 6 Punctuation: 3, 6 Irregular verbs: 4 Verb tense: 4	Editing: 3 Paragraph writing: 6	
Lesson 89		Main idea: 5, 7	Capitalization: 2, 6 Punctuation: 2, 6 Subject/predicate: 3 Pronouns: 4	Editing: 2 Paragraph writing: 6	
Lesson 90		Main idea: 7	Capitalization: 2, 6 Punctuation: 2, 6 Pronouns: 3 Verb tense: 4 Irregular verbs: 4 Subject/predicate: 5	Editing: 2 Paragraph writing: 6	
Lesson 91			Capitalization: 2 Punctuation: 2 Verb tense: 3 Irregular verbs: 3 Pronouns: 4 Subject/predicate: 6	Editing: 2 Paragraph writing: 5 Sentences: 7	
Lesson 92		Main idea: 6	Subject/predicate: 2 Verb tense: 3 Irregular verbs: 3 Pronouns: 4	Sentences: 5 Paragraph writing: 7	

Lesson 93		Main idea: 6	Capitalization: 2, 7 Punctuation: 2, 7 Subject/predicate: 3 Pronouns: 4 Verb tense: 5 Irregular verbs: 5	Editing: 2 Paragraph writing: 7	
Lesson 94		Main idea: 5	Capitalization: 2, 4, 7 Punctuation: 2, 6 Pronouns: 3 Verb tense: 6 Irregular verbs: 6	Editing: 2 Paragraph writing: 7	
Lesson 95	Prepositions: 2	Main idea: 2, 4	Verb tense: 3 Irregular verbs: 3 Subject/predicate: 4 Capitalization: 4 Punctuation: 4 Pronouns: 4	Editing: 4	
Lesson 96	Prepositions: 4	Main idea: 4	Capitalization: 1, 2 Punctuation: 2 Run-on sentences: 2 Verb tense: 3 Irregular verbs: 3 Subject/predicate: 5	Editing: 2 Paragraph writing: 6	
Lesson 97		Main idea: 5	Capitalization: 2, 4 Pronouns: 3 Punctuation: 4 Run-on sentences: 4 Subject/predicate: 6	Editing: 4, 5 Paragraph writing: 5	
Lesson 98			Capitalization: 2, 4 Pronouns: 3 Punctuation: 4 Subject/predicate: 5 Verb tense: 6 Irregular verbs: 6	Editing: 4 Revising for clarity: 7	
Lesson 99			Subject/predicate: 2 Capitalization: 3, 5 Punctuation: 3 Pronouns: 4	Editing: 3 Revising for clarity: 6, 7 Sentences: 8	
Lesson 100			Capitalization: 2 Pronouns: 3 Verb tense: 4 Irregular verbs: 4 Subject/predicate: 6	Editing: 3 Revising for clarity: 6, 7 Sentences: 8	
Lesson 101			Capitalization: 2, 5 Verb tense: 3 Irregular verbs: 3 Pronouns: 4 Punctuation: 5	Editing: 2 Revising for clarity: 4 Paragraph writing: 6	
Lesson 102			Capitalization: 2 Pronouns: 4 Verb tense: 5 Irregular verbs: 5	Editing: 2, 3 Revising for clarity: 4 Sentences: 6 Paragraph writing: 7	
Lesson 103		Supporting facts: 5	Subject/predicate: 2 Capitalization: 3 Verb tense: 4 Irregular verbs: 4	Editing: 3 Paragraph writing: 6	
Lesson 104		Main idea: 5	Capitalization: 2 Punctuation: 2 Run-on sentences: 3 Pronouns: 4	Editing: 2, 3 Revising for clarity: 4 Sentences: 6 Paragraph writing: 7	
Lesson 105			Run-on sentence: 2 Verbs: 3 Predicates: 3 Capitalization: 4 Pronouns: 4 Subject/predicate: 4	Editing: 2	
Lesson 106			Pronouns: 1 Run-on sentences: 2 Verbs: 3, 4 Subject/Predicate: 4 Capitalization: 5	Editing: 2, 5 Paragraph writing: 6	

Lesson 107			Subject/predicate: 2 Run-on sentences: 3 Verb tense: 4 Irregular verbs: 4 Pronouns: 5	Editing: 3 Paragraph writing: 6	
Lesson 108		Main ideas: 5	Subject/predicate: 2 Run-on sentence: 3 Pronouns: 4, 5	Editing: 3 Paragraph writing: 6	
Lesson 109		Main ideas: 5	Run-on sentences: 2 Verbs: 3 Possessives: 4	Sentences: 5 Paragraph writing: 6	
Lesson 110		Main ideas: 5	Run-on sentences: 2 Verbs: 3 Possessives: 4 Compound predicate: 6	Sentences: 5 Paragraph writing: 7